Nodame Cantabile

11

TOMOKO NINOMIYA

TRANSLATED AND ADAPTED BY
David and Eriko Walsh

LETTERED BY
North Market Street Graphics

CHASE BRANCH LIBRARY
17731 W. SEVEN MILE RD.
DETROIT, MI 48235

DEL
REY

BALLANTINE BOOKS • NEW YORK

Nodame Cantabile volume 11 is a work of fiction. Names, characters, places, and incidents are the products of the author's imagination or are used fictitiously. Any resemblance to actual events, locales, or persons, living or dead, is entirely coincidental.

A Del Rey Manga/Kodansha Trade Paperback Original

Nodame Cantabile copyright © 2004 by Tomoko Ninomiya
English translation copyright © 2007 by Tomoko Ninomiya

All rights reserved.

Published in the United States by Del Rey Books, an imprint of The Random House Publishing Group, a division of Random House, Inc., New York.

DEL REY is a registered trademark and the Del Rey colophon is a trademark of Random House, Inc.

Publication rights arranged through Kodansha Ltd.

First published in Japan in 2005 by Kodansha Ltd., Tokyo.

ISBN 978-0-345-49399-6

Printed in the United States of America

www.delreymanga.com

9 8 7 6 5 4 3 2 1

Translator and adaptor: David and Eriko Walsh
Letterer: North Market Street Graphics

Contents

A Note from the Author

I have never worked on a manga with so many characters. I really enjoy coming up with different names.

TOMOKO NINOMIYA

Honorifics Explained

Throughout the Del Rey Manga books, you will find Japanese honorifics left intact in the translations. For those not familiar with how the Japanese use honorifics and, more important, how they differ from American honorifics, we present this brief overview.

Politeness has always been a critical facet of Japanese culture. Ever since the feudal era, when Japan was a highly stratified society, use of honorifics—which can be defined as polite speech that indicates relationship or status—has played an essential role in the Japanese language. When addressing someone in Japanese, an honorific usually takes the form of a suffix attached to one's name (example: "Asuna-san"), is used as a title at the end of one's name, or appears in place of the name itself (example: "Negi-sensei," or simply "Sensei!").

Honorifics can be expressions of respect or endearment. In the context of manga and anime, honorifics give insight into the nature of the relationship between characters. Many English translations leave out these important honorifics and therefore distort the feel of the original Japanese. Because Japanese honorifics contain nuances that English honorifics lack, it is our policy at Del Rey not to translate them. Here, instead, is a guide to some of the honorifics you may encounter in Del Rey Manga.

-san: This is the most common honorific and is equivalent to Mr., Miss, Ms., or Mrs. It is the all-purpose honorific and can be used in any situation where politeness is required.

-sama: This is one level higher than "-san" and is used to confer great respect.

-dono: This comes from the word "tono," which means "lord." It is an even higher level than "-sama" and confers utmost respect.

-kun: This suffix is used at the end of boys' names to express familiarity or endearment. It is also sometimes used by men among friends, or when addressing someone younger or of a lower station.

-chan: This is used to express endearment, mostly toward girls. It is also used for little boys, pets, and even among lovers. It gives a sense of childish cuteness.

Bozu: This is an informal way to refer to a boy, similar to the English terms "kid" and "squirt."

Sempai/Senpai: This title suggests that the addressee is one's senior in a group or organization. It is most often used in a school setting, where underclassmen refer to their upperclassmen as "sempai." It can also be used in the workplace, such as when a newer employee addresses an employee who has seniority in the company.

Kohai: This is the opposite of "sempai" and is used toward underclassmen in school or newcomers in the workplace. It connotes that the addressee is of a lower station.

Sensei: Literally meaning "one who has come before," this title is used for teachers, doctors, or masters of any profession or art.

[blank]: This is usually forgotten in these lists, but it is perhaps the most significant difference between Japanese and English. The lack of honorific means that the speaker has permission to address the person in a very intimate way. Usually, only family, spouses, or very close friends have this kind of permission. Known as *yobisute*, it can be gratifying when someone who has earned the intimacy starts to call one by one's name without an honorific. But when that intimacy hasn't been earned, it can be very insulting.

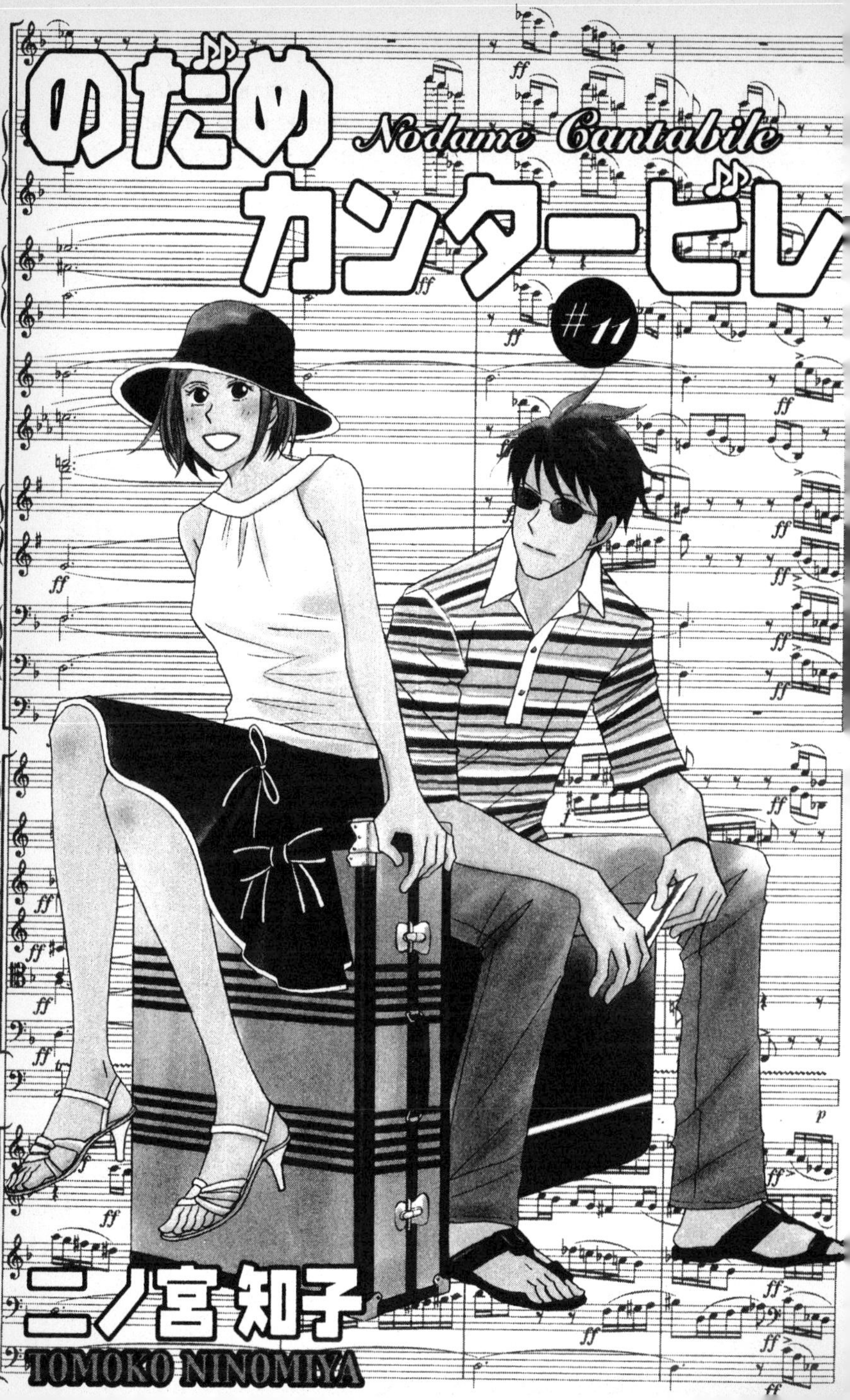
のだめカンタービレ
Nodame Cantabile
#11
二ノ宮知子
TOMOKO NINOMIYA

The Performers in

NODAME'S RHAPSODY ♥

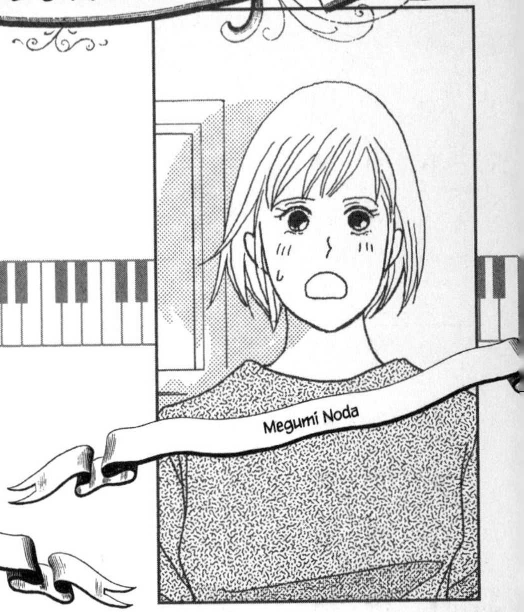
Megumi Noda

A musical prodigy, she's known for her unique performance as well as her struggles with sight reading. She's accepted to a Conservatoire in Paris with Chiaki after her dazzling performance during the Piano Competition at Momogaoka University during her senior year.

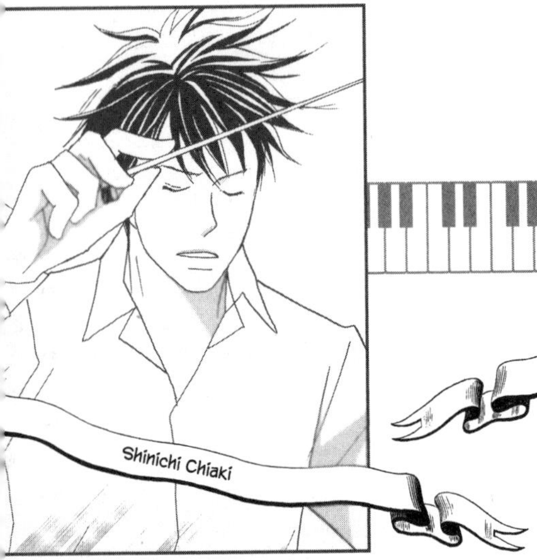
Shinichi Chiaki

His extreme fear of flying has stopped him from studying overseas, but he's finally overcome his phobia and is studying in Paris. He considers himself to be Viera's student, but in Japan, he's known as Stresemann's student. He likes to forge his own path.

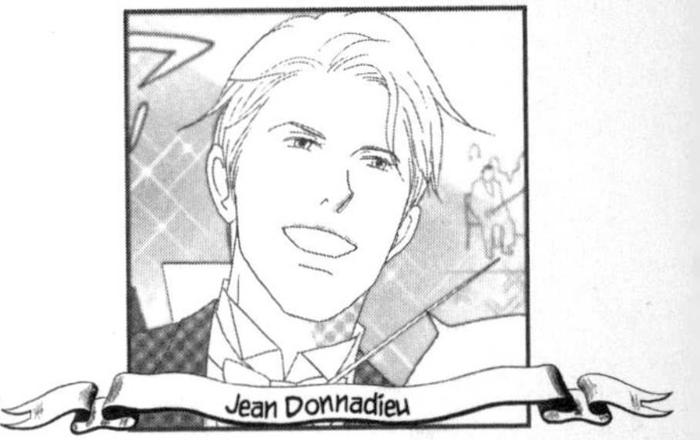
Jean Donnadieu

The winner of the competition at Belgium, he's Chiaki's main rival and a student of Sebastiano Viera. He's a very confident up-and-coming conductor.

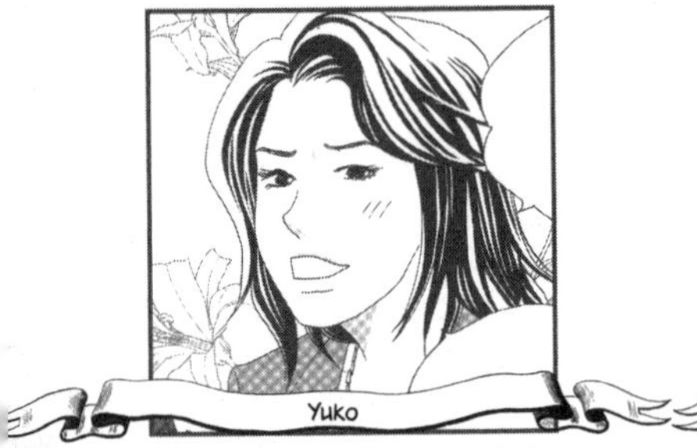
Yuko

She's Jean's girlfriend. Jean calls her "his lucky Venus." She's very motherly toward Jean, while she enjoys intimidating his competition.

Franz von Stresemann

AKA Milch Holstein, he's a world-famous German conductor and Chiaki's teacher. He's a horny old man and enjoys relaxing at cabarets.

Sebastiano Viera

An internationally renowned conductor, he's been a role model for Chiaki since Chiaki was very young. He does not think well of Stresemann after he hit on his wife and stole his toy.

Hajime Katahira

Another Japanese conductor participating in the current competition with Chiaki. He's 30 years old and a faithful family man. He's known for calculating the duration of his "jumps" during performances.

Elise

Stresemann's capable but somewhat flaky manager. She's addicted to beef jerky and has left poor Chiaki to deal with her horny client while she takes a relaxing vacation.

Franck Lantoine

A French student who lives in the same apartment building as Chiaki and Nodame. He's a huge fan of anime and Puri Gorota. He's got a crush on Nodame, but it's unlikely that anthing will happen...

Tanya

She's a sexy, boy-crazy Russian student who lives in the same apartment building as Nodame and Chiaki. She recently broke up with her boyfriend, but she's hoping Chiaki might mend her broken heart.

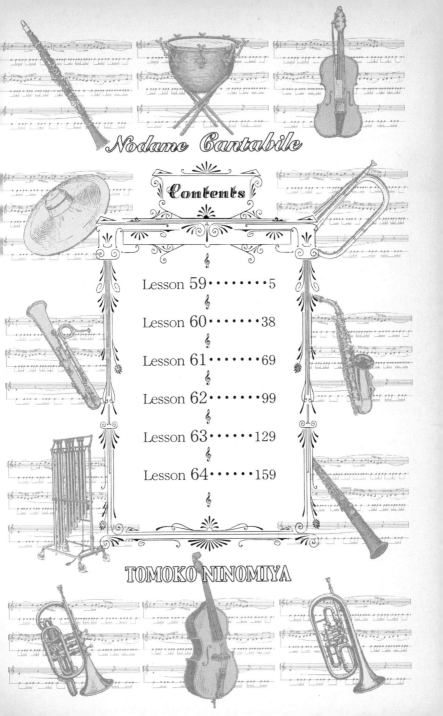

Nodame Cantabile

Contents

TOMOKO NINOMIYA

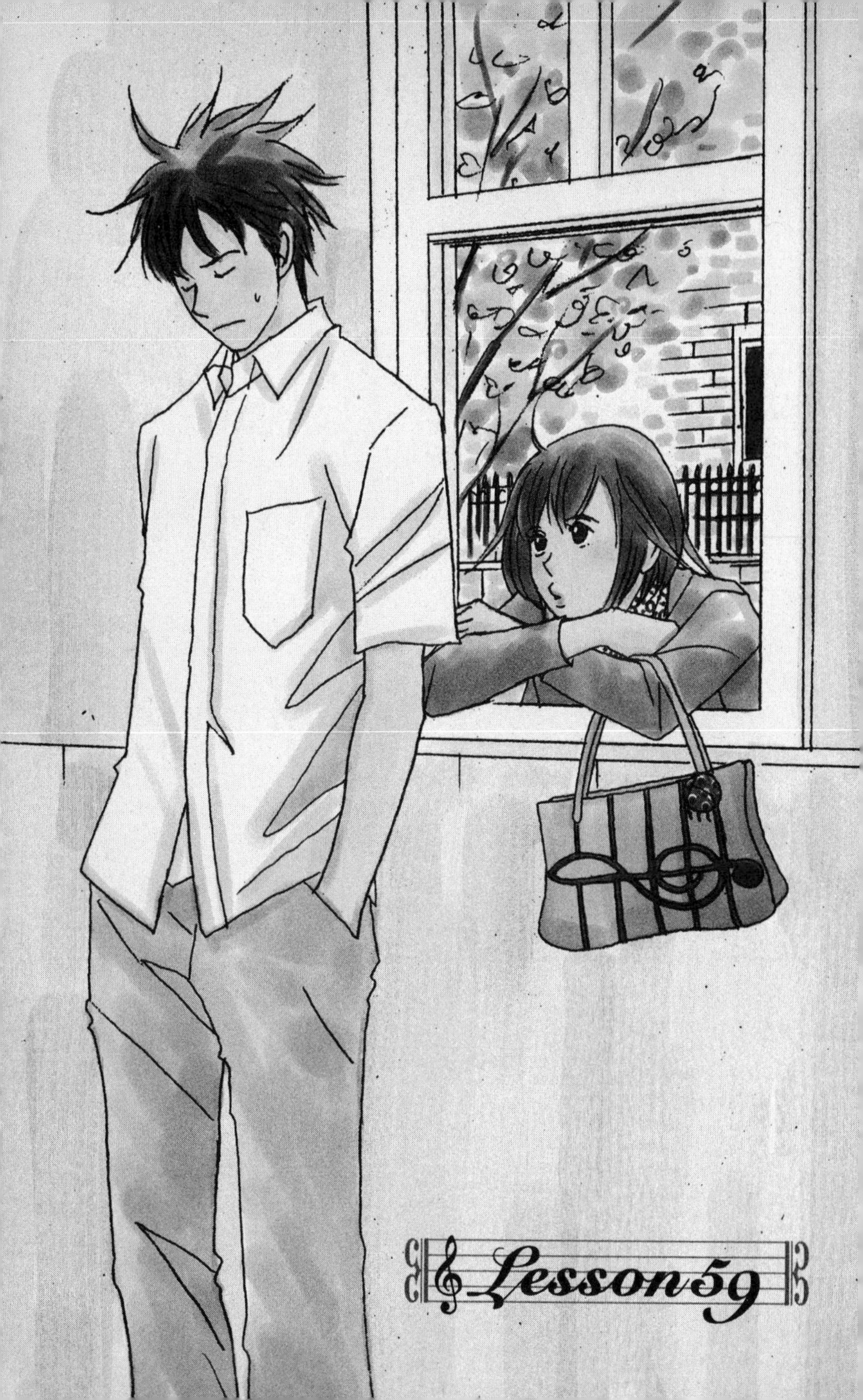
Lesson 59

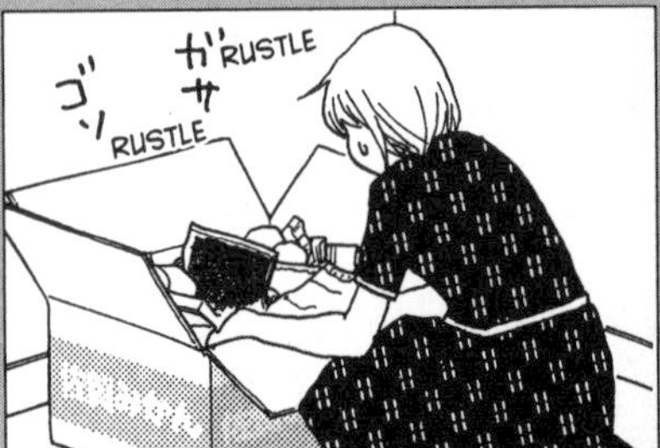
ガサ
RUSTLE
ゴソ
RUSTLE

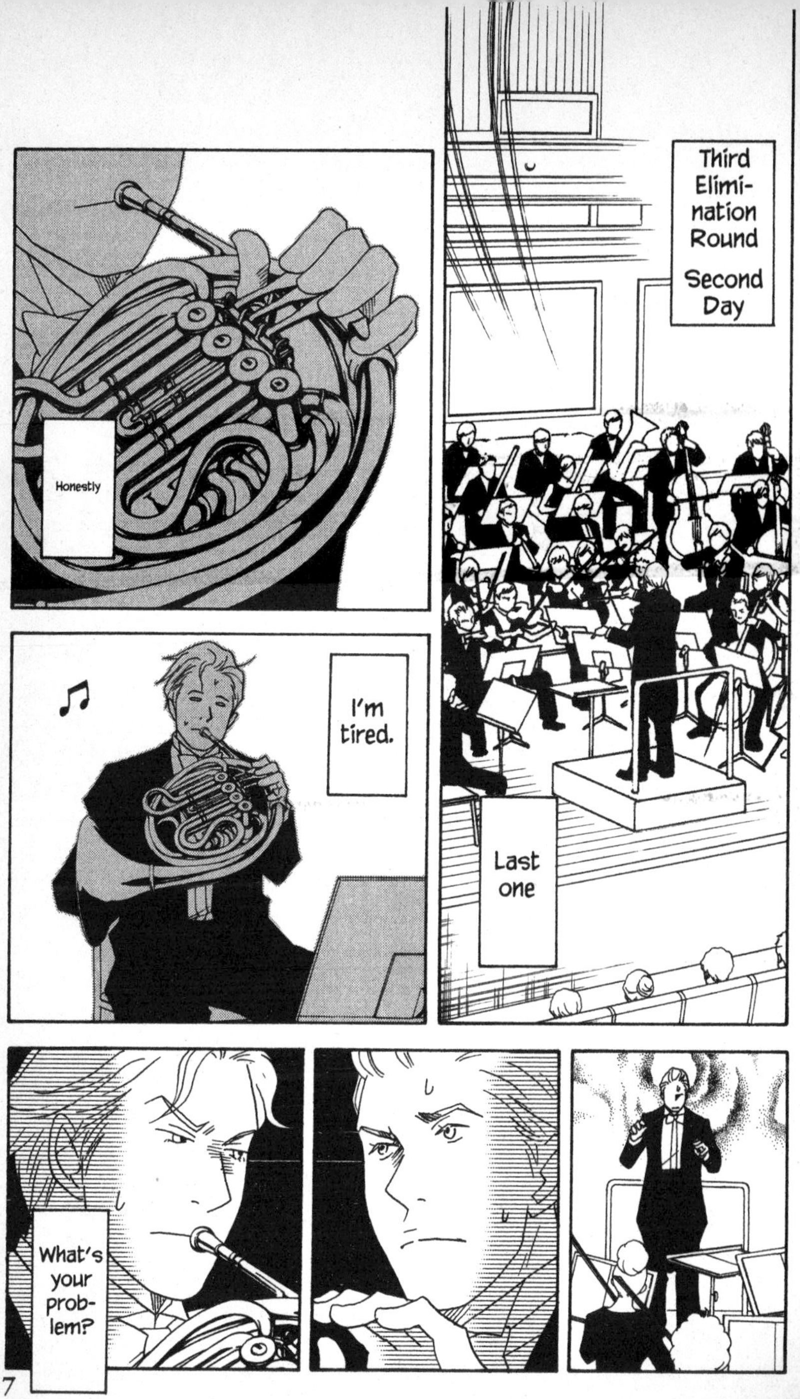
Third Elimination Round
Second Day
Last one
Honestly
I'm tired.
What's your problem?

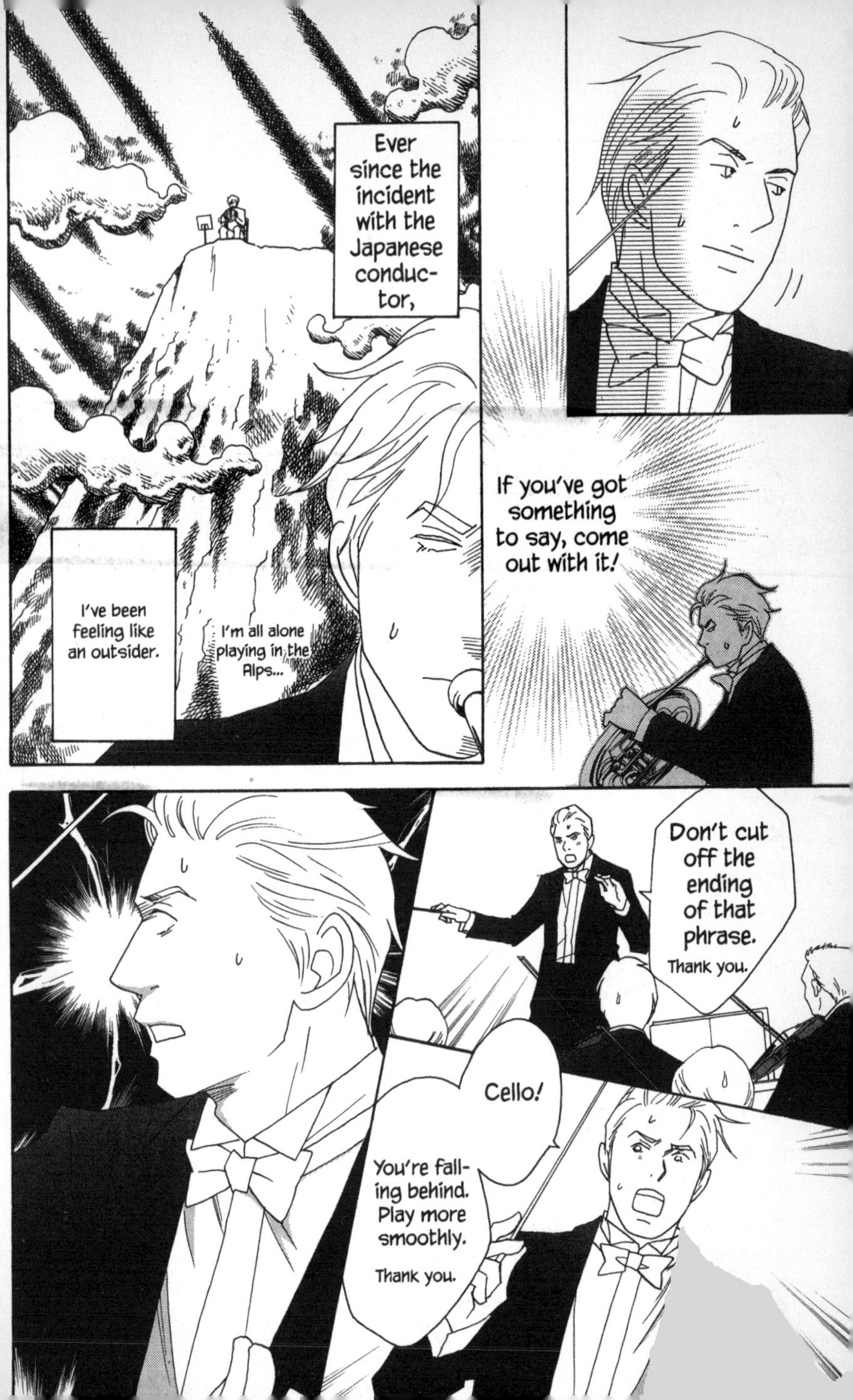
If you've got something to say, come out with it!
Ever since the incident with the Japanese conductor,
I've been feeling like an outsider.
I'm all alone playing in the Alps...
Don't cut off the ending of that phrase.
Thank you.
Cello!
You're falling behind. Play more smoothly.
Thank you.

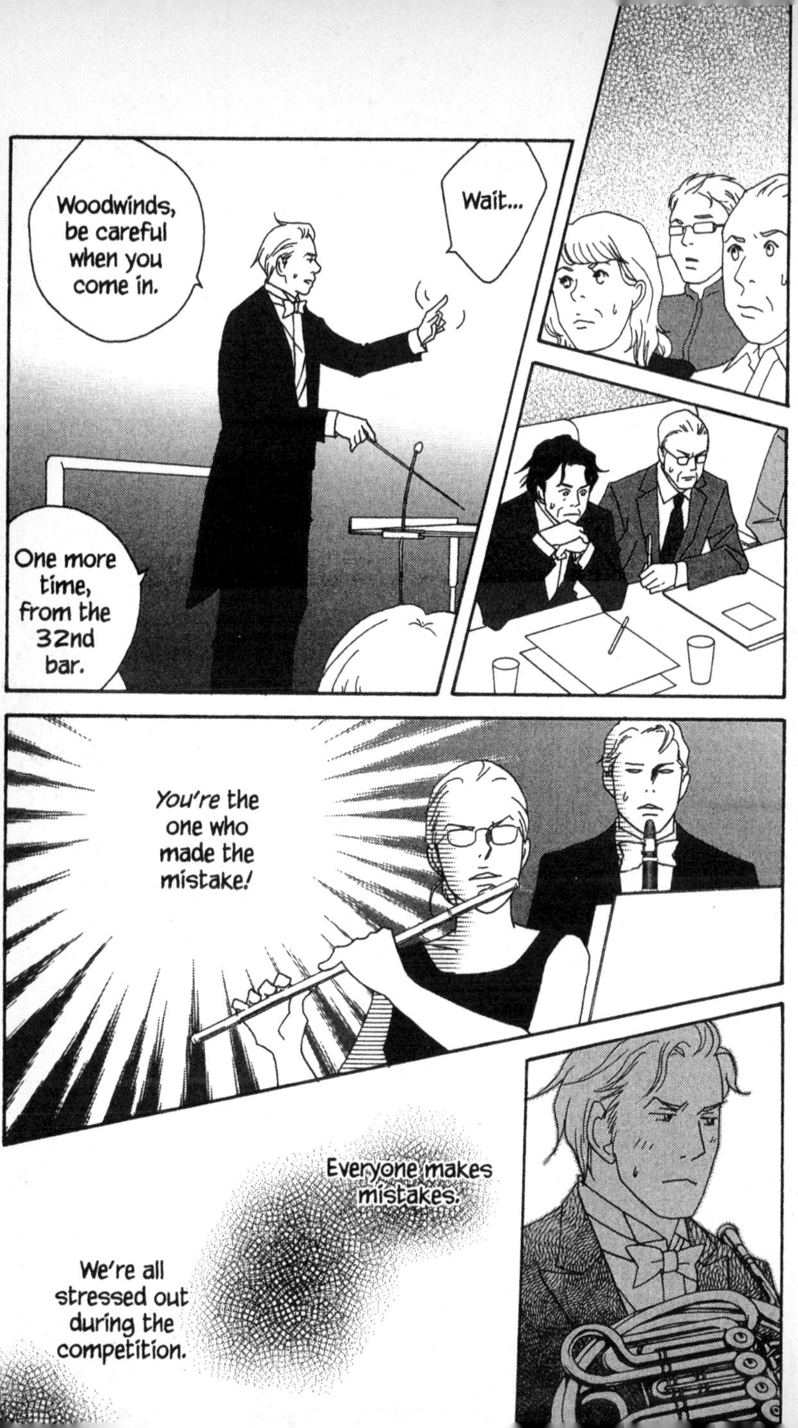
Wait...
Woodwinds, be careful when you come in.
One more time, from the 32nd bar.
You're the one who made the mistake!
Everyone makes mistakes.
We're all stressed out during the competition.

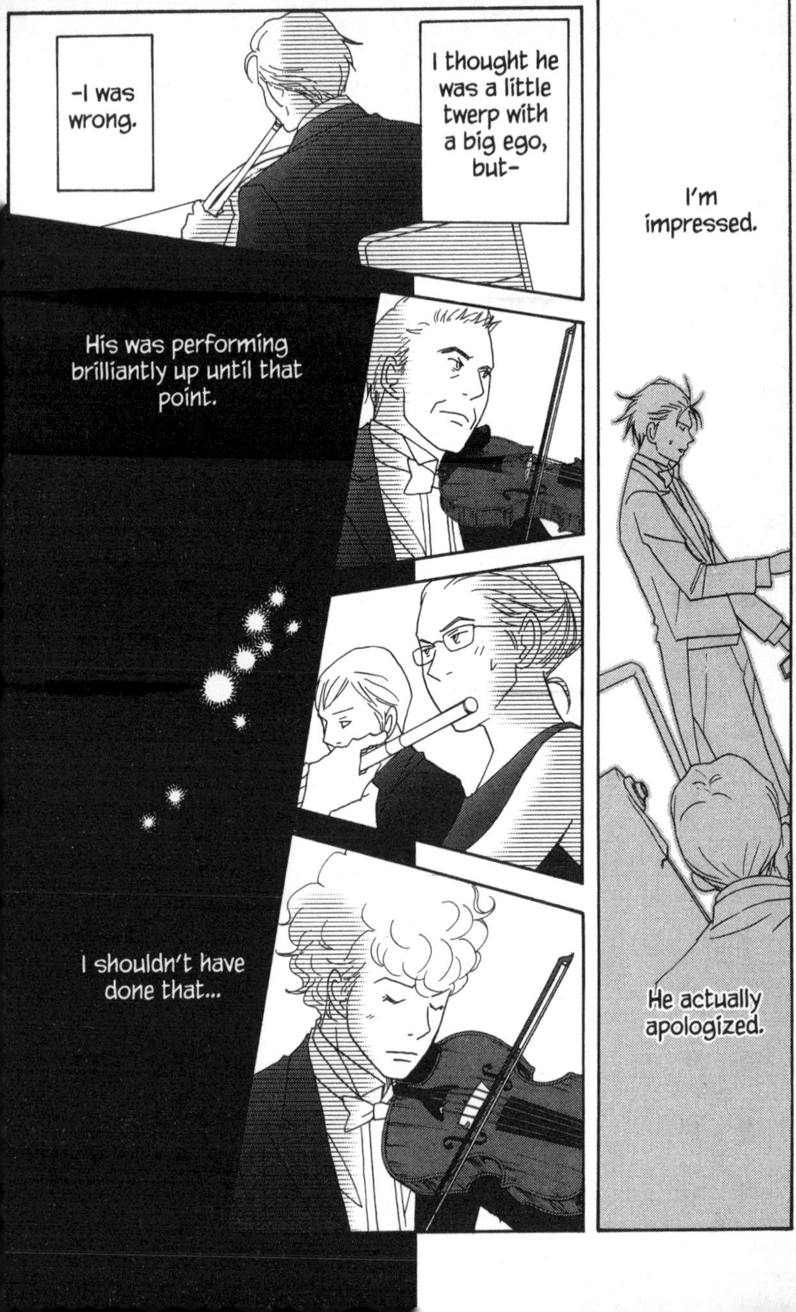
I'm impressed.
He actually apologized.
I thought he was a little twerp with a big ego, but-
-I was wrong.
His was performing brilliantly up until that point.
I shouldn't have done that...

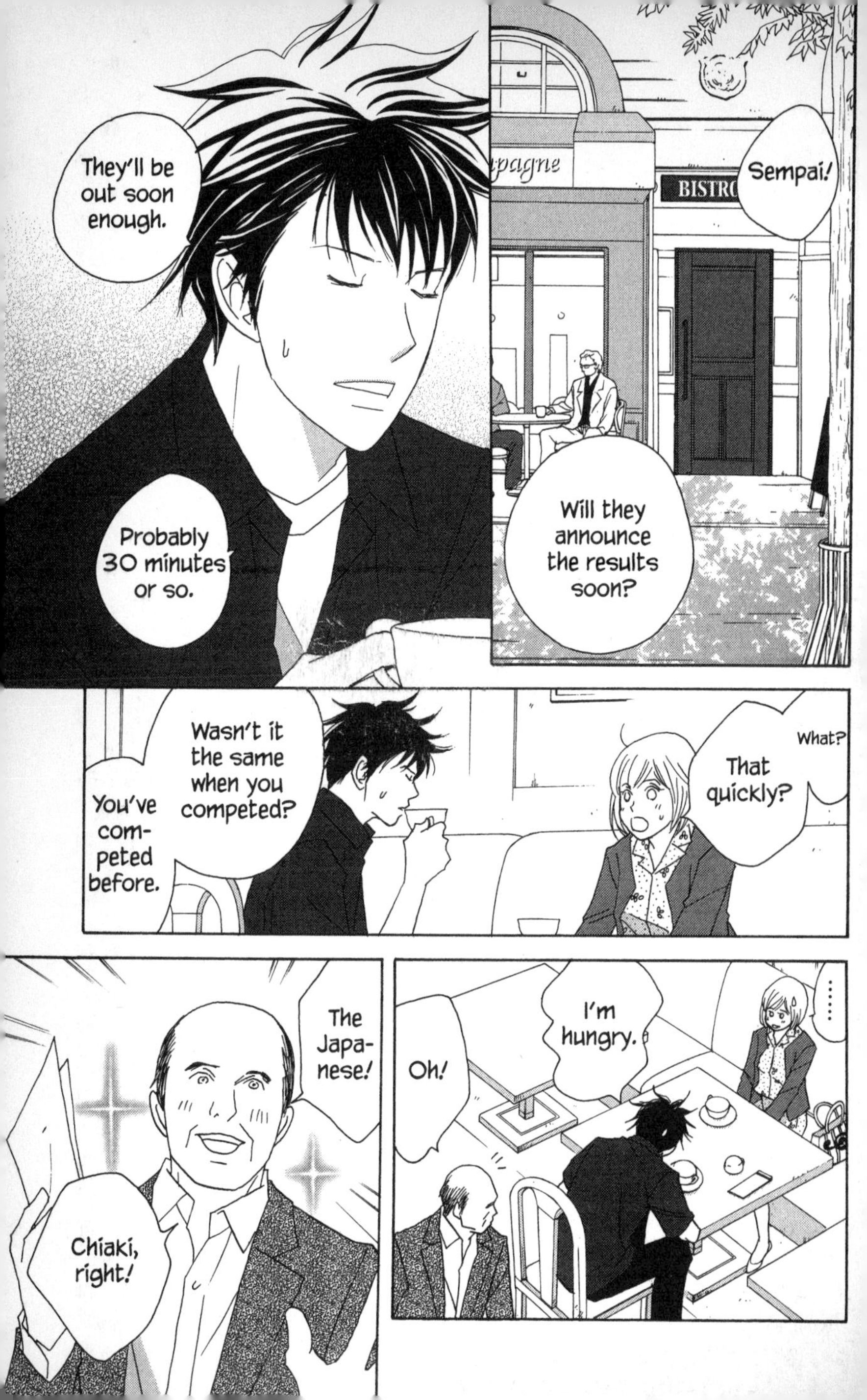
Sempai!
Will they announce the results soon?
They'll be out soon enough.
Probably 30 minutes or so.
What?
That quickly?
Wasn't it the same when you competed?
You've competed before.
……
I'm hungry.
Oh!
The Japanese!
Chiaki, right!

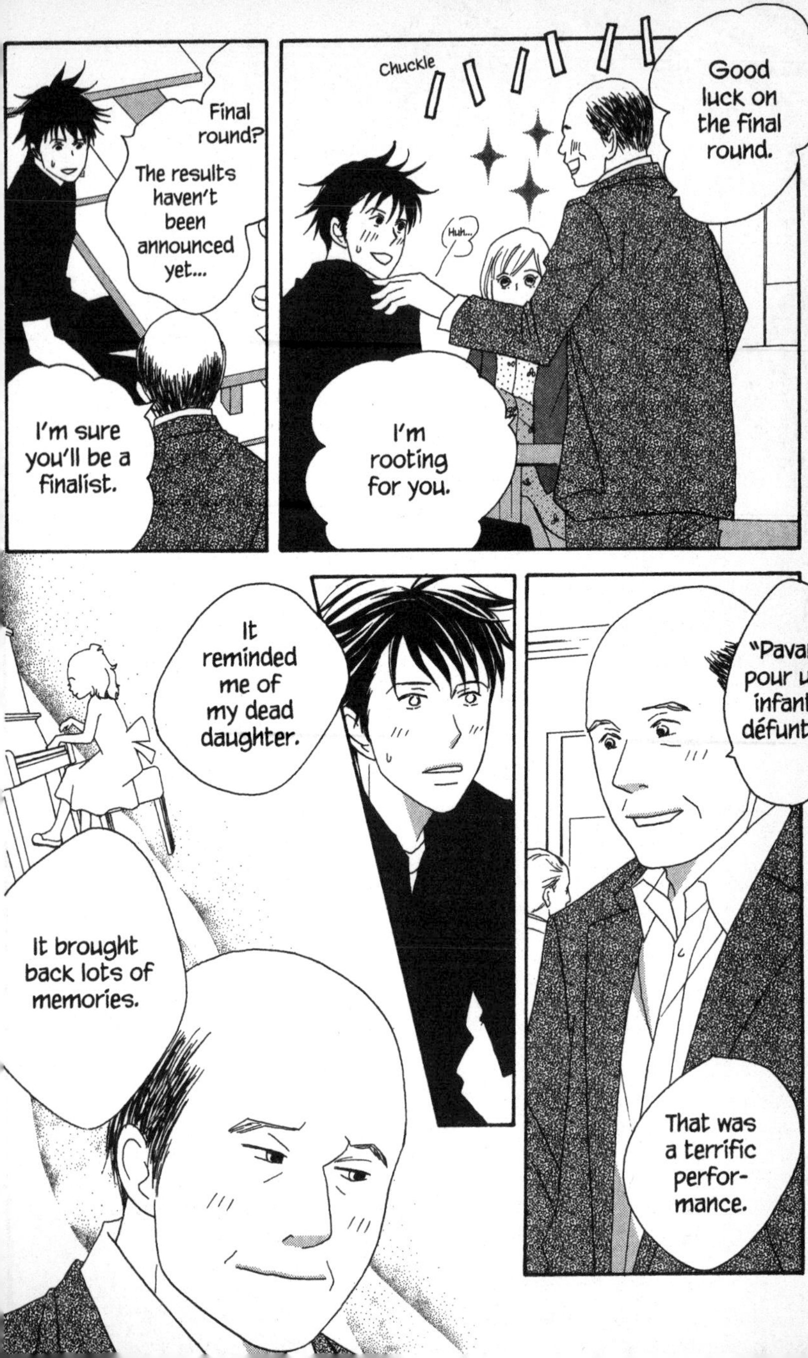
Good luck on the final round.
Chuckle
Huh...
I'm rooting for you.
Final round?
The results haven't been announced yet...
I'm sure you'll be a finalist.
"Pavane pour une infante défunte."
That was a terrific performance.
It reminded me of my dead daughter.
It brought back lots of memories.

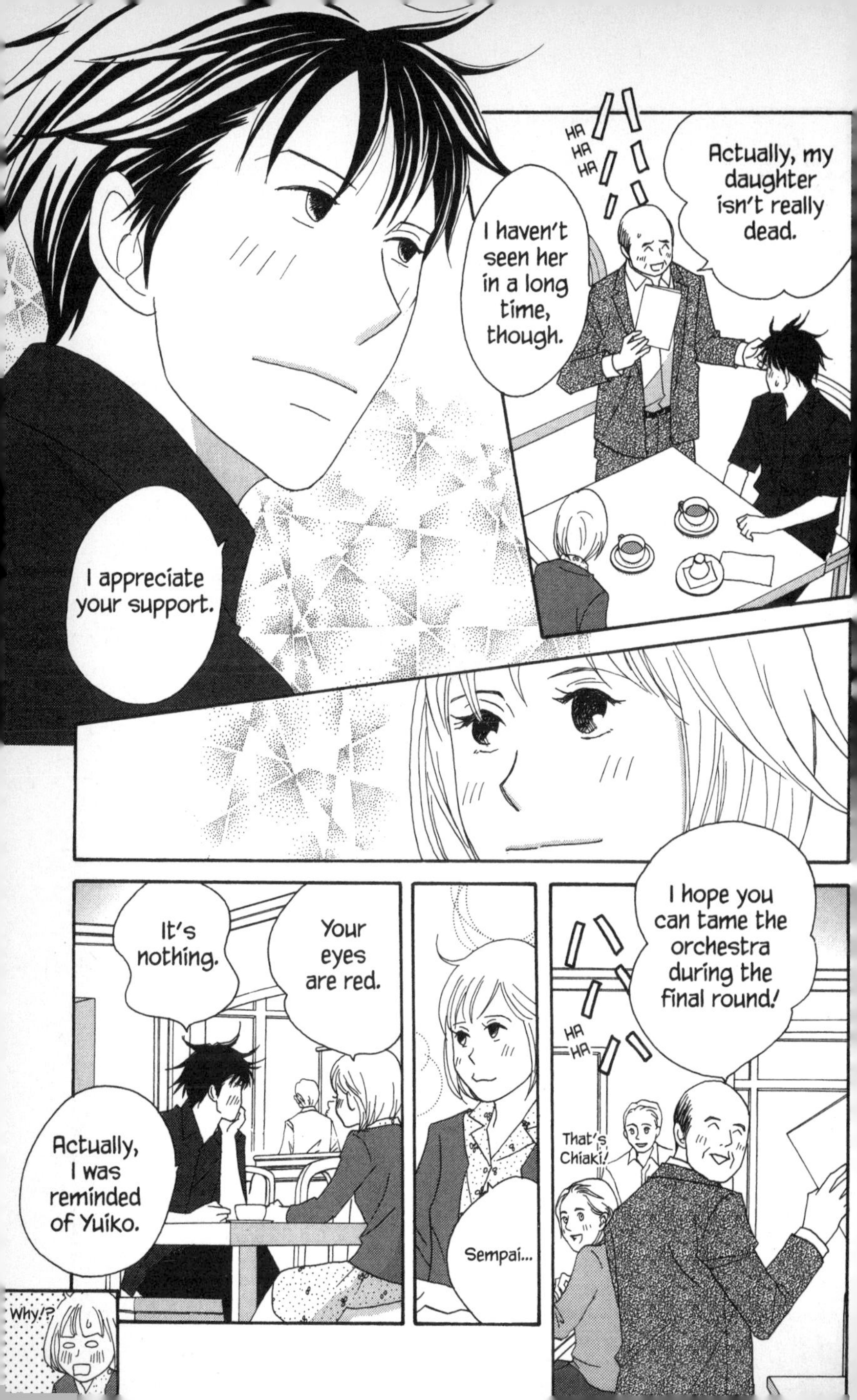
Actually, my daughter isn't really dead.
HA HA HA
I haven't seen her in a long time, though.
I appreciate your support.
I hope you can tame the orchestra during the final round!
HA HA
That's Chiaki!
Sempai...
Your eyes are red.
It's nothing.
Actually, I was reminded of Yuiko.
Why!?

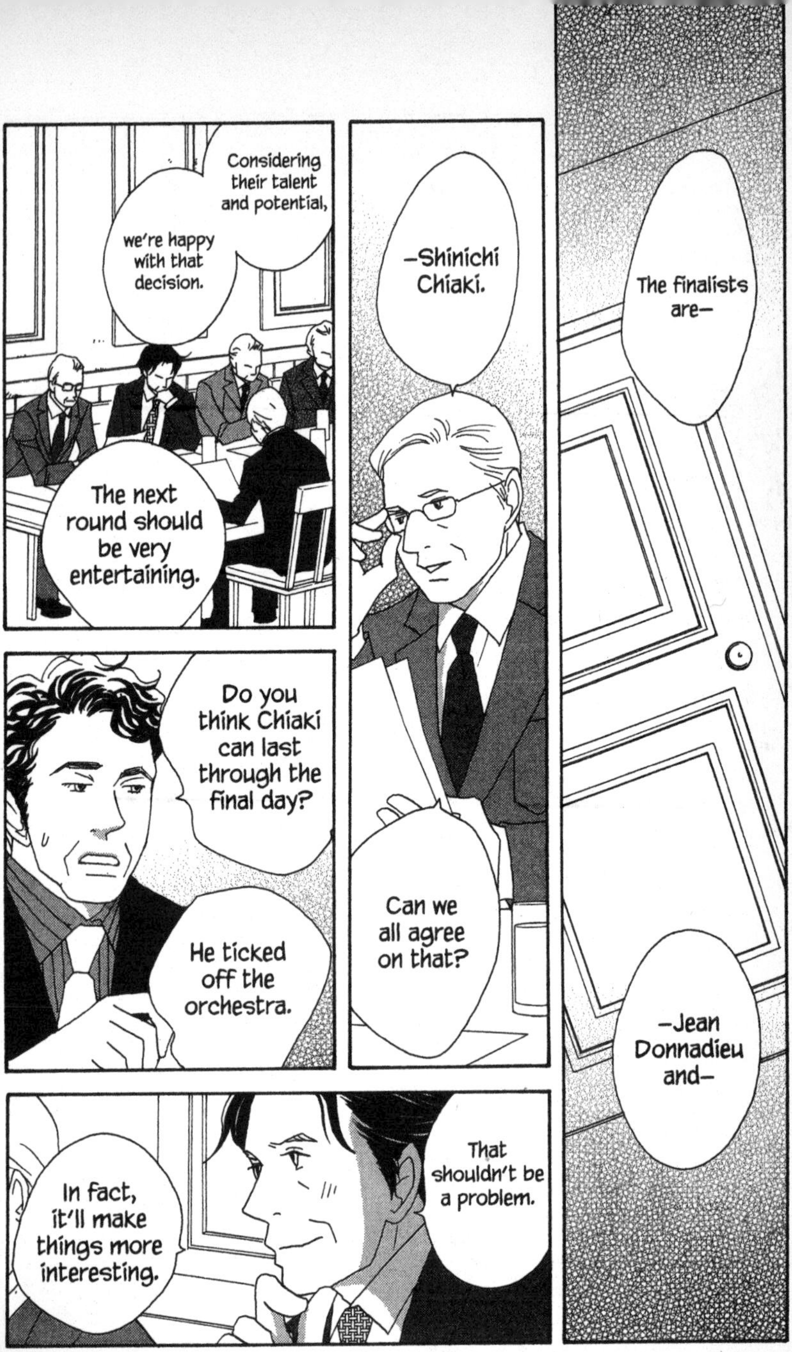
The finalists are—
—Jean Donnadieu and—
—Shinichi Chiaki.
Can we all agree on that?
Considering their talent and potential,
we're happy with that decision.
The next round should be very entertaining.
Do you think Chiaki can last through the final day?
He ticked off the orchestra.
That shouldn't be a problem.
In fact, it'll make things more interesting.

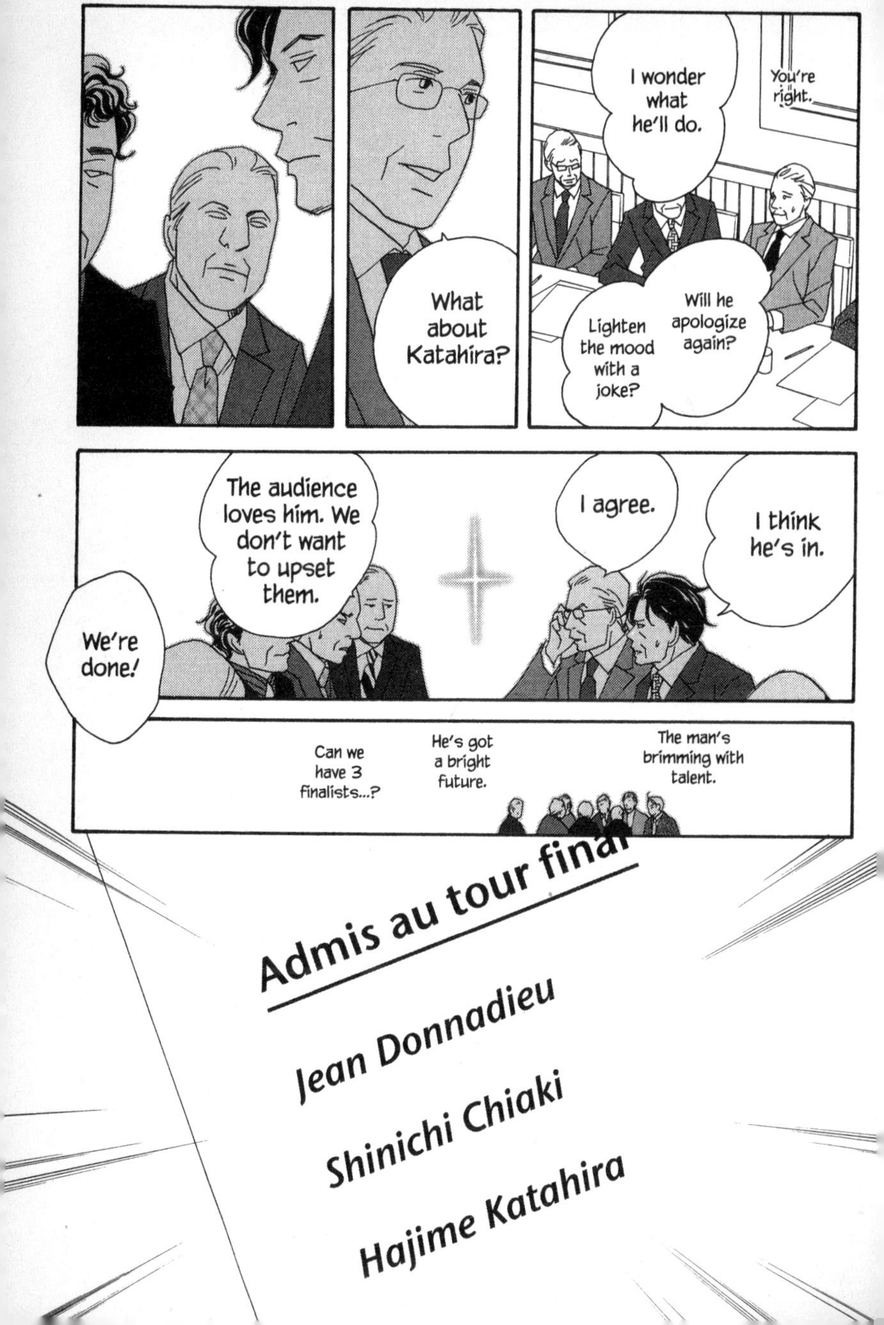
You're right.
I wonder what he'll do.
Will he apologize again?
Lighten the mood with a joke?
What about Katahira?
I think he's in.
I agree.
The audience loves him. We don't want to upset them.
We're done!
The man's brimming with talent.
He's got a bright future.
Can we have 3 finalists...?
Admis au tour final
Jean Donnadieu
Shinichi Chiaki
Hajime Katahira

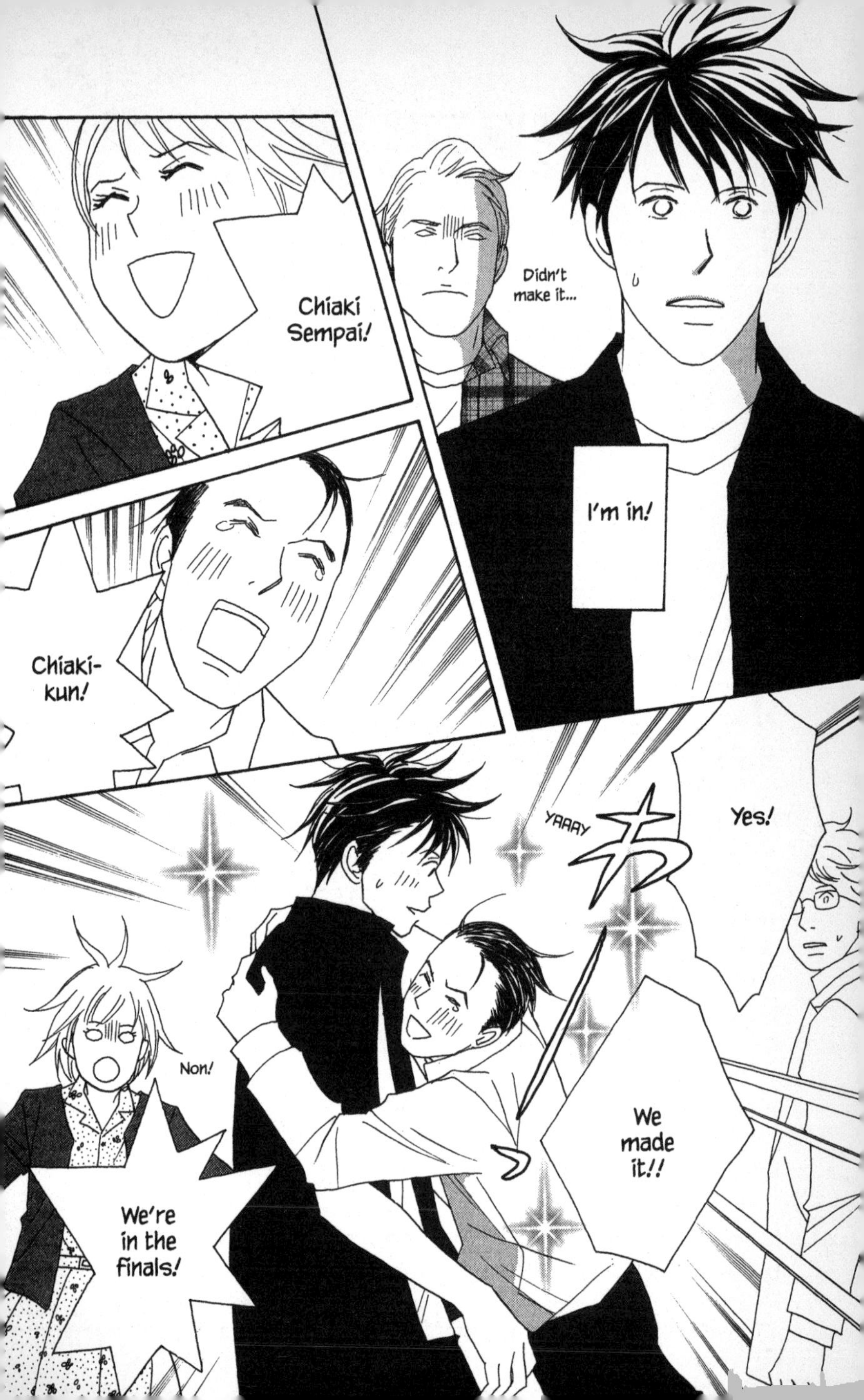
Didn't make it...
I'm in!
Chiaki Sempai!
Chiaki-kun!
Yes!
YAAAY
We made it!!
Non!
We're in the finals!

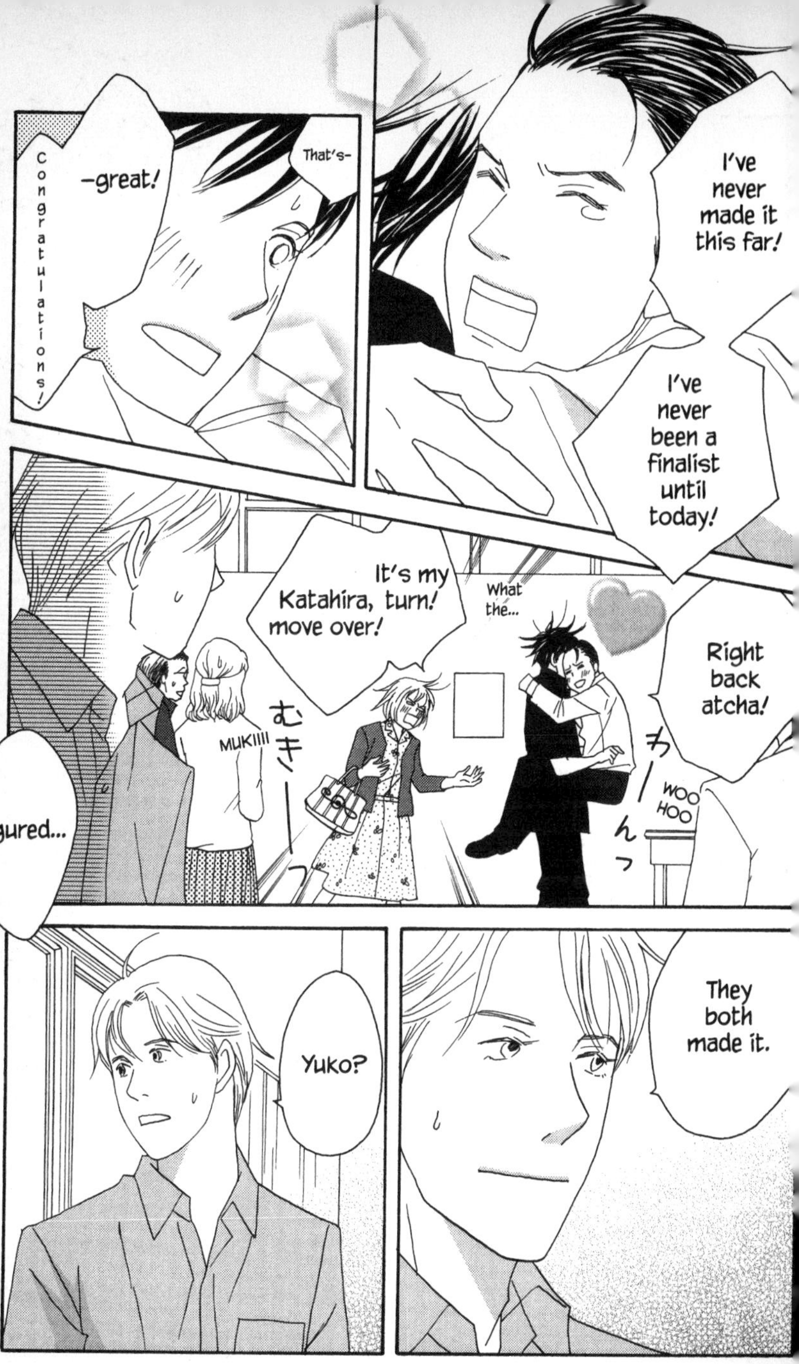
I've never made it this far!
I've never been a finalist until today!
That's-
-great!
Congratulations!
Right back atcha!
わーんっ
WOO HOO
What the...
It's my turn! Katahira, move over!
むきーっ
MUKIIII
I figured...
They both made it.
Yuko?

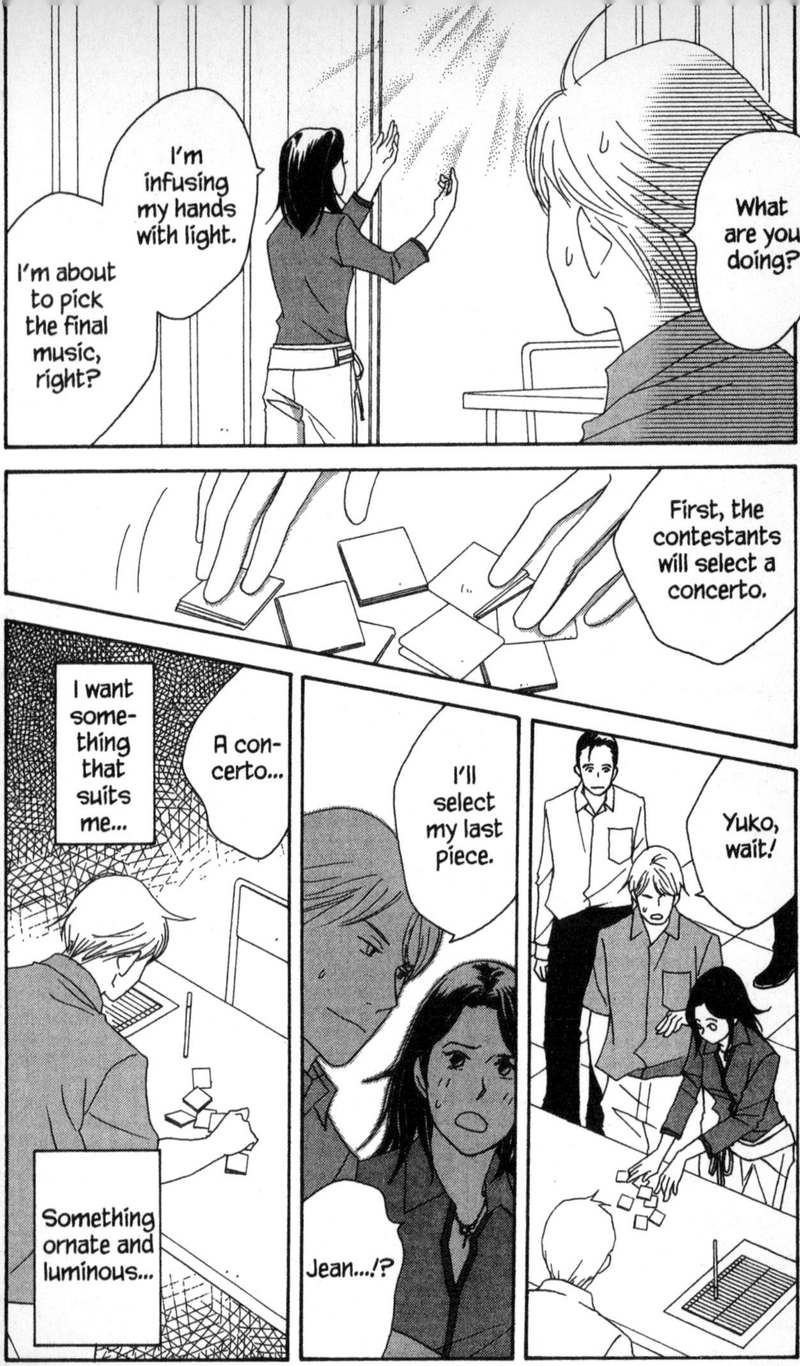
What are you doing?
I'm infusing my hands with light.
I'm about to pick the final music, right?
First, the contestants will select a concerto.
Yuko, wait!
I'll select my last piece.
Jean...!?
A con-certo...
I want some-thing that suits me...
Something ornate and luminous...

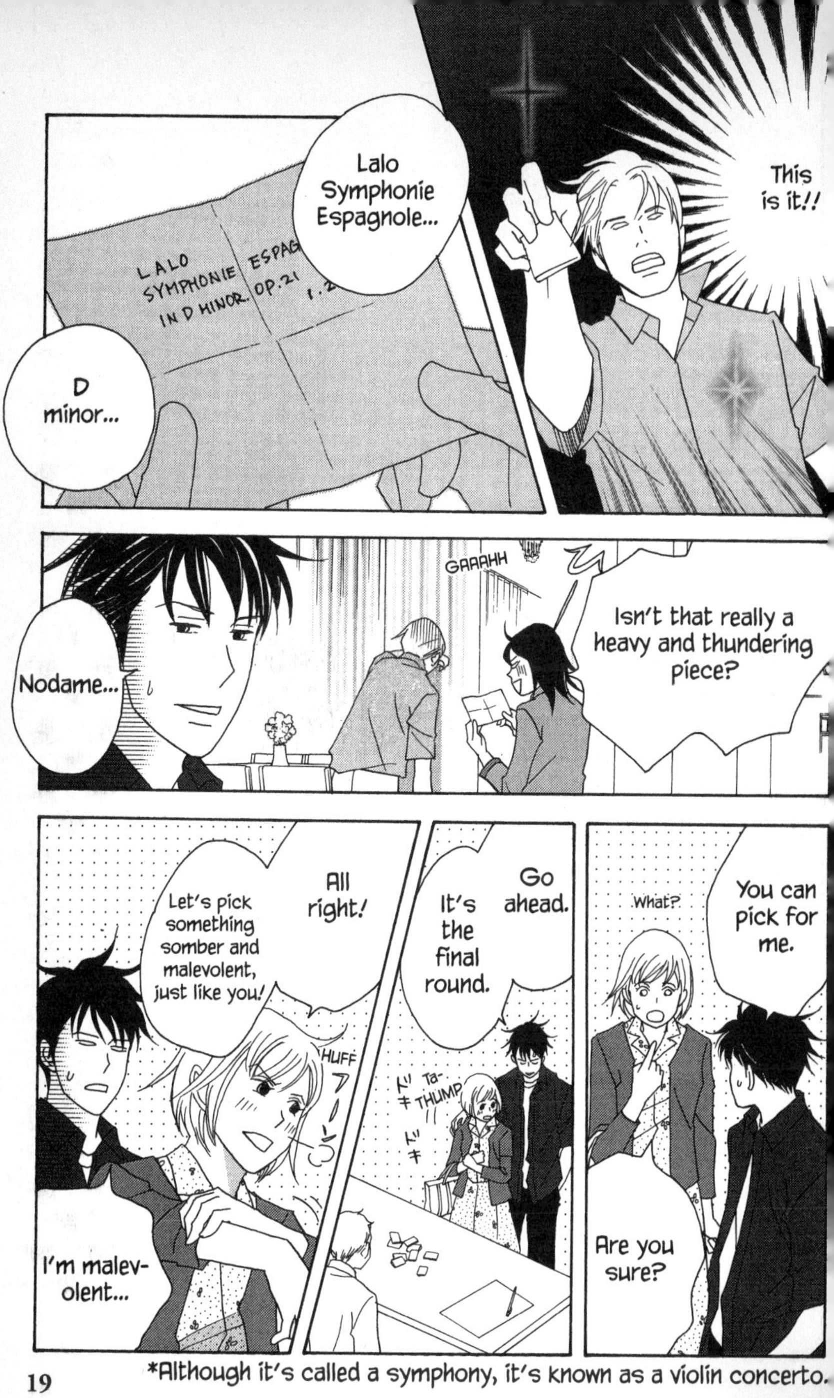
This is it!!
LALO SYMPHONIE ESPAG IN D MINOR. OP.21
Lalo Symphonie Espagnole...
D minor...
Isn't that really a heavy and thundering piece?
GAAAHH
Nodame...
You can pick for me.
What?
Are you sure?
Go ahead.
It's the final round.
Ta-THUMP
All right!
Let's pick something somber and malevolent, just like you!
HUFF
I'm malevolent...

*Although it's called a symphony, it's known as a violin concerto.

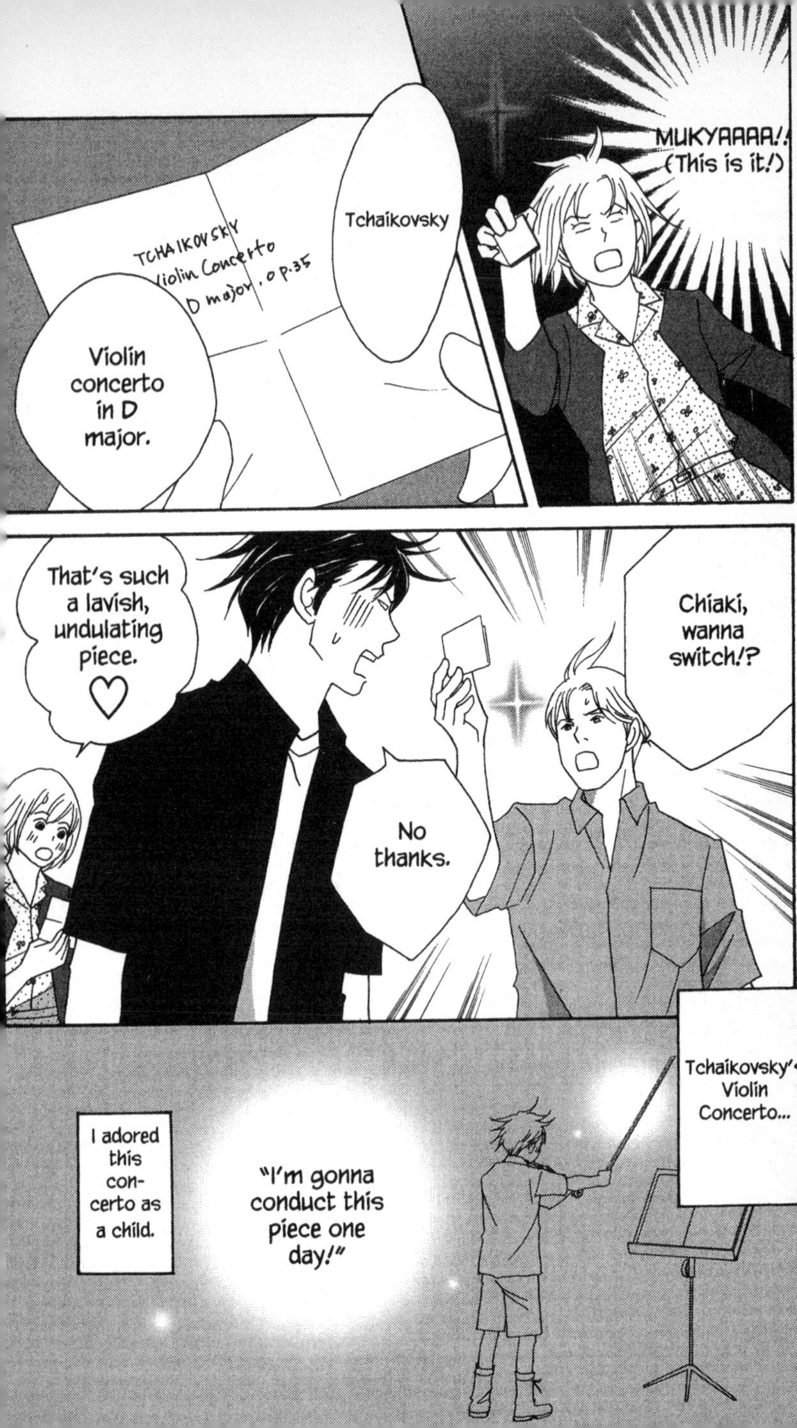
MUKYAAAA!!
(This is it!)
TCHAIKOVSKY
Violin Concerto
D major, op.35
Tchaikovsky
Violin concerto in D major.
Chiaki, wanna switch!?
That's such a lavish, undulating piece. ♡
No thanks.
Tchaikovsky's Violin Concerto...
I adored this con-certo as a child.
"I'm gonna conduct this piece one day!"

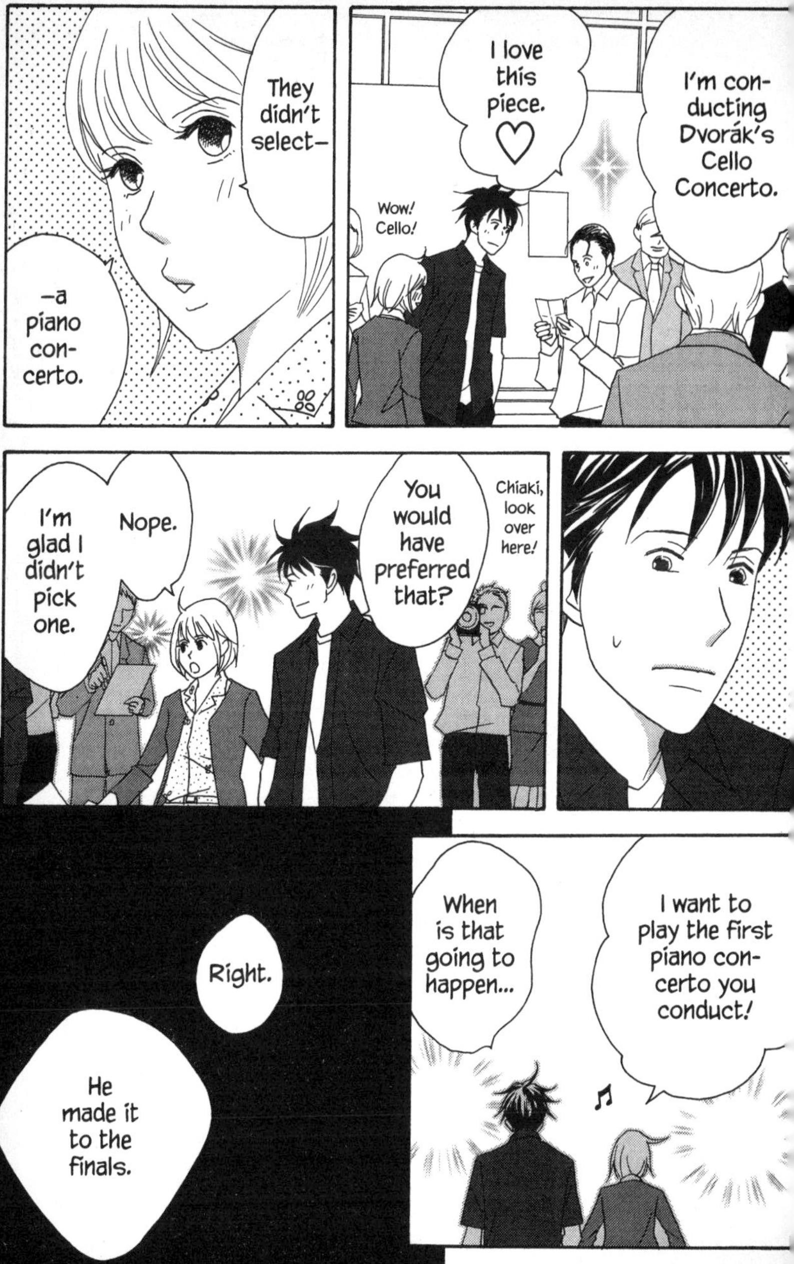
I'm conducting Dvorák's Cello Concerto.
I love this piece. ♡
Wow! Cello!
They didn't select—
—a piano concerto.
Chiaki, look over here!
You would have preferred that?
Nope.
I'm glad I didn't pick one.
I want to play the first piano concerto you conduct!
When is that going to happen...
Right.
He made it to the finals.

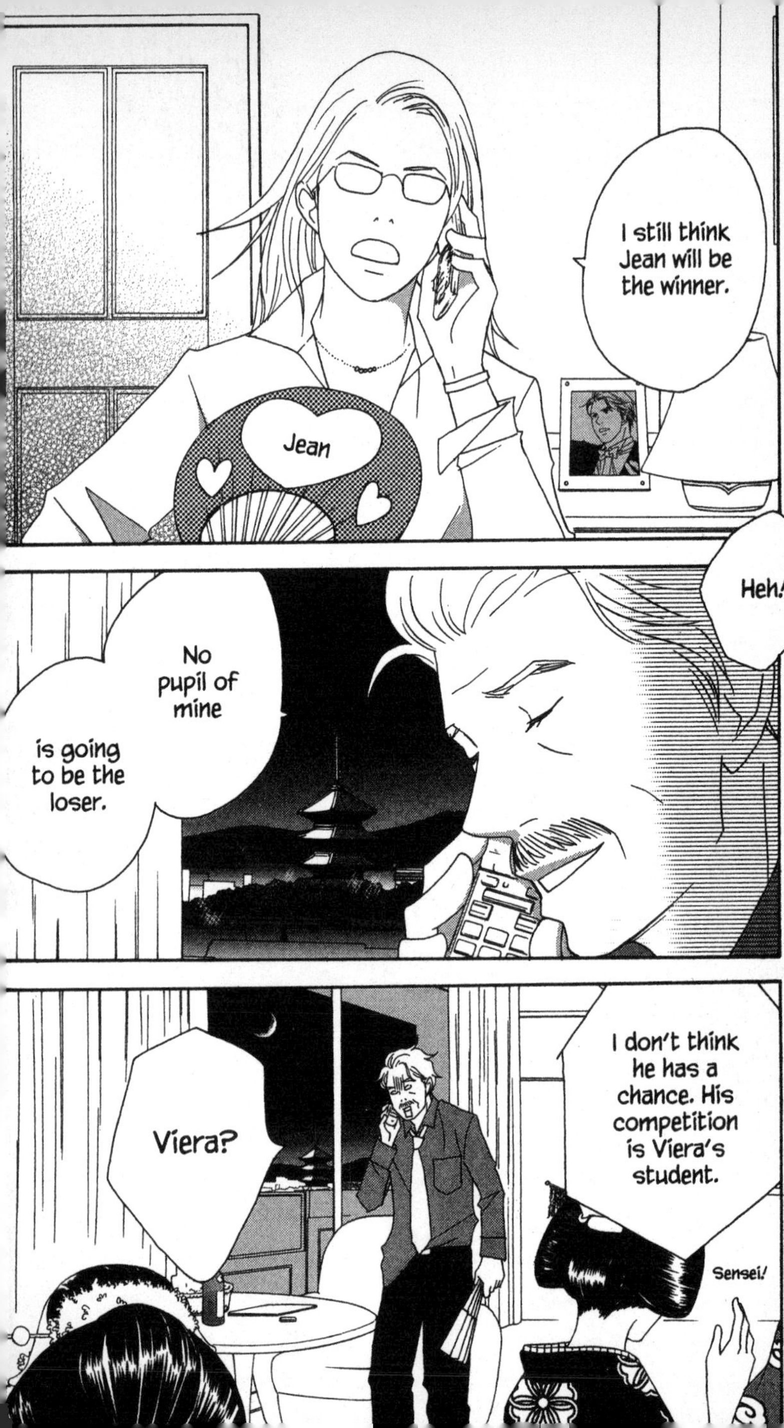
I still think Jean will be the winner.
Jean
Heh!
No pupil of mine
is going to be the loser.
I don't think he has a chance. His competition is Viera's student.
Sensei!
Viera?

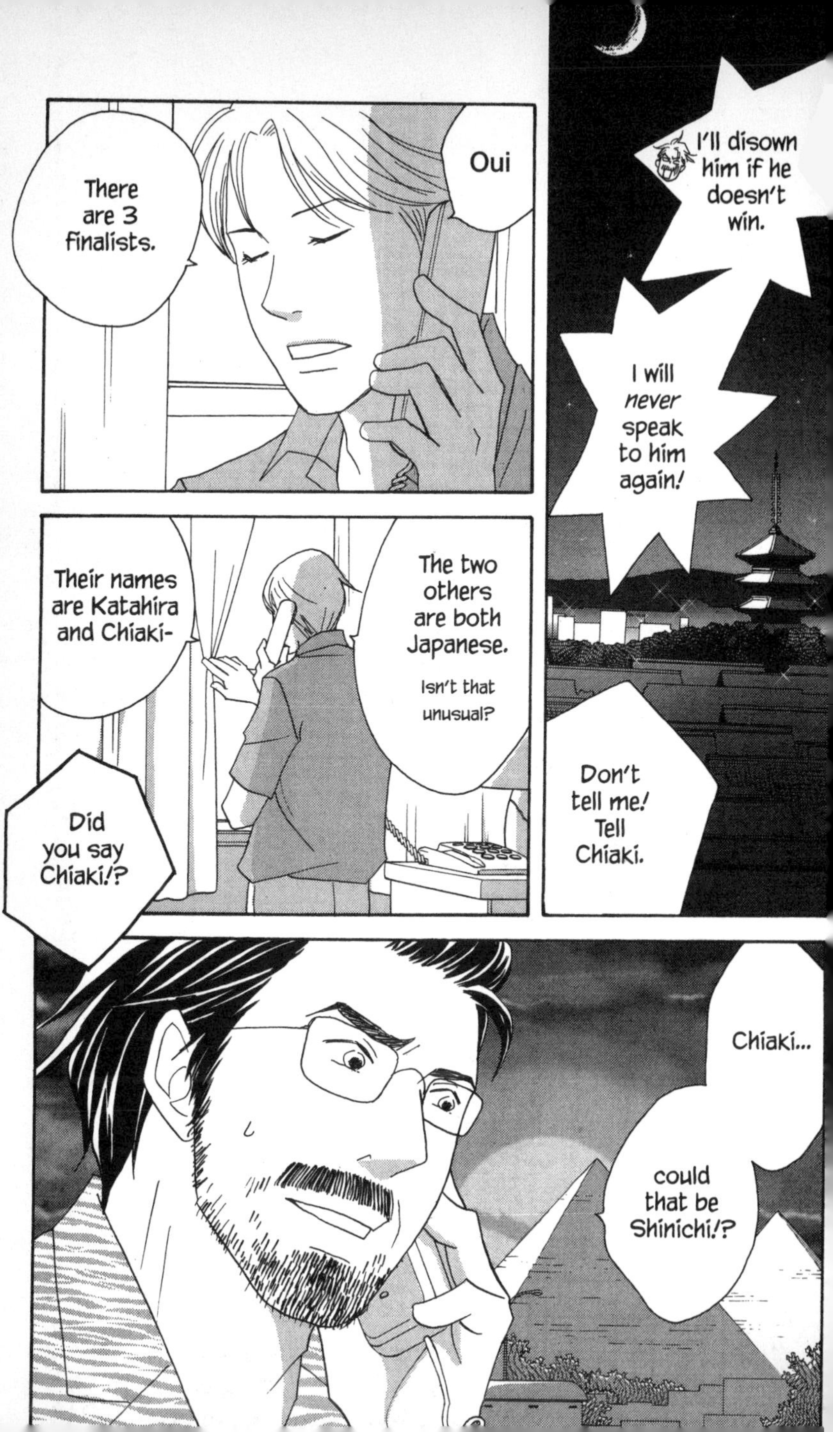
I'll disown him if he doesn't win.
I will *never* speak to him again!
Don't tell me! Tell Chiaki.
Oui
There are 3 finalists.
The two others are both Japanese.
Isn't that unusual?
Their names are Katahira and Chiaki-
Did you say Chiaki!?
Chiaki...
could that be Shinichi!?

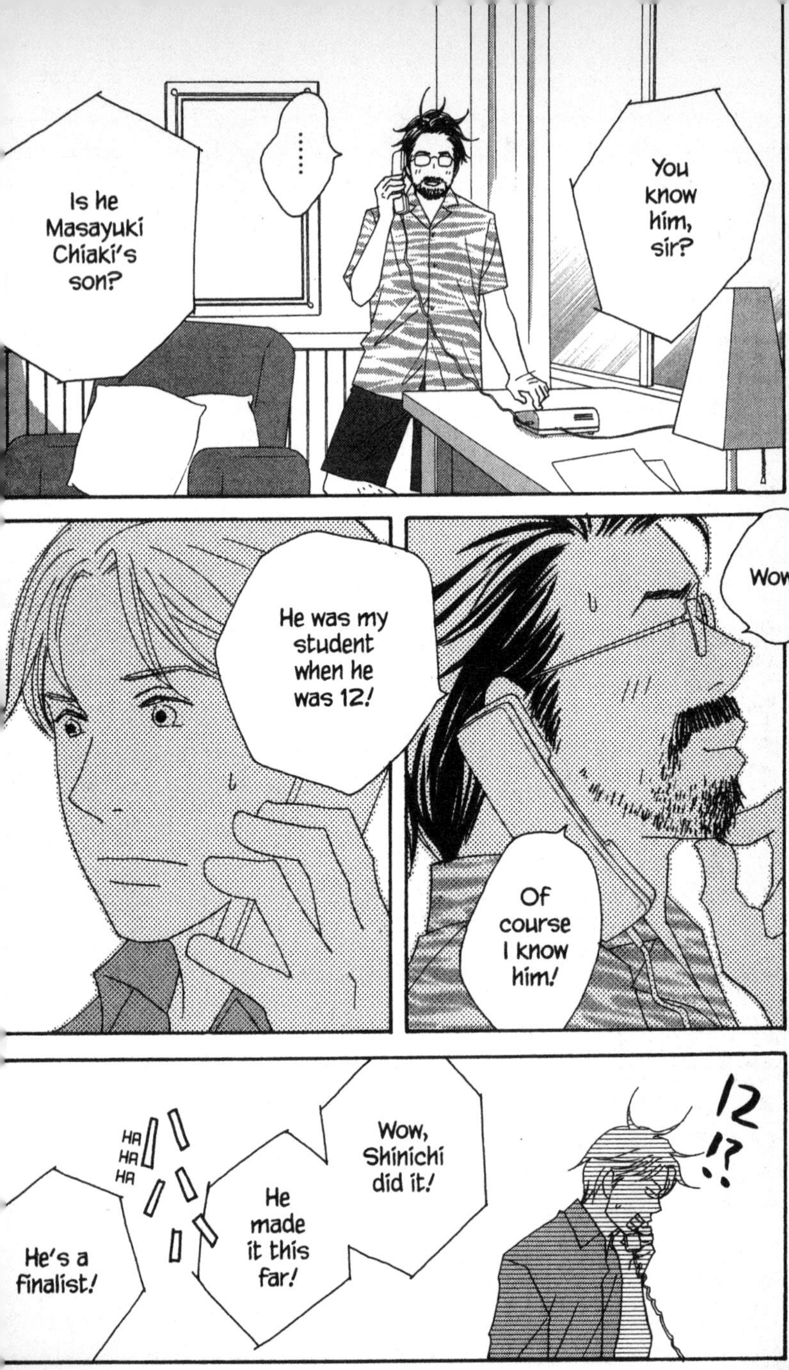
You know him, sir?
......
Is he Masayuki Chiaki's son?
Wow!
Of course I know him!
He was my student when he was 12!
12!?
Wow, Shinichi did it!
He made it this far!
HA HA HA
He's a finalist!

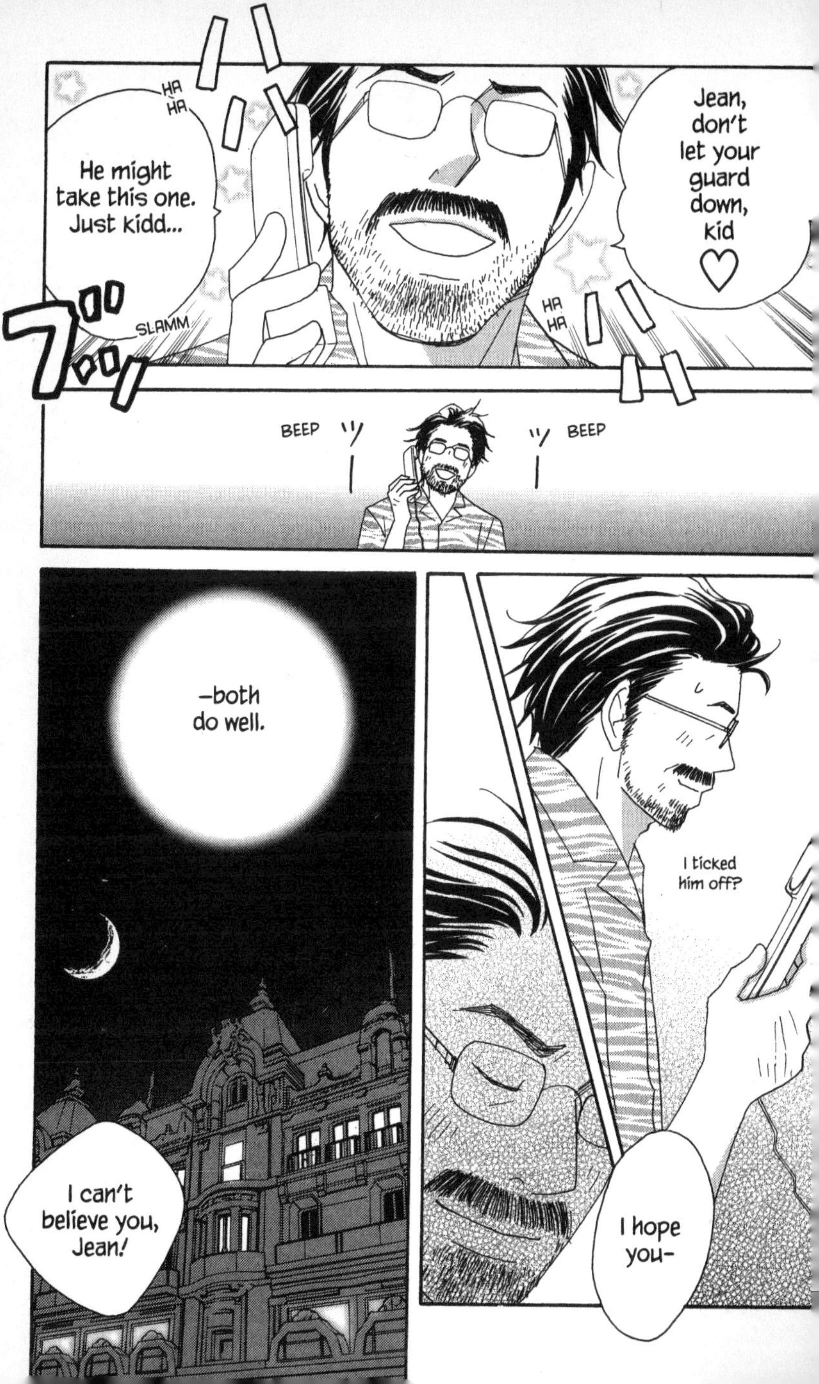
Jean, don't let your guard down, kid ♥
HA HA
HA HA
He might take this one. Just kidd...
SLAMM
BEEP
BEEP
I ticked him off?
I hope you-
-both do well.
I can't believe you, Jean!

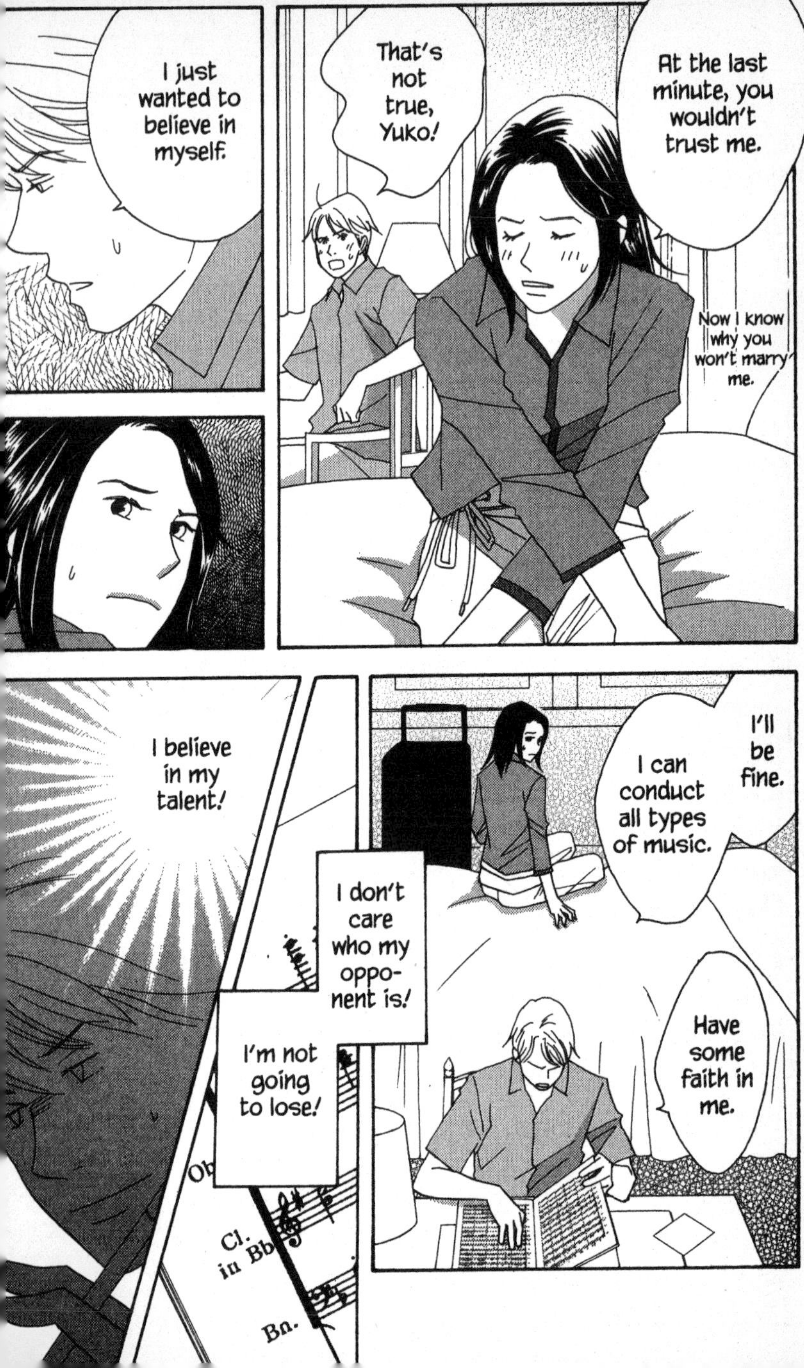
At the last minute, you wouldn't trust me.
That's not true, Yuko!
Now I know why you won't marry me.
I just wanted to believe in myself.
I'll be fine.
I can conduct all types of music.
Have some faith in me.
I believe in my talent!
I don't care who my opponent is!
I'm not going to lose!
Ob
Cl. in Bb
Bn.

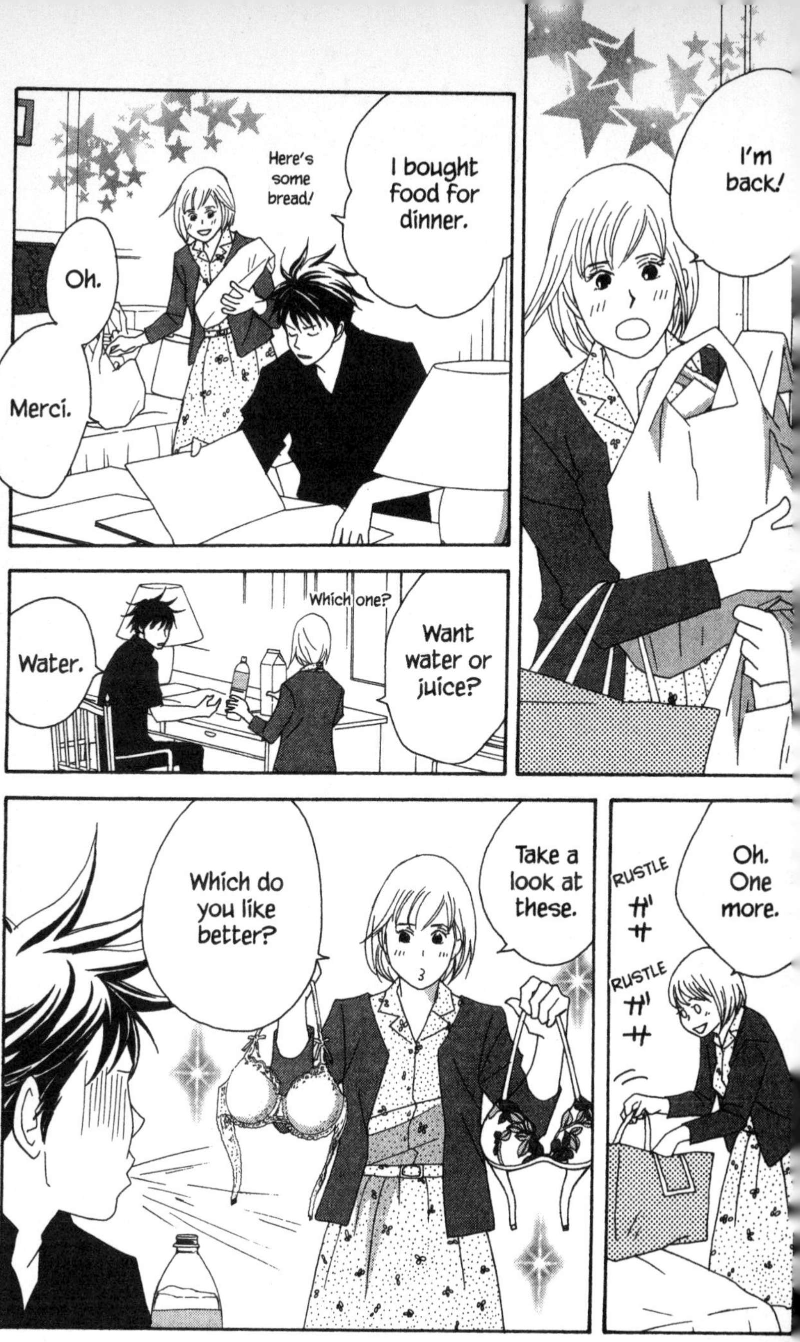
I'm back!
I bought food for dinner.
Here's some bread!
Oh.
Merci.
Want water or juice?
Which one?
Water.
Oh. One more.
RUSTLE
ガサ
RUSTLE
ガサ
Take a look at these.
Which do you like better?

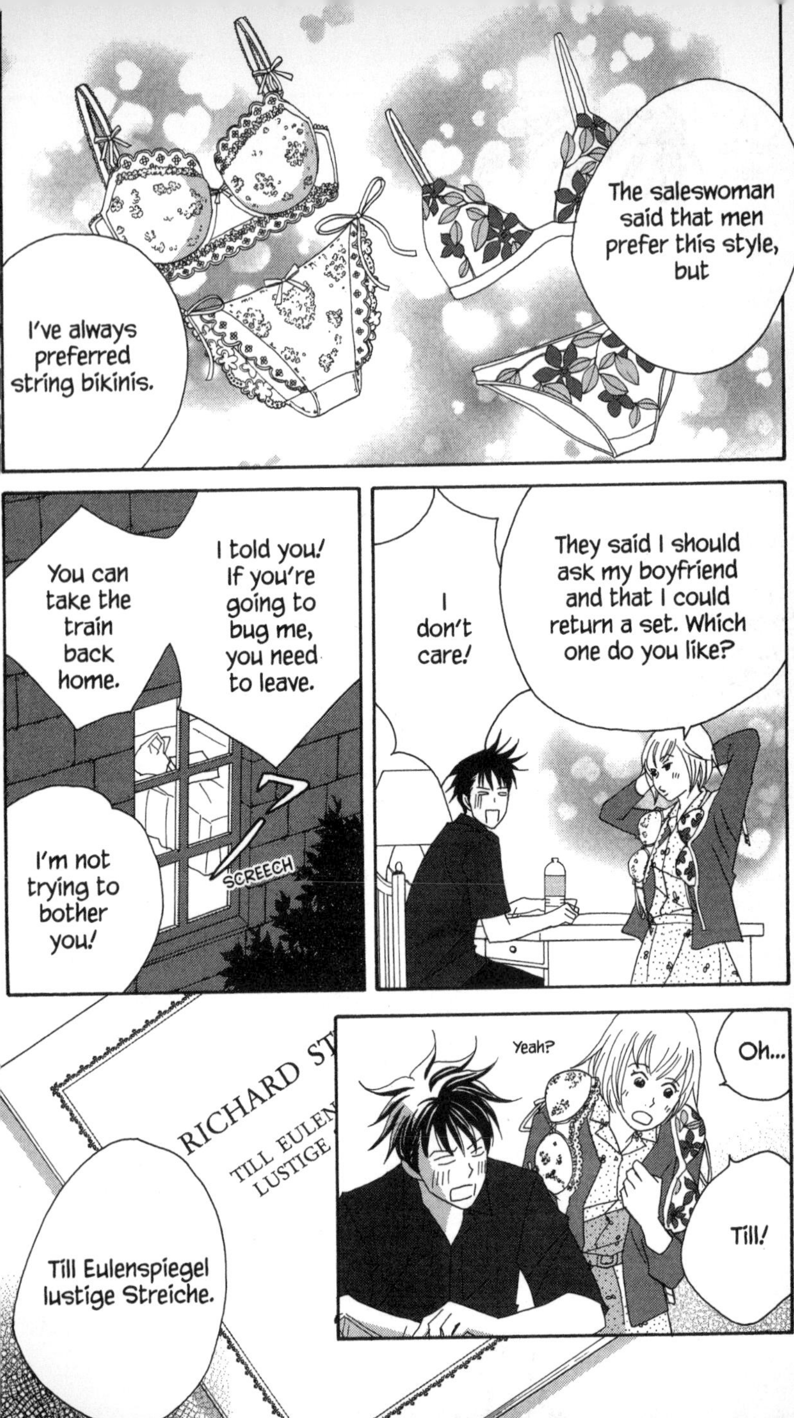
The saleswoman said that men prefer this style, but
I've always preferred string bikinis.
They said I should ask my boyfriend and that I could return a set. Which one do you like?
I don't care!
I told you! If you're going to bug me, you need to leave.
You can take the train back home.
SCREECH
I'm not trying to bother you!
Oh...
Yeah?
Till!
Till Eulenspiegel lustige Streiche.

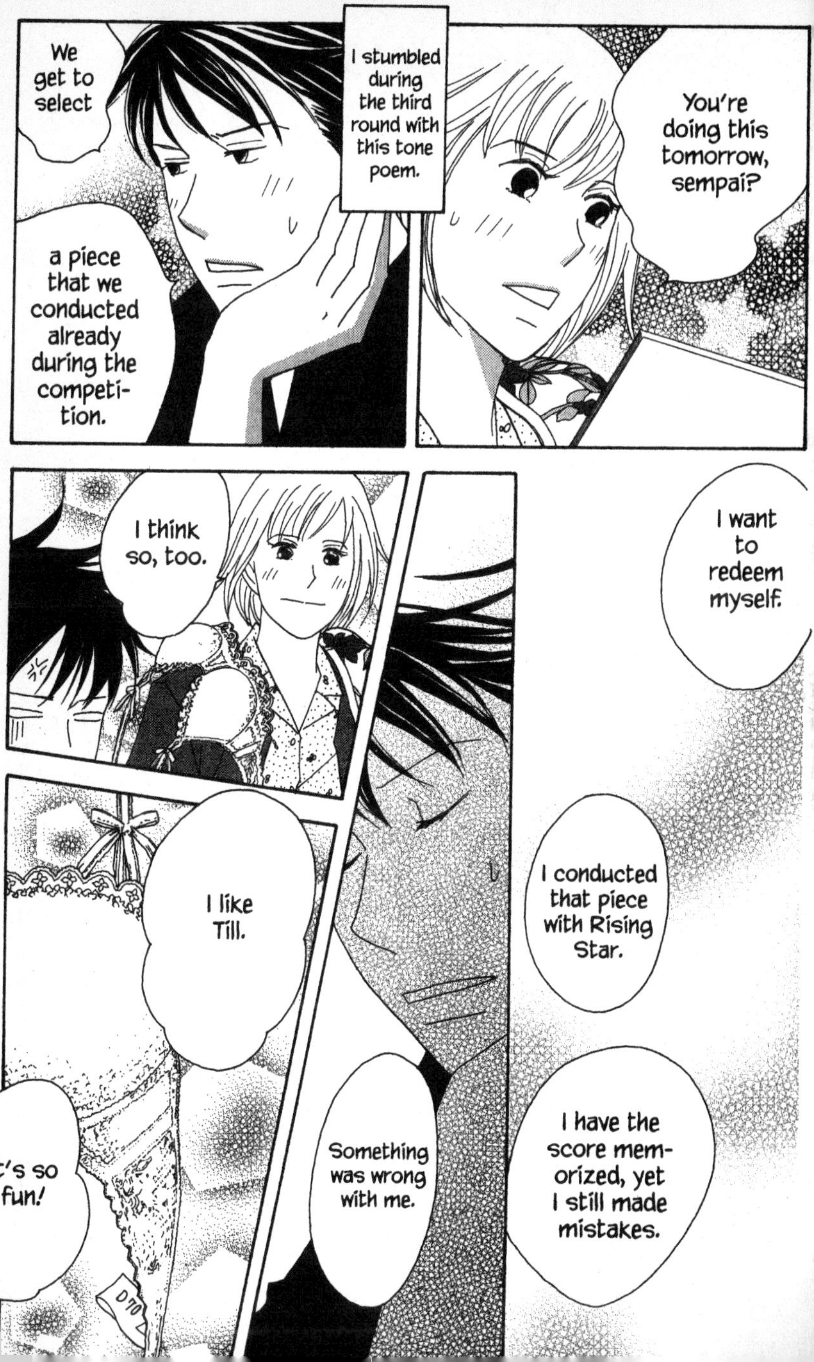
You're doing this tomorrow, sempai?
I stumbled during the third round with this tone poem.
We get to select
a piece that we conducted already during the competition.
I want to redeem myself.
I conducted that piece with Rising Star.
I have the score memorized, yet I still made mistakes.
Something was wrong with me.
I think so, too.
I like Till.
It's so fun!

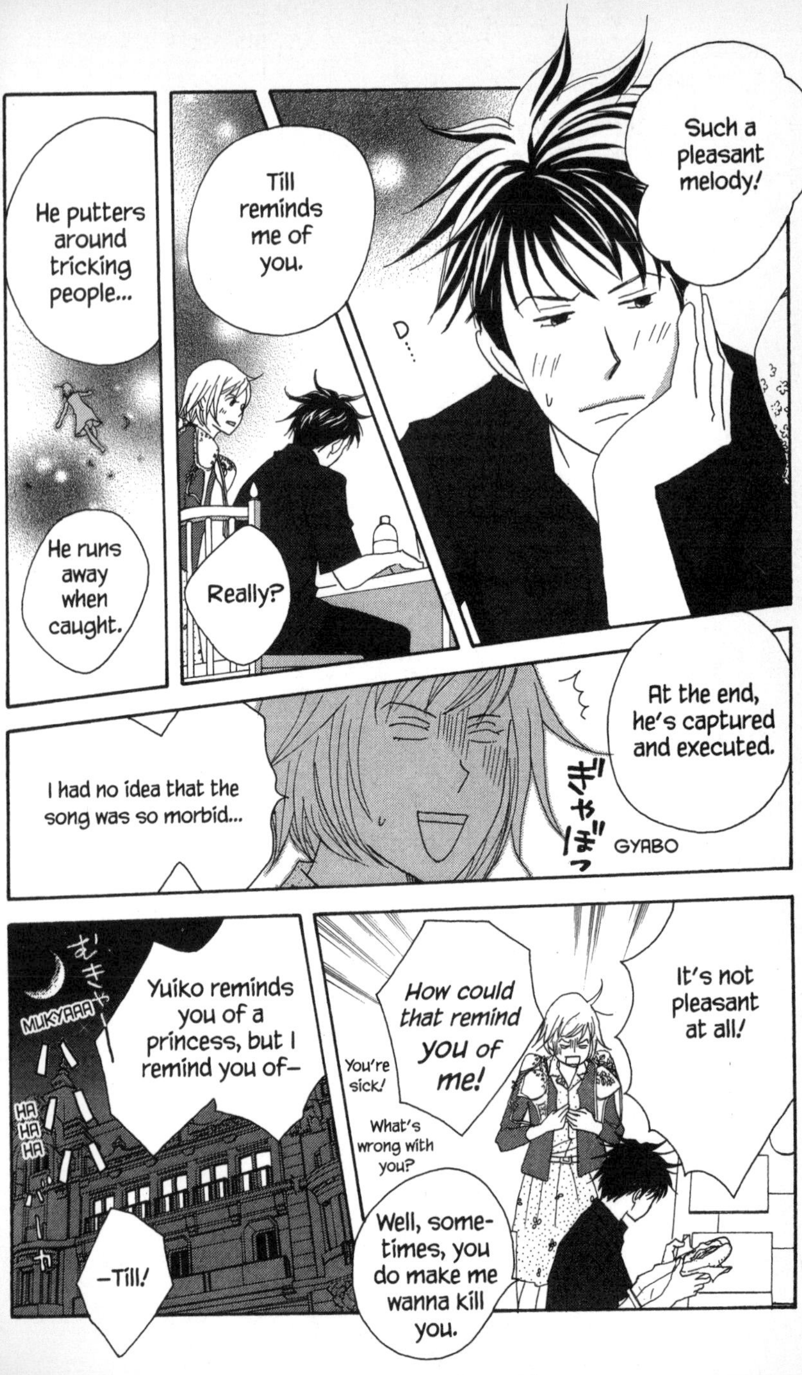
Such a pleasant melody!
D...
Till reminds me of you.
Really?
He putters around tricking people...
He runs away when caught.
At the end, he's captured and executed.
ぎゃぼっ
GYABO
I had no idea that the song was so morbid...
It's not pleasant at all!
How could that remind you of me!
You're sick!
What's wrong with you?
Well, some-times, you do make me wanna kill you.
むきゃー
MUKYAAA
Yuiko reminds you of a princess, but I remind you of–
–Till!
ハハハ
HA HA HA

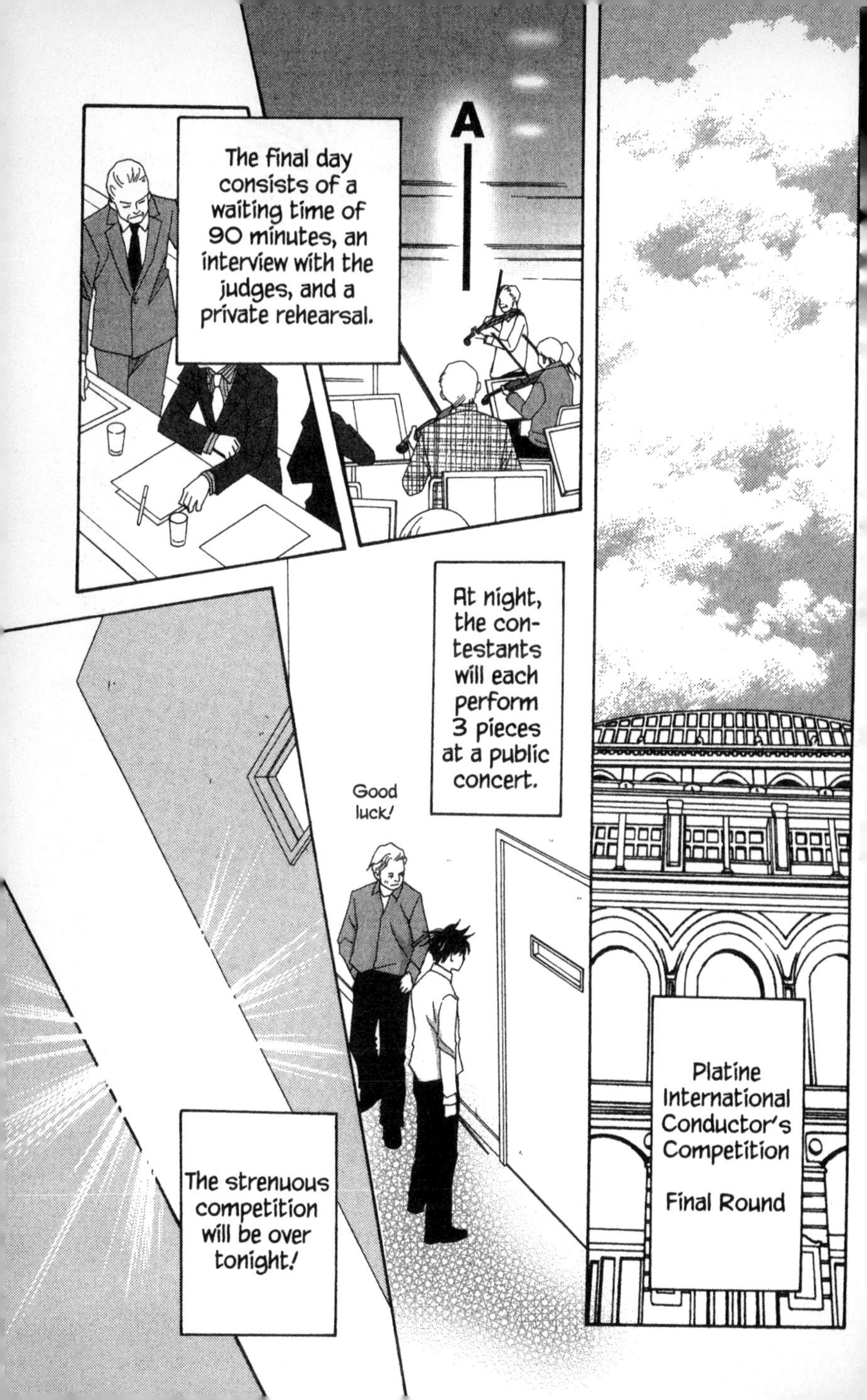
Platine International Conductor's Competition
Final Round
The final day consists of a waiting time of 90 minutes, an interview with the judges, and a private rehearsal.
A
At night, the contestants will each perform 3 pieces at a public concert.
Good luck!
The strenuous competition will be over tonight!

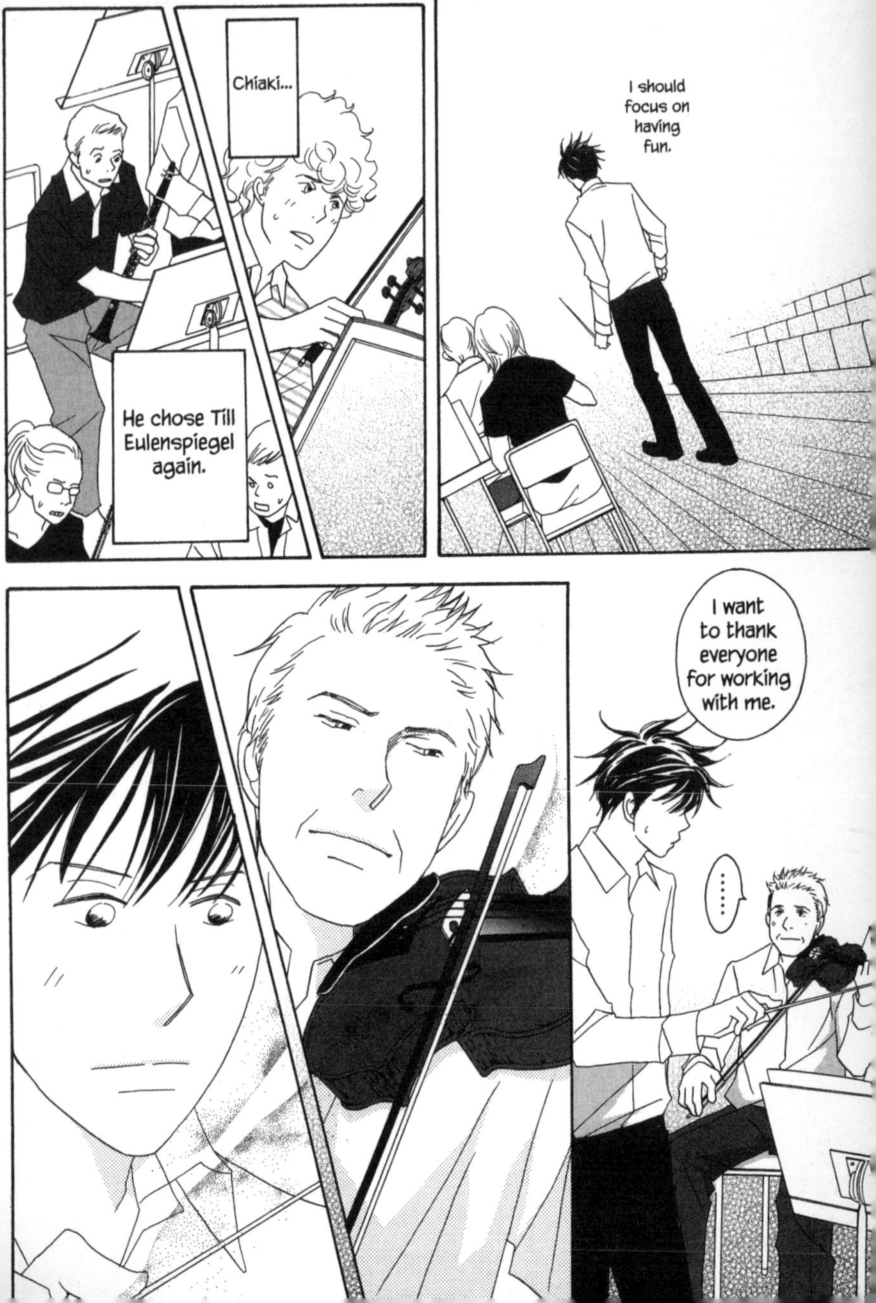
I should focus on having fun.
Chiaki...
He chose Till Eulenspiegel again.
I want to thank everyone for working with me.
......

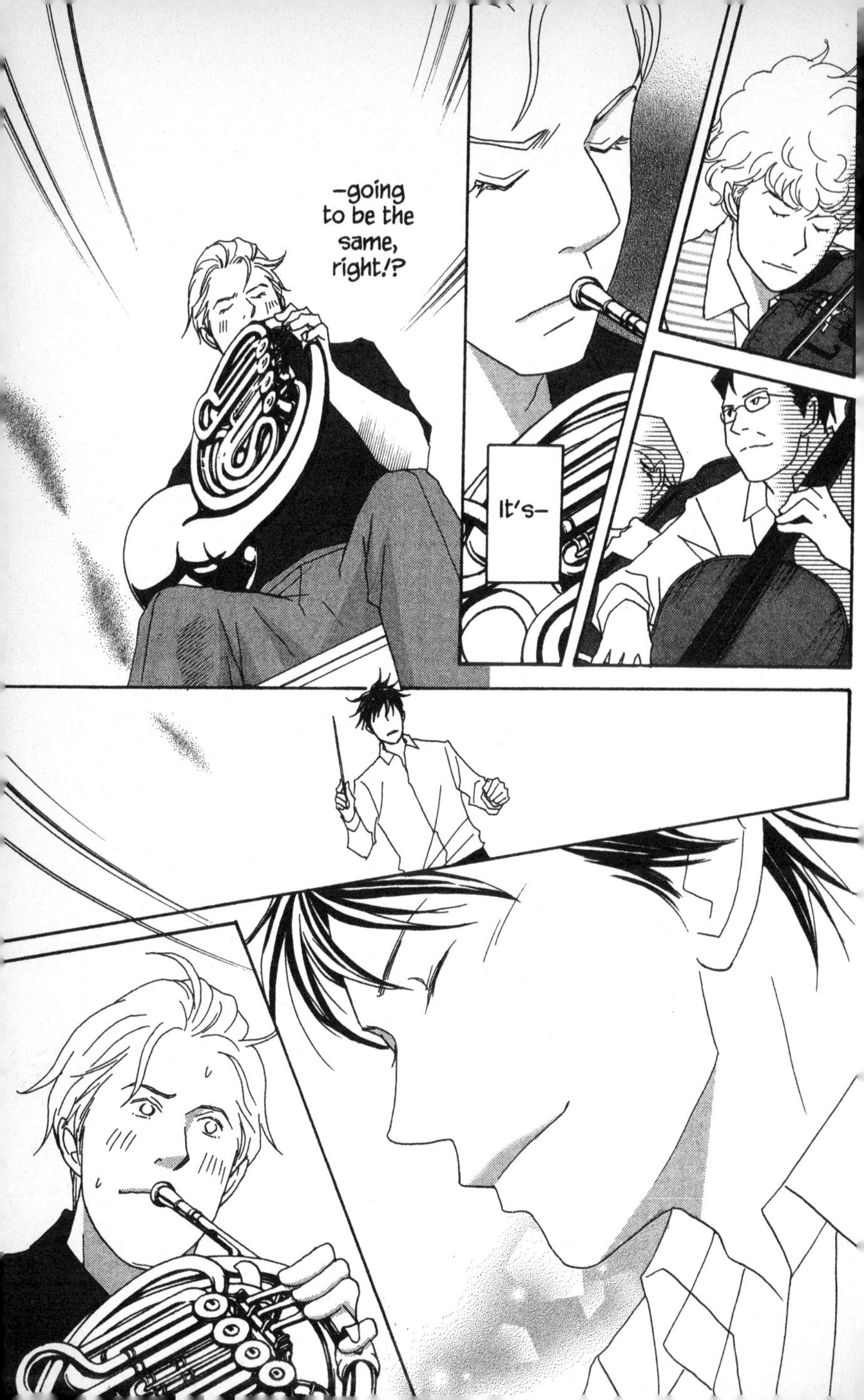
It's–
–going to be the same, right!?

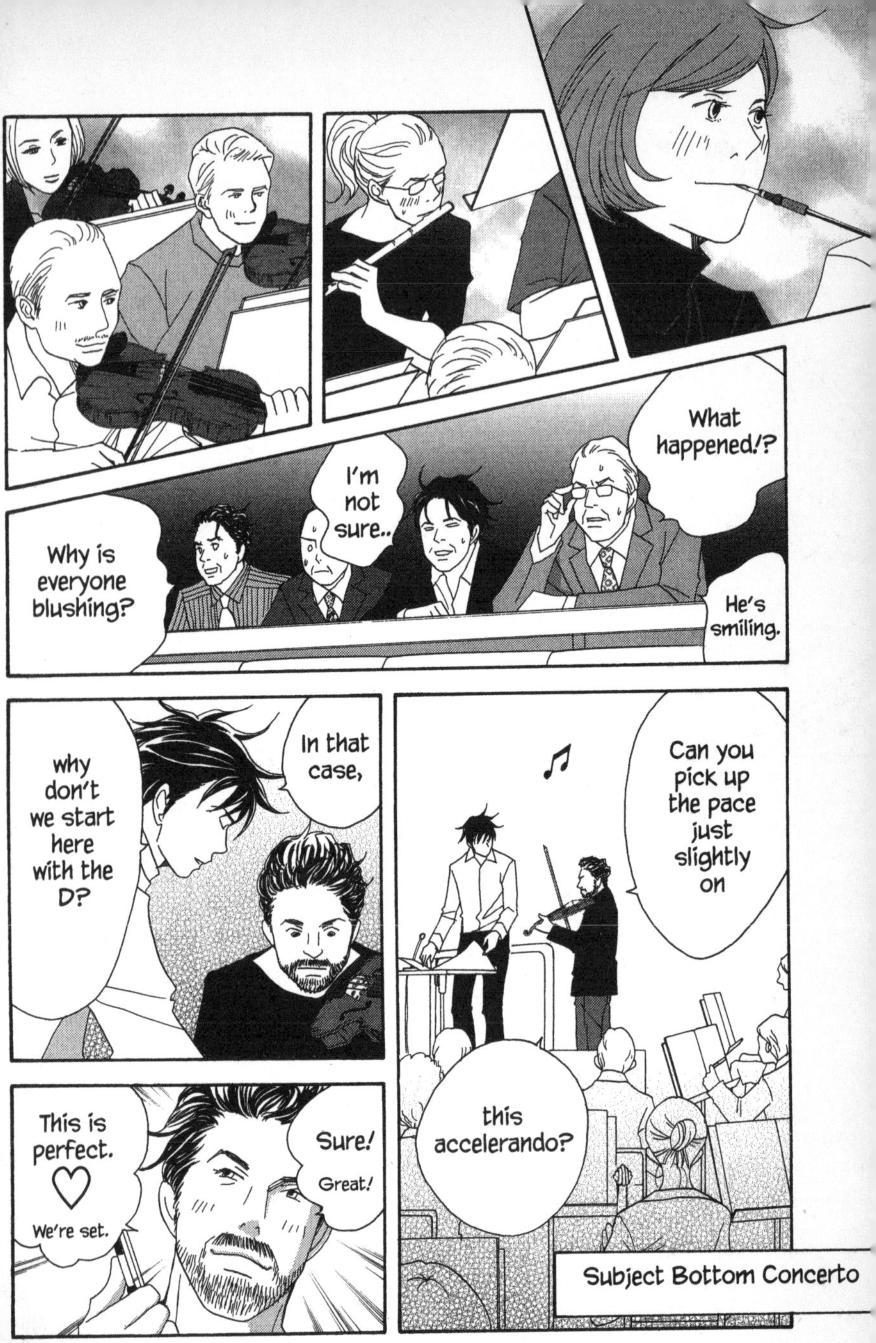

What happened!?
He's smiling.
I'm not sure..
Why is everyone blushing?
Can you pick up the pace just slightly on
this accelerando?
Subject Bottom Concerto
In that case,
why don't we start here with the D?
Sure!
Great!
This is perfect. ♡
We're set.

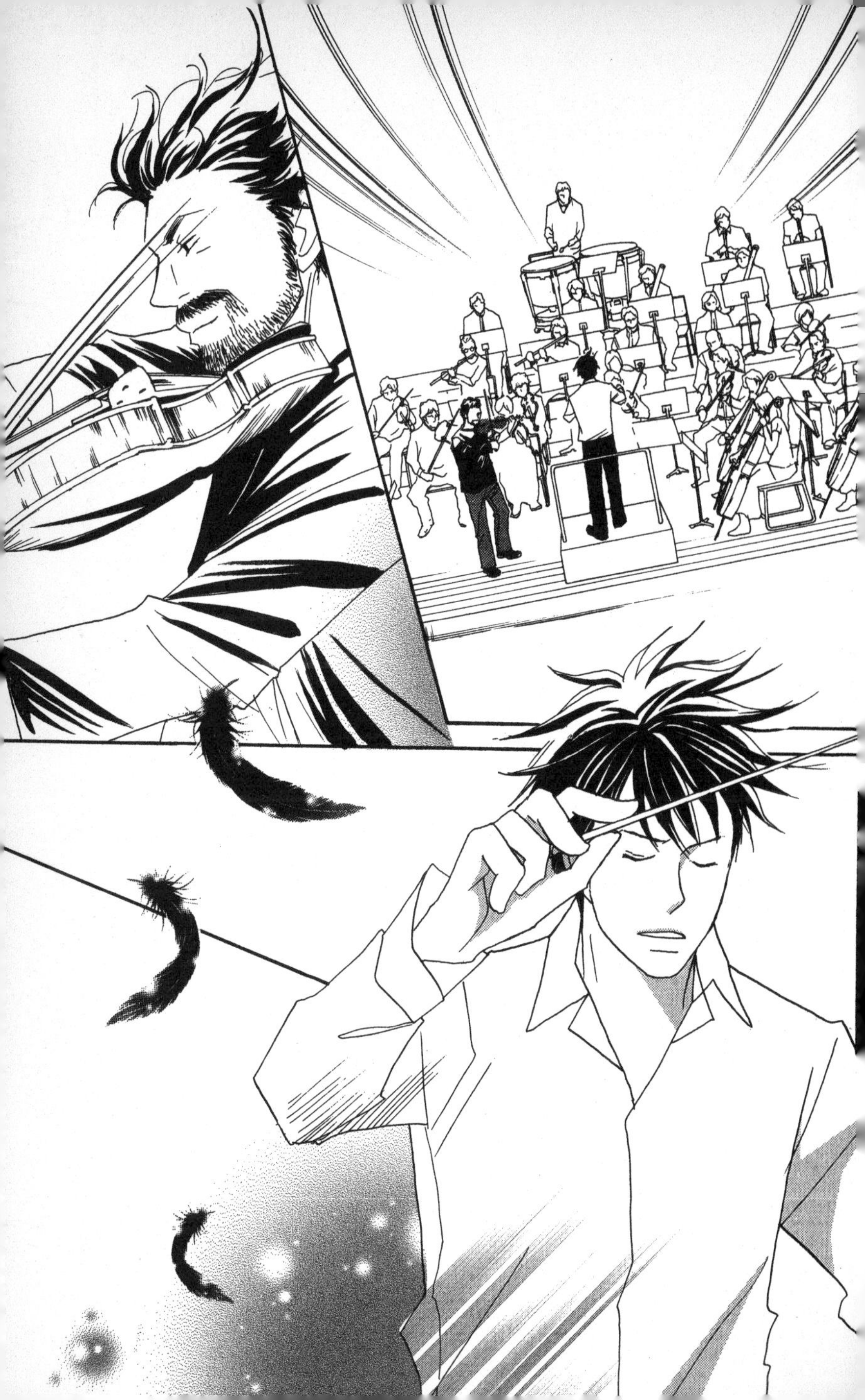

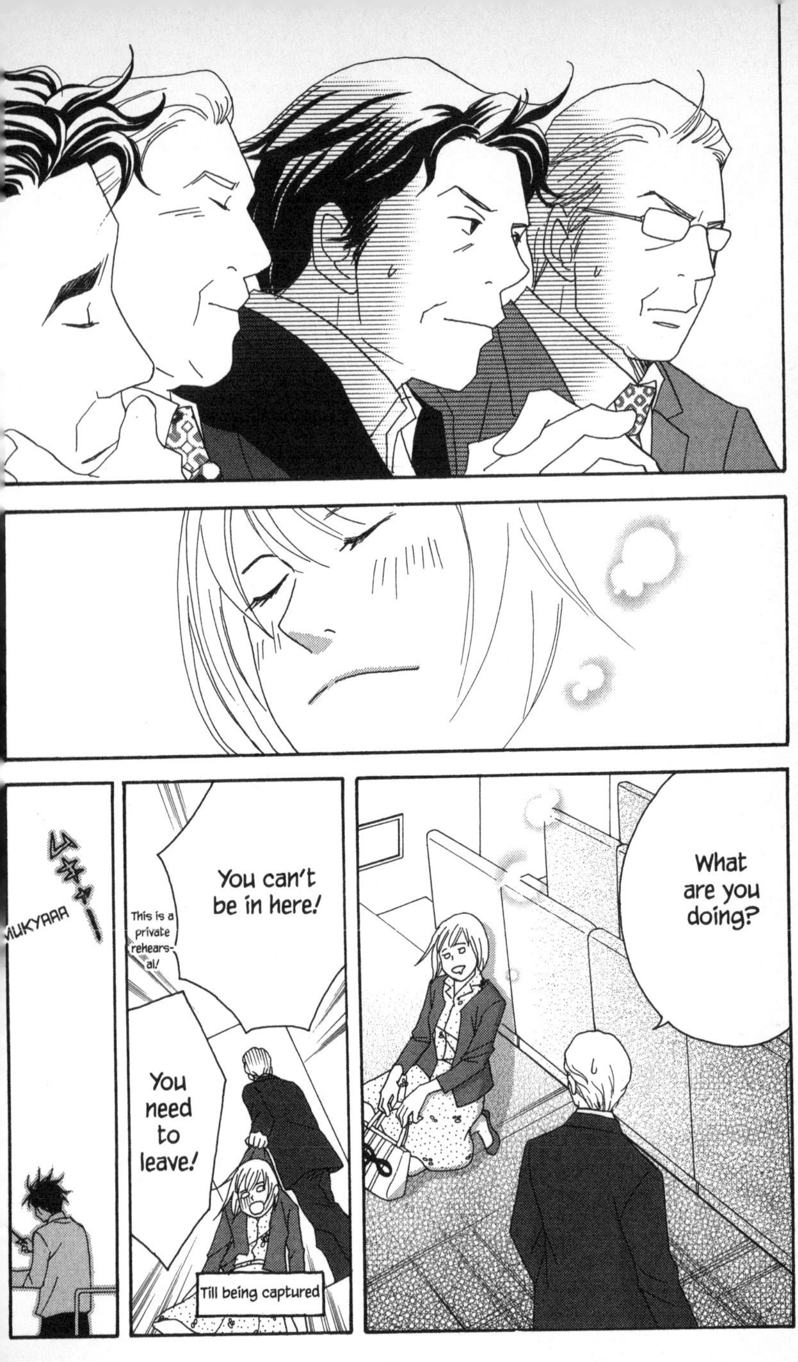
What are you doing?
You can't be in here!
This is a private rehears-al!
You need to leave!
Till being captured
MUKYAAA

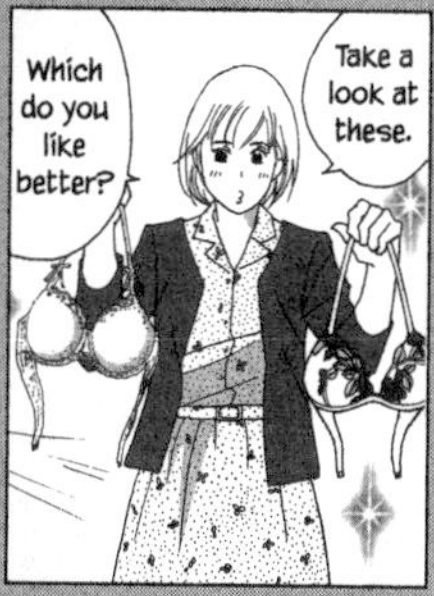
Take a look at these.
Which do you like better?

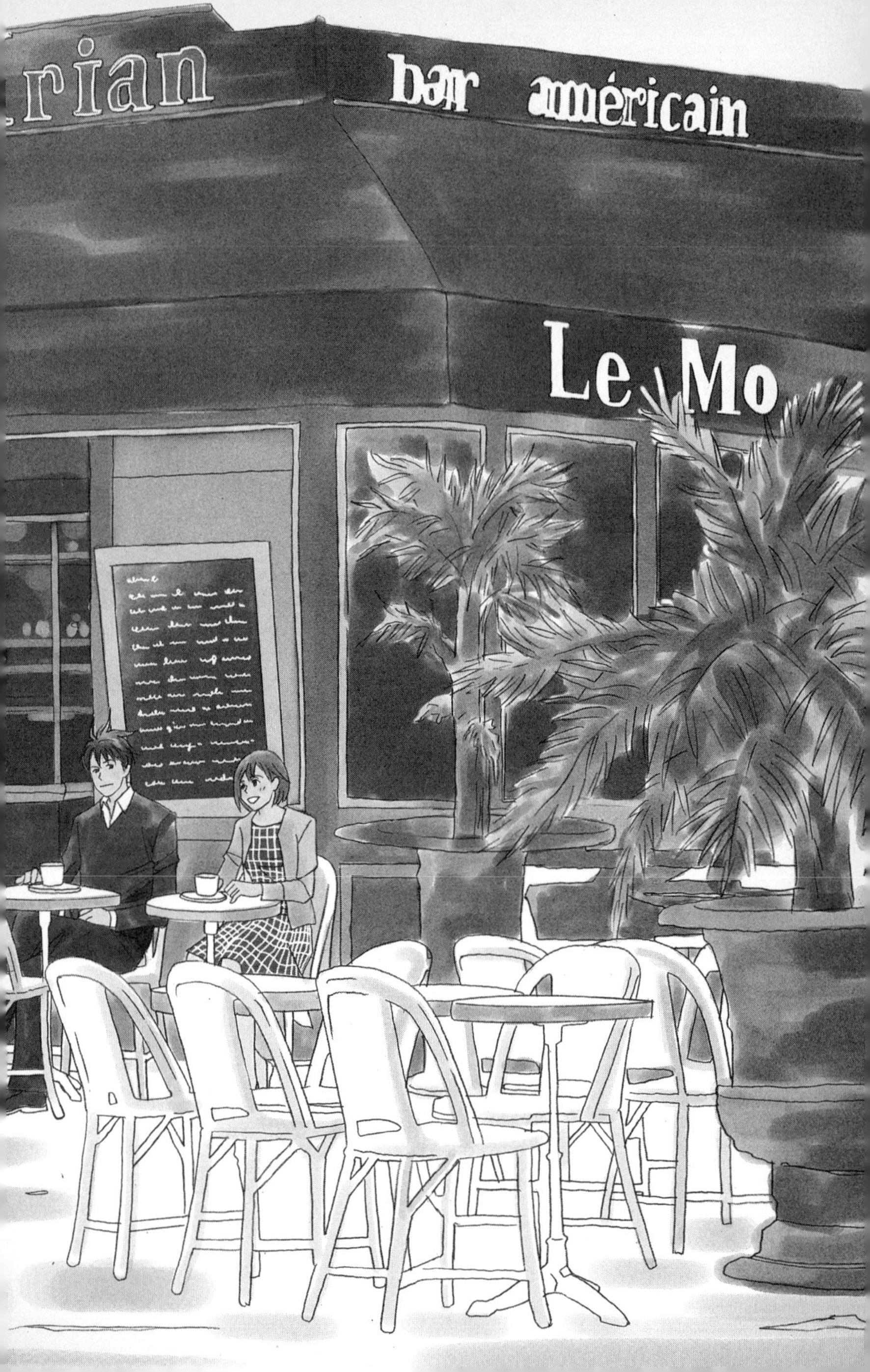
Le Mo
bar américain
rian

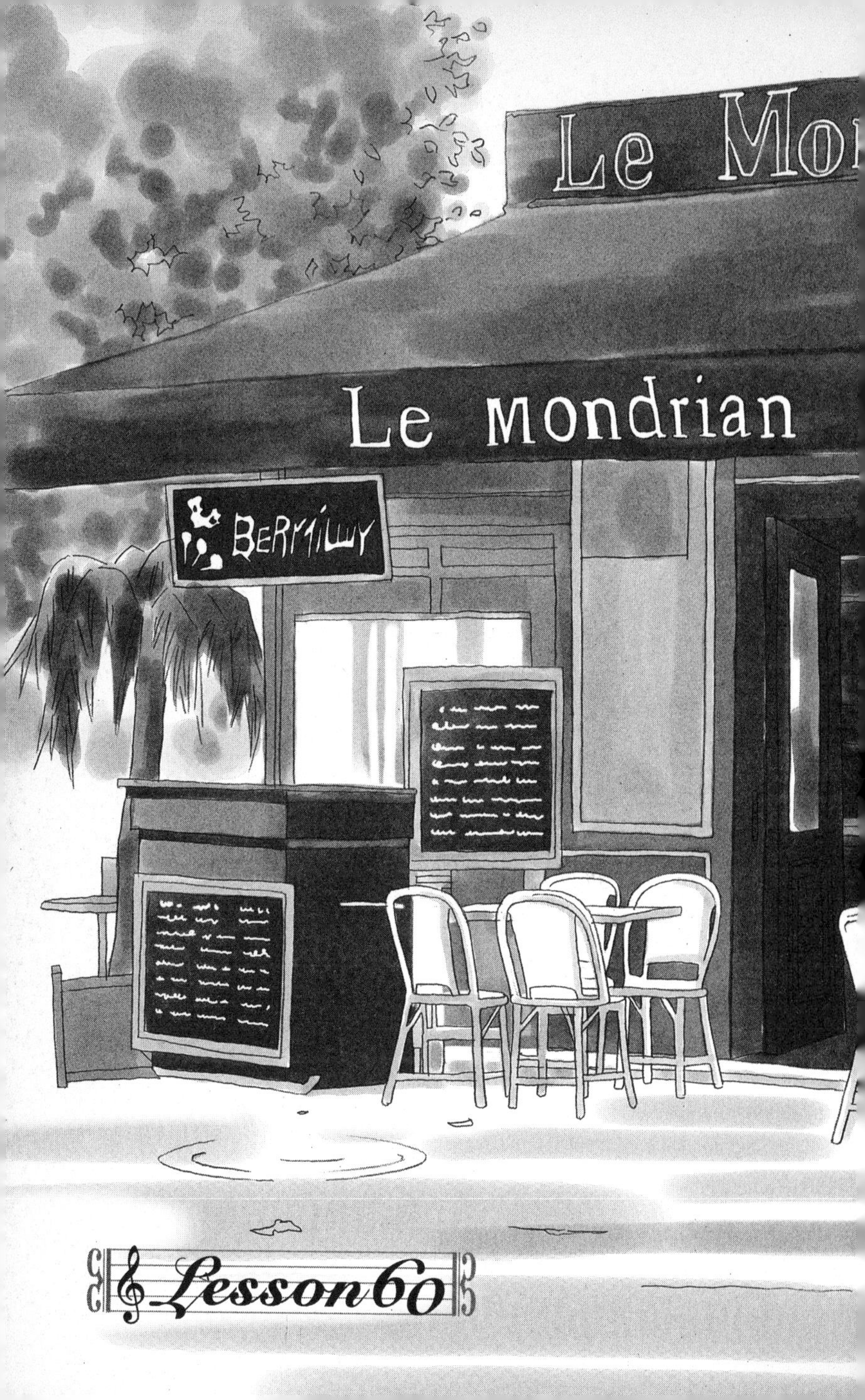
Le mondrian
Lesson 60

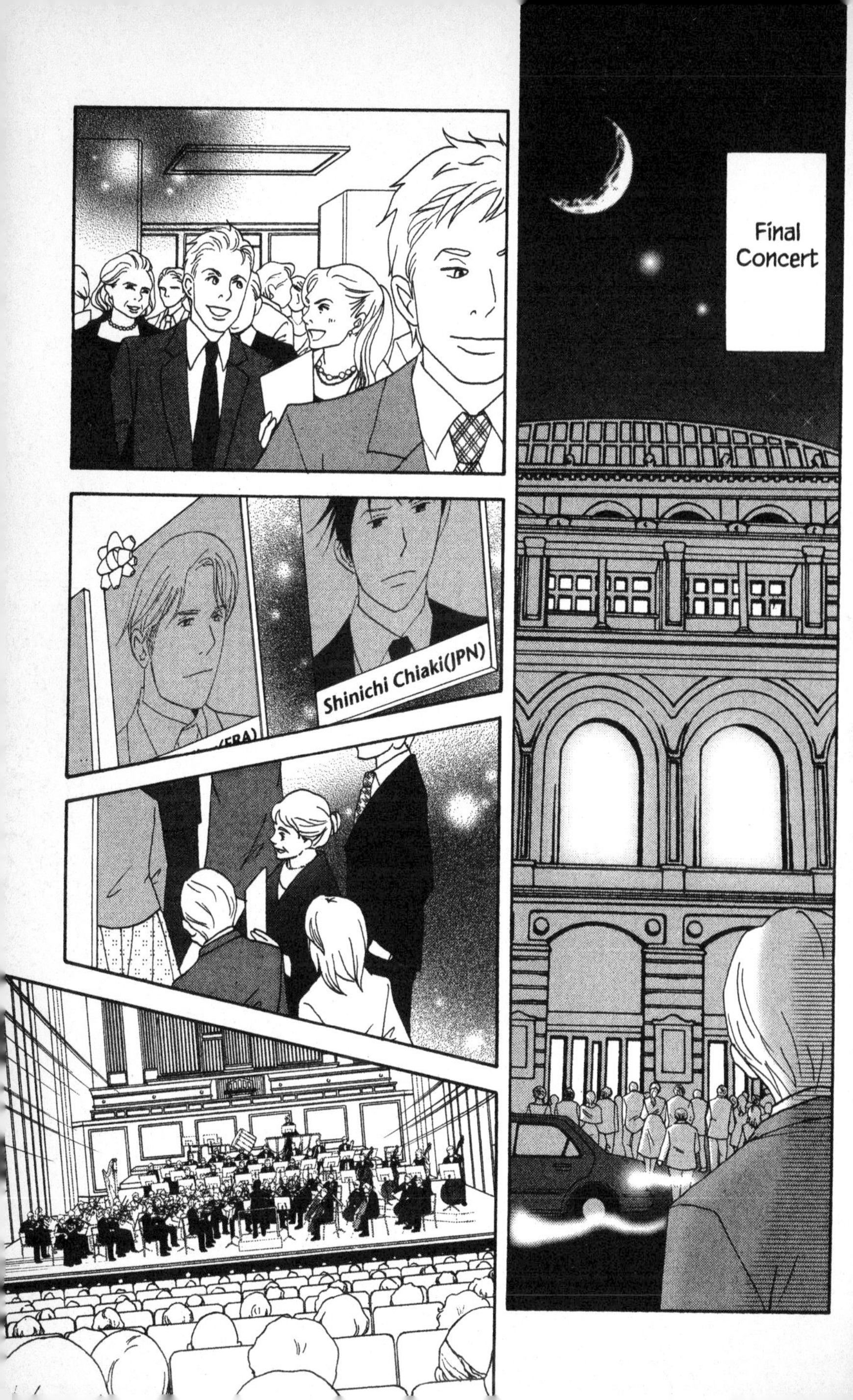
Final Concert
Shinichi Chiaki(JPN)

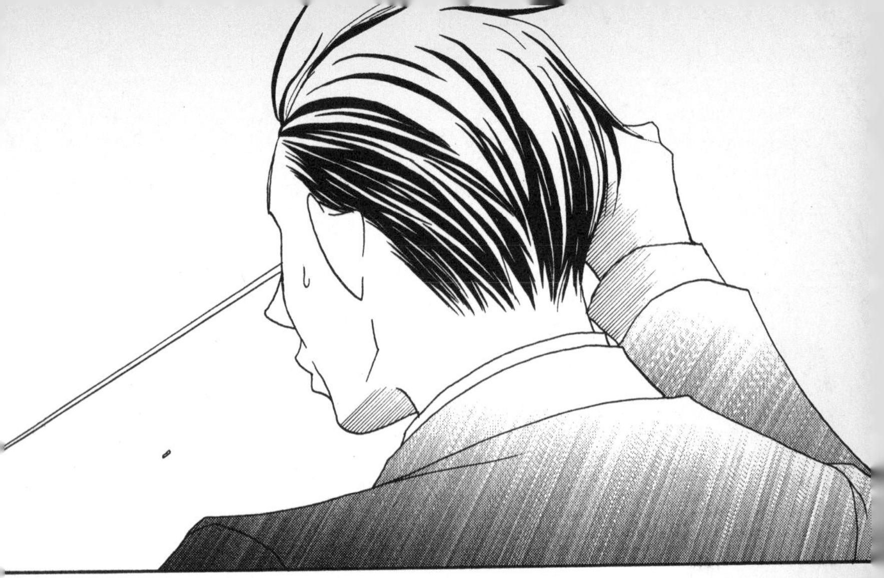

Final Concert Subject A (Judge's Selection)

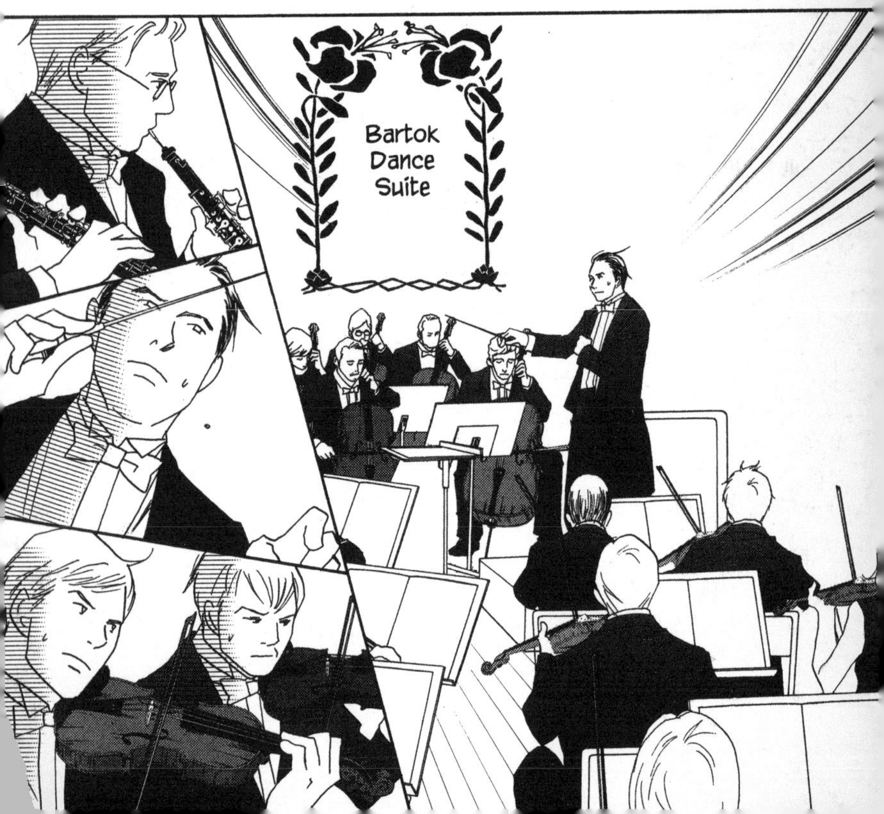
Bartok Dance Suite

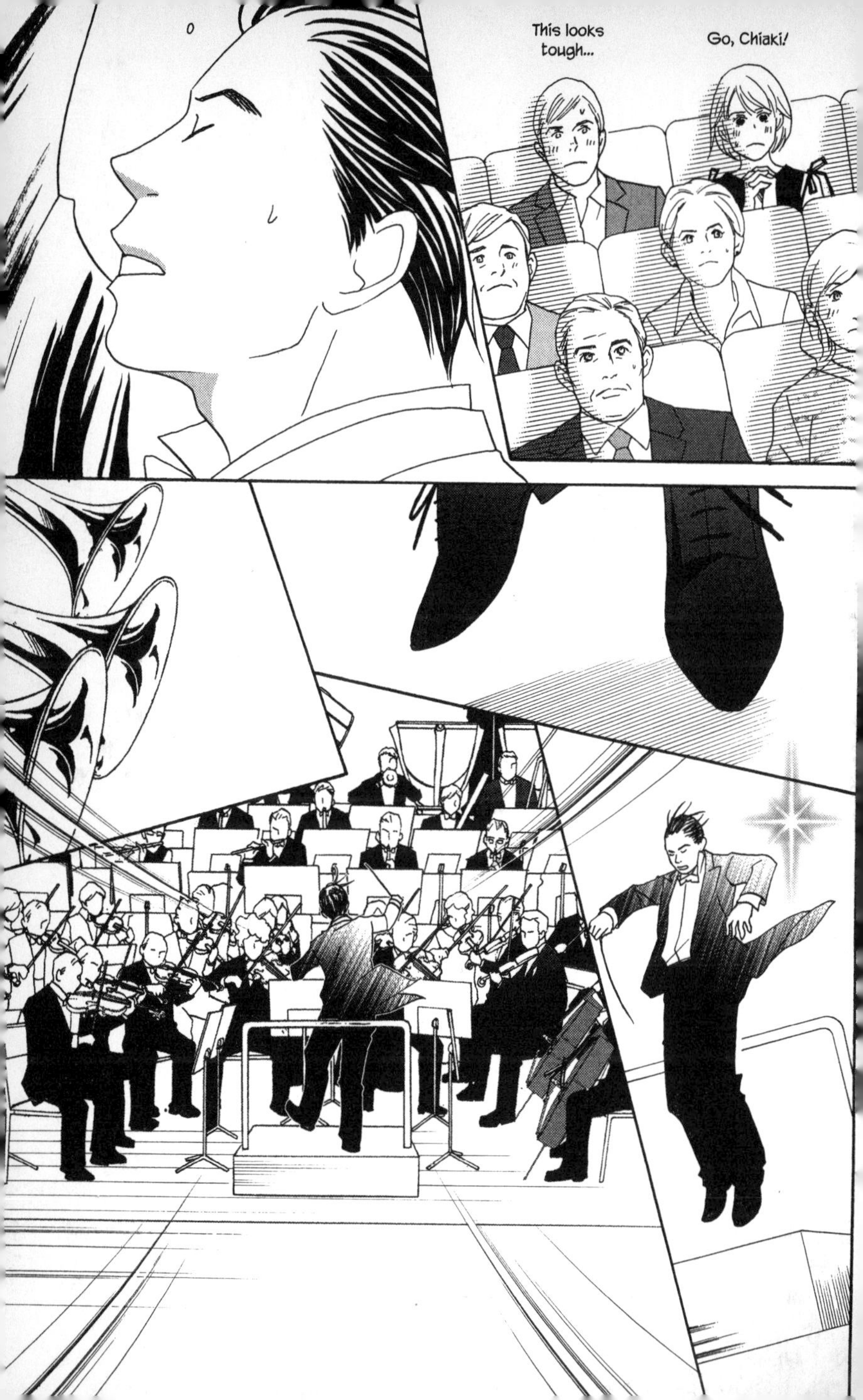
Go, Chiaki!
This looks tough...

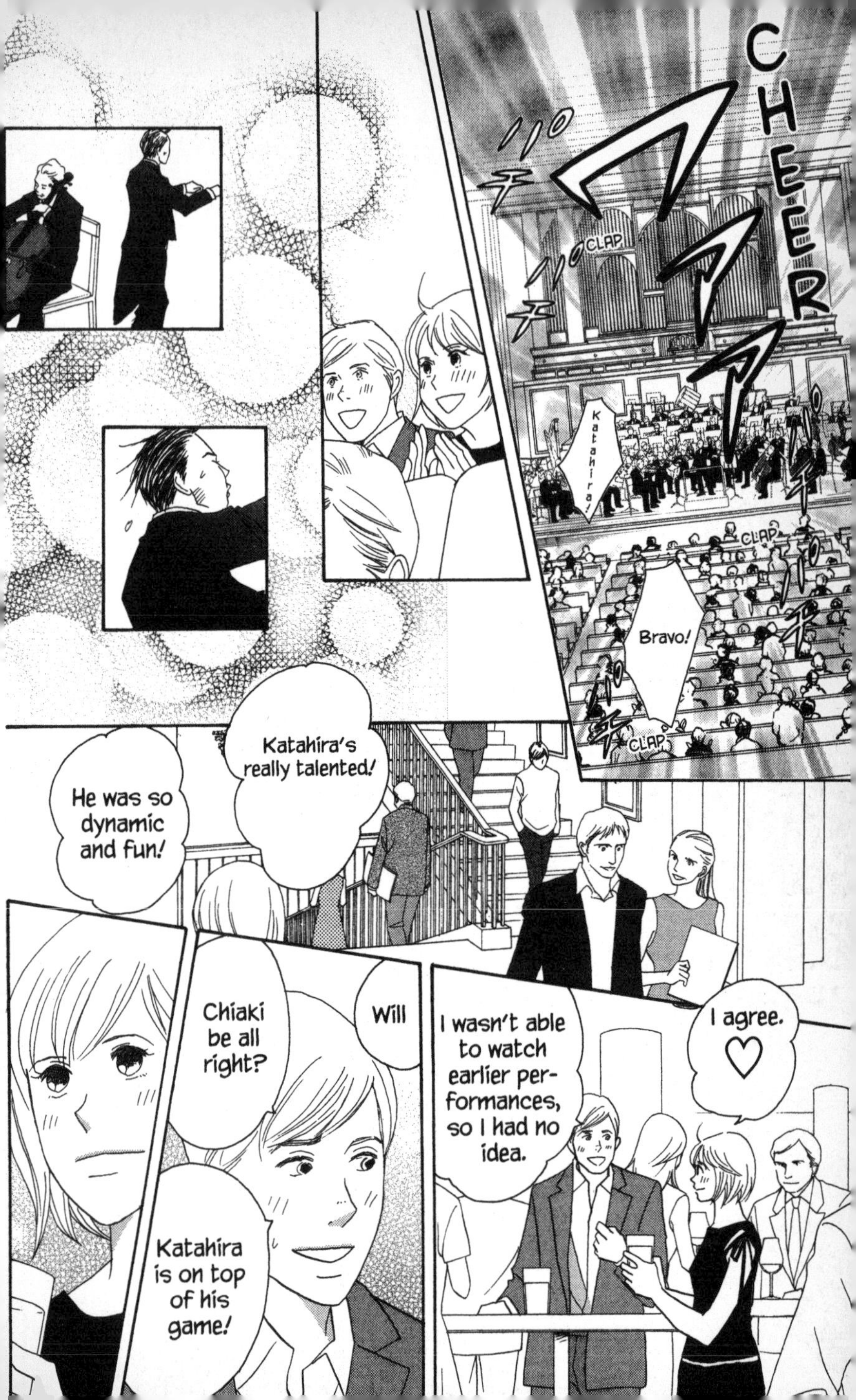
CHEER
CLAP
Katahira!
CLAP
Bravo!
CLAP
Katahira's really talented!
He was so dynamic and fun!
I agree. ♡
I wasn't able to watch earlier performances, so I had no idea.
Will
Chiaki be all right?
Katahira is on top of his game!

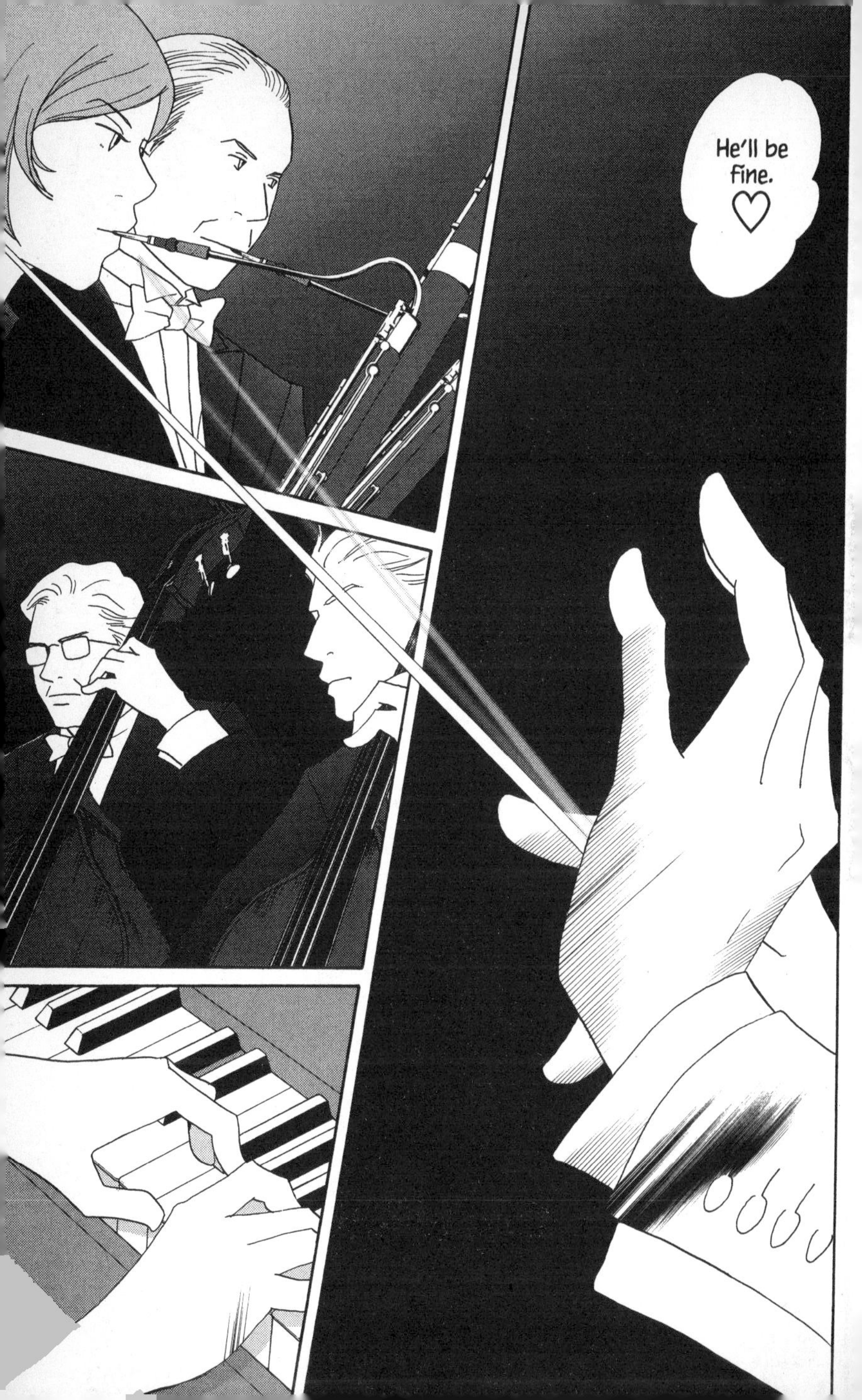
He'll be fine. ♡

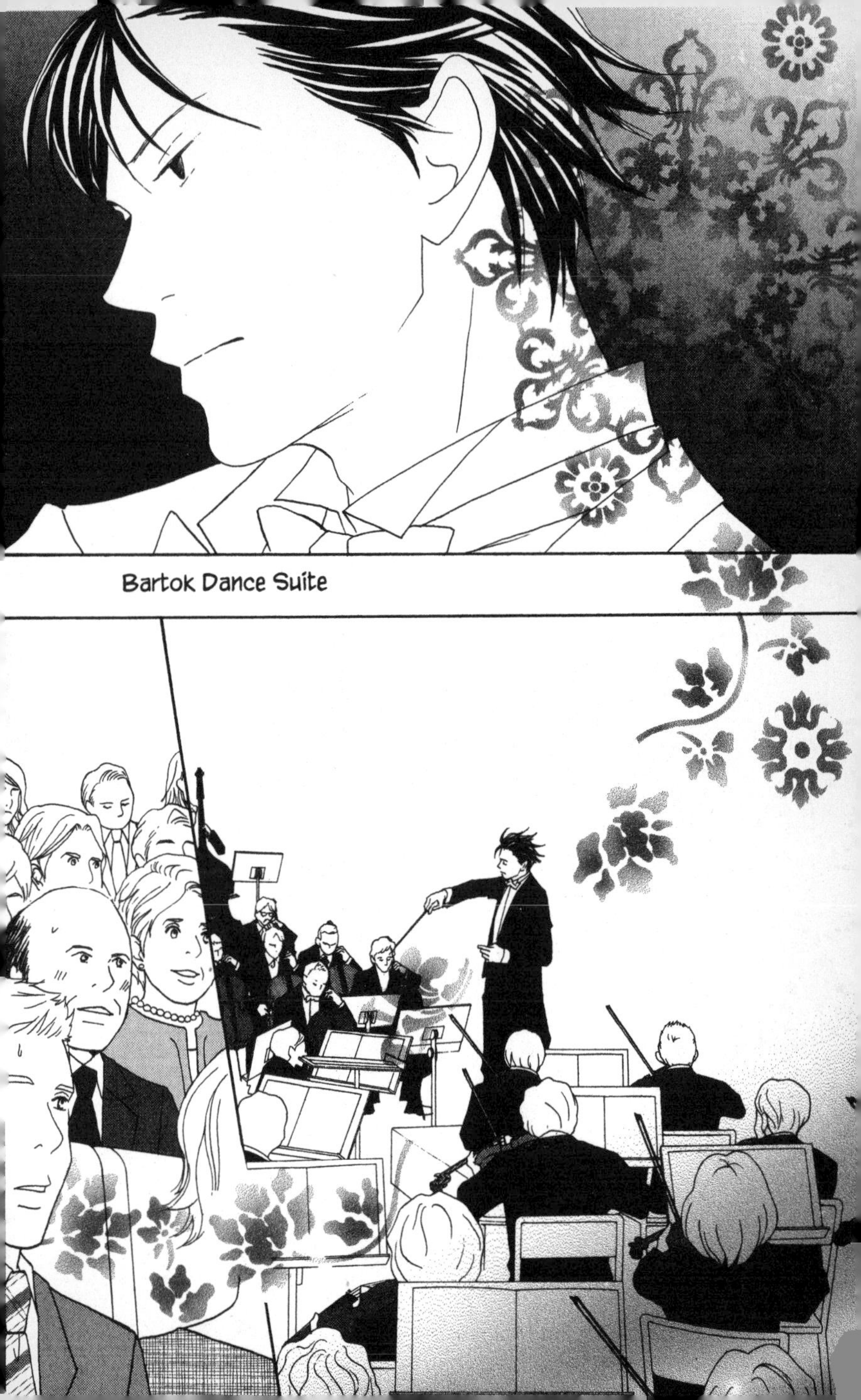
Bartok Dance Suite

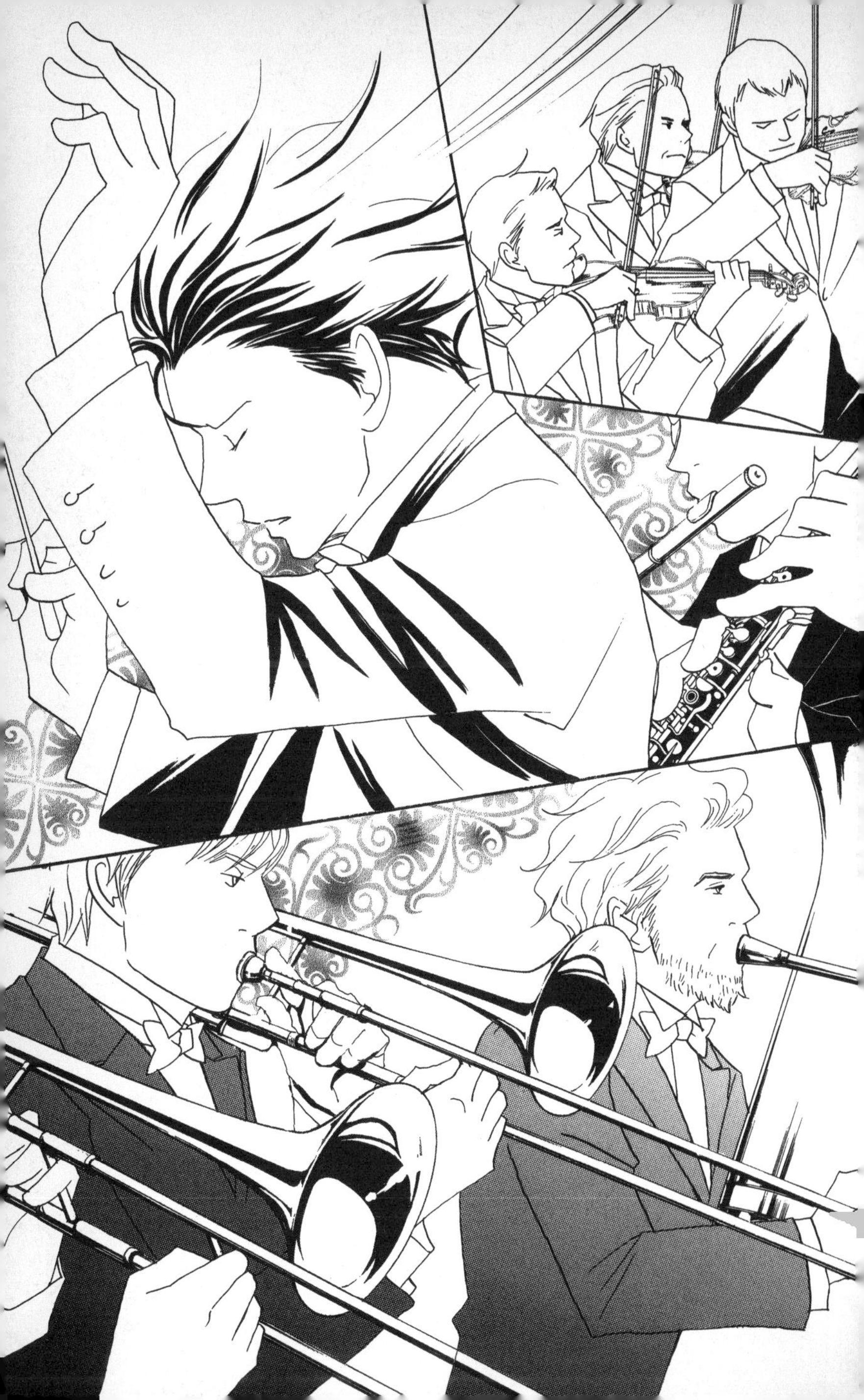

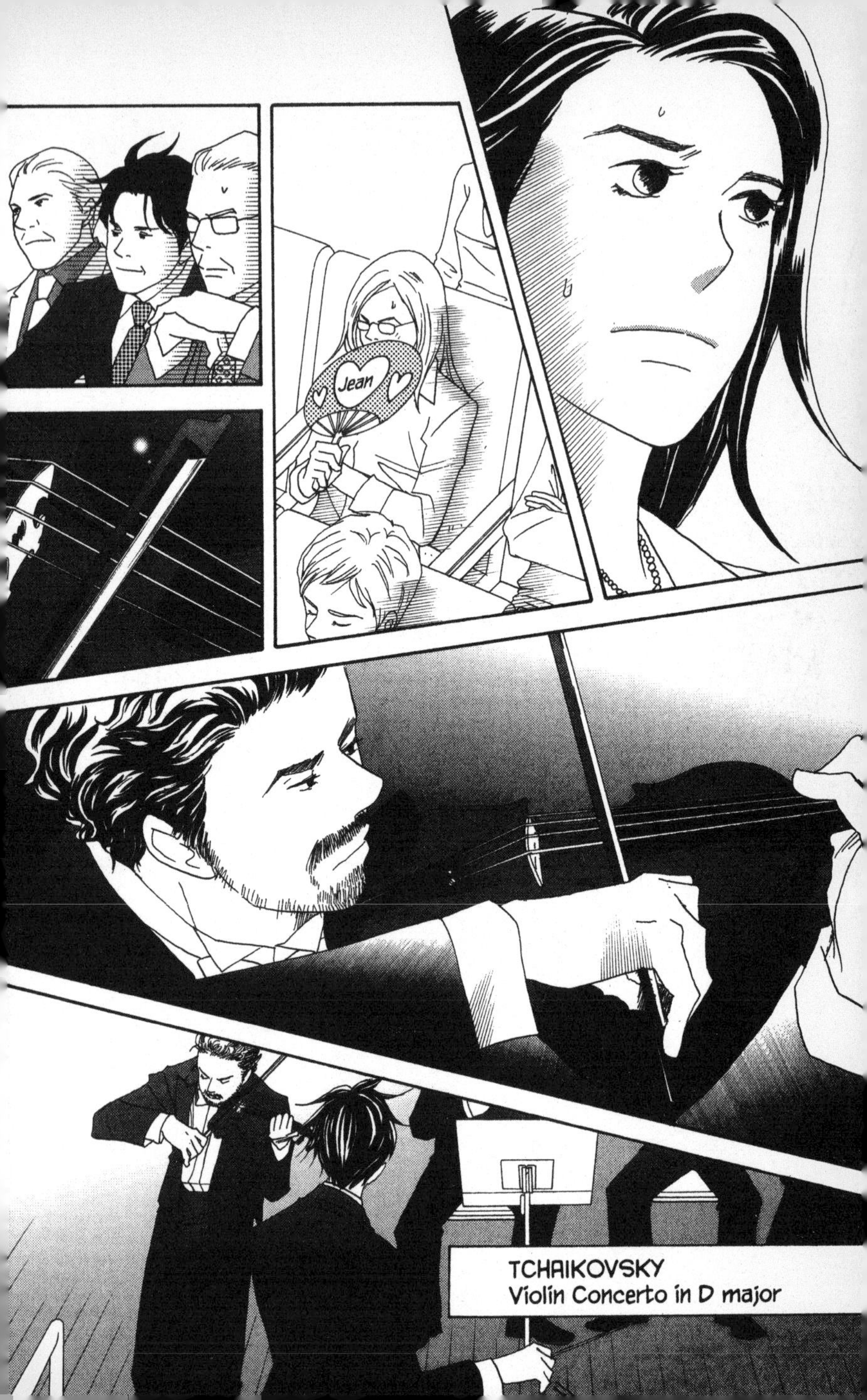
Jean
TCHAIKOVSKY
Violin Concerto in D major

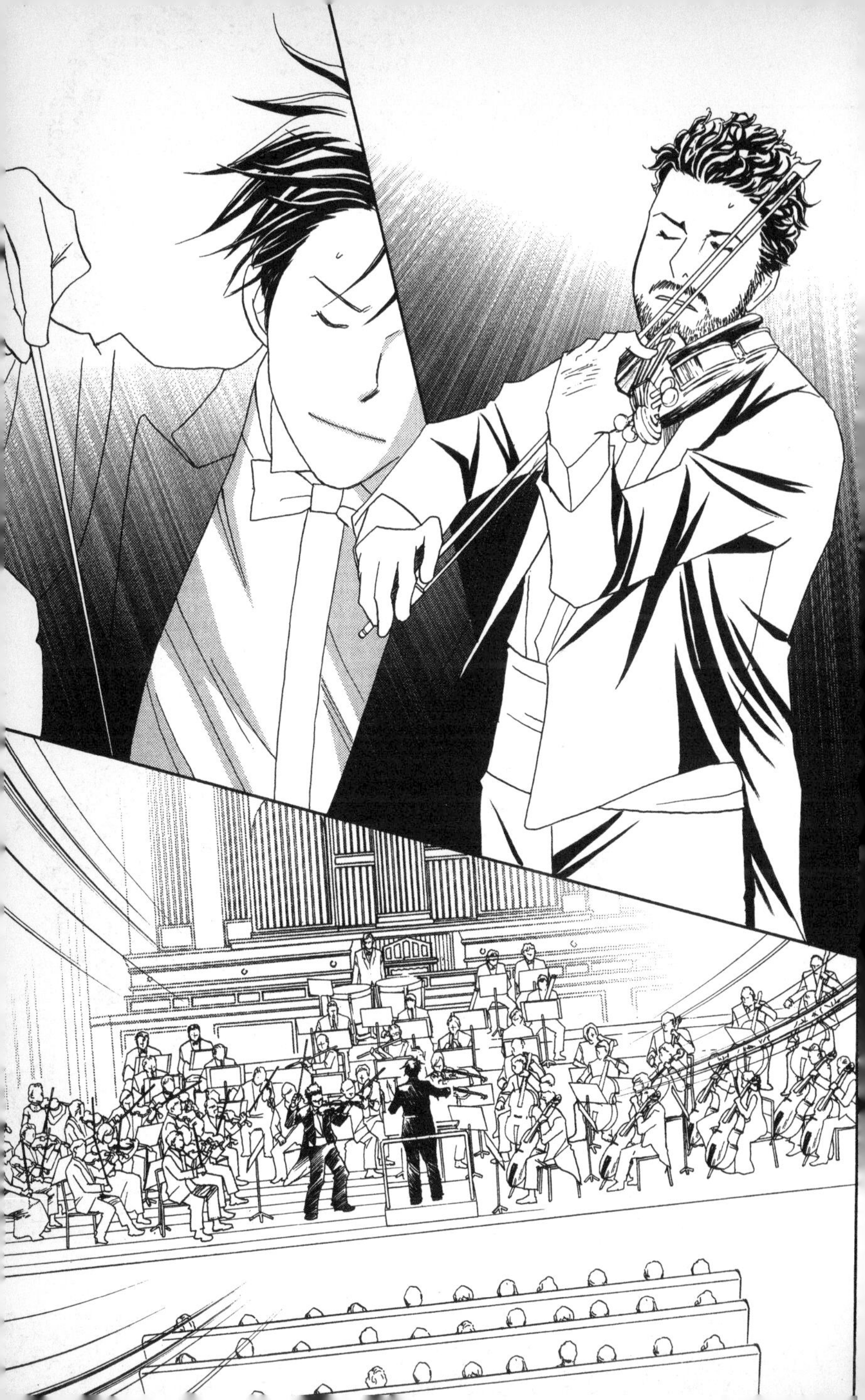

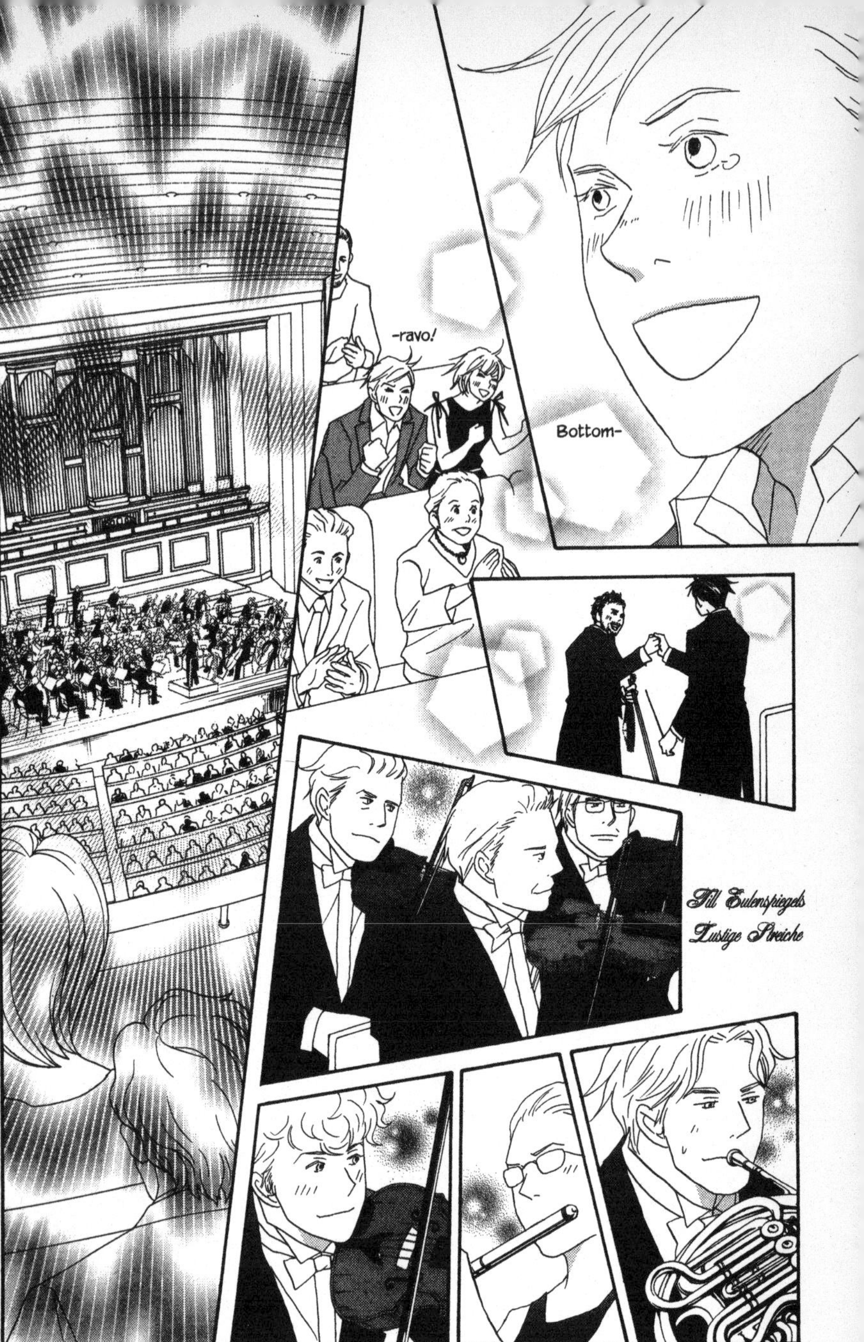
Bottom-
-ravo!
Till Eulenspiegels
Lustige Streiche

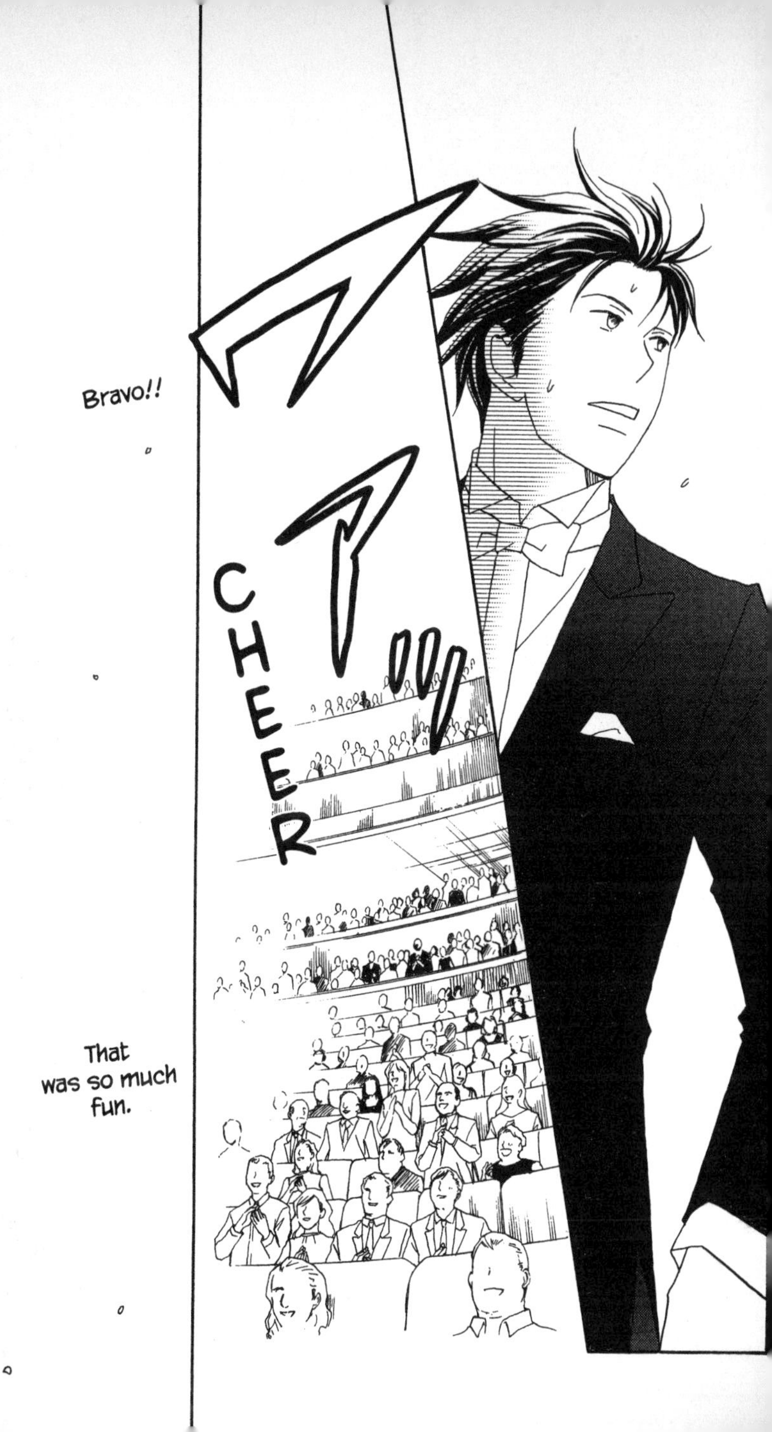
Bravo!!
That was so much fun.
CHEER

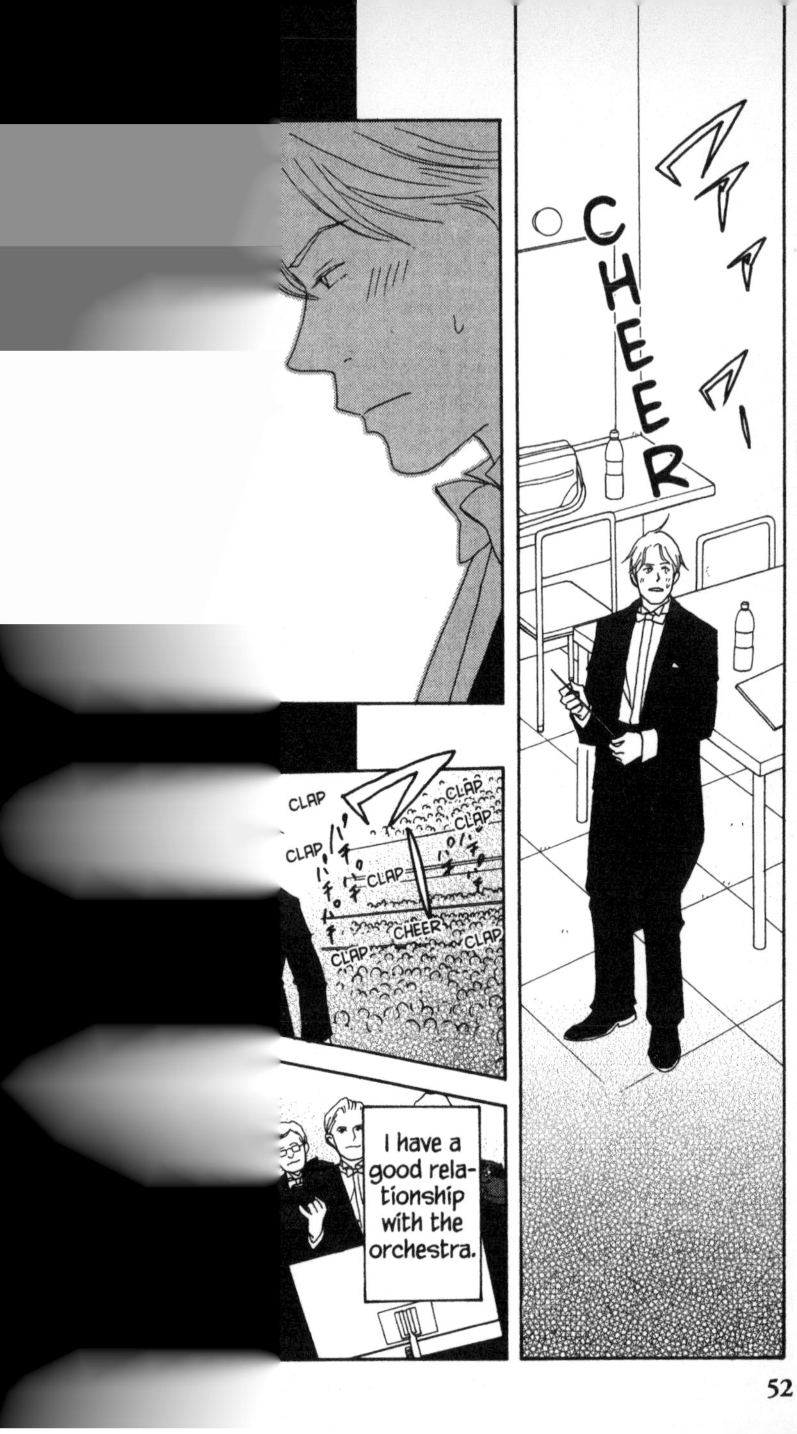
CHEER
CLAP
CLAP
CLAP
CLAP
CLAP
CLAP
CHEER
CLAP
I have a good relationship with the orchestra.

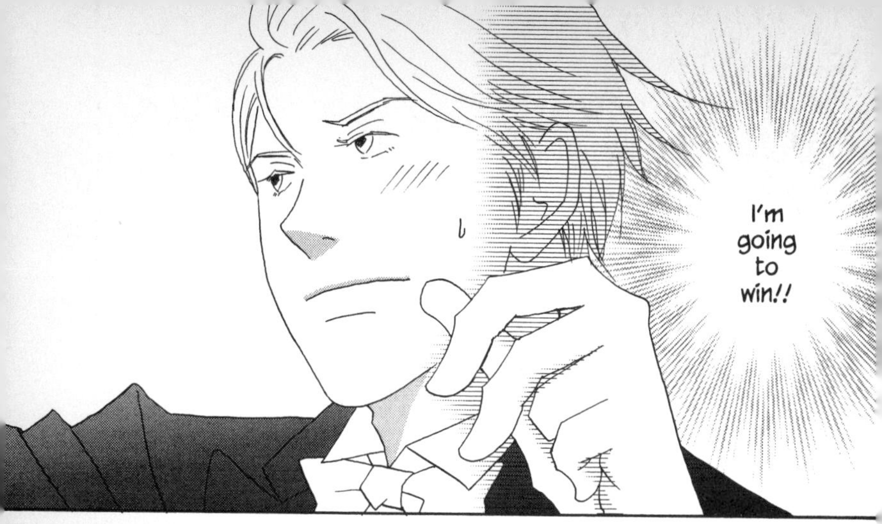
I'm going to win!!

Bartók Dance Suite

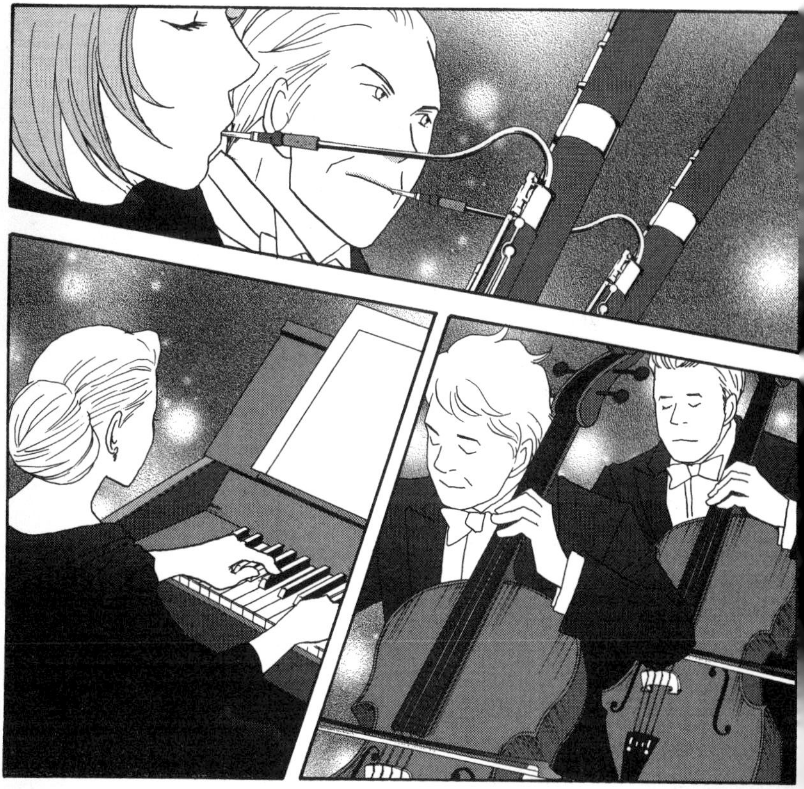

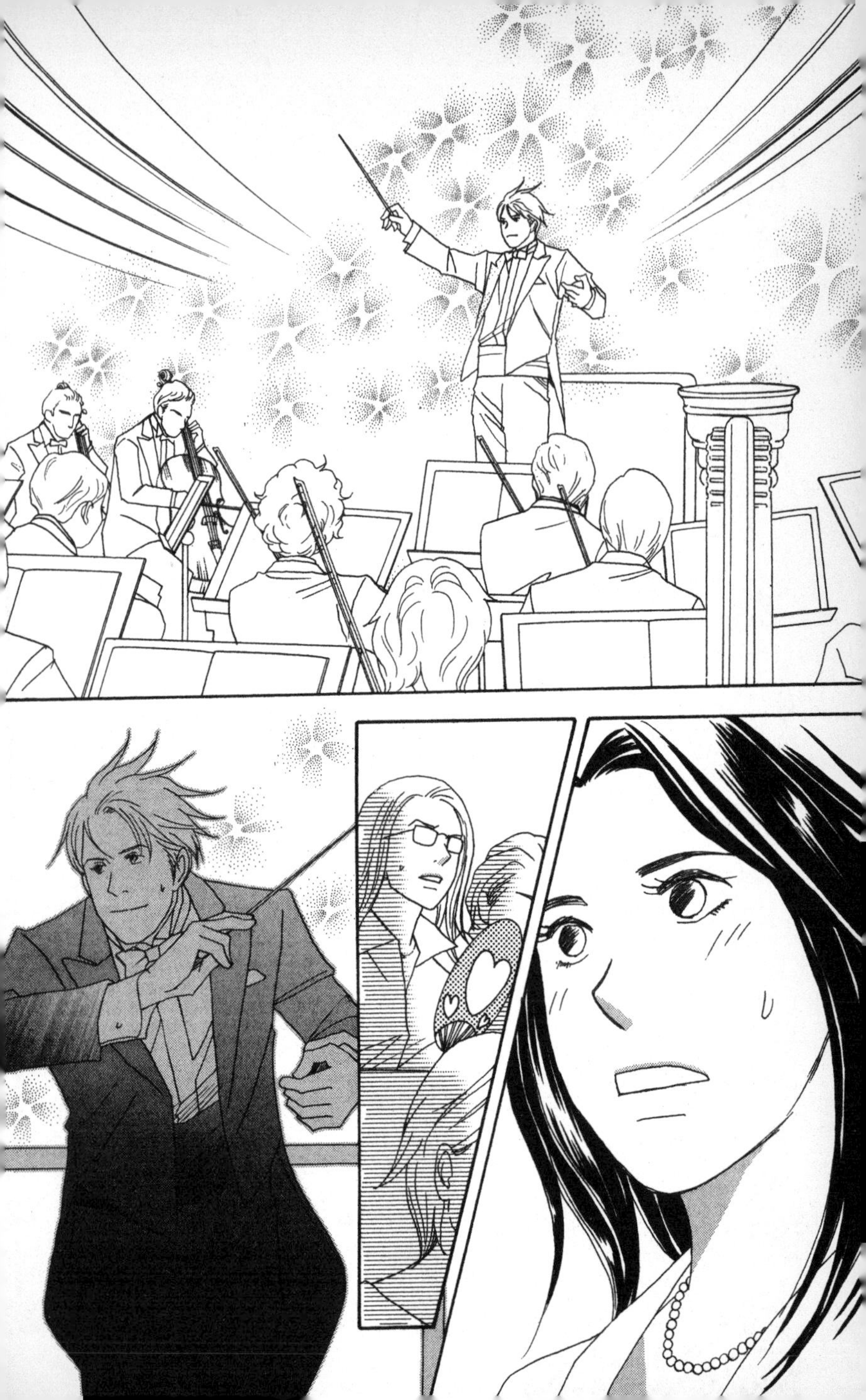

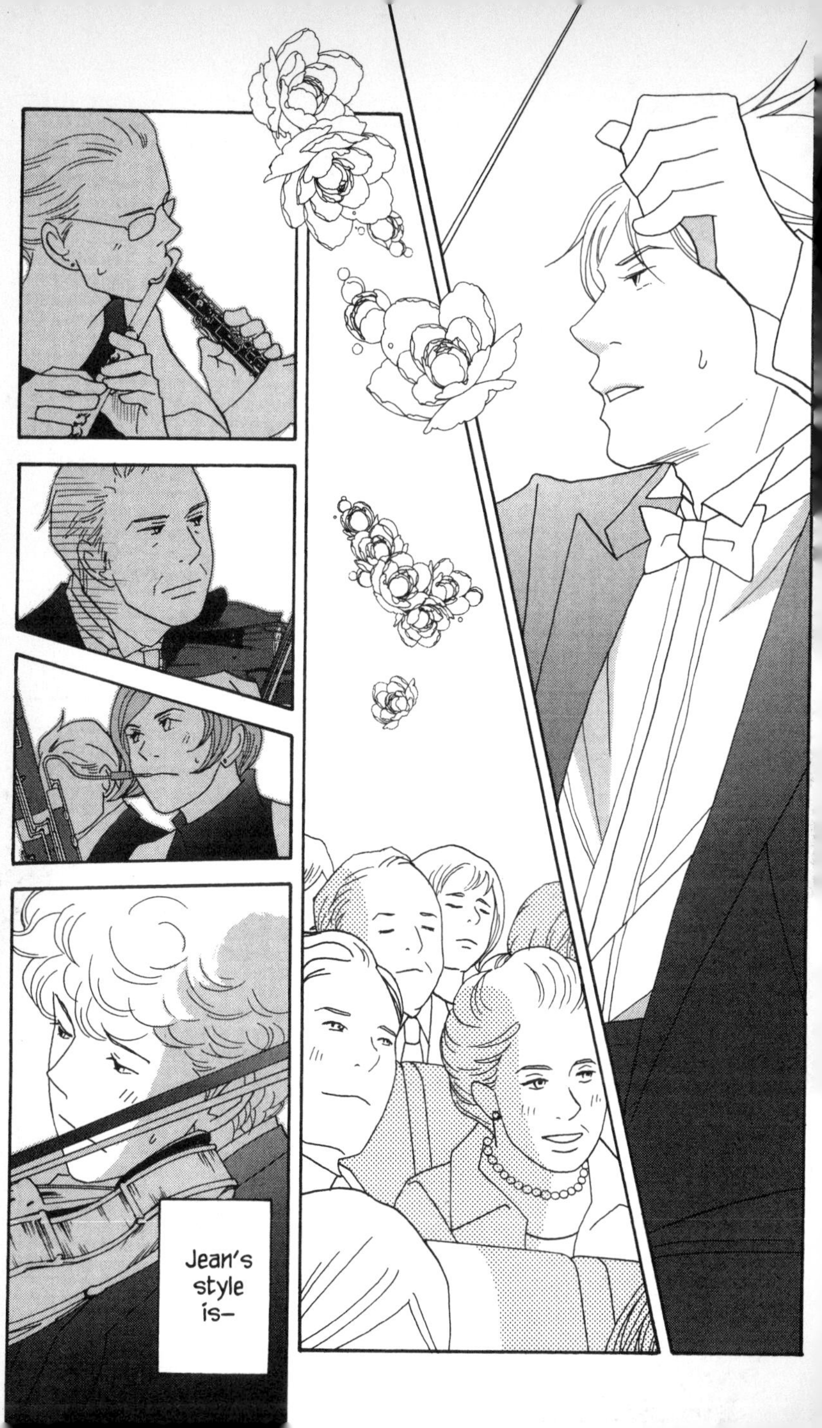
Jean's style is–

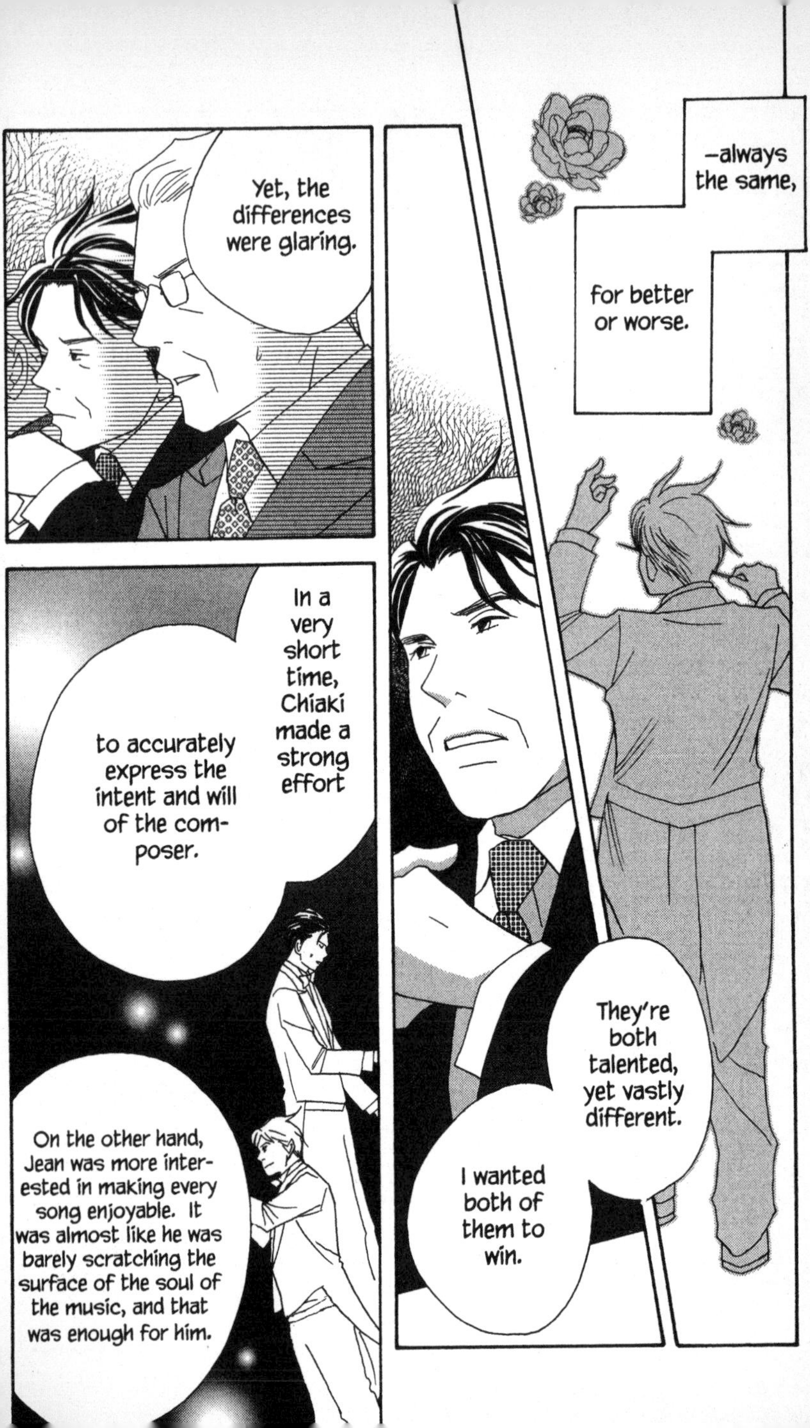
—always the same,
for better or worse.
They're both talented, yet vastly different.
I wanted both of them to win.
Yet, the differences were glaring.
In a very short time, Chiaki made a strong effort
to accurately express the intent and will of the com-poser.
On the other hand, Jean was more inter-ested in making every song enjoyable. It was almost like he was barely scratching the surface of the soul of the music, and that was enough for him.

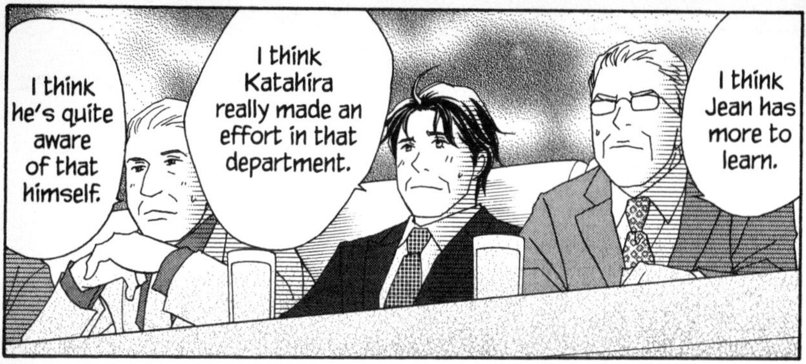
I think Jean has more to learn.
I think Katahira really made an effort in that department.
I think he's quite aware of that himself.

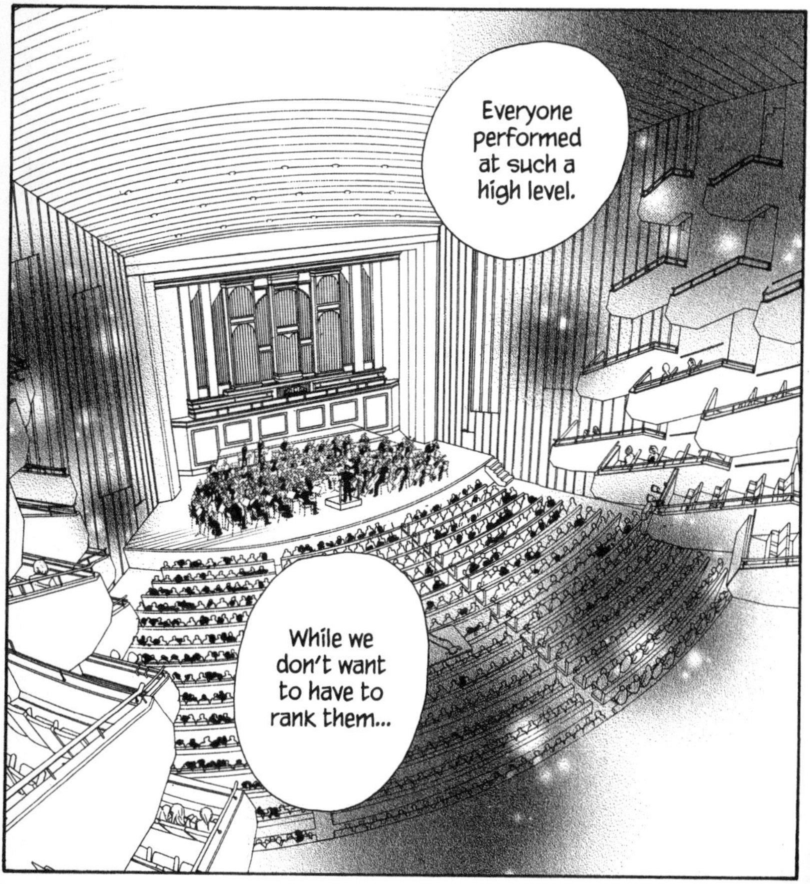
Everyone performed at such a high level.
While we don't want to have to rank them...

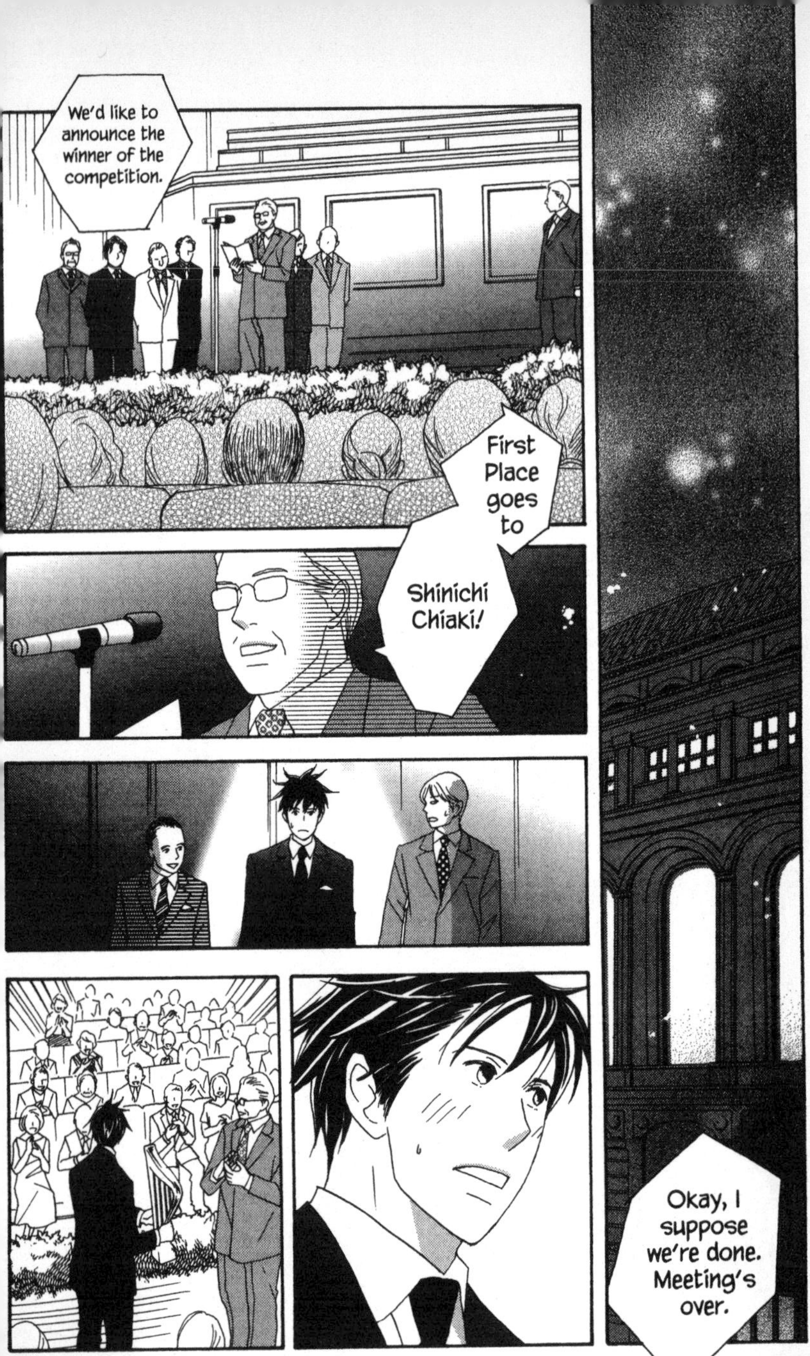
We'd like to announce the winner of the competition.
First Place goes to
Shinichi Chiaki!
Okay, I suppose we're done. Meeting's over.

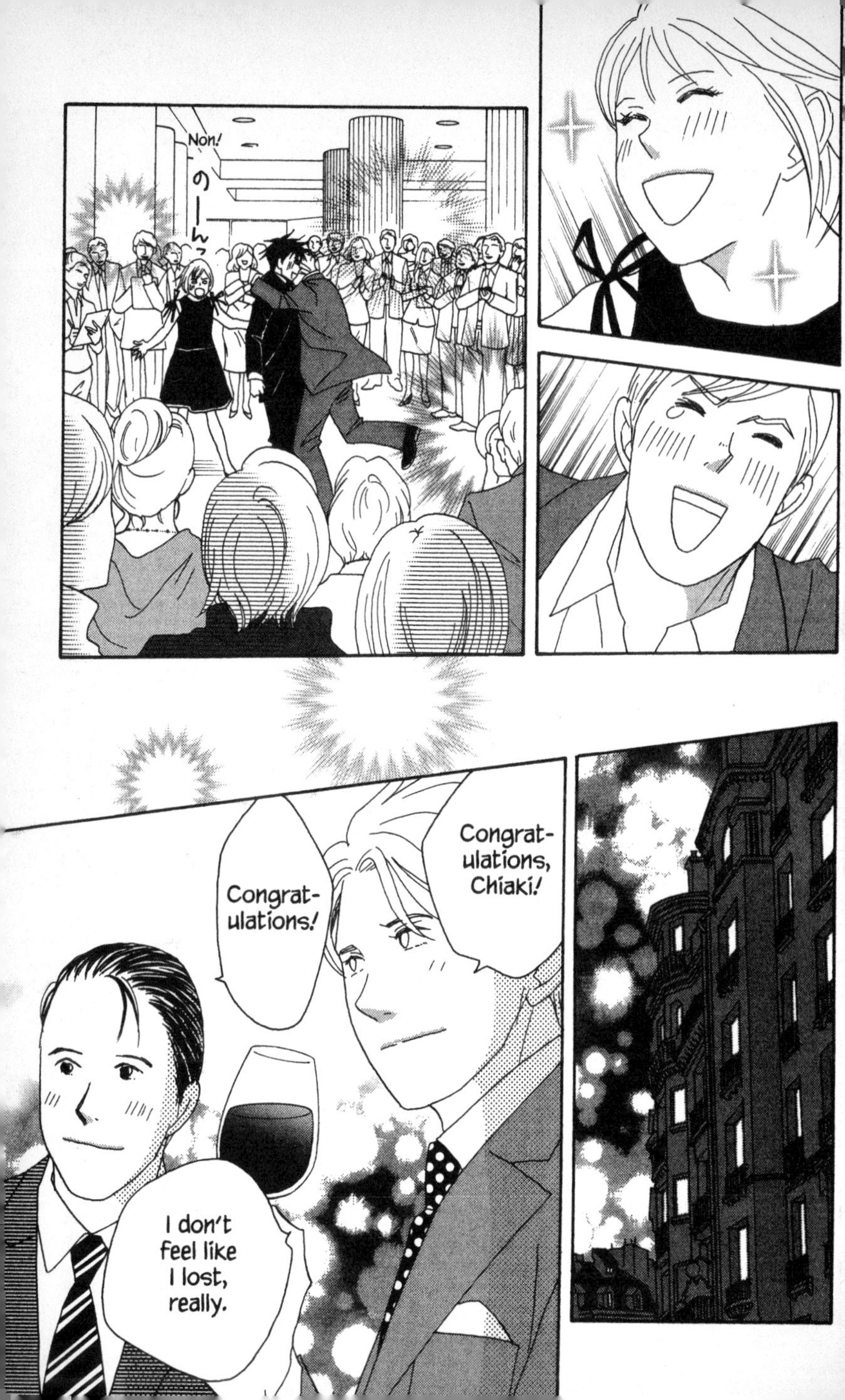
Non!
のーんっ
Congrat-ulations, Chiaki!
Congrat-ulations!
I don't feel like I lost, really.

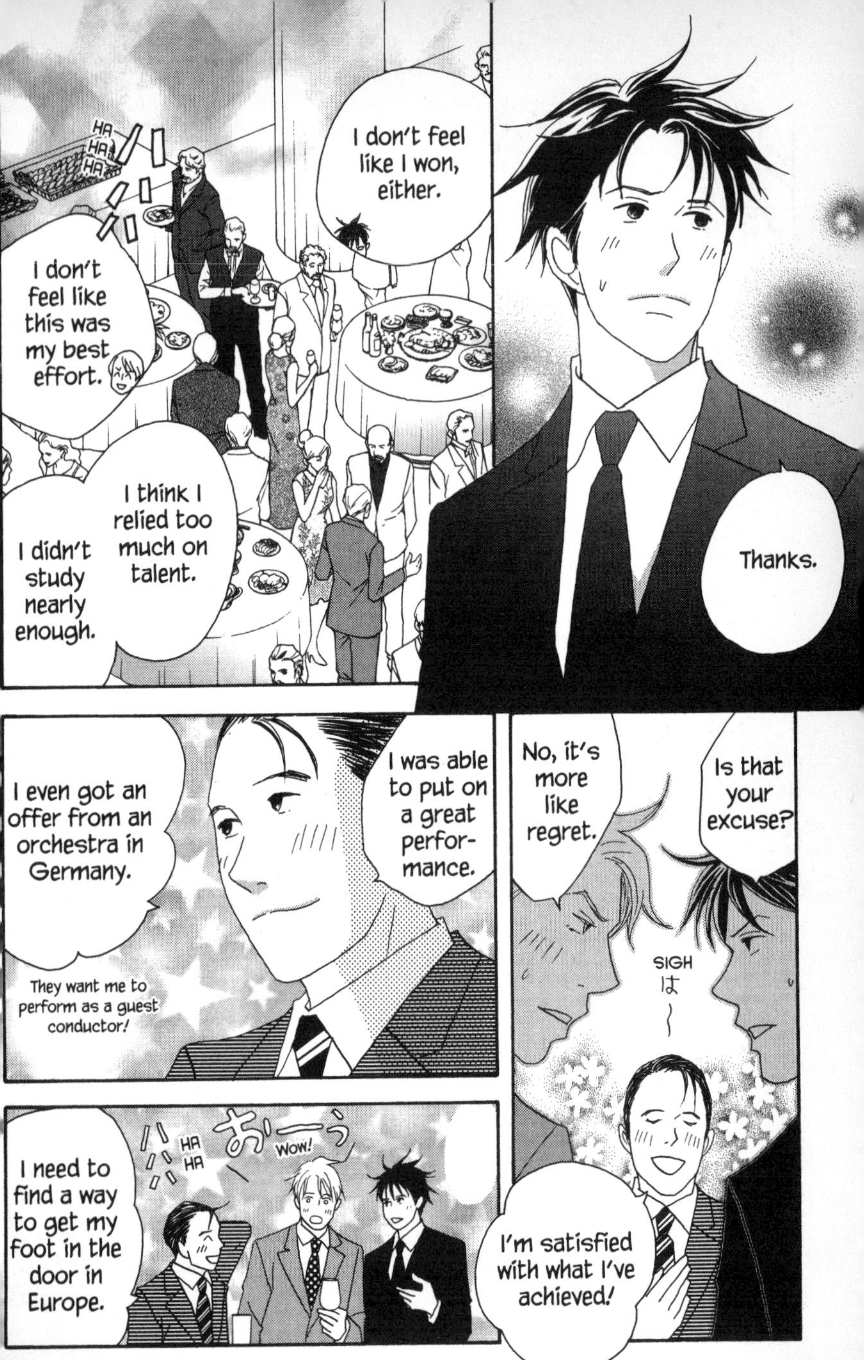
Thanks.
I don't feel like I won, either.
HA HA HA
I don't feel like this was my best effort.
I think I relied too much on talent.
I didn't study nearly enough.
Is that your excuse?
No, it's more like regret.
SIGH
は〜
I'm satisfied with what I've achieved!
I was able to put on a great perfor-mance.
I even got an offer from an orchestra in Germany.
They want me to perform as a guest conductor!
おーう
WOW!
ハハ
HA HA
I need to find a way to get my foot in the door in Europe.

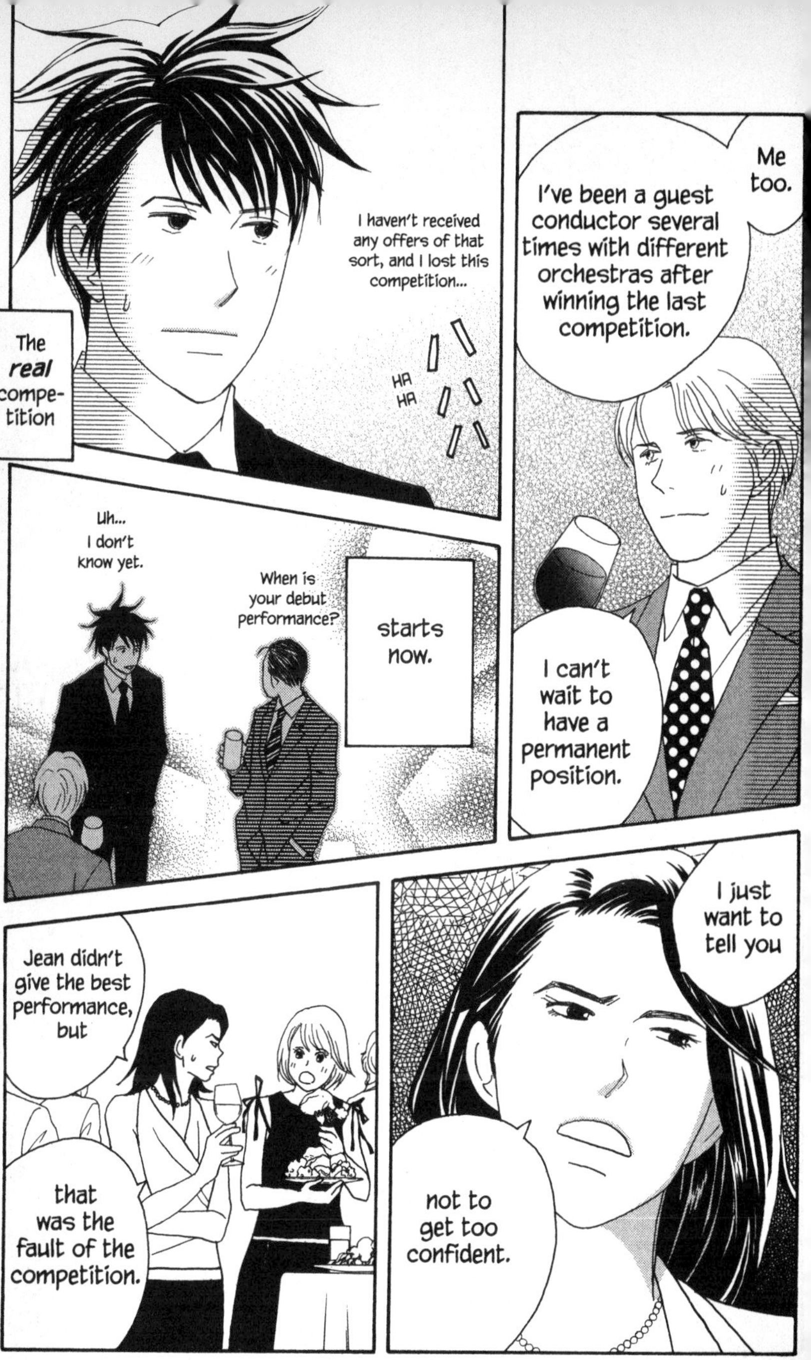
Me too.
I've been a guest conductor several times with different orchestras after winning the last competition.
I can't wait to have a permanent position.
I haven't received any offers of that sort, and I lost this competition...
HA HA
The *real* compe-tition
starts now.
When is your debut performance?
Uh... I don't know yet.
I just want to tell you
not to get too confident.
Jean didn't give the best performance, but
that was the fault of the competition.

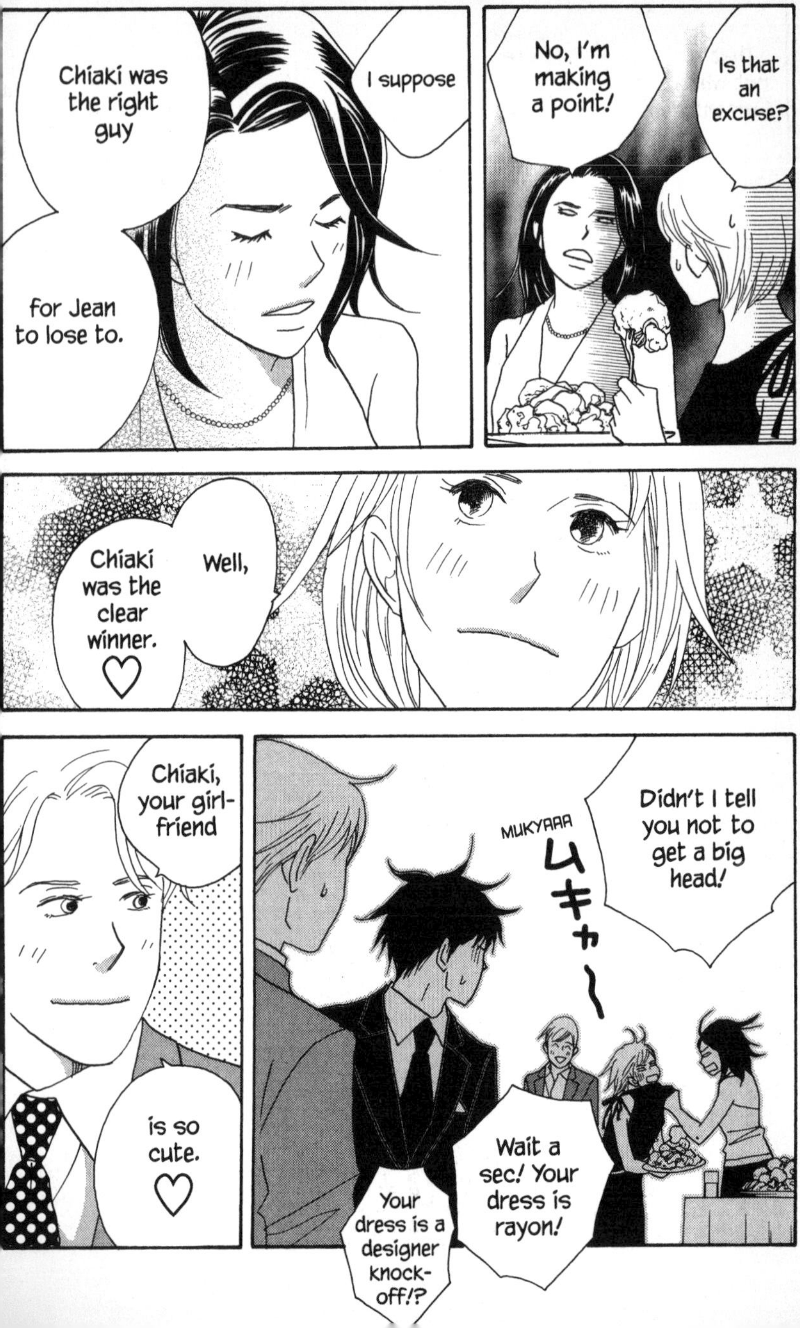
Is that an excuse?
No, I'm making a point!
I suppose
Chiaki was the right guy
for Jean to lose to.
Well,
Chiaki was the clear winner. ♡
Didn't I tell you not to get a big head!
MUKYAAA
ムキャ〜
Wait a sec! Your dress is rayon!
Your dress is a designer knock-off!?
Chiaki, your girl-friend
is so cute. ♡

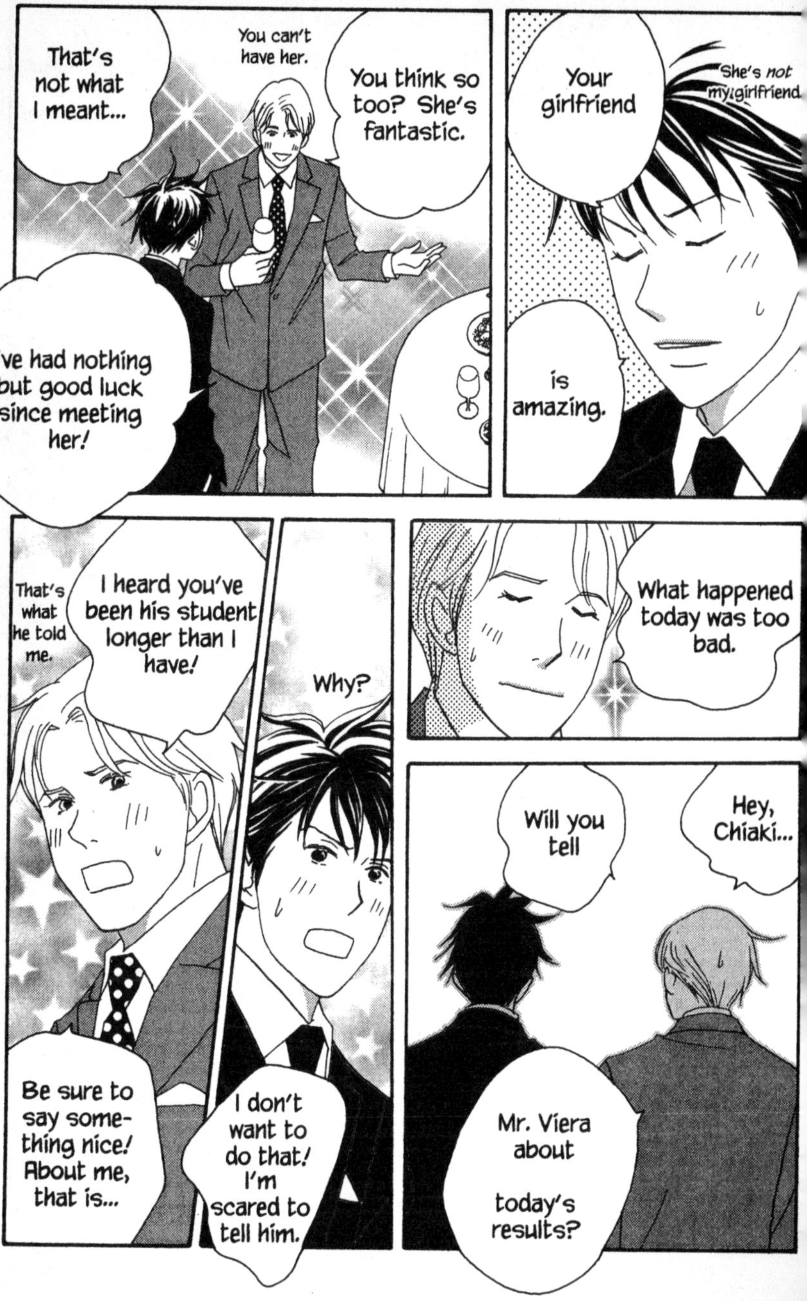
Your girlfriend
is amazing.
She's *not* my girlfriend.
You think so too? She's fantastic.
You can't have her.
That's not what I meant...
I've had nothing but good luck since meeting her!
What happened today was too bad.
Hey, Chiaki...
Will you tell
Mr. Viera about
today's results?
Why?
I don't want to do that! I'm scared to tell him.
I heard you've been his student longer than I have!
That's what he told me.
Be sure to say some-thing nice! About me, that is...

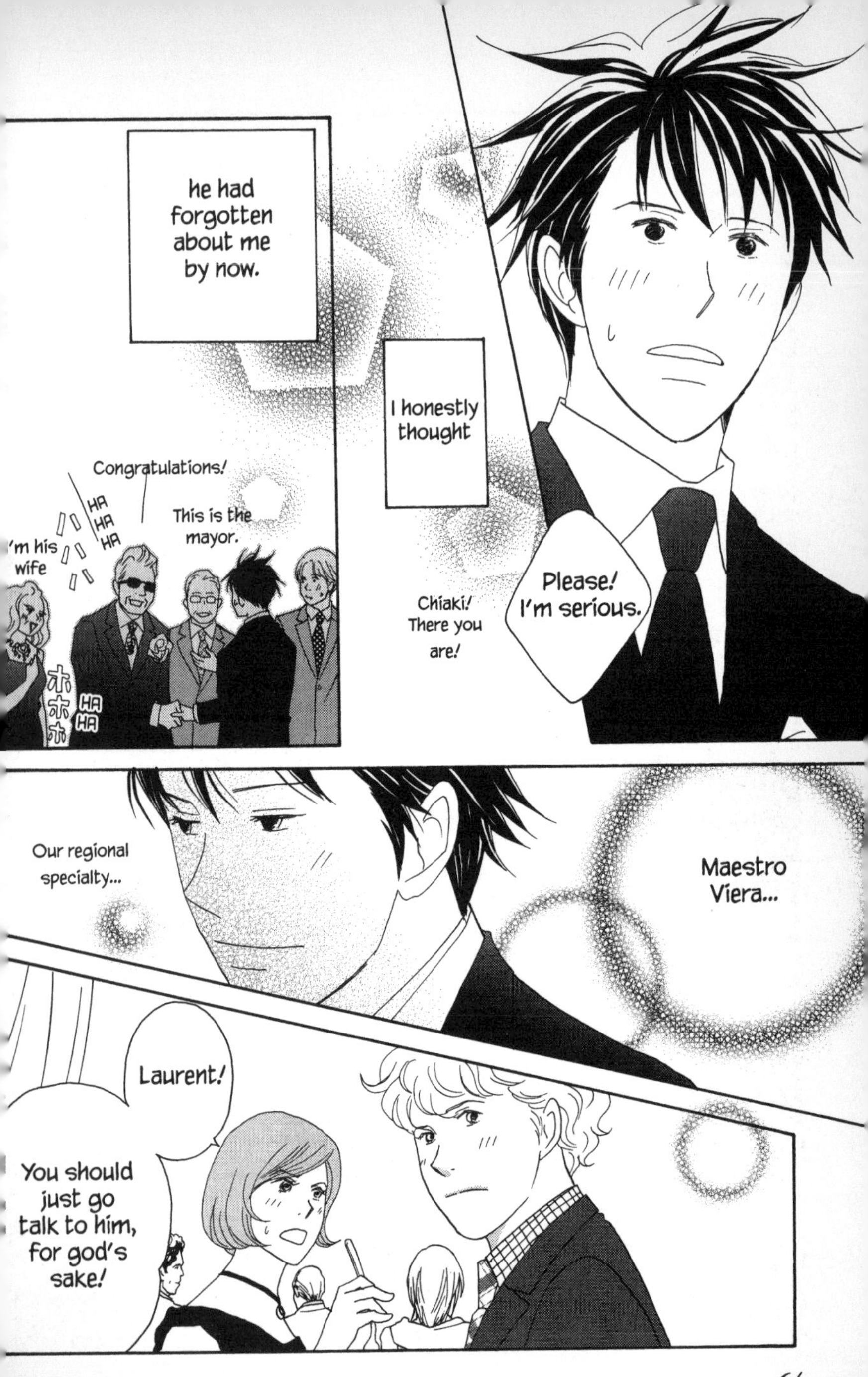
I honestly thought
Please! I'm serious.
Chiaki! There you are!
he had forgotten about me by now.
This is the mayor.
Congratulations!
HA HA HA
I'm his wife
ホホホ
HA HA
Maestro Viera...
Our regional specialty...
Laurent!
You should just go talk to him, for god's sake!

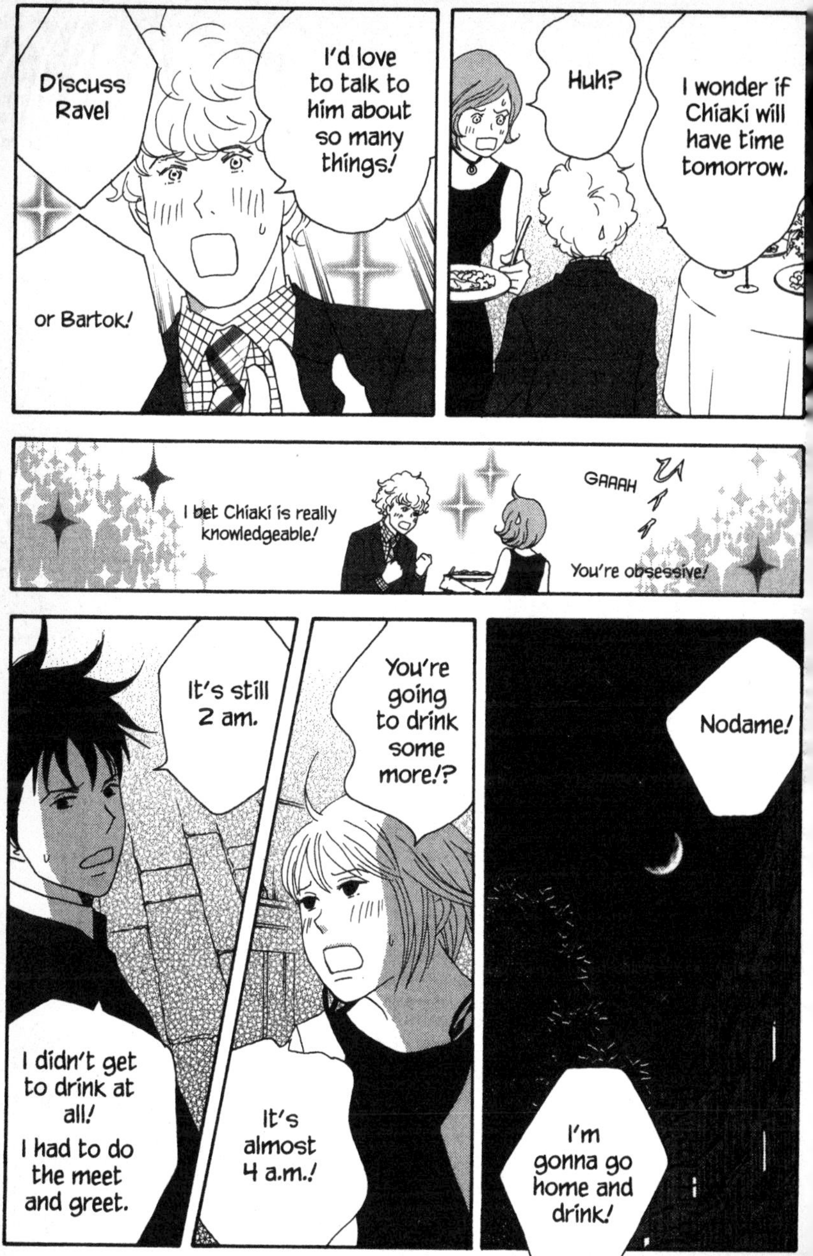
I wonder if Chiaki will have time tomorrow.
Huh?
I'd love to talk to him about so many things!
Discuss Ravel
or Bartok!
GAAAH
You're obsessive!
I bet Chiaki is really knowledgeable!
Nodame!
I'm gonna go home and drink!
You're going to drink some more!?
It's almost 4 a.m.!
It's still 2 am.
I didn't get to drink at all!
I had to do the meet and greet.

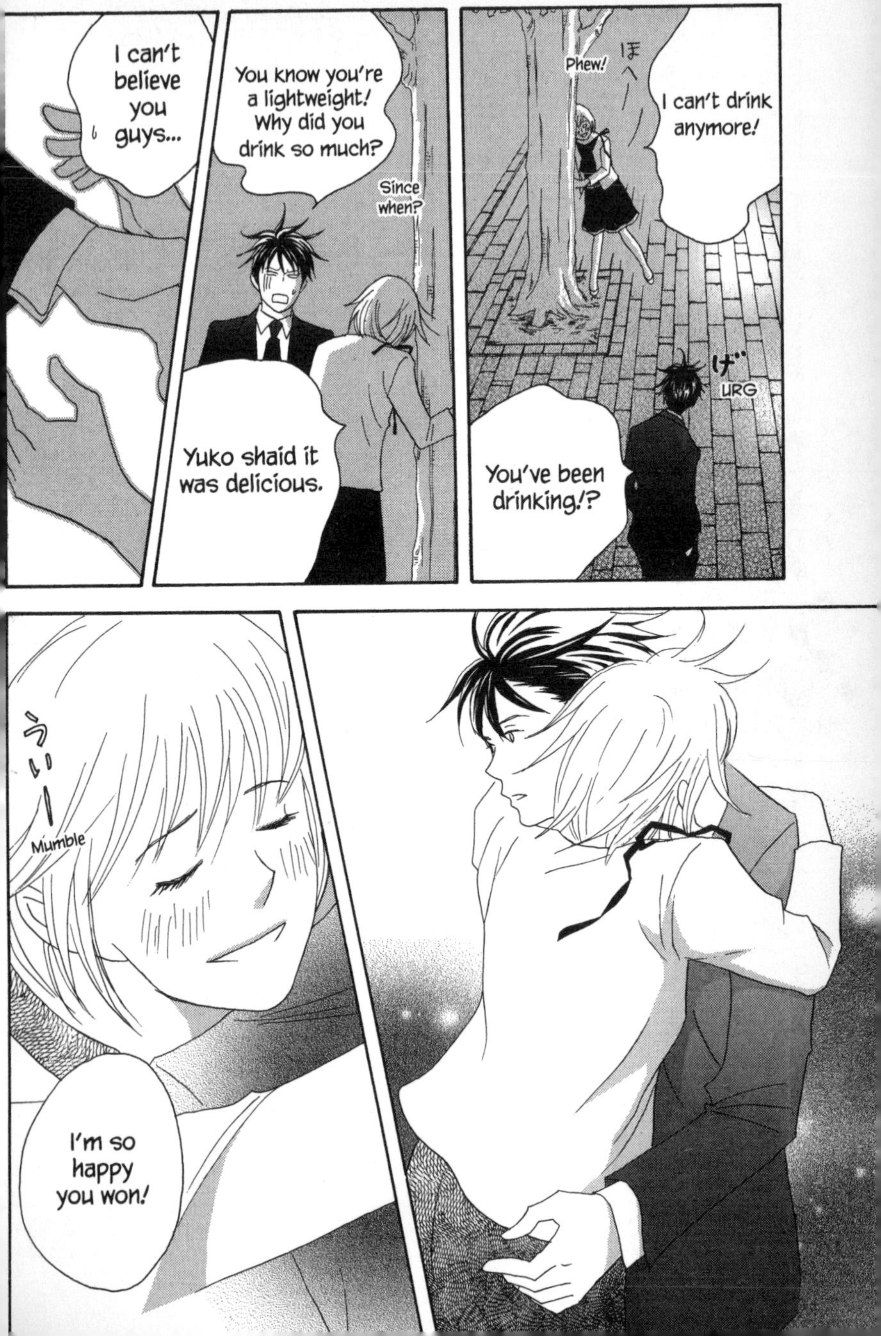
ほへ
Phew!
I can't drink anymore!
げ
URG
You've been drinking!?
You know you're a lightweight! Why did you drink so much?
Since when?
Yuko shaid it was delicious.
I can't believe you guys...
うぃー
Mumble
I'm so happy you won!

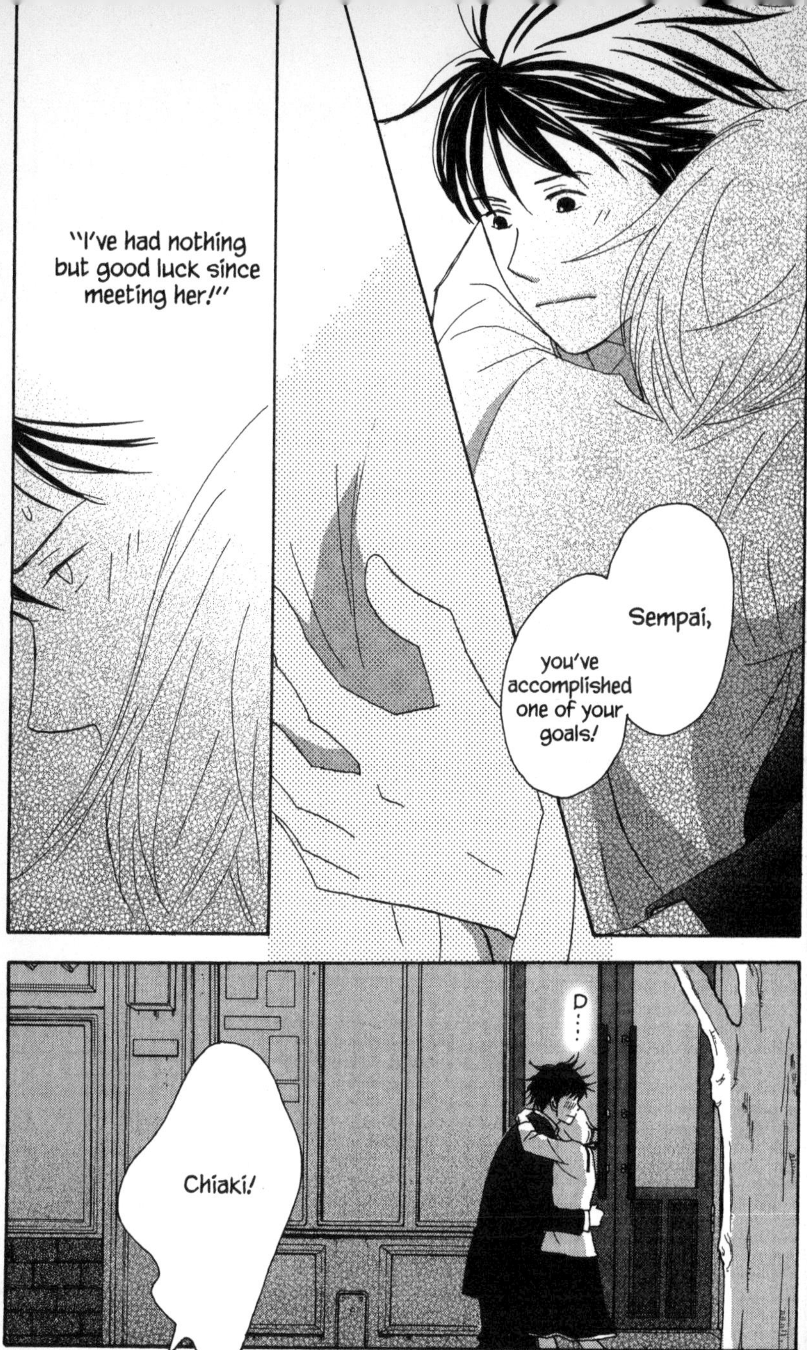
Sempai, you've accomplished one of your goals!
"I've had nothing but good luck since meeting her!"
D...
Chiaki!

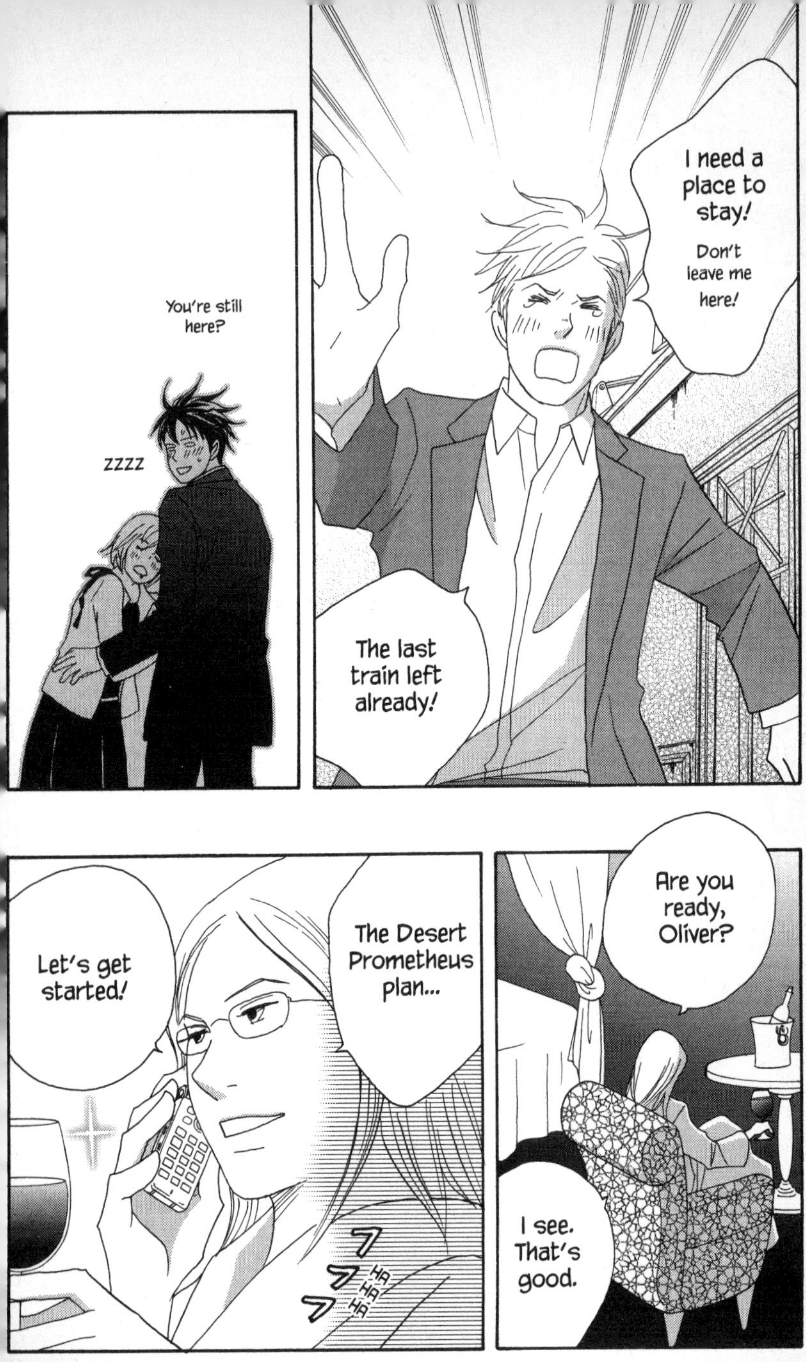
I need a place to stay!
Don't leave me here!
The last train left already!
You're still here?
ZZZZ
Are you ready, Oliver?
I see. That's good.
The Desert Prometheus plan...
Let's get started!
HA HA HA

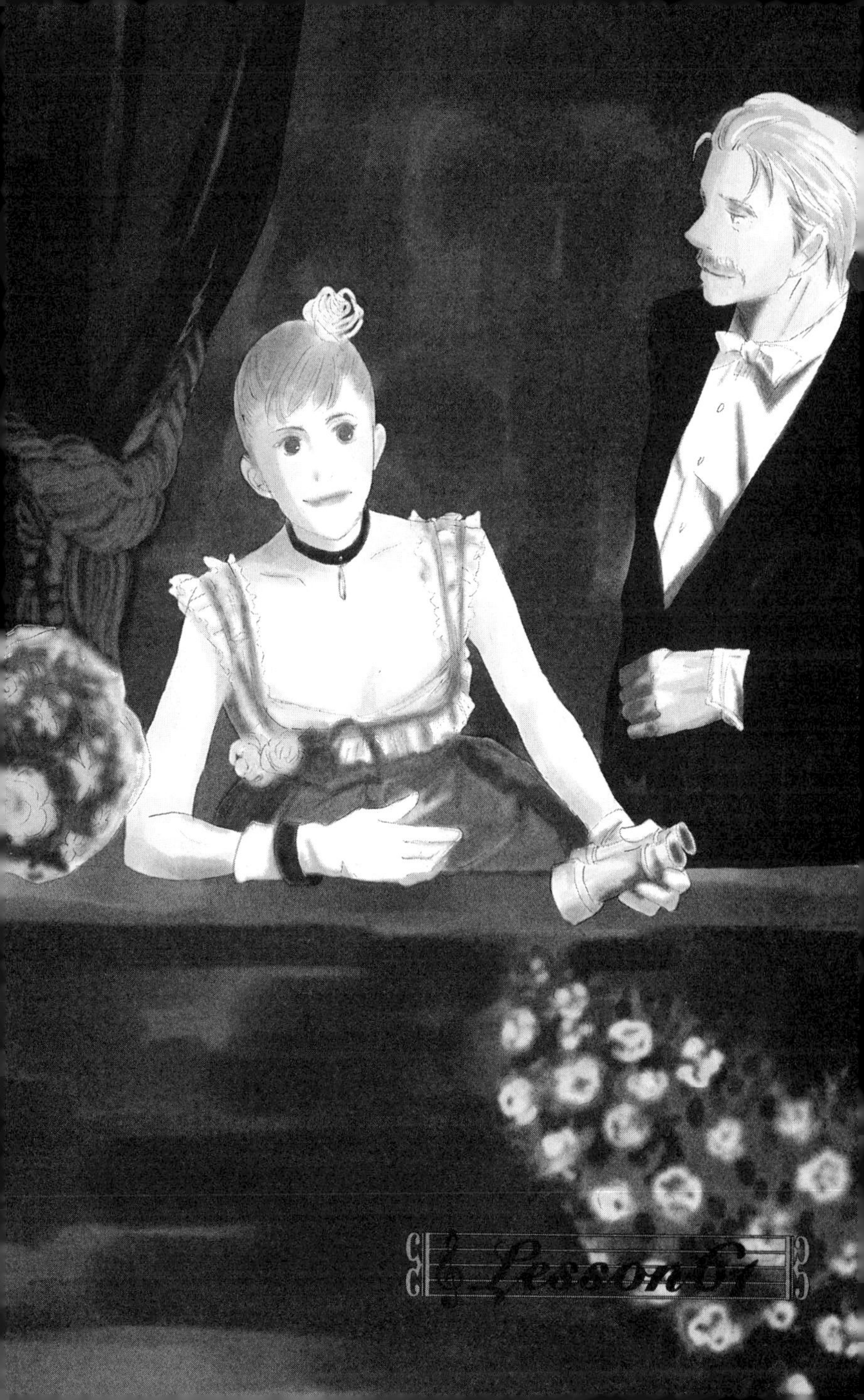
Lesson 61

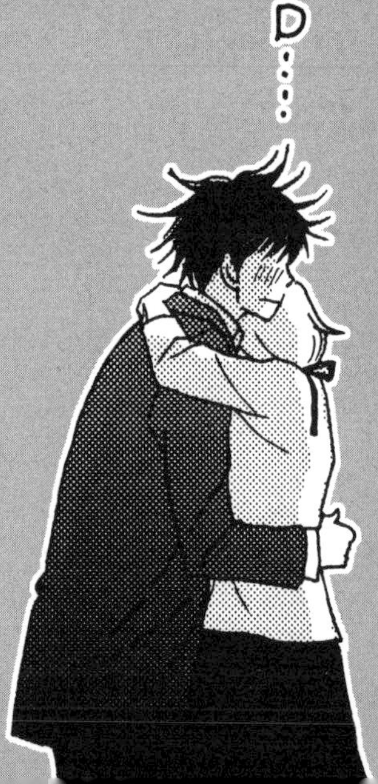
D....

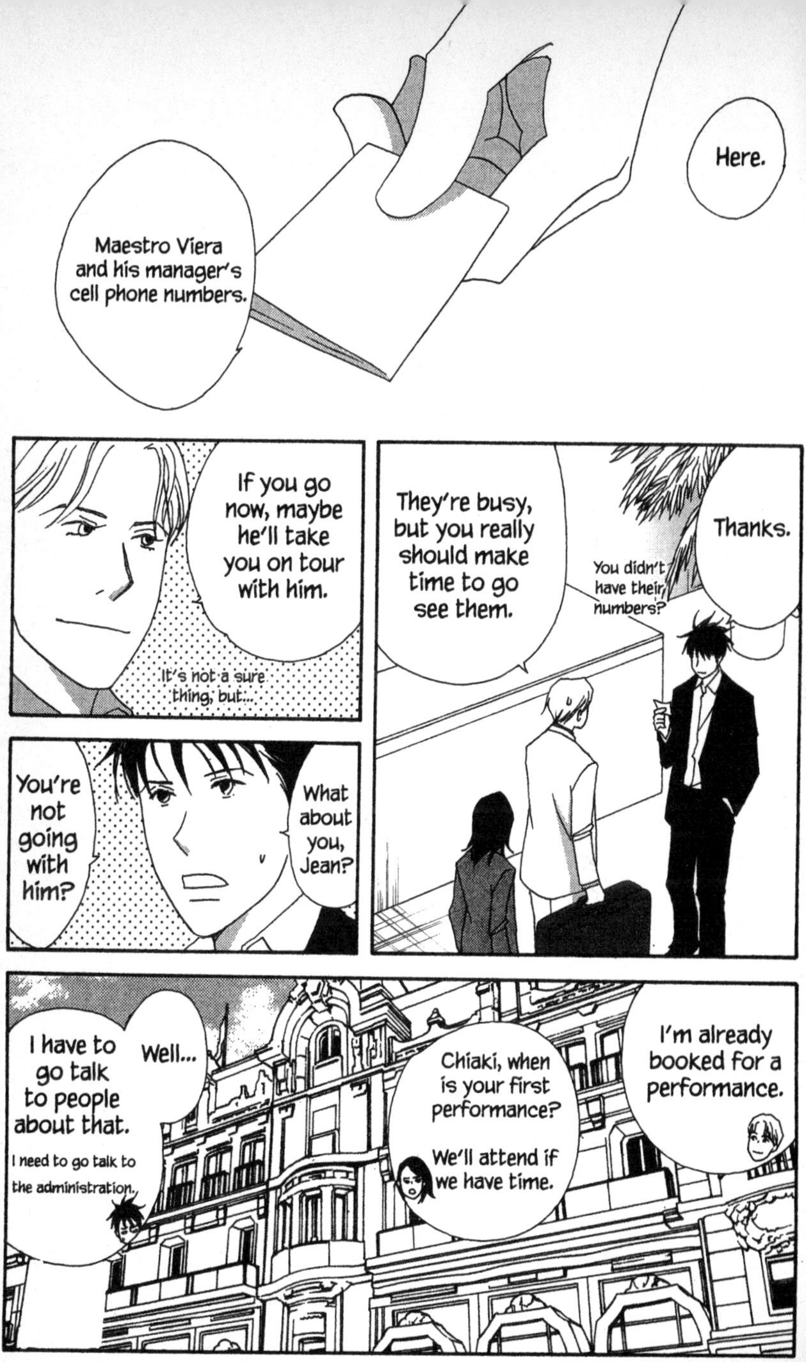
Here.
Maestro Viera and his manager's cell phone numbers.
Thanks.
You didn't have their numbers?
They're busy, but you really should make time to go see them.
If you go now, maybe he'll take you on tour with him.
It's not a sure thing, but...
What about you, Jean?
You're not going with him?
I'm already booked for a performance.
Chiaki, when is your first performance?
We'll attend if we have time.
Well...
I have to go talk to people about that.
I need to go talk to the administration.

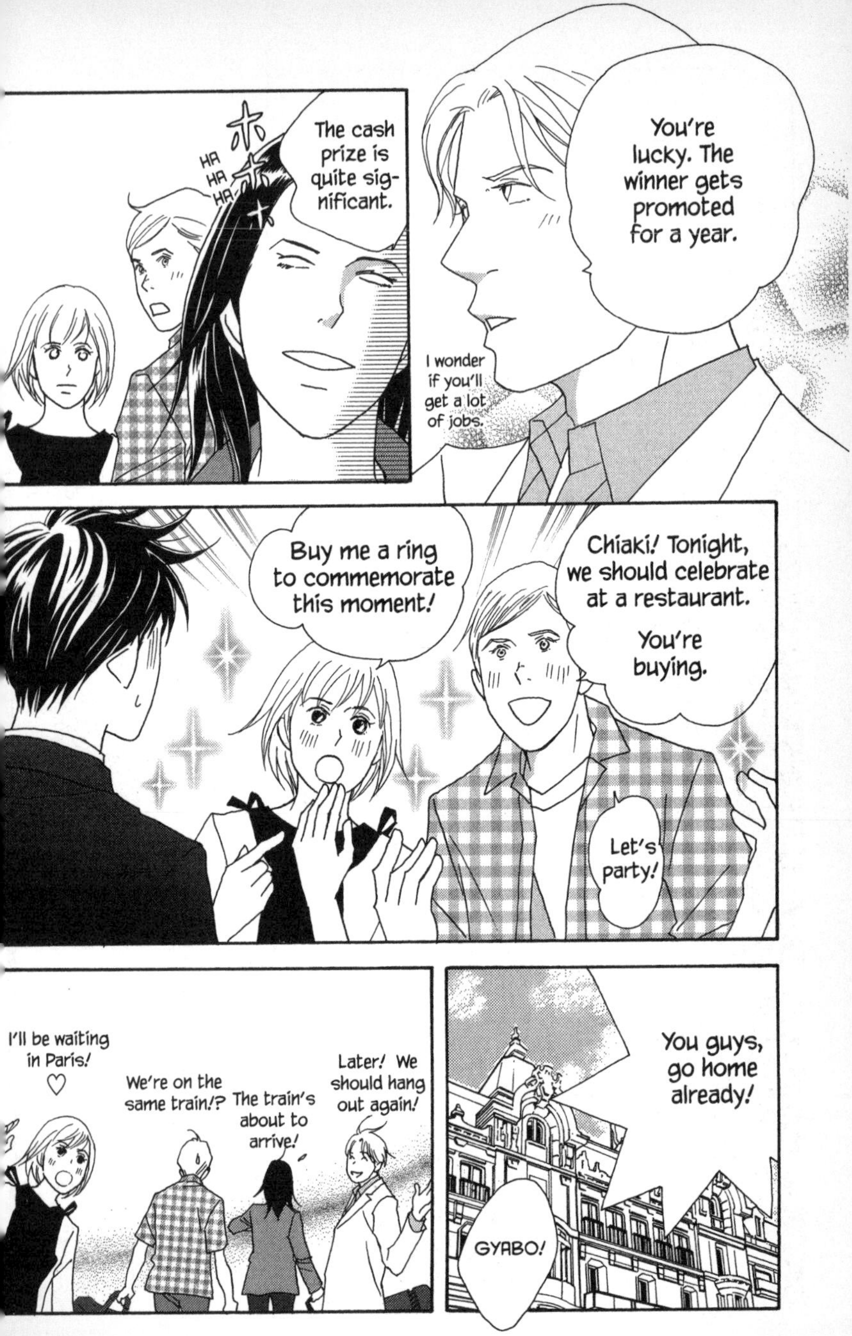
You're lucky. The winner gets promoted for a year.
I wonder if you'll get a lot of jobs.
The cash prize is quite significant.
HA HA HA
Chiaki! Tonight, we should celebrate at a restaurant.
You're buying.
Let's party!
Buy me a ring to commemorate this moment!
You guys, go home already!
GYABO!
Later! We should hang out again!
The train's about to arrive!
We're on the same train!?
I'll be waiting in Paris! ♡

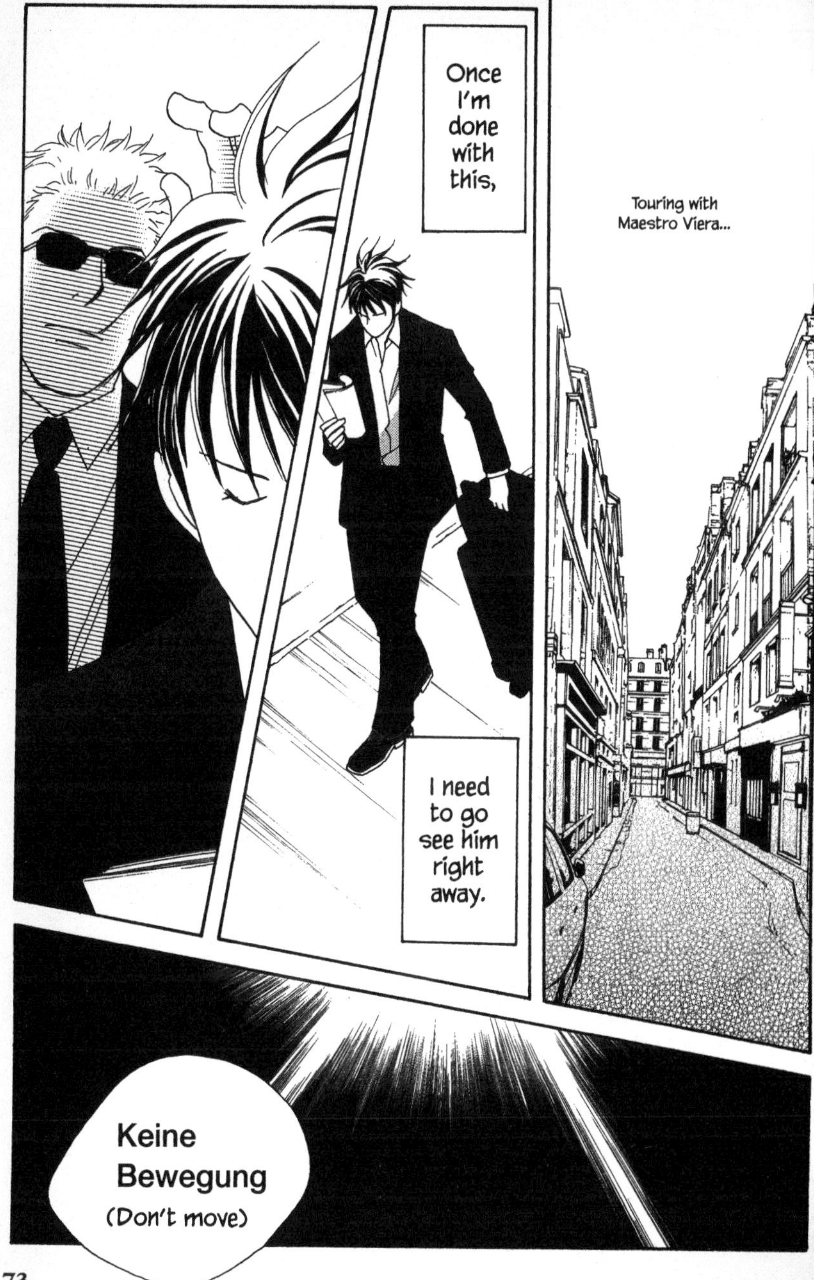
Touring with Maestro Viera...
Once I'm done with this,
I need to go see him right away.
Keine Bewegung
(Don't move)

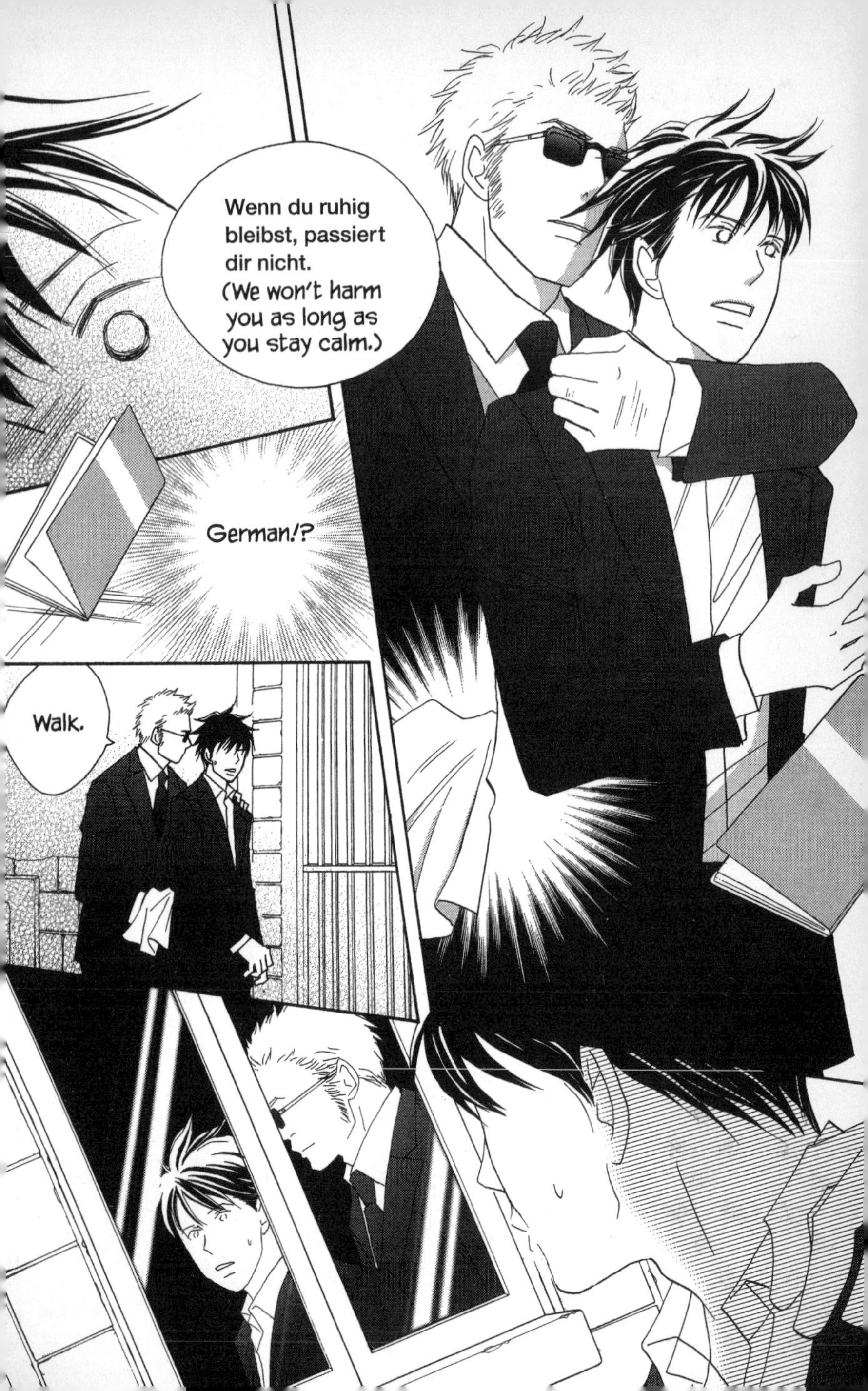
Wenn du ruhig bleibst, passiert dir nicht. (We won't harm you as long as you stay calm.)
German!?
Walk.

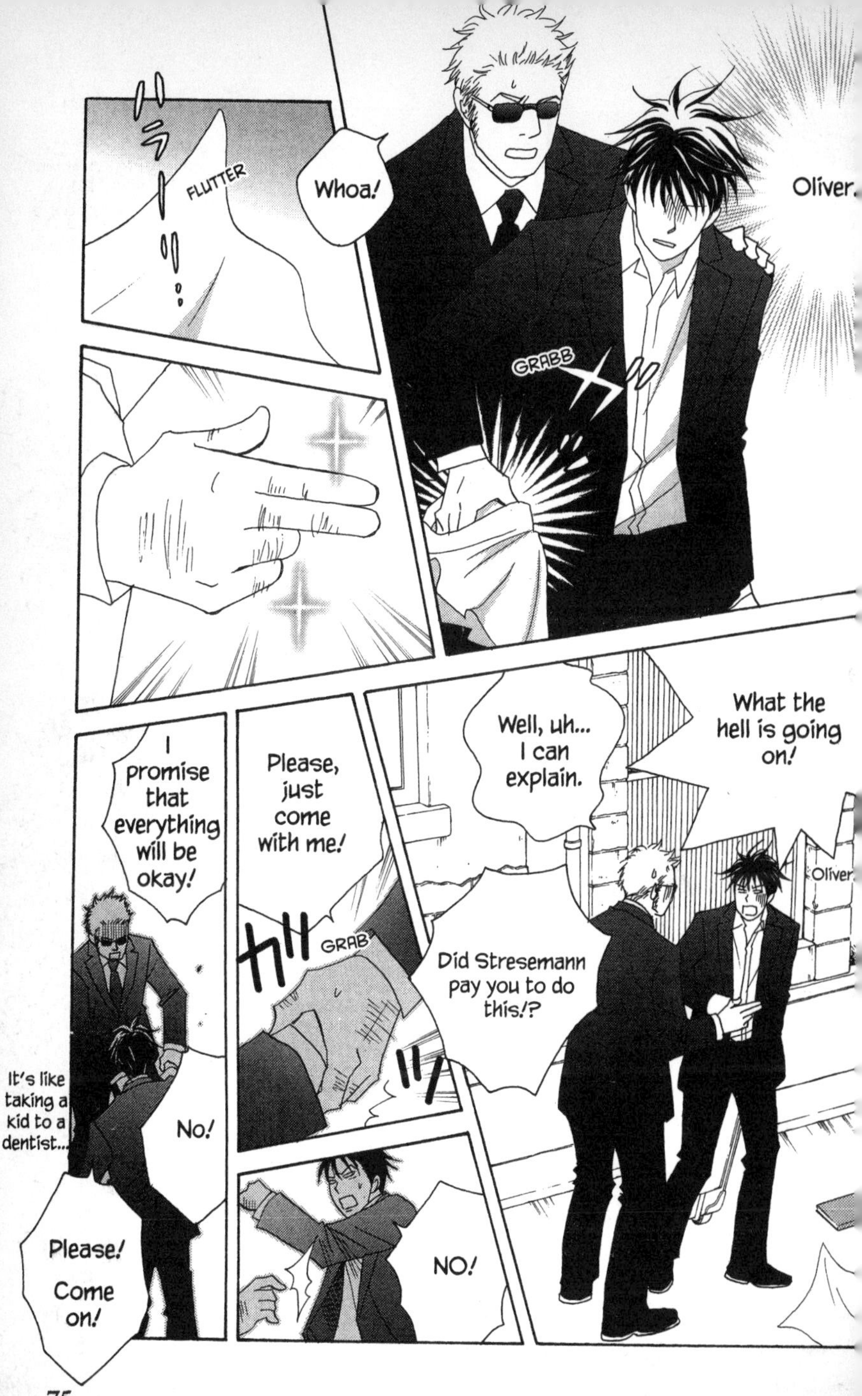
Oliver.
Whoa!
GRABB
FLUTTER
What the hell is going on!
Well, uh... I can explain.
Oliver
Did Stresemann pay you to do this!?
Please, just come with me!
GRAB
NO!
I promise that everything will be okay!
No!
It's like taking a kid to a dentist...
Please! Come on!

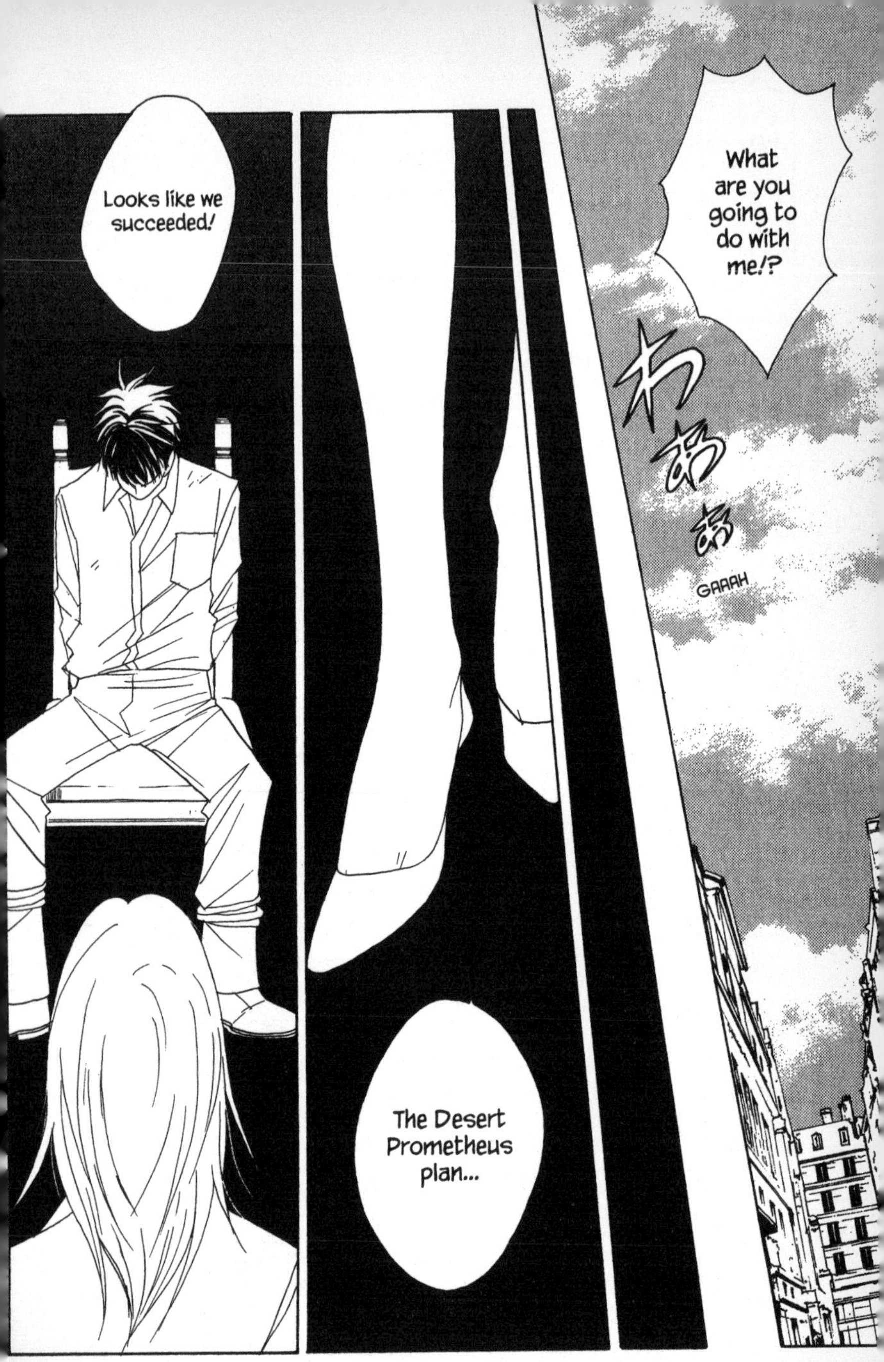

What are you going to do with me!?
わああ
GAAAH
The Desert Prometheus plan...
Looks like we succeeded!

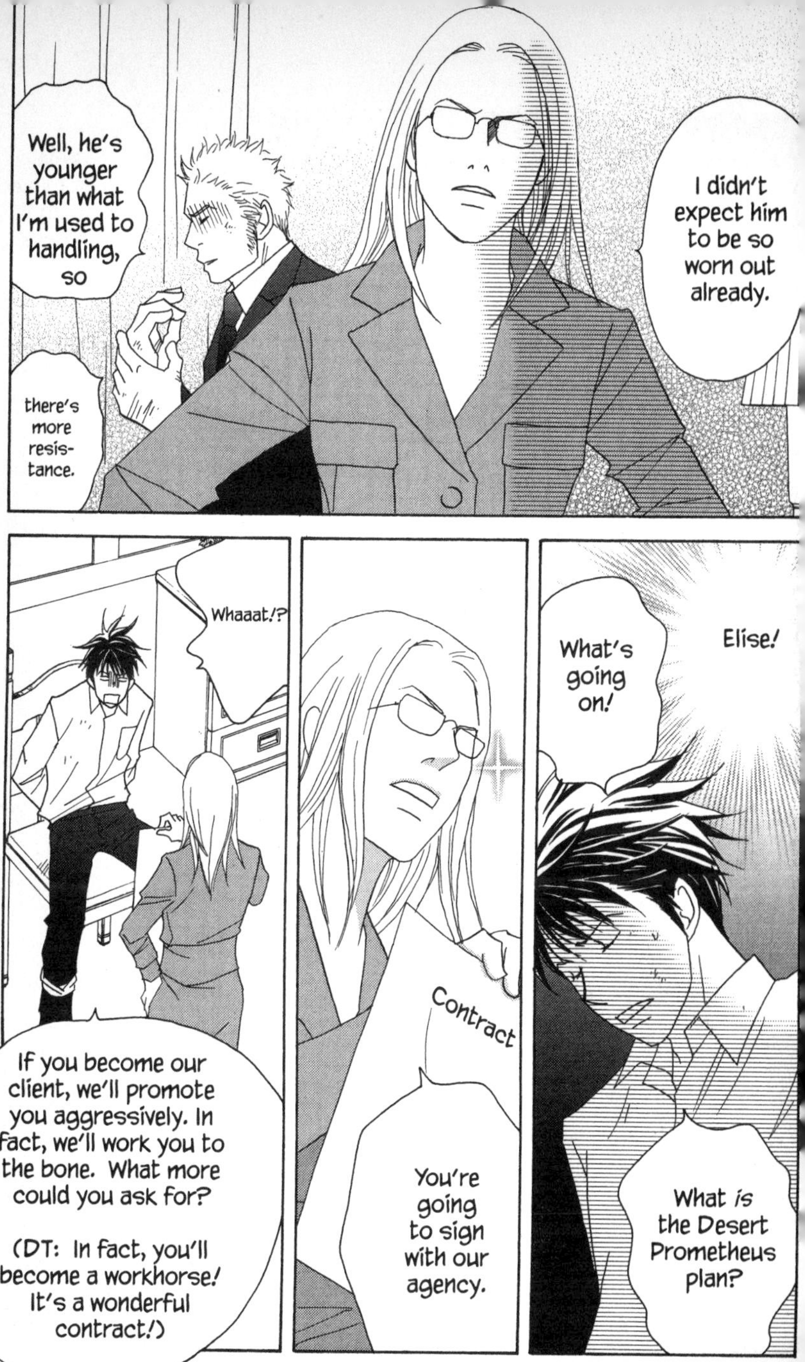
I didn't expect him to be so worn out already.
Well, he's younger than what I'm used to handling, so
there's more resis-tance.
Elise!
What's going on!
What *is* the Desert Prometheus plan?
Contract
You're going to sign with our agency.
Whaaat!?
If you become our client, we'll promote you aggressively. In fact, we'll work you to the bone. What more could you ask for?
(DT: In fact, you'll become a workhorse! It's a wonderful contract!)

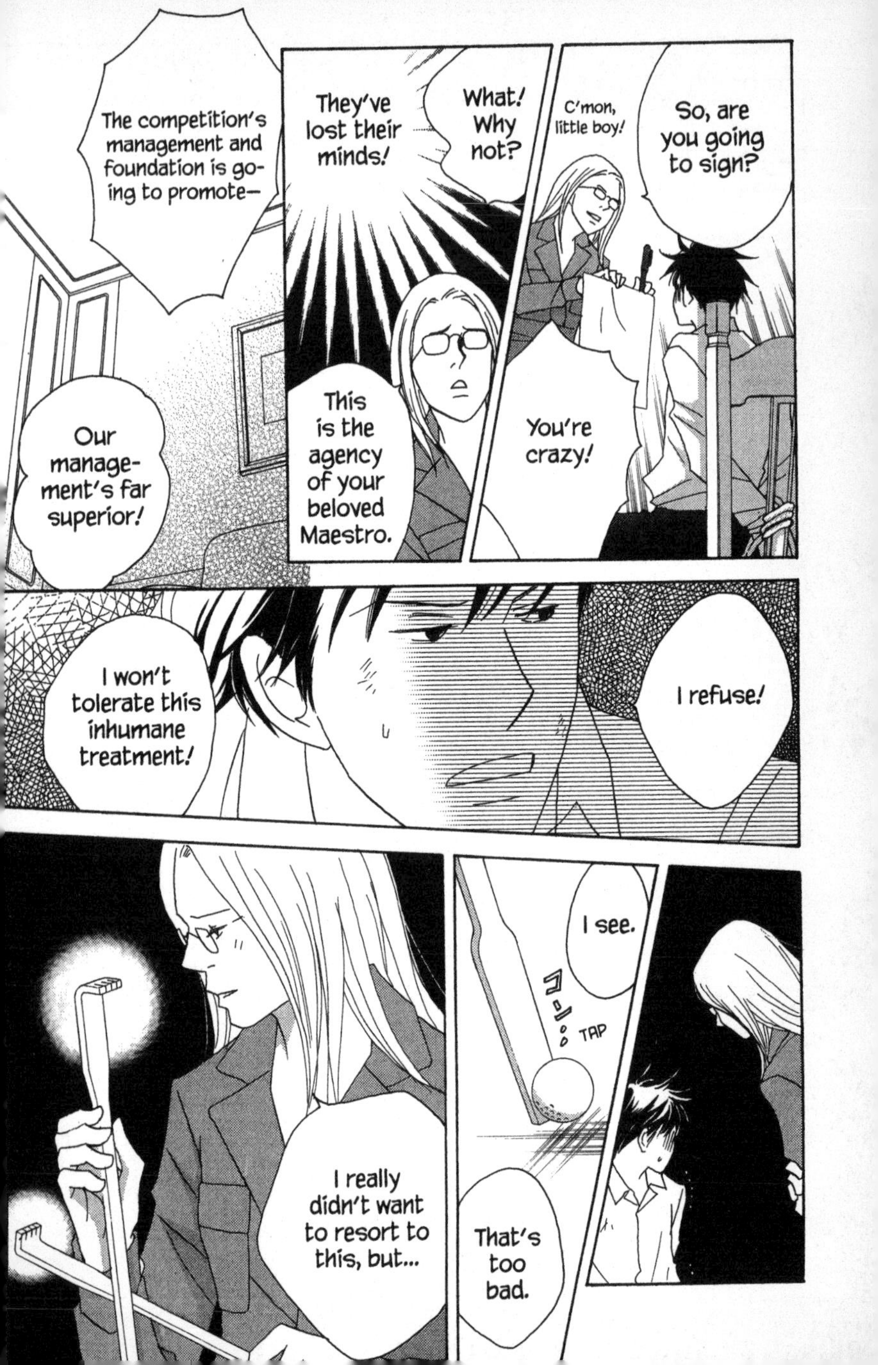
So, are you going to sign?
C'mon, little boy!
You're crazy!
What! Why not?
They've lost their minds!
This is the agency of your beloved Maestro.
The competition's management and foundation is going to promote—
Our management's far superior!
I refuse!
I won't tolerate this inhumane treatment!
I see.
TAP
That's too bad.
I really didn't want to resort to this, but...

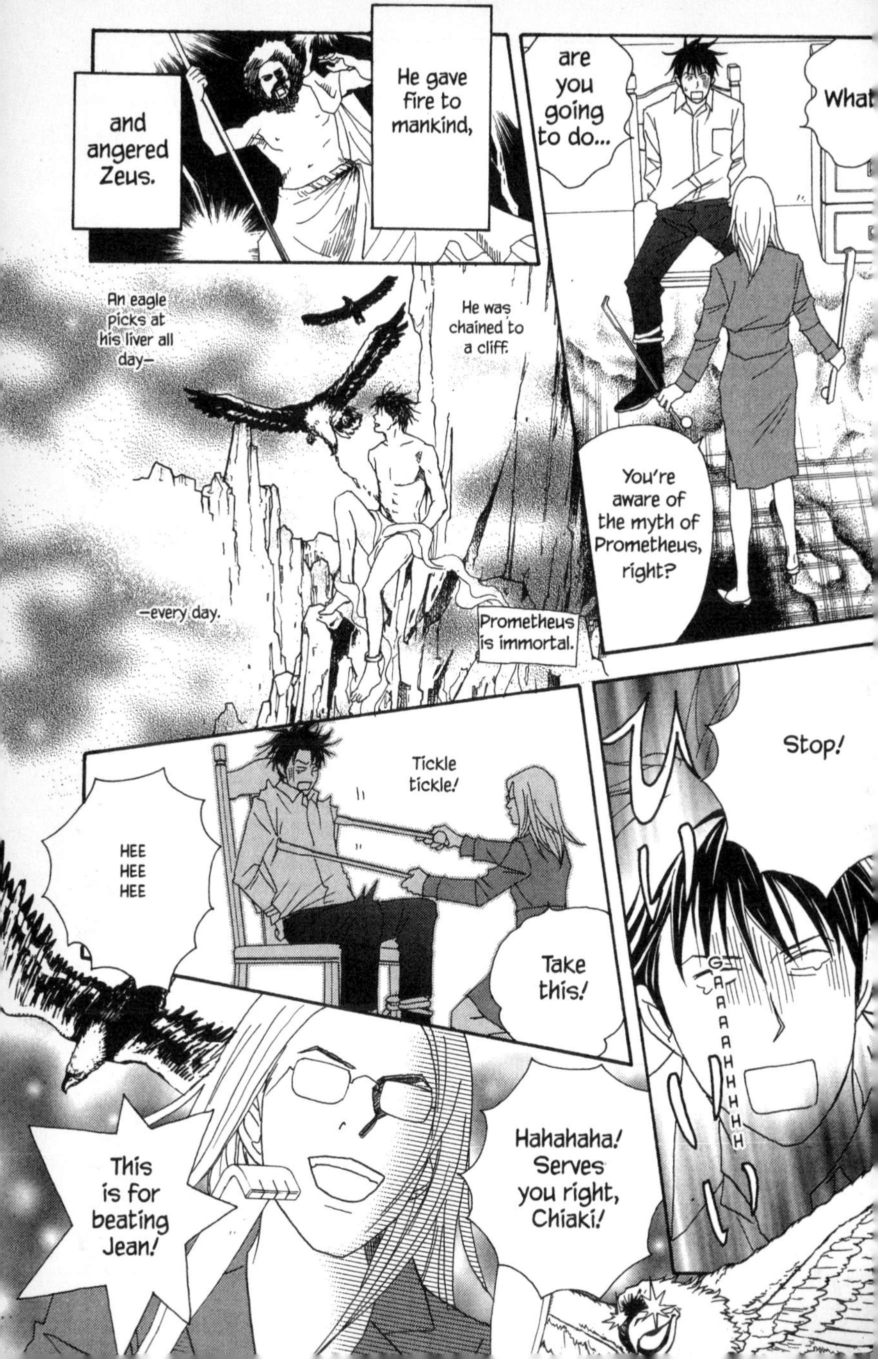
What
are you going to do...
You're aware of the myth of Prometheus, right?
He gave fire to mankind,
and angered Zeus.
He was chained to a cliff.
An eagle picks at his liver all day—
Prometheus is immortal.
—every day.
Stop!
GAAAAAHHHHHHH
Tickle tickle!
HEE HEE HEE
Take this!
Hahahaha! Serves you right, Chiaki!
This is for beating Jean!

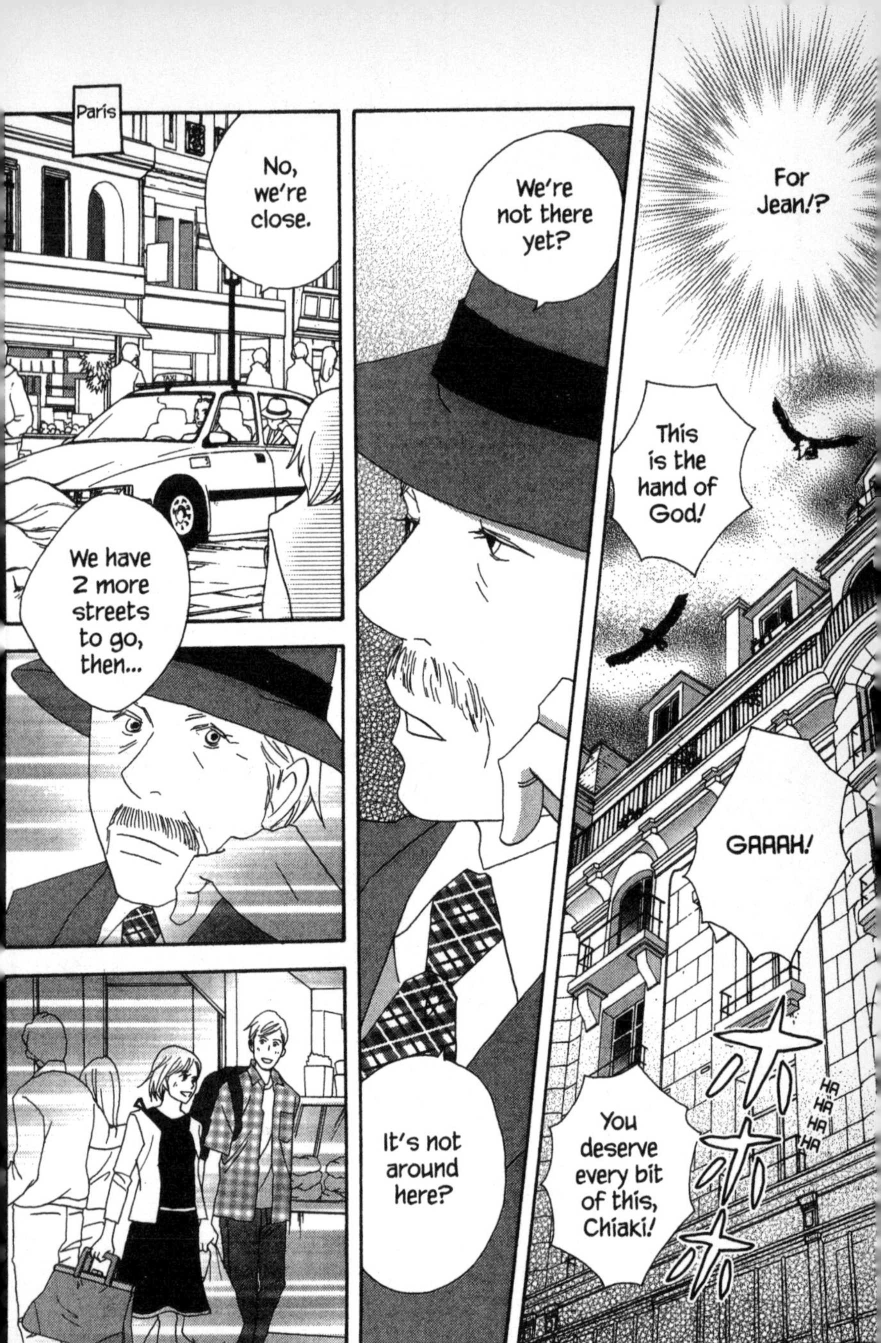
For Jean!?
This is the hand of God!
GAAAH!
HA HA HA HA
You deserve every bit of this, Chiaki!
We're not there yet?
It's not around here?
Paris
No, we're close.
We have 2 more streets to go, then...

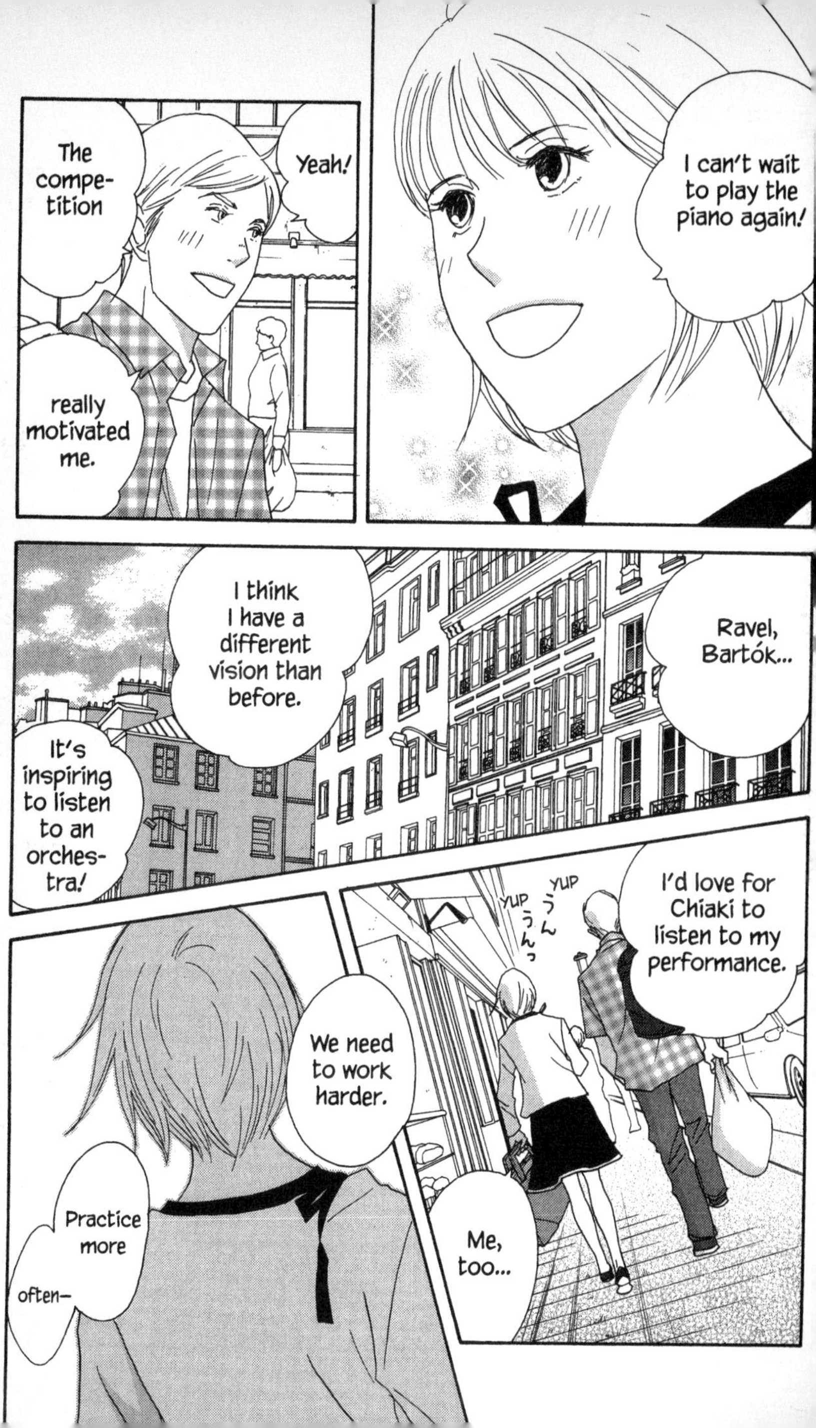

I can't wait to play the piano again!
Yeah!
The competition
really motivated me.
Ravel, Bartók...
I think I have a different vision than before.
It's inspiring to listen to an orchestra!
I'd love for Chiaki to listen to my performance.
YUP うん
YUP うんっ
We need to work harder.
Me, too...
Practice more
often—

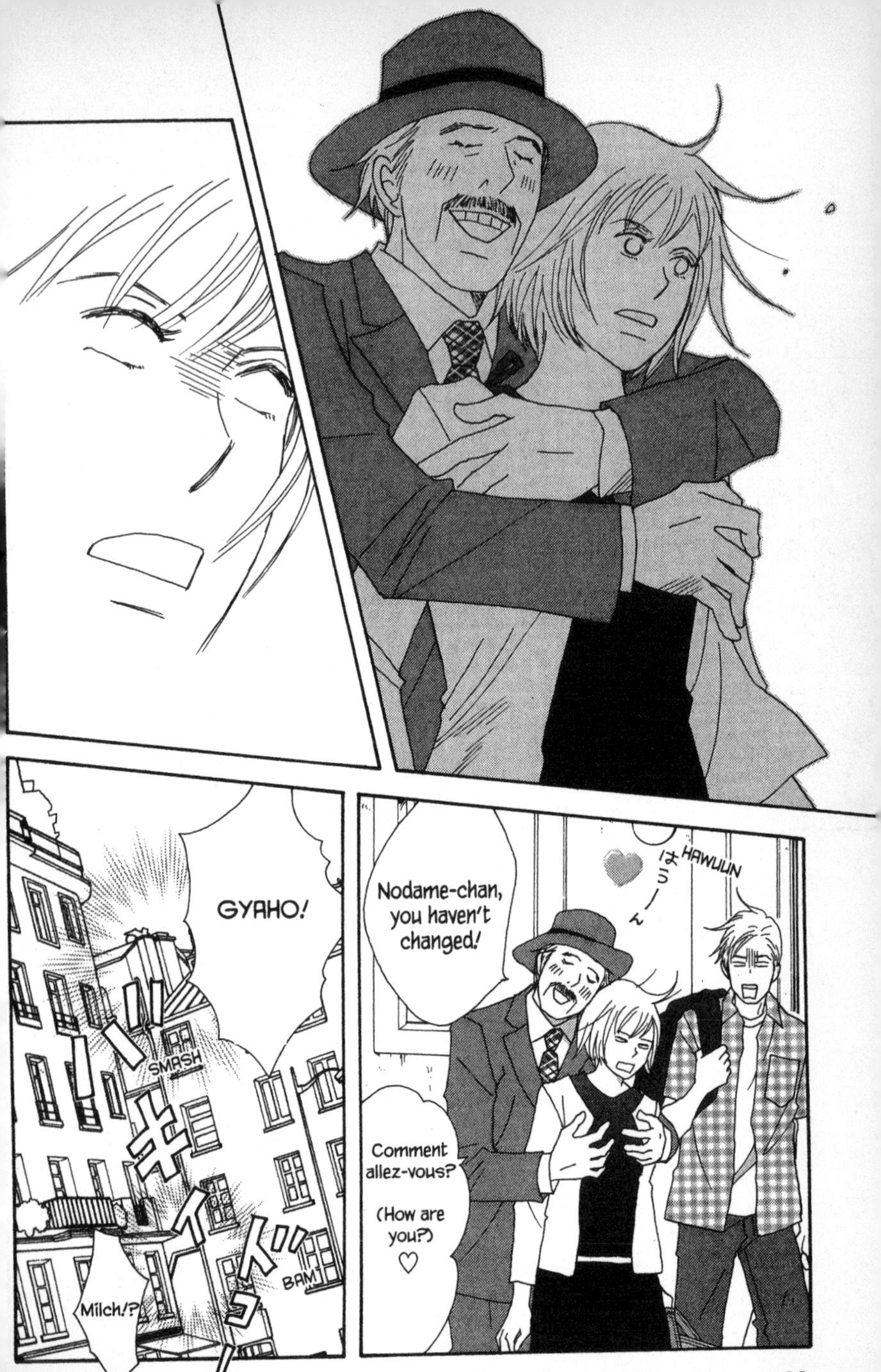
HAWUUN
はら〜ん
Nodame-chan, you haven't changed!
Comment allez-vous?
(How are you?) ♡
GYAHO!
SMASH
BAM
Milch!?

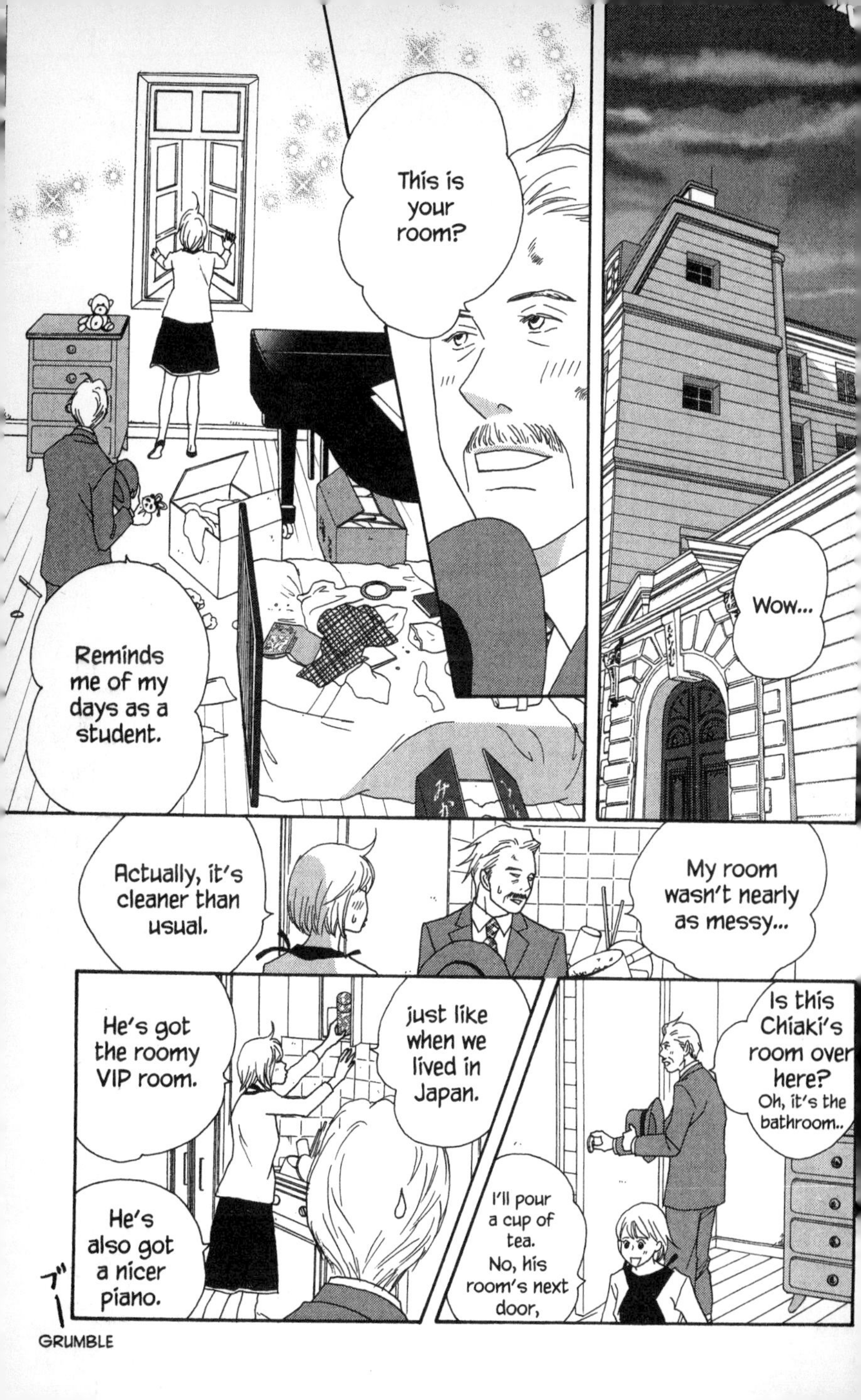
Wow...
This is your room?
Reminds me of my days as a student.
My room wasn't nearly as messy...
Actually, it's cleaner than usual.
Is this Chiaki's room over here?
Oh, it's the bathroom..
I'll pour a cup of tea.
No, his room's next door,
just like when we lived in Japan.
He's got the roomy VIP room.
He's also got a nicer piano.
GRUMBLE

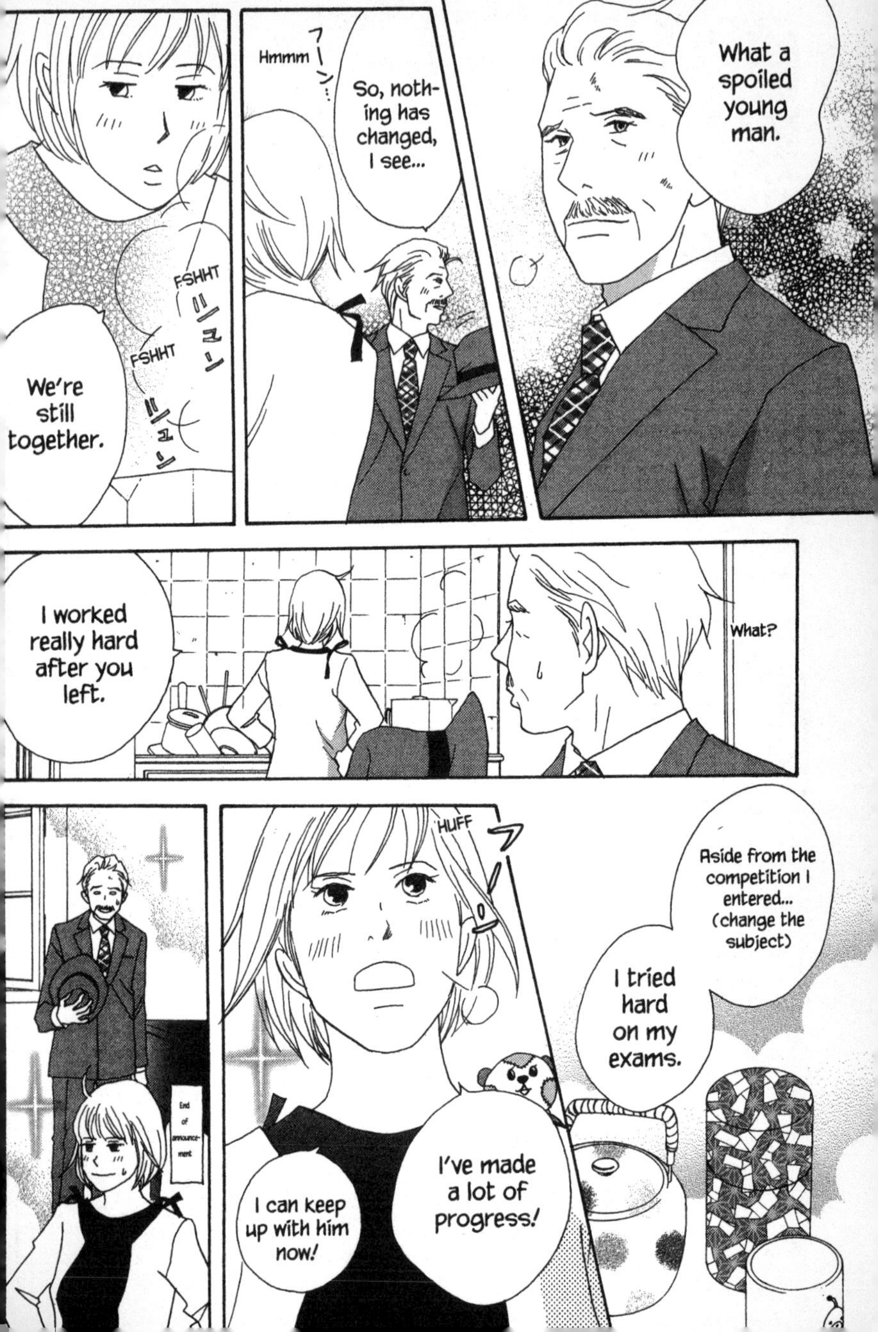

What a spoiled young man.
Hmmm
So, nothing has changed, I see...
FSHHT
FSHHT
We're still together.
What?
I worked really hard after you left.
Aside from the competition I entered... (change the subject)
I tried hard on my exams.
HUFF
I've made a lot of progress!
I can keep up with him now!
End of announcement

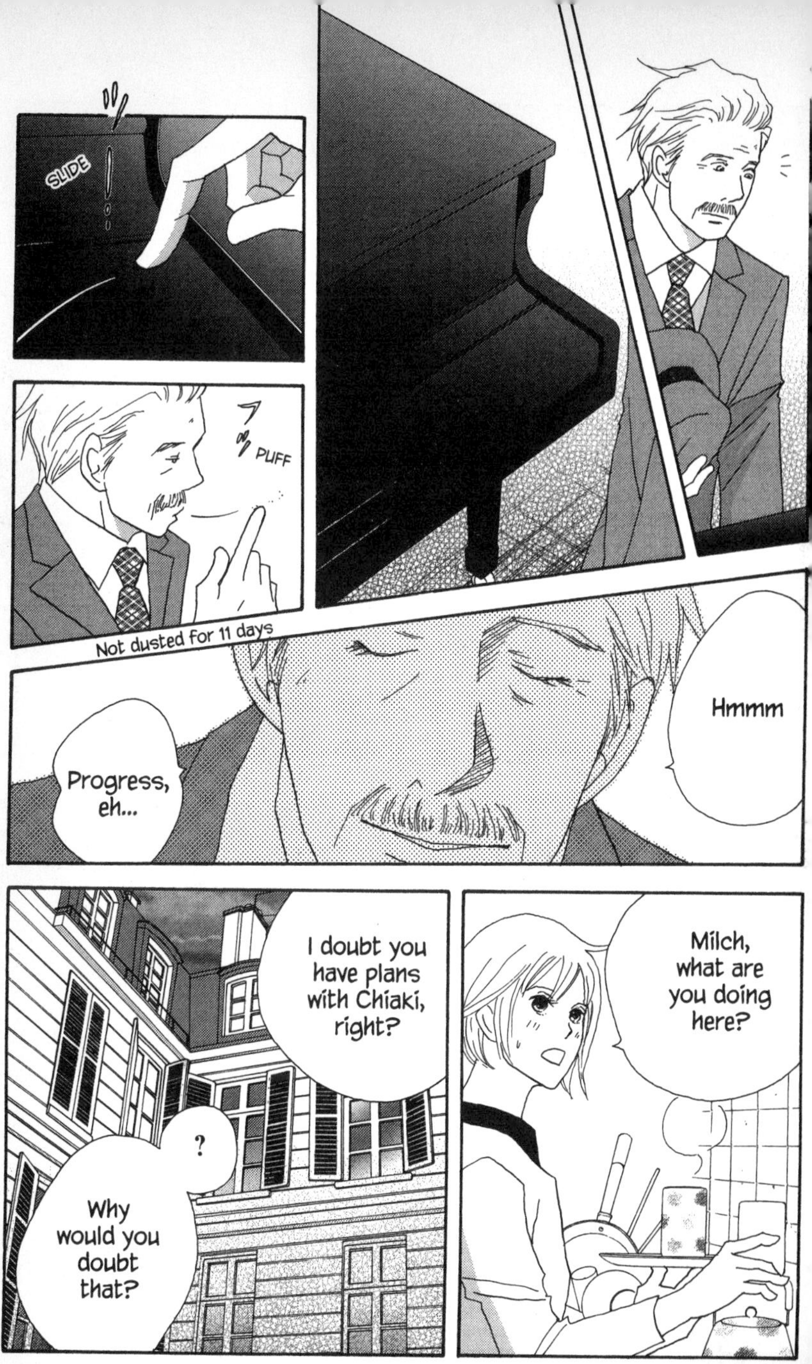
SLIDE
PUFF
Not dusted for 11 days
Hmmm
Progress, eh...
Milch, what are you doing here?
I doubt you have plans with Chiaki, right?
?
Why would you doubt that?

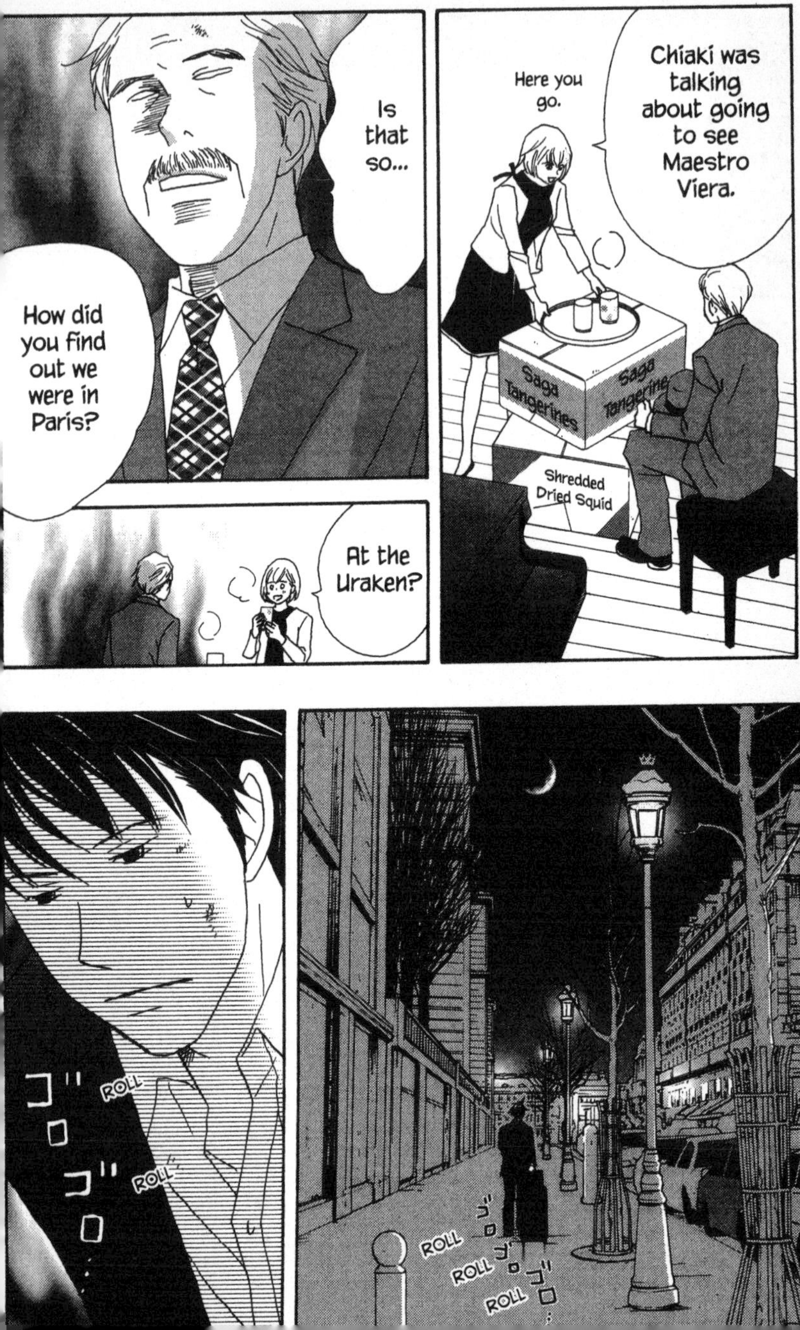
Chiaki was talking about going to see Maestro Viera.
Here you go.
Saga Tangerines
Saga Tangerine
Shredded Dried Squid
Is that so...
How did you find out we were in Paris?
At the Uraken?
ROLL
ROLL
ROLL
ROLL
ROLL

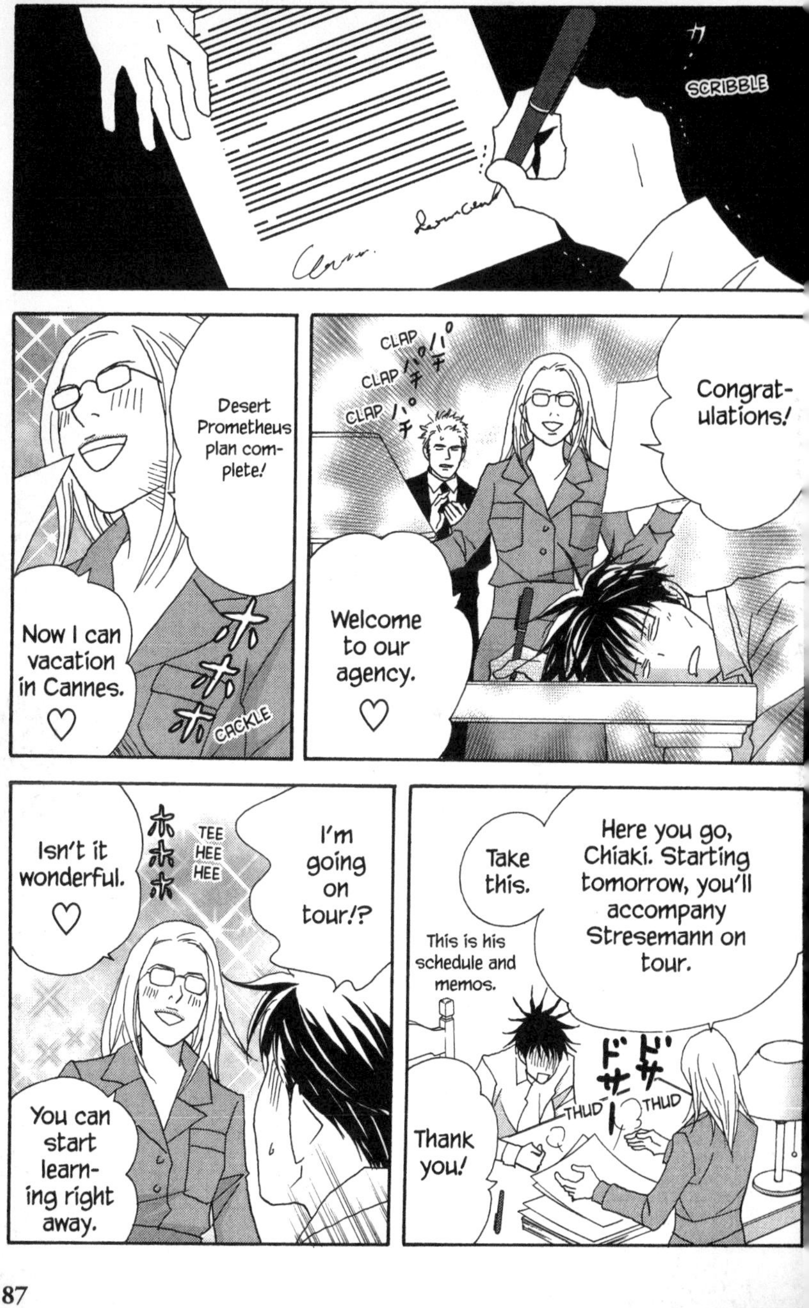
SCRIBBLE
Congrat-ulations!
CLAP CLAP CLAP
Welcome to our agency. ♡
Desert Prometheus plan complete!
CACKLE
Now I can vacation in Cannes. ♡
Here you go, Chiaki. Starting tomorrow, you'll accompany Stresemann on tour.
Take this.
This is his schedule and memos.
THUD THUD
Thank you!
I'm going on tour!?
TEE HEE HEE
Isn't it wonderful. ♡
You can start learning right away.

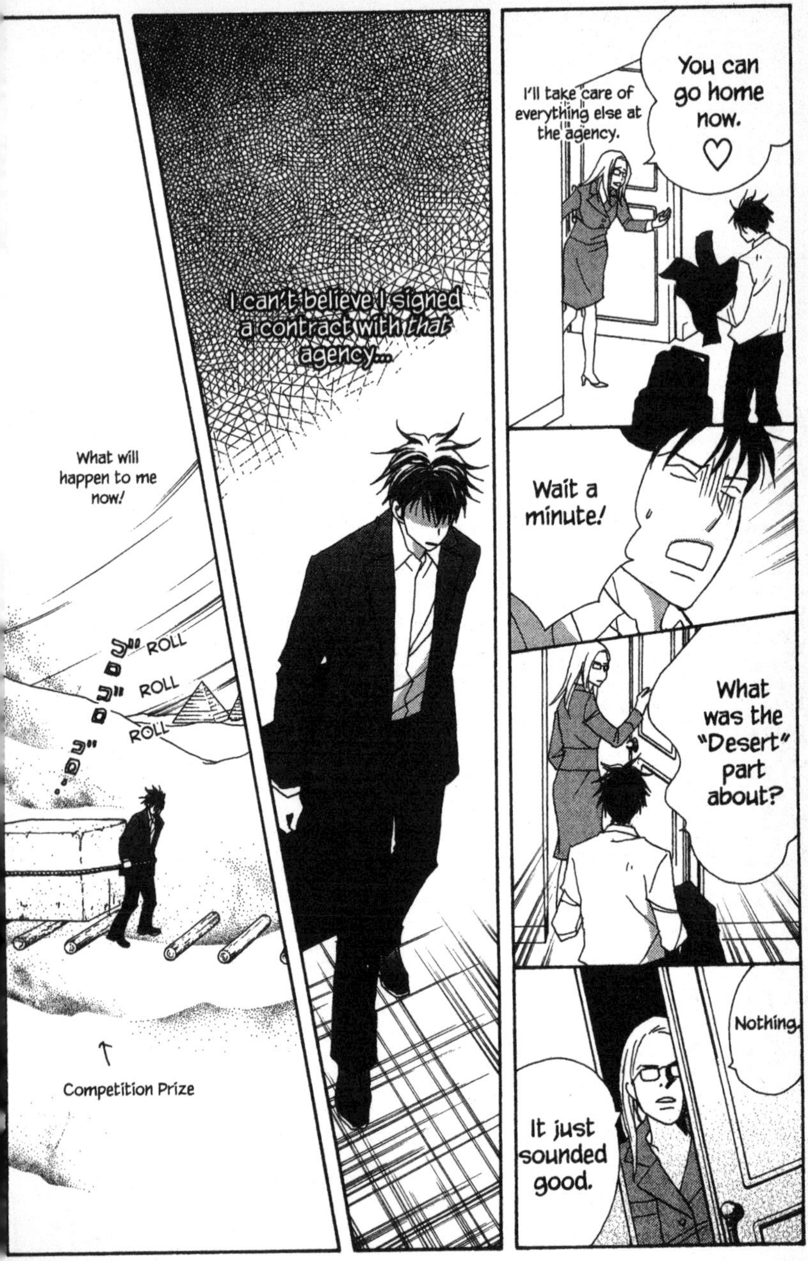
You can go home now. ♡
I'll take care of everything else at the agency.
Wait a minute!
What was the "Desert" part about?
Nothing.
It just sounded good.
I can't believe I signed a contract with *that* agency...
What will happen to me now!
ROLL
ROLL
ROLL
Competition Prize

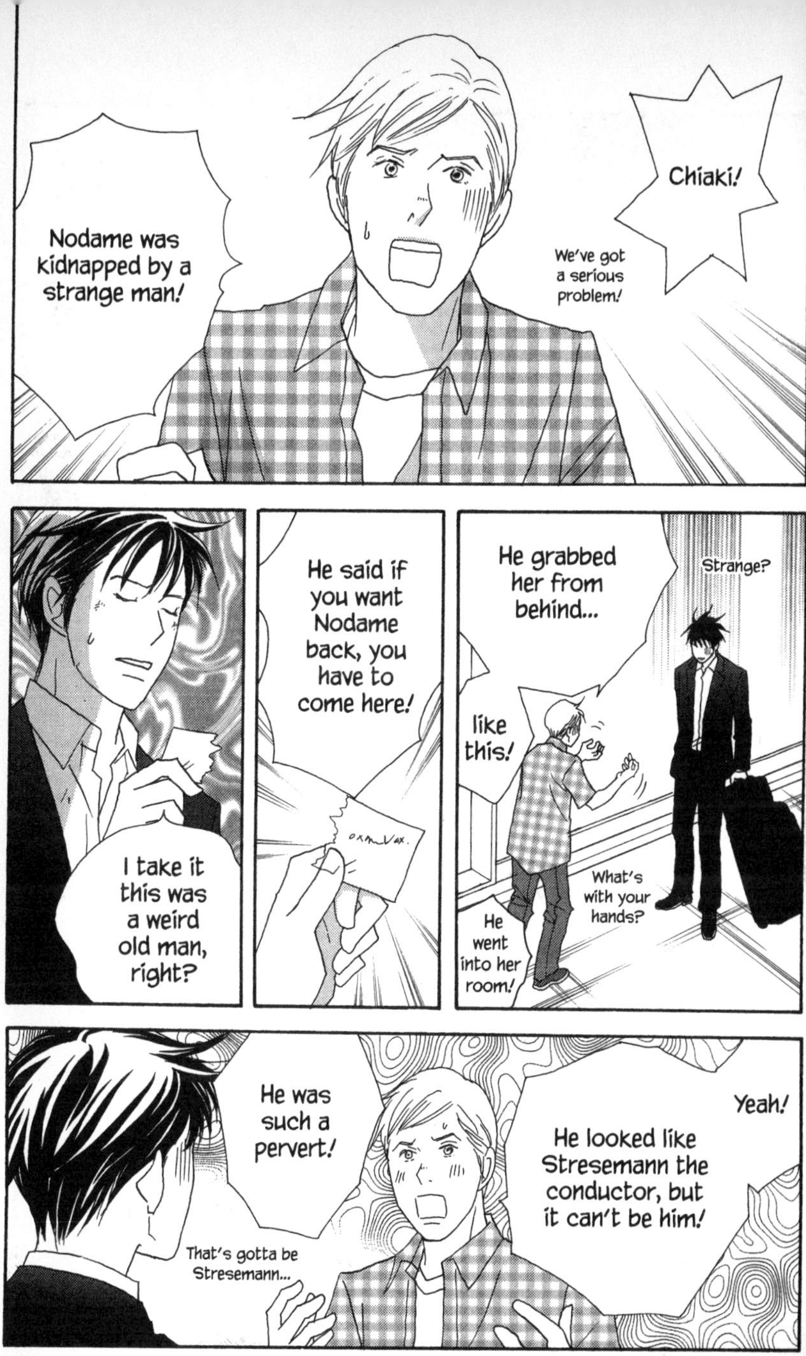
Chiaki!
We've got a serious problem!
Nodame was kidnapped by a strange man!
Strange?
He grabbed her from behind...
like this!
What's with your hands?
He went into her room!
He said if you want Nodame back, you have to come here!
I take it this was a weird old man, right?
Yeah!
He looked like Stresemann the conductor, but it can't be him!
He was such a pervert!
That's gotta be Stresemann...

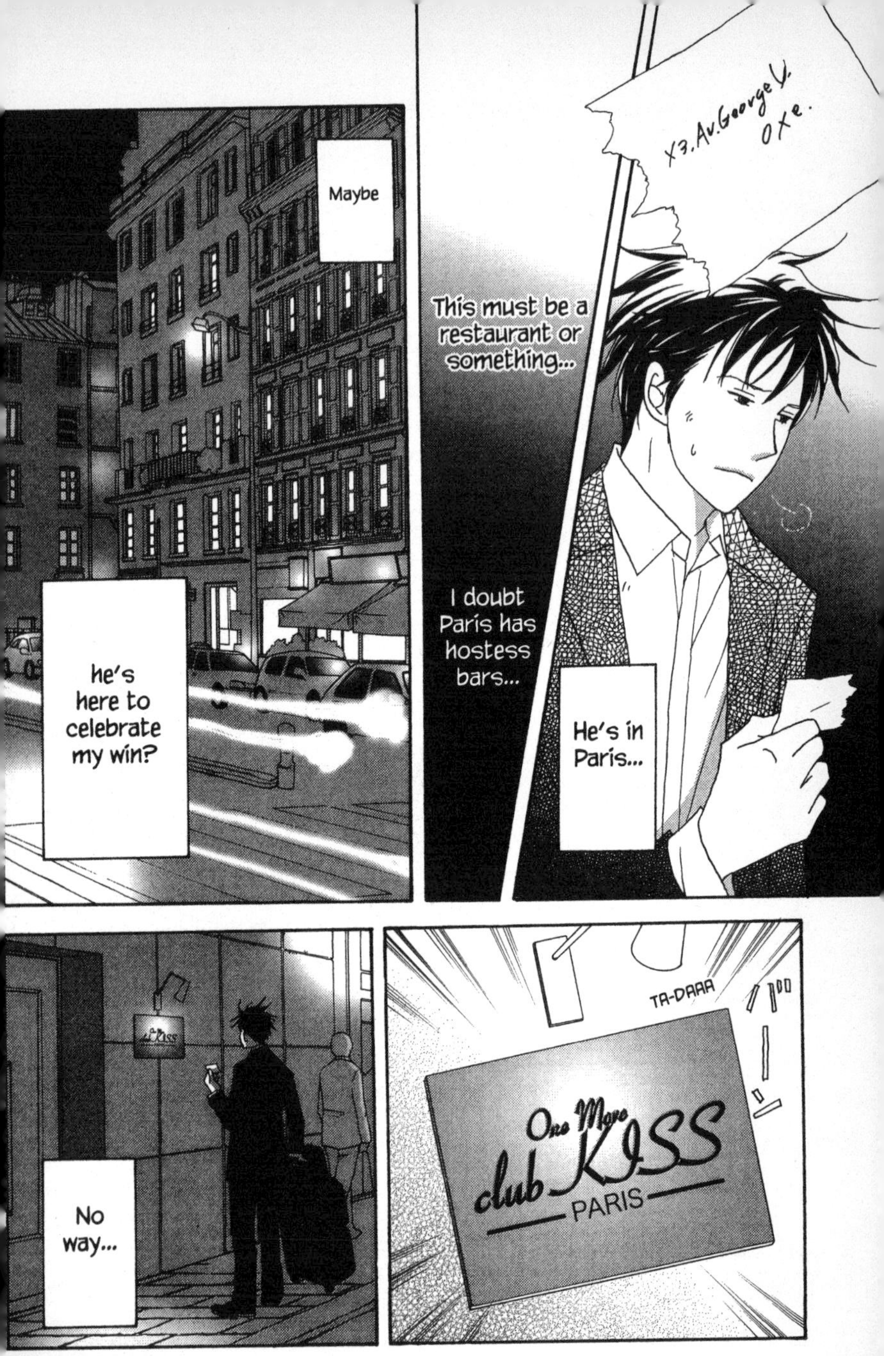
X3. Av. George V.
This must be a restaurant or something...
I doubt Paris has hostess bars...
He's in Paris...
Maybe
he's here to celebrate my win?
TA-DAAA
One More club KISS PARIS
No way...

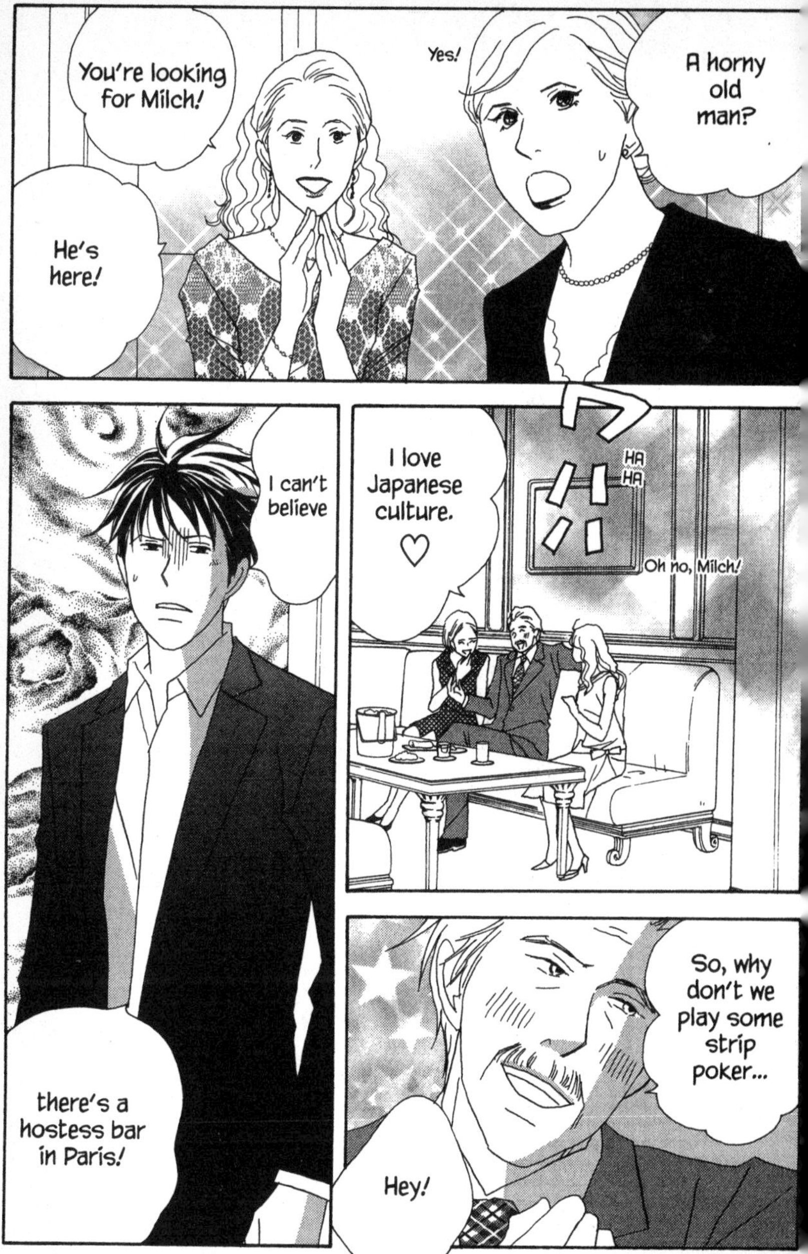
A horny old man?
Yes!
You're looking for Milch!
He's here!
I love Japanese culture. ♡
HA HA
Oh no, Milch!
So, why don't we play some strip poker...
Hey!
I can't believe
there's a hostess bar in Paris!

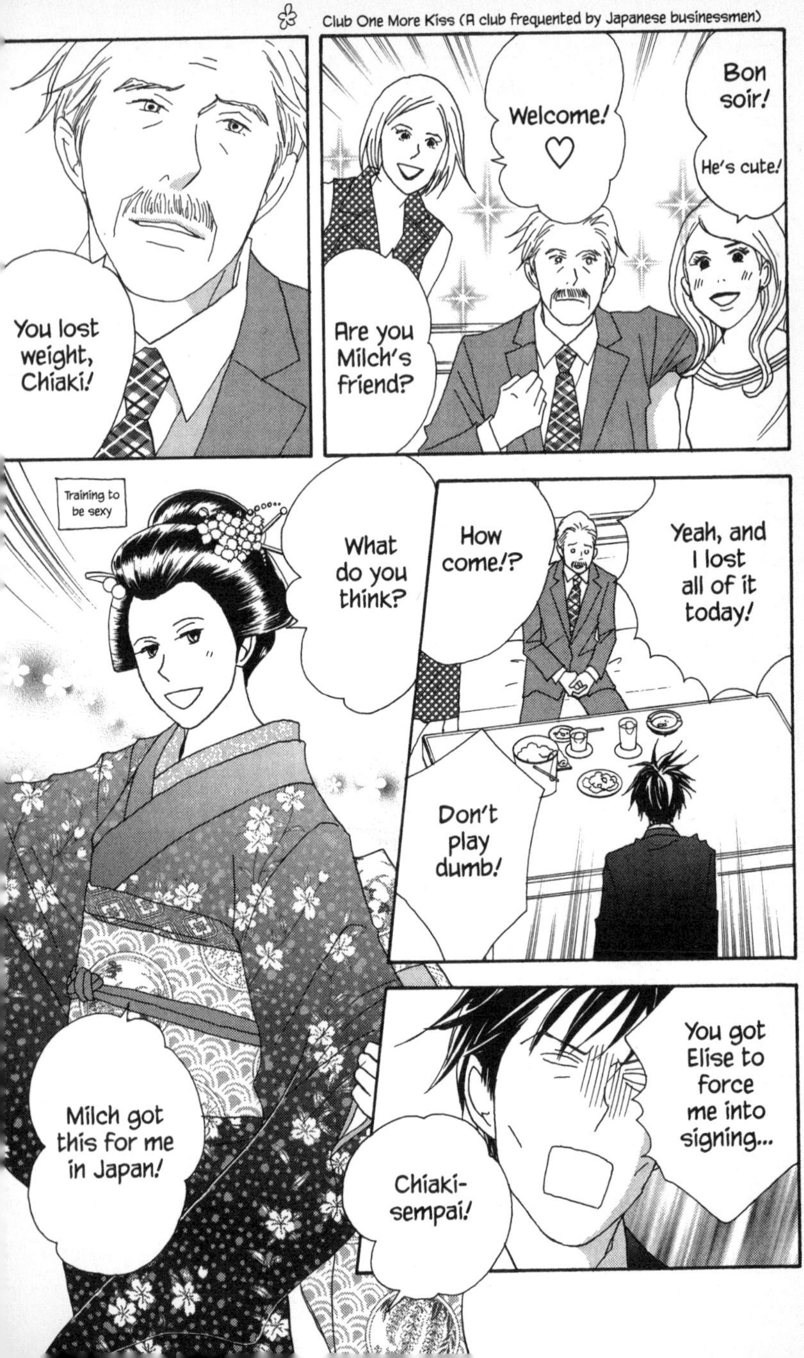

Club One More Kiss (A club frequented by Japanese businessmen)
Bon soir!
He's cute!
Welcome! ♥
Are you Milch's friend?
You lost weight, Chiaki!
Yeah, and I lost all of it today!
How come!?
Don't play dumb!
You got Elise to force me into signing...
Chiaki-sempai!
Training to be sexy
What do you think?
Milch got this for me in Japan!

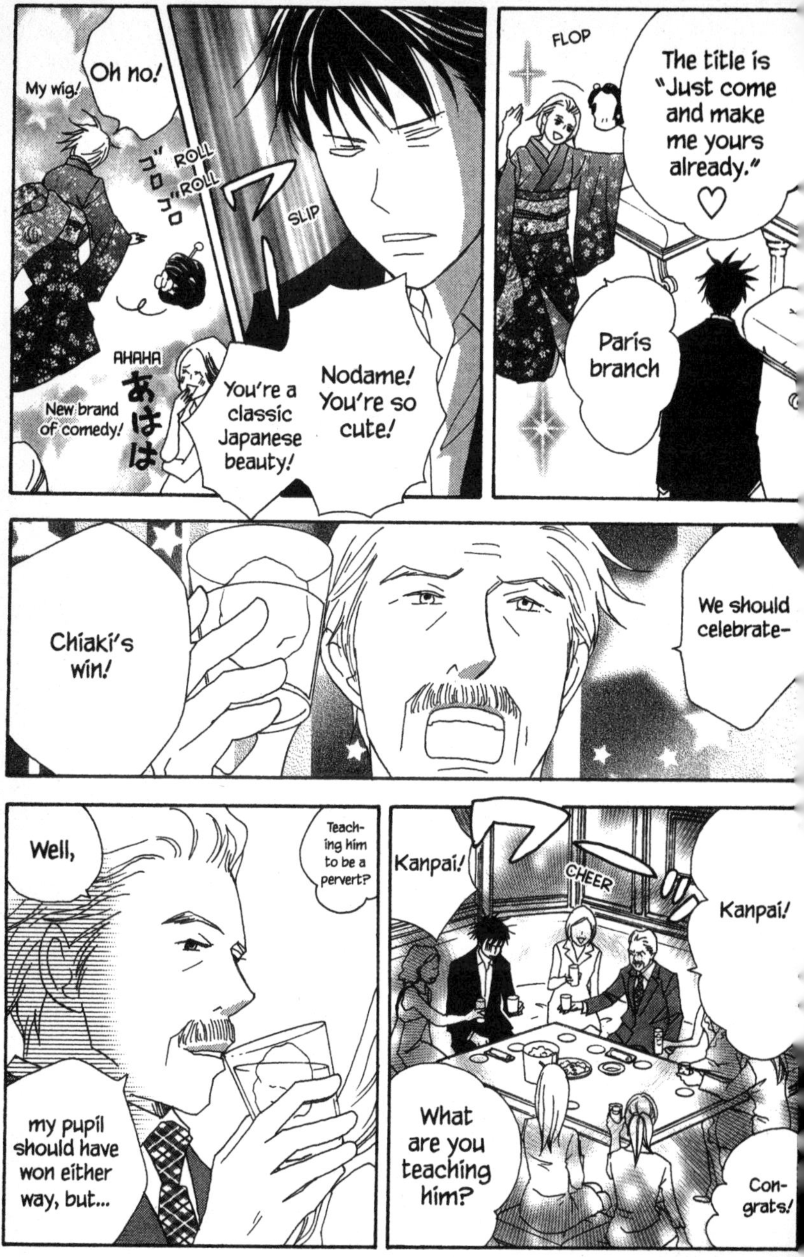

The title is "Just come and make me yours already." ♥
FLOP
Paris branch
SLIP
Nodame! You're so cute!
You're a classic Japanese beauty!
Oh no!
My wig!
ゴロゴロ ROLL ROLL
あはは AHAHA
New brand of comedy!
We should celebrate-
Chiaki's win!
Kanpai!
CHEER
Kanpai!
What are you teaching him?
Con-grats!
Teach-ing him to be a pervert?
Well,
my pupil should have won either way, but...

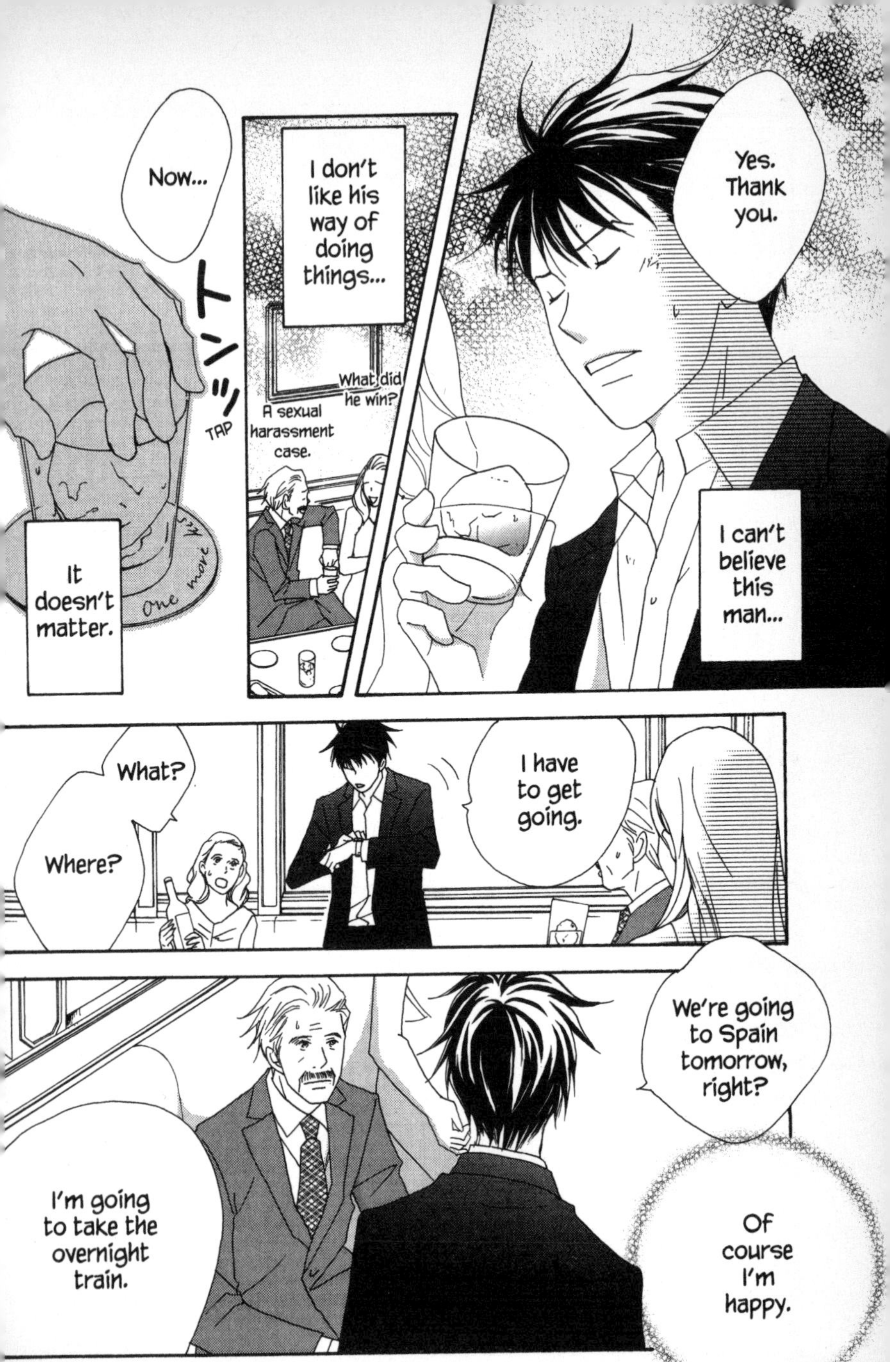
Yes. Thank you.
I can't believe this man...
I don't like his way of doing things...
What did he win?
A sexual harassment case.
Now...
TAP
It doesn't matter.
I have to get going.
What?
Where?
We're going to Spain tomorrow, right?
Of course I'm happy.
I'm going to take the overnight train.

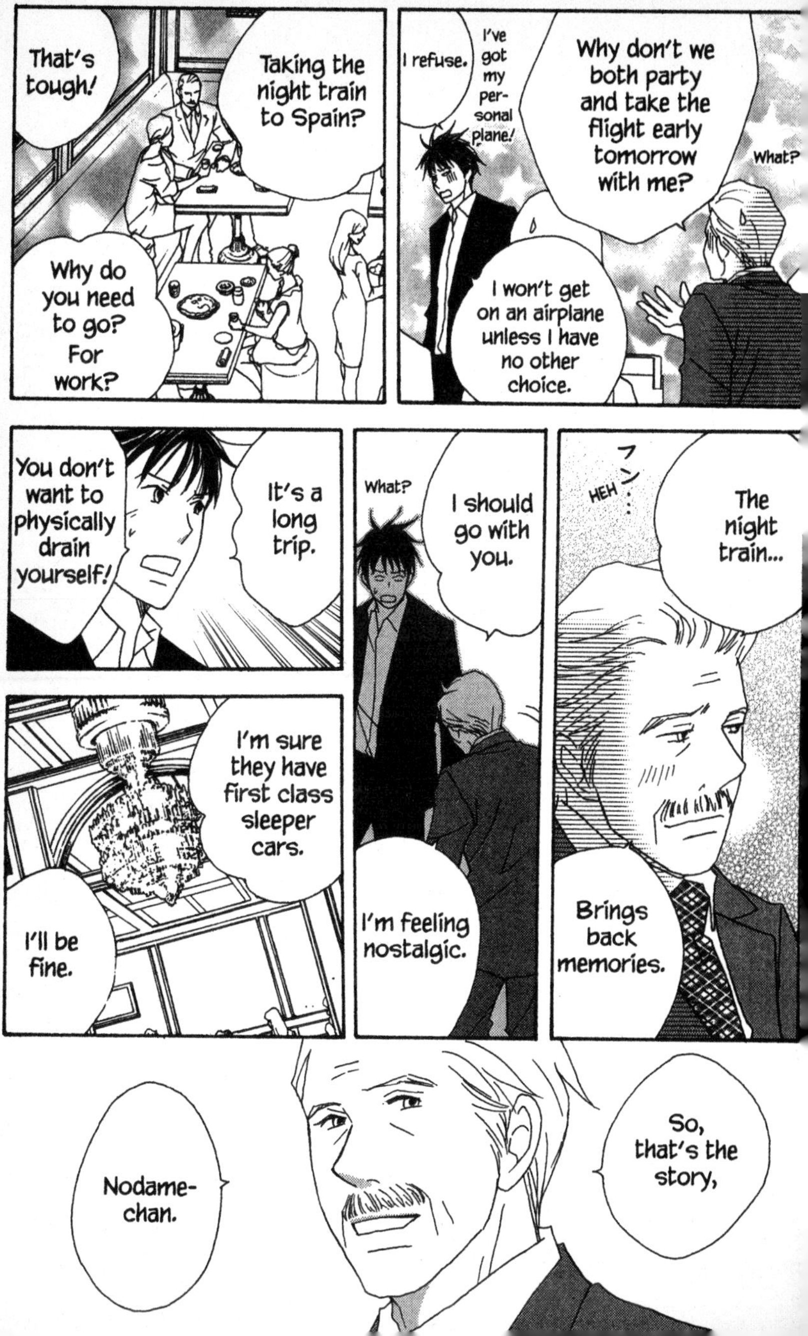
Why don't we both party and take the flight early tomorrow with me?
What?
I've got my personal plane!
I refuse.
I won't get on an airplane unless I have no other choice.
Taking the night train to Spain?
That's tough!
Why do you need to go? For work?
The night train...
HEH フン...
Brings back memories.
I should go with you.
What?
I'm feeling nostalgic.
It's a long trip.
You don't want to physically drain yourself!
I'm sure they have first class sleeper cars.
I'll be fine.
So, that's the story,
Nodame-chan.

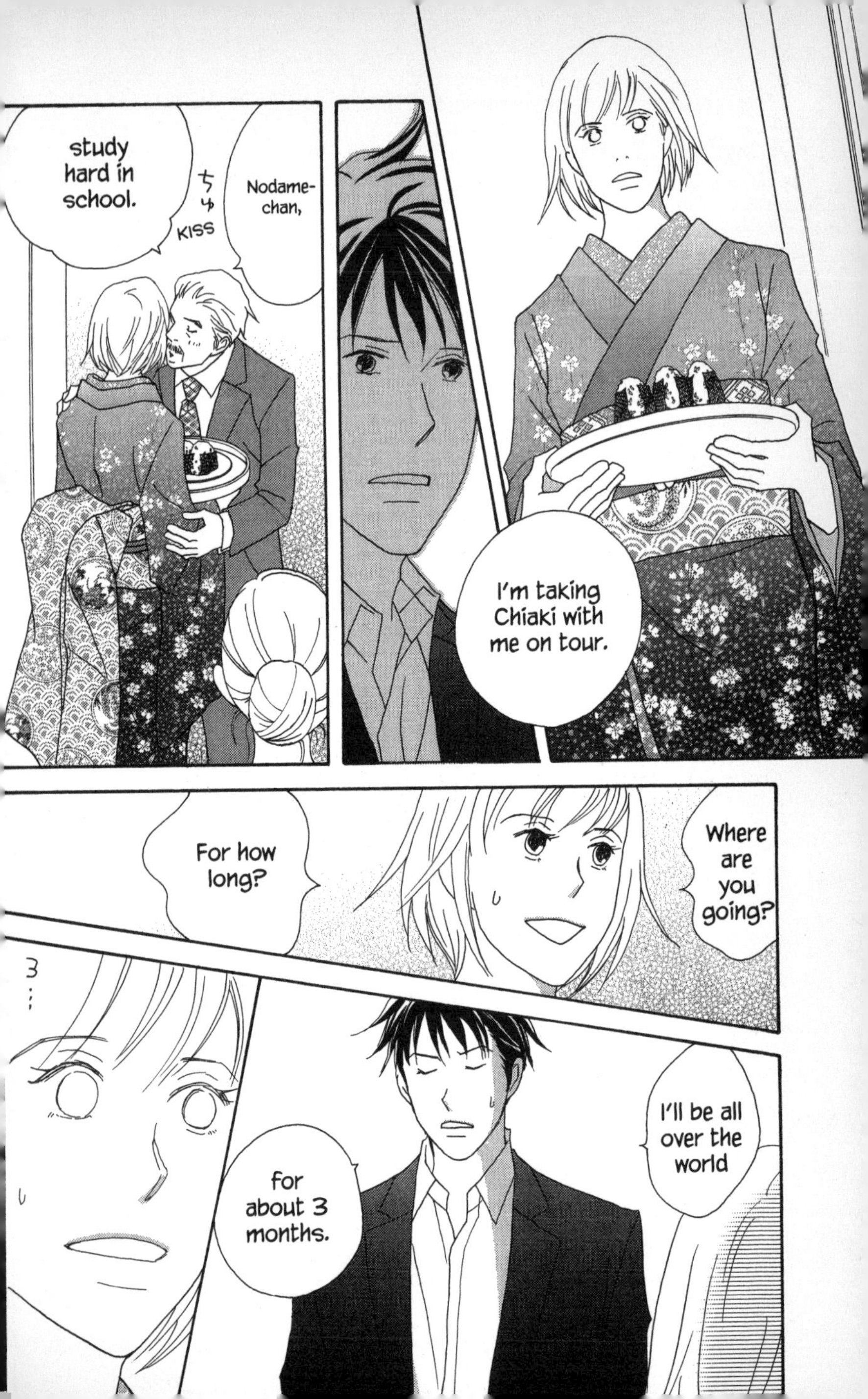
I'm taking Chiaki with me on tour.
Nodame-chan,
ちゅ
KISS
study hard in school.
Where are you going?
For how long?
I'll be all over the world
for about 3 months.
3…

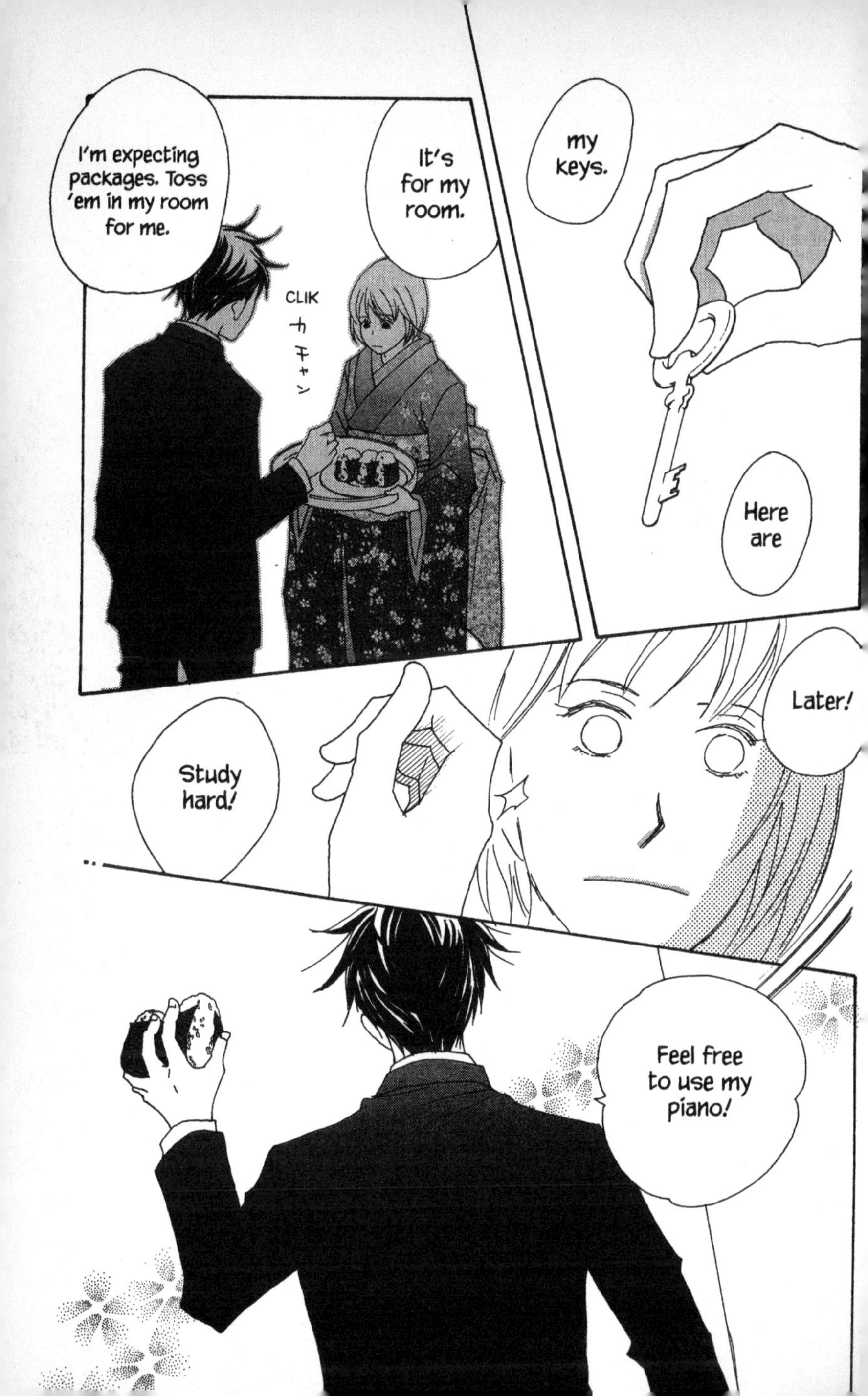
Here are
my keys.
It's for my room.
I'm expecting packages. Toss 'em in my room for me.
CLIK
カチャン
Later!
Study hard!
Feel free to use my piano!

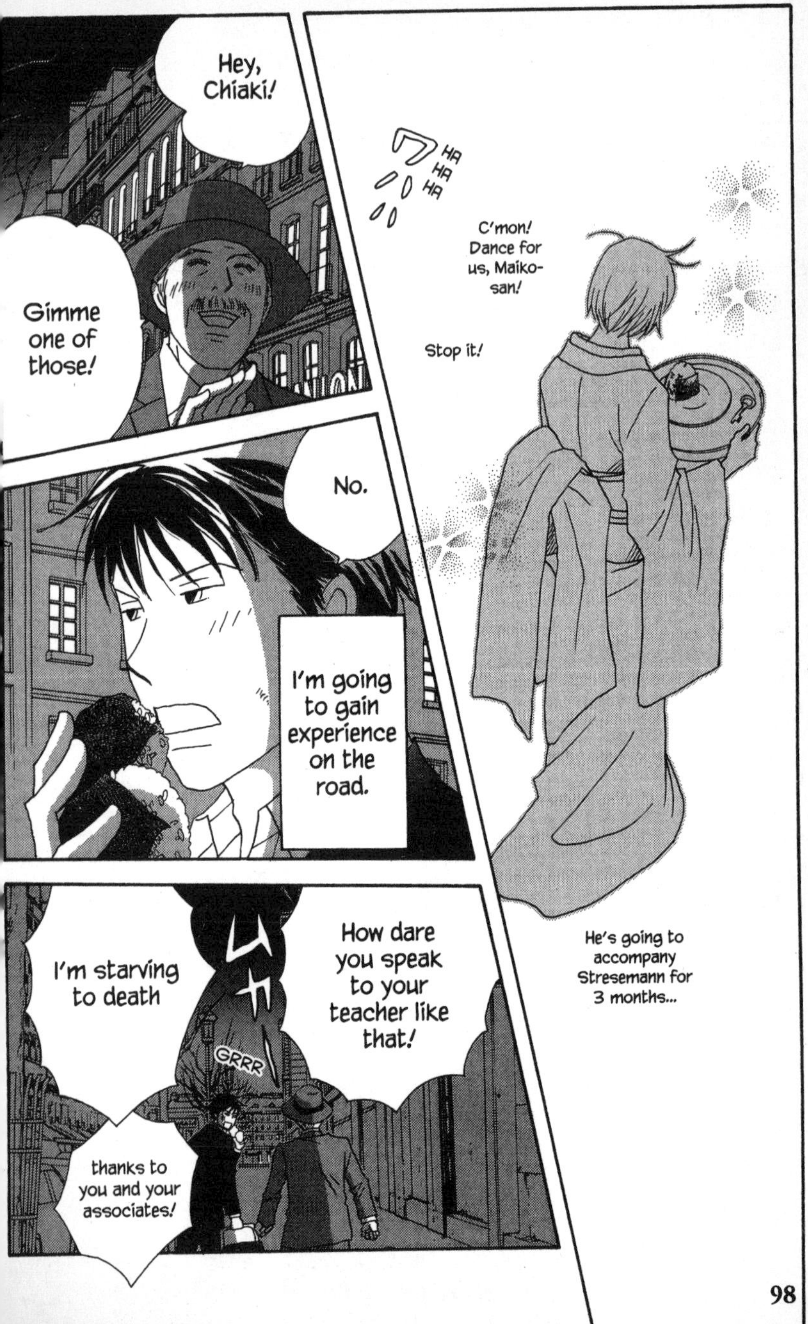
HA HA HA
C'mon! Dance for us, Maiko-san!
Stop it!
He's going to accompany Stresemann for 3 months...
Hey, Chiaki!
Gimme one of those!
No.
I'm going to gain experience on the road.
How dare you speak to your teacher like that!
GRRR
I'm starving to death
thanks to you and your associates!

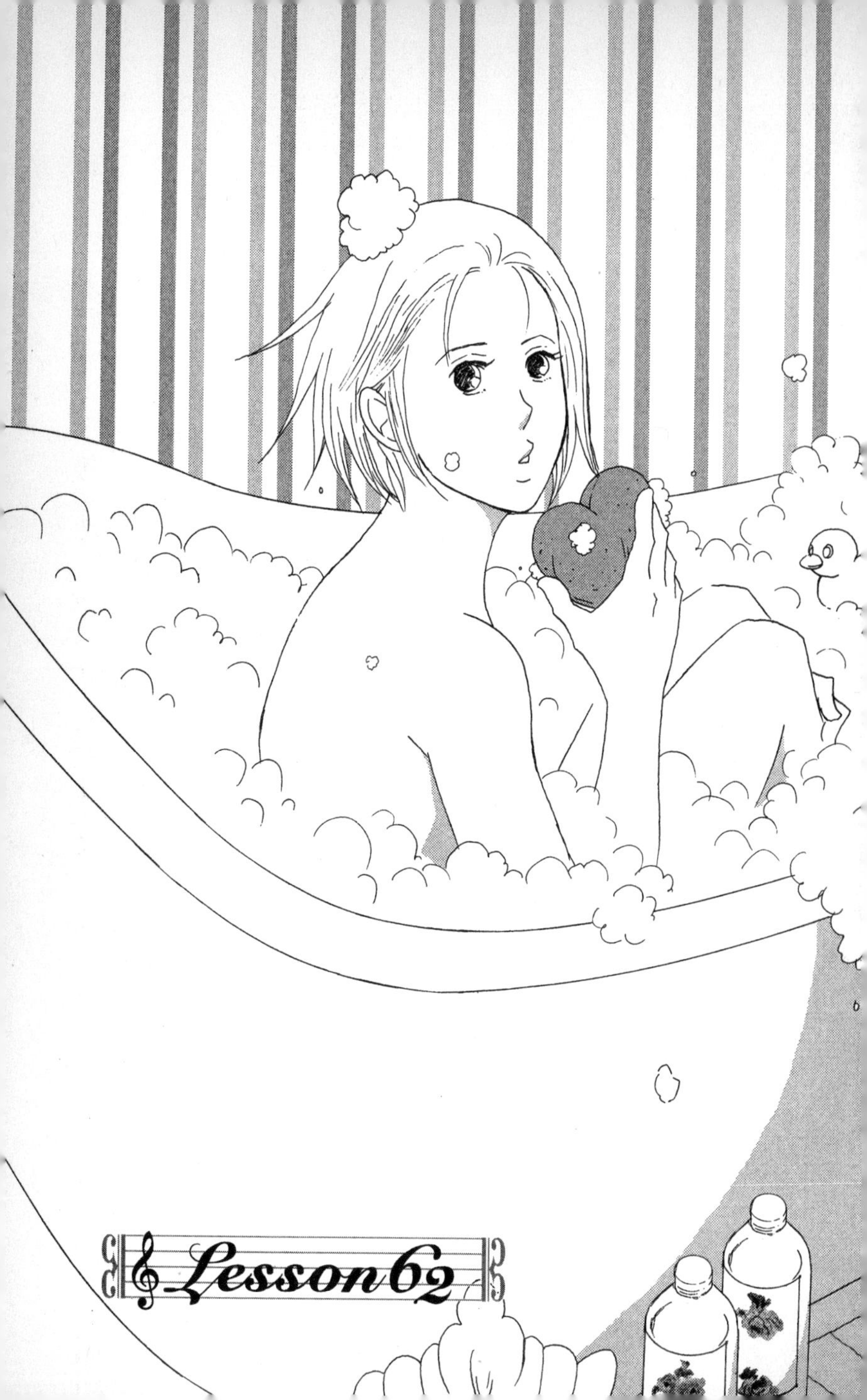
Lesson 62

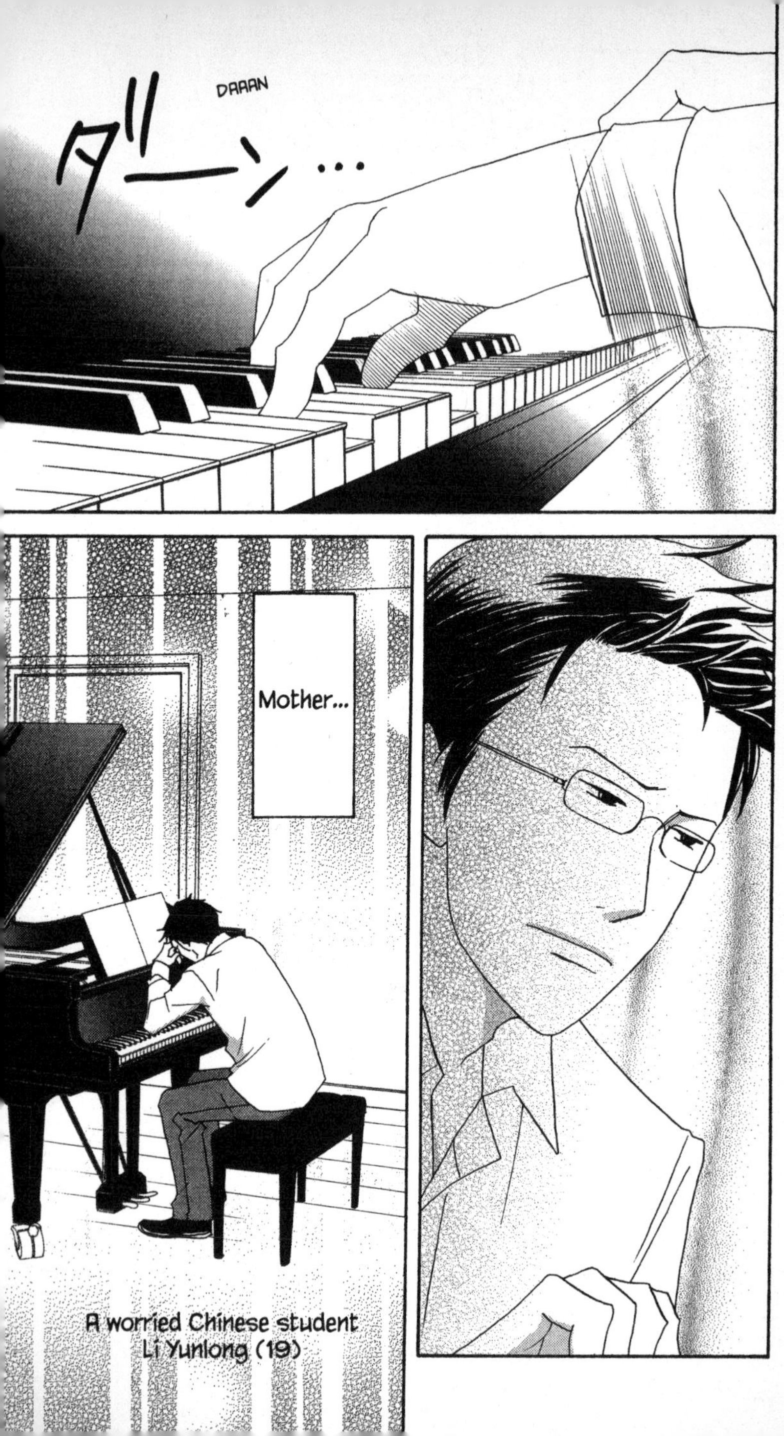
DAAAN
ダーン…
Mother...
A worried Chinese student
Li Yunlong (19)

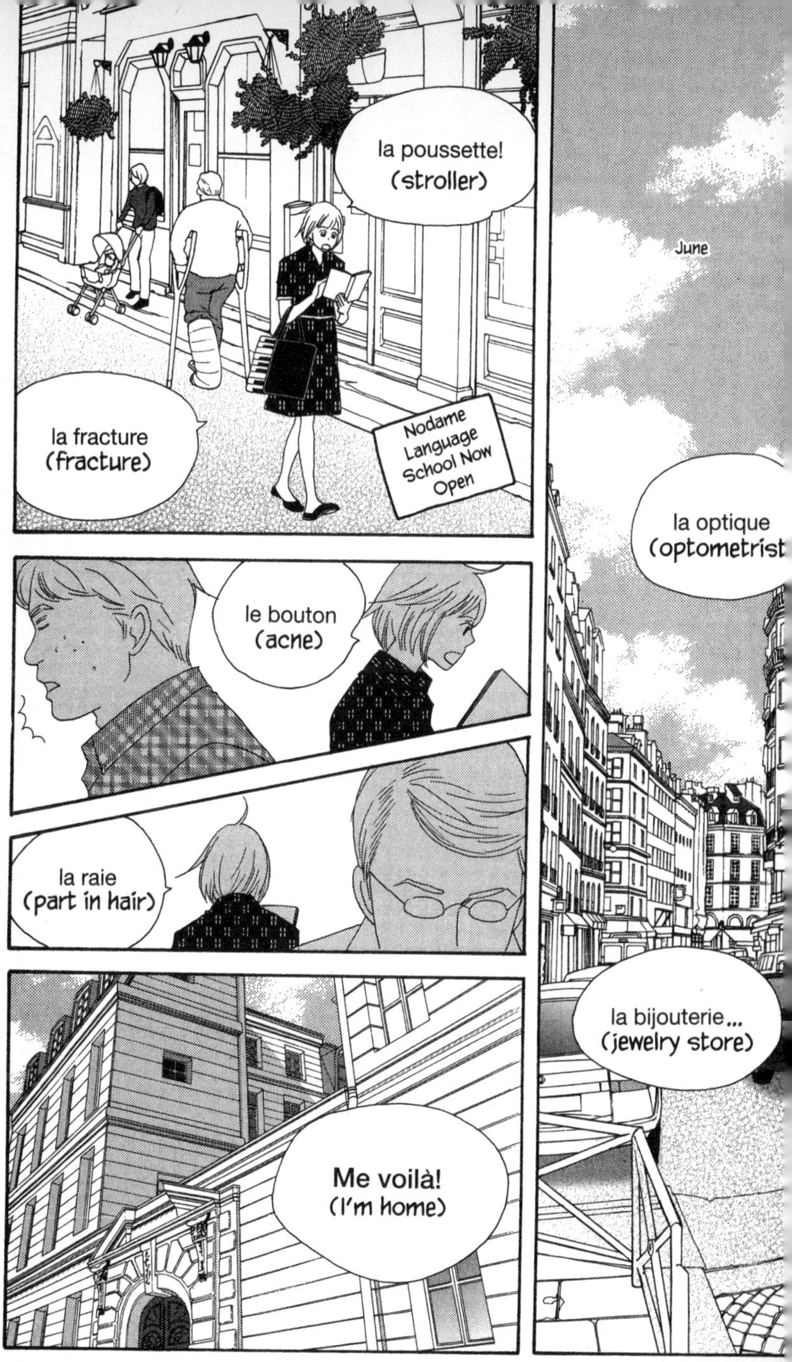
June
la optique
(optometrist
la bijouterie...
(jewelry store)
la poussette!
(stroller)
Nodame Language School Now Open
la fracture
(fracture)
le bouton
(acne)
la raie
(part in hair)
Me voilà!
(I'm home)

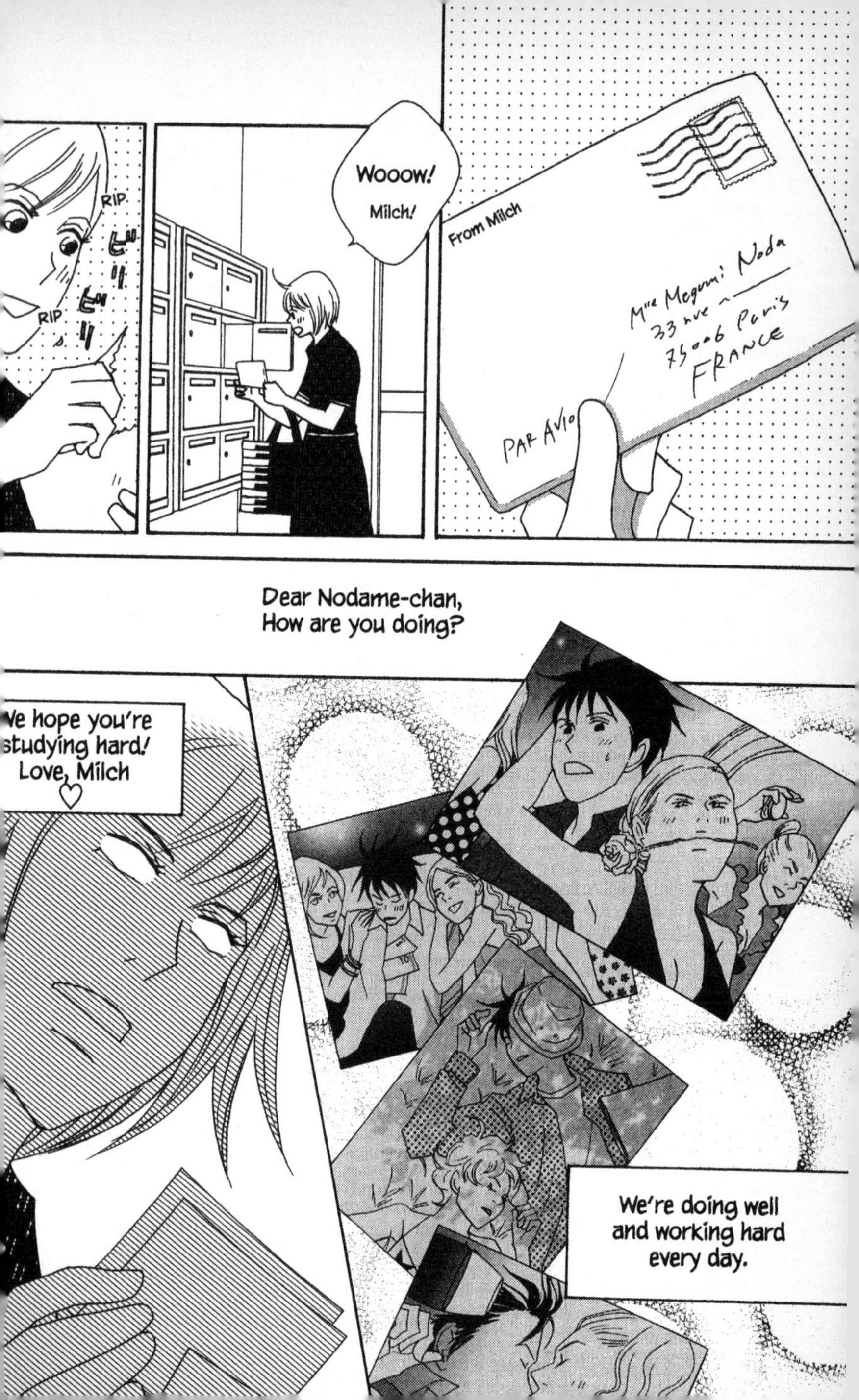
From Milch
Mlle Megumi Noda
33 ave ~
75006 Paris
FRANCE
PAR AVIO
Wooow!
Milch!
RIP
ビリ
ビリ
RIP
Dear Nodame-chan,
How are you doing?
We're doing well and working hard every day.
We hope you're studying hard! Love, Milch ♡

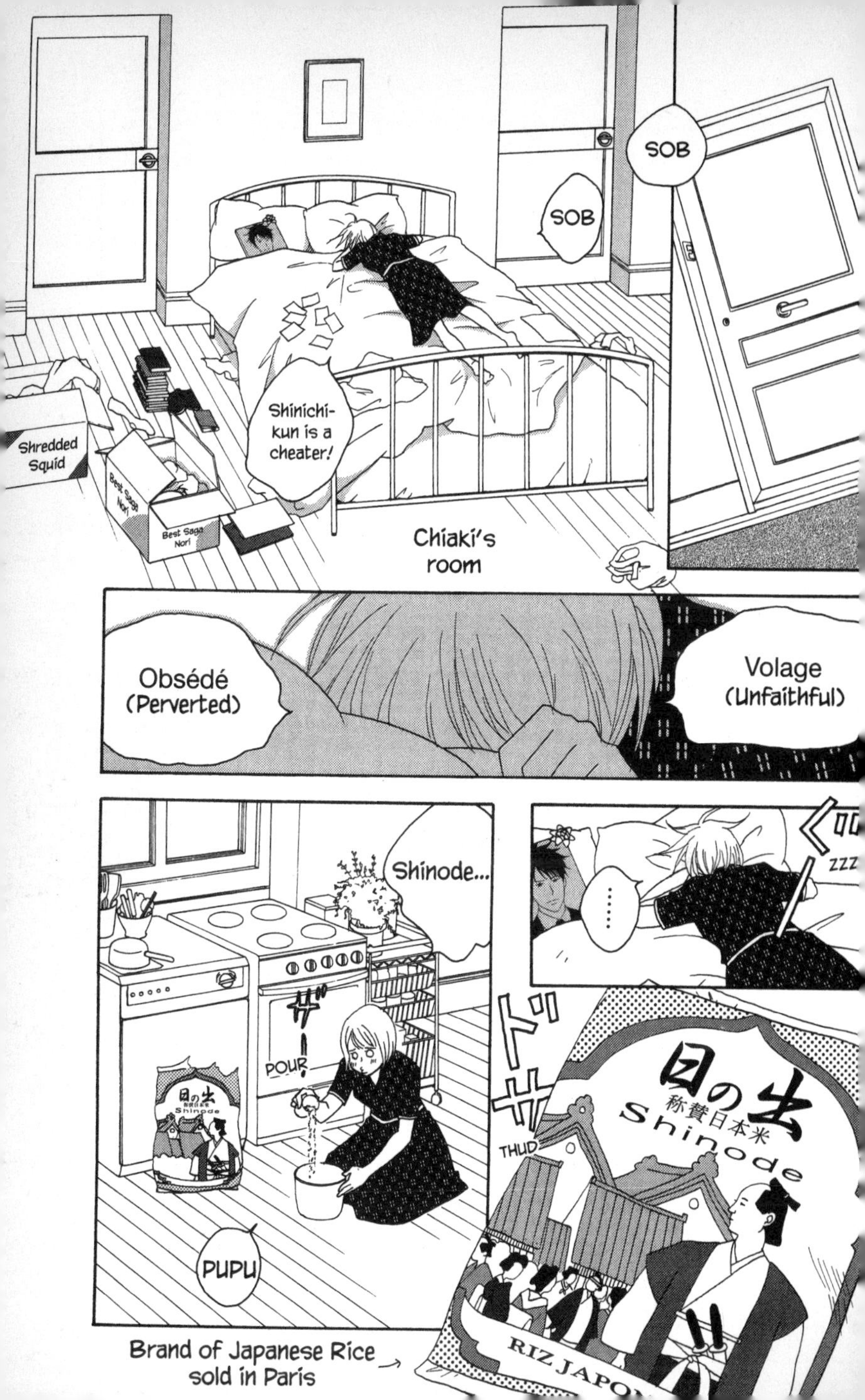
SOB
SOB
Shinichi-kun is a cheater!
Shredded Squid
Best Saga Nori
Best Saga Nori
Chiaki's room
Volage (Unfaithful)
Obsédé (Perverted)
......
ZZZ
ドサ
THUD
日の出
称賛日本米
Shinode
RIZ JAPO
Shinode...
ザー
POUR
日の出
Shinode
PUPU
Brand of Japanese Rice sold in Paris

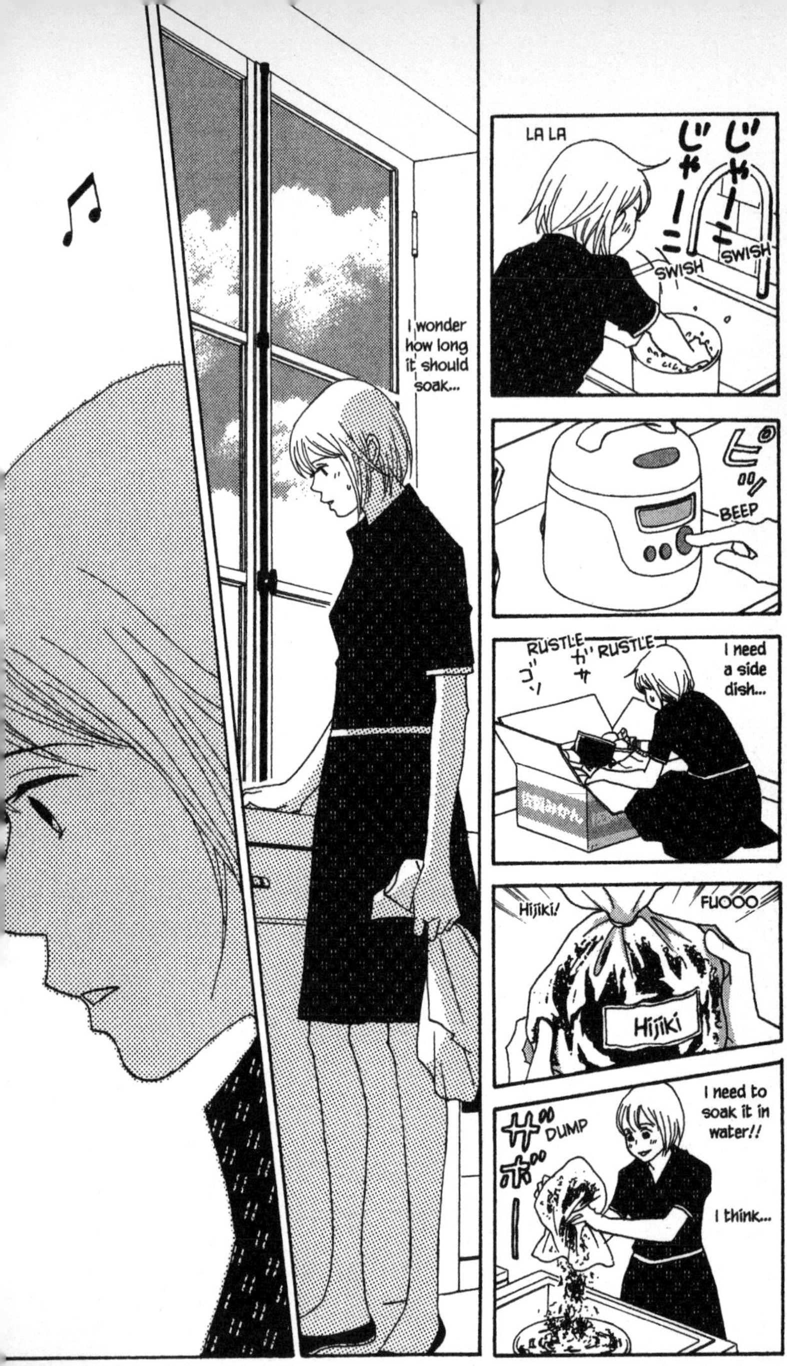
LA LA
じゃーー
SWISH
じゃーー
SWISH
ピッ
BEEP
RUSTLE
ガサ
RUSTLE
ゴソ
I need a side dish...
Hijiki!
FUOOO
Hijiki
I need to soak it in water!!
I think...
サッ
DUMP
ポー
I wonder how long it should soak...

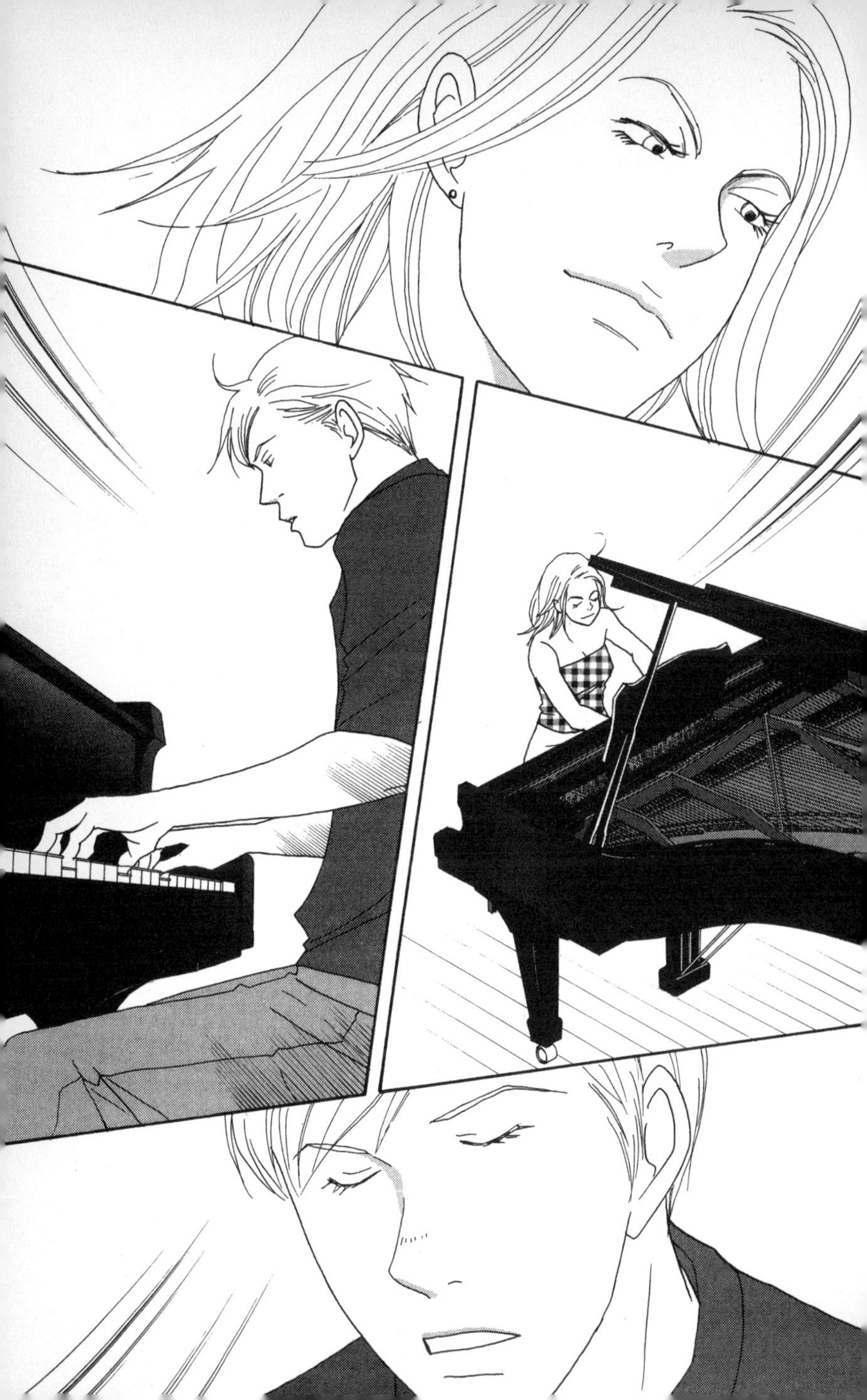

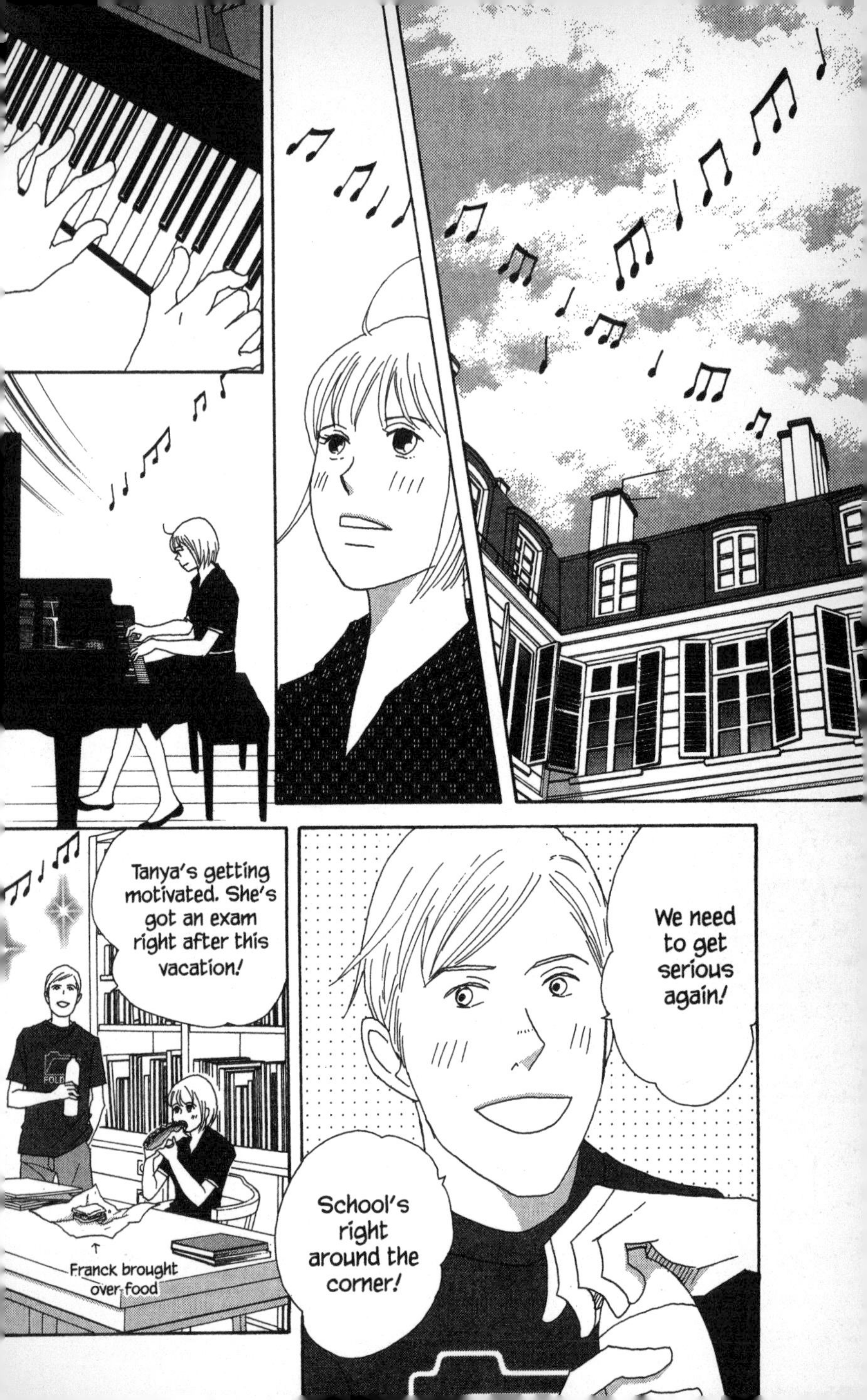
We need to get serious again!
School's right around the corner!
Tanya's getting motivated. She's got an exam right after this vacation!
Franck brought over food

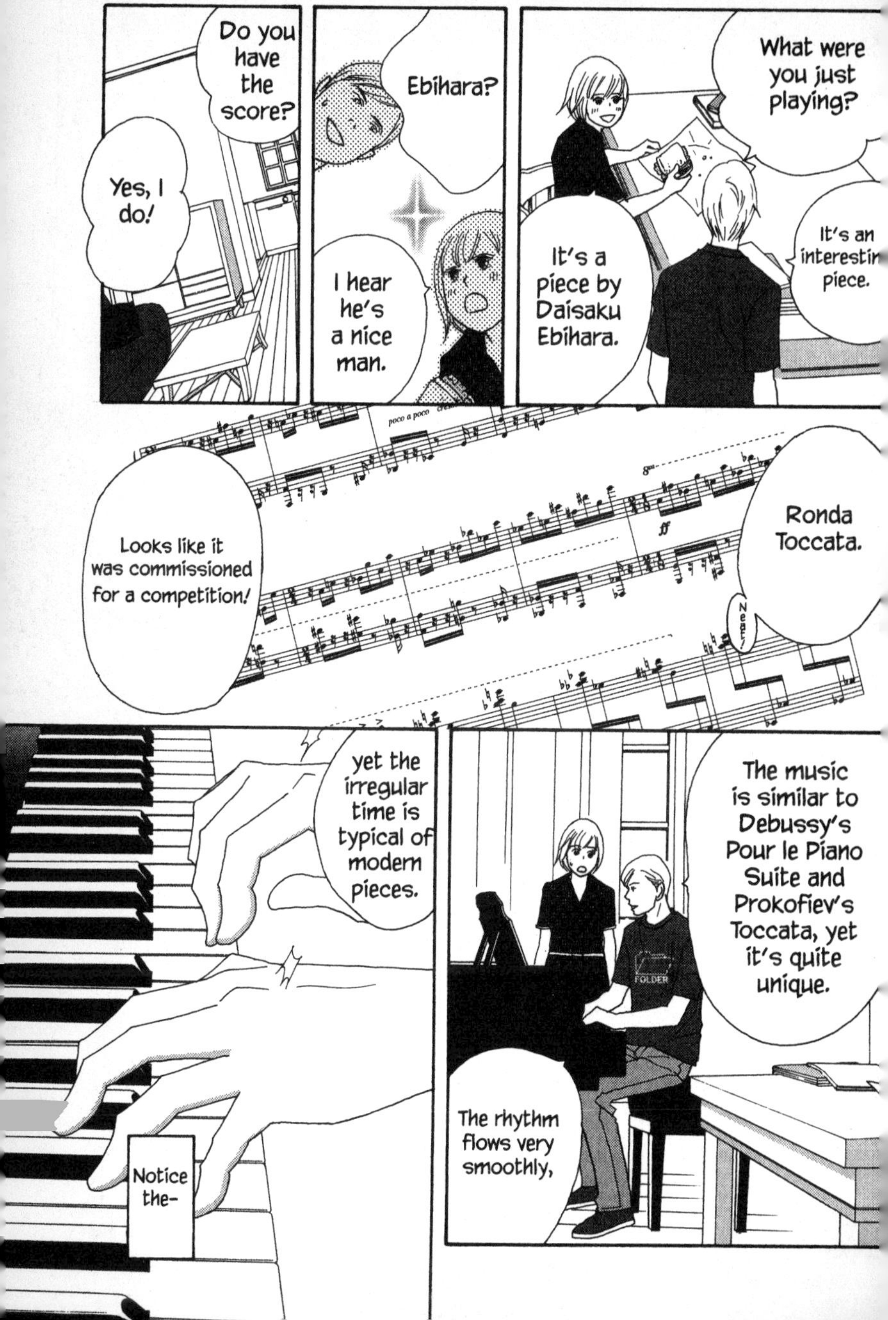
What were you just playing?
It's an interestin piece.
It's a piece by Daisaku Ebihara.
Ebihara?
I hear he's a nice man.
Do you have the score?
Yes, I do!
poco a poco
Ronda Toccata.
Looks like it was commissioned for a competition!
The music is similar to Debussy's Pour le Piano Suite and Prokofiev's Toccata, yet it's quite unique.
FOLDER
The rhythm flows very smoothly,
yet the irregular time is typical of modern pieces.
Notice the-

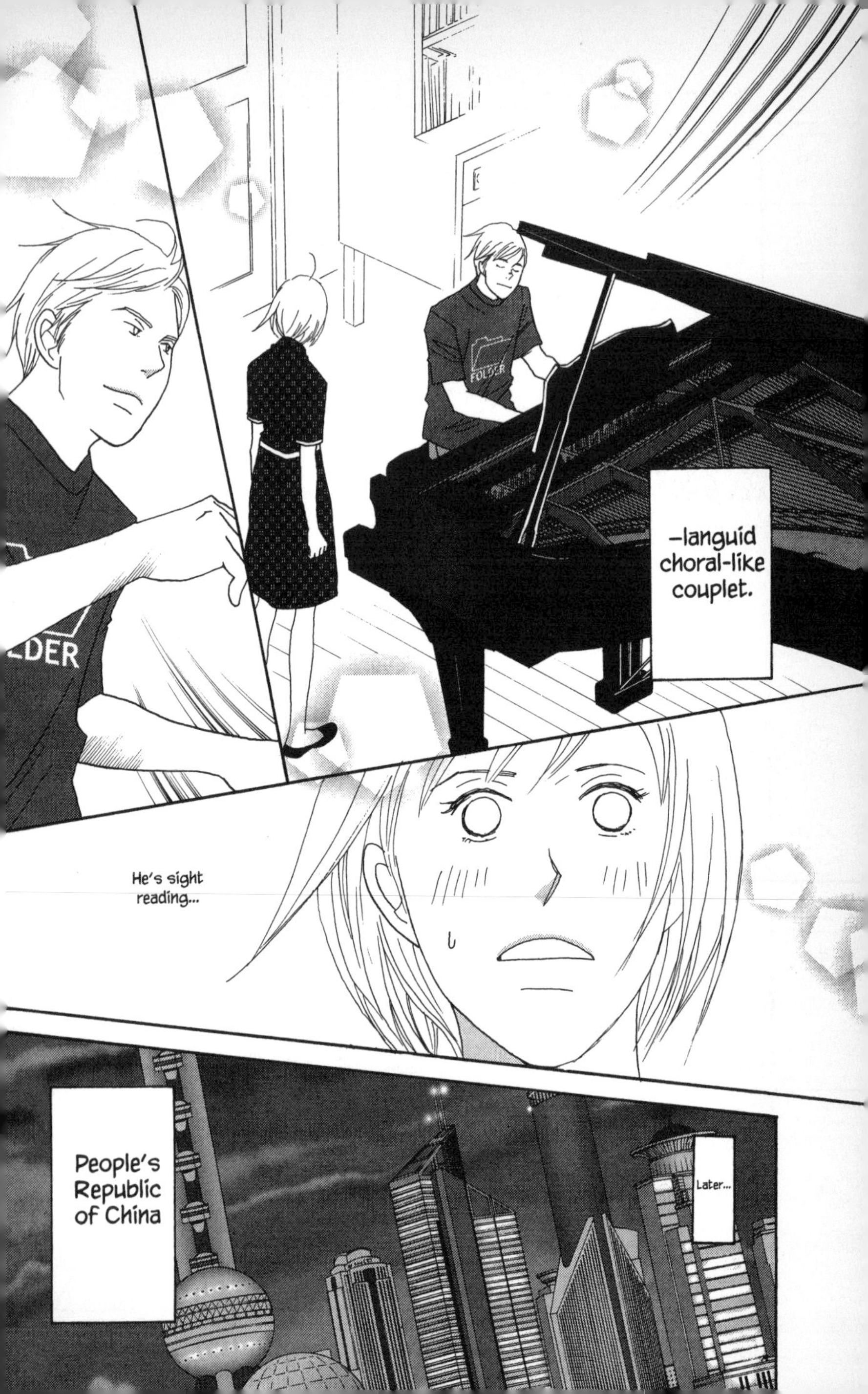
–languid choral-like couplet.
FOLDER
FOLDER
He's sight reading...
Later...
People's Republic of China

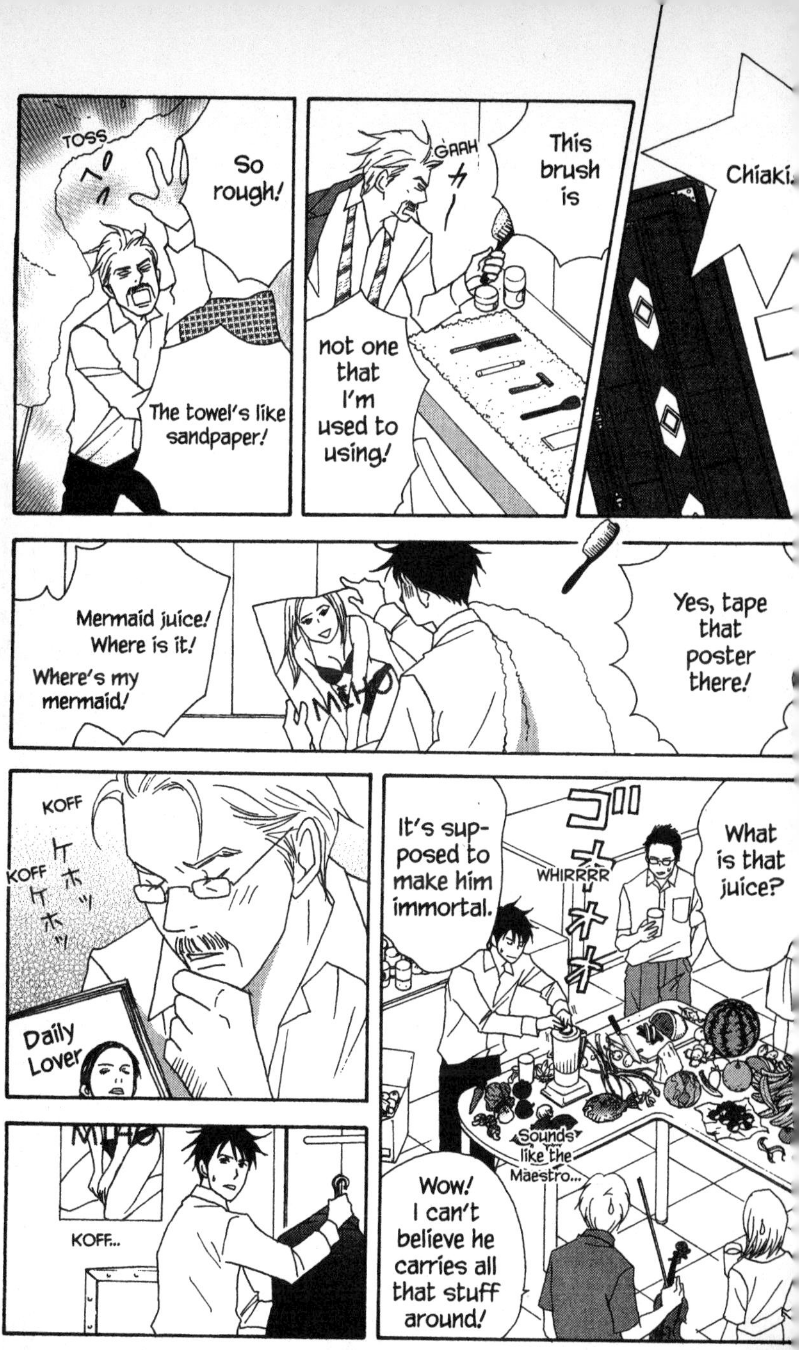
Chiaki...
This brush is
GAAH
not one that I'm used to using!
TOSS
So rough!
The towel's like sandpaper!
Yes, tape that poster there!
Mermaid juice! Where is it!
Where's my mermaid!
MIHO
What is that juice?
WHIRRRR
It's sup-posed to make him immortal.
Sounds like the Maestro...
Wow! I can't believe he carries all that stuff around!
KOFF
KOFF
Daily Lover
MIHO
KOFF...

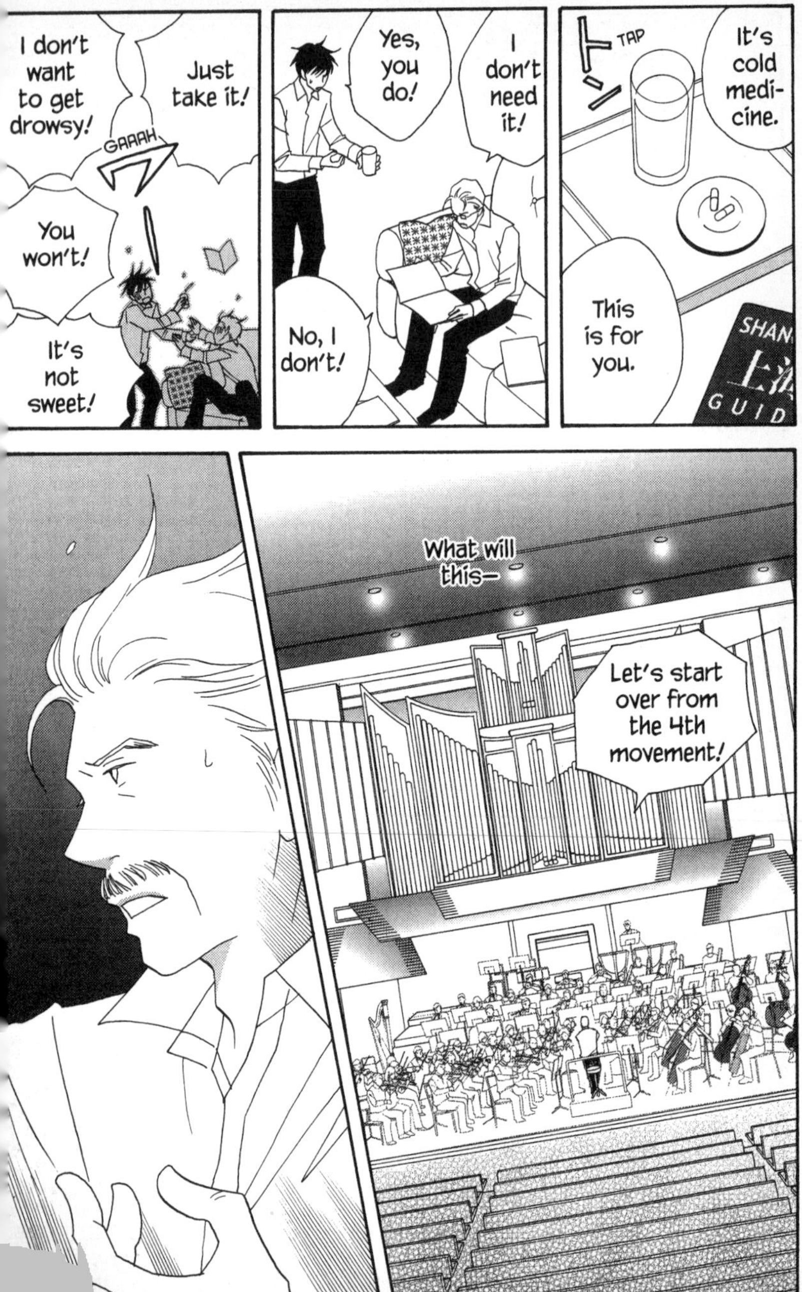
It's cold medicine.
TAP
This is for you.
SHAN
GUID
I don't need it!
Yes, you do!
No, I don't!
Just take it!
I don't want to get drowsy!
GAAAH
You won't!
It's not sweet!
What will this—
Let's start over from the 4th movement!

Shinichi Chiaki Learning Life Lessons

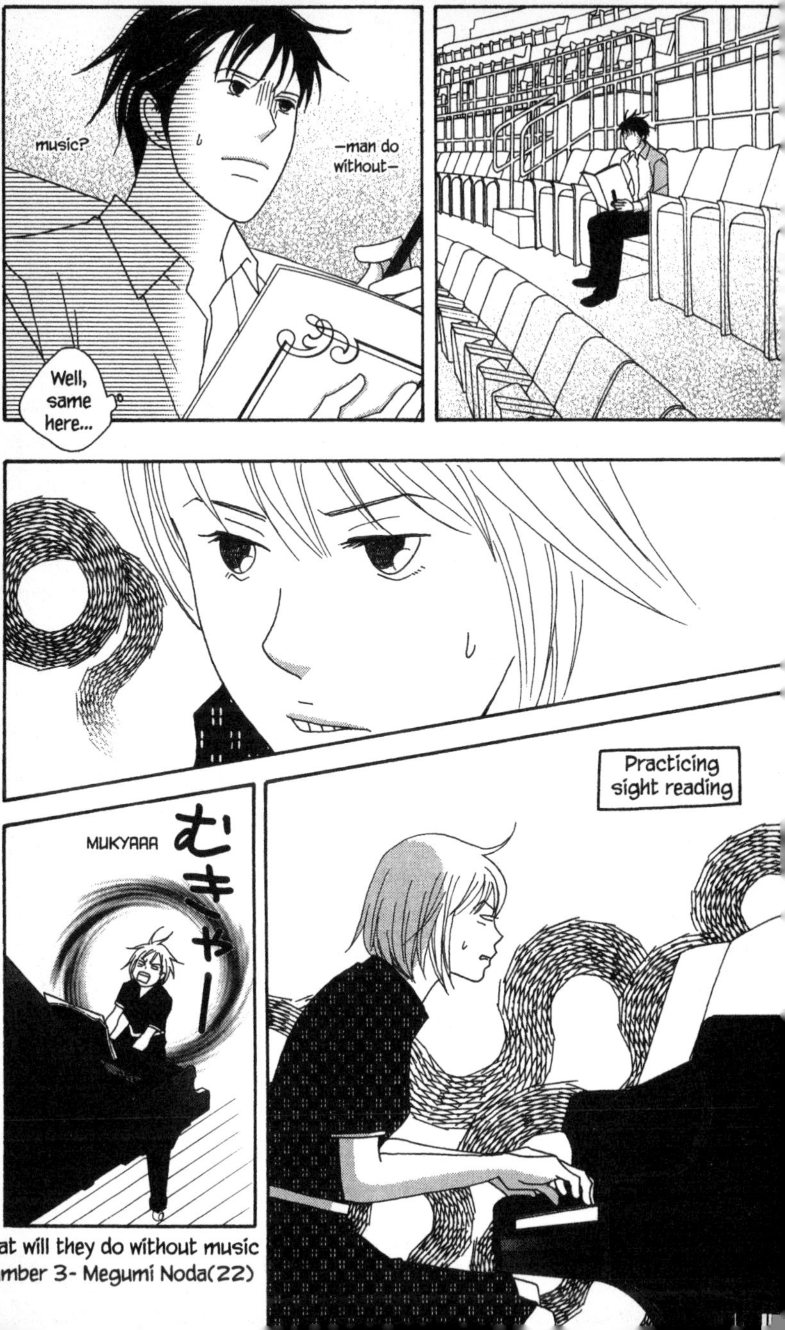
—man do without—
music?
Well, same here...
Practicing sight reading
むきゃー
MUKYAAA

What will they do without music
Number 3- Megumi Noda(22)

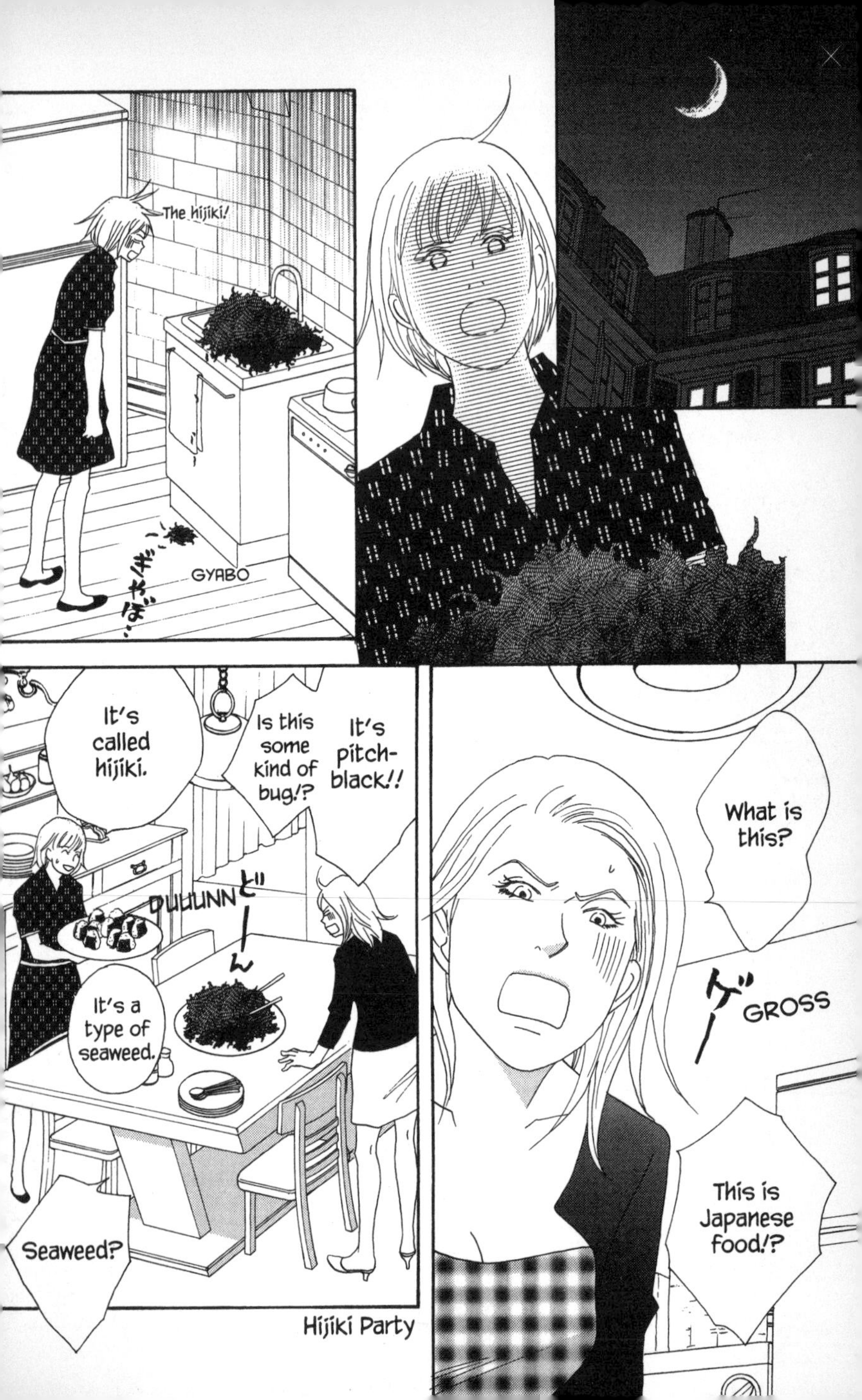
The hijiki!
GYABO
ぎゃぼ‥
What is this?
ゲー
GROSS
This is Japanese food!?
It's pitch-black!!
Is this some kind of bug!?
It's called hijiki.
DUUUNN
どーん
It's a type of seaweed.
Seaweed?

Hijiki Party

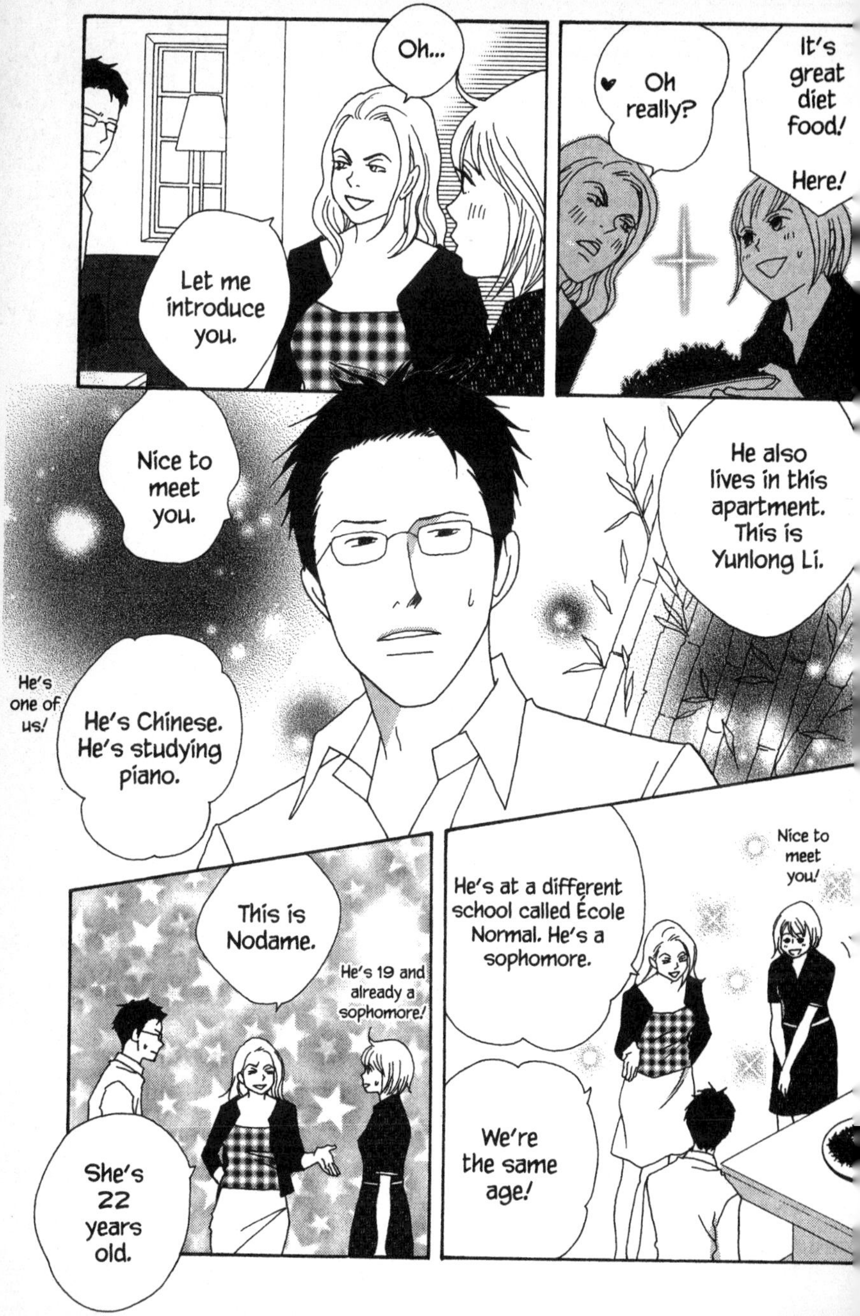
It's great diet food!
Here!
Oh really?
Oh...
Let me introduce you.
He also lives in this apartment. This is Yunlong Li.
Nice to meet you.
He's Chinese. He's studying piano.
He's one of us!
Nice to meet you!
He's at a different school called École Normal. He's a sophomore.
We're the same age!
This is Nodame.
He's 19 and already a sophomore!
She's 22 years old.

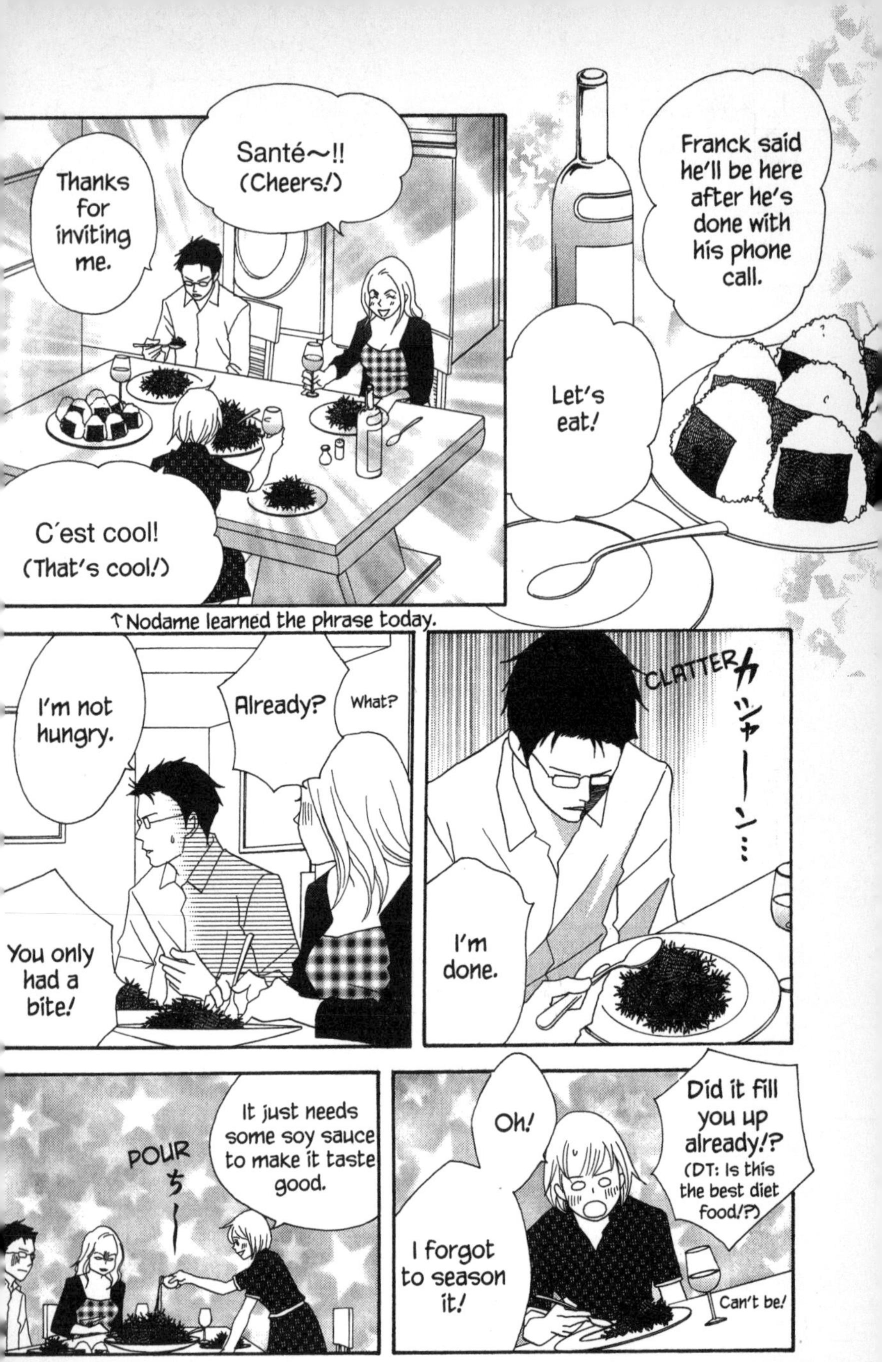

Franck said he'll be here after he's done with his phone call.
Let's eat!
Santé~!! (Cheers!)
Thanks for inviting me.
C'est cool! (That's cool!)
↑Nodame learned the phrase today.
CLATTER カシャーン…
I'm done.
What?
Already?
I'm not hungry.
You only had a bite!
Did it fill you up already!? (DT: Is this the best diet food!?)
Oh!
I forgot to season it!
Can't be!
It just needs some soy sauce to make it taste good.
POUR ちー

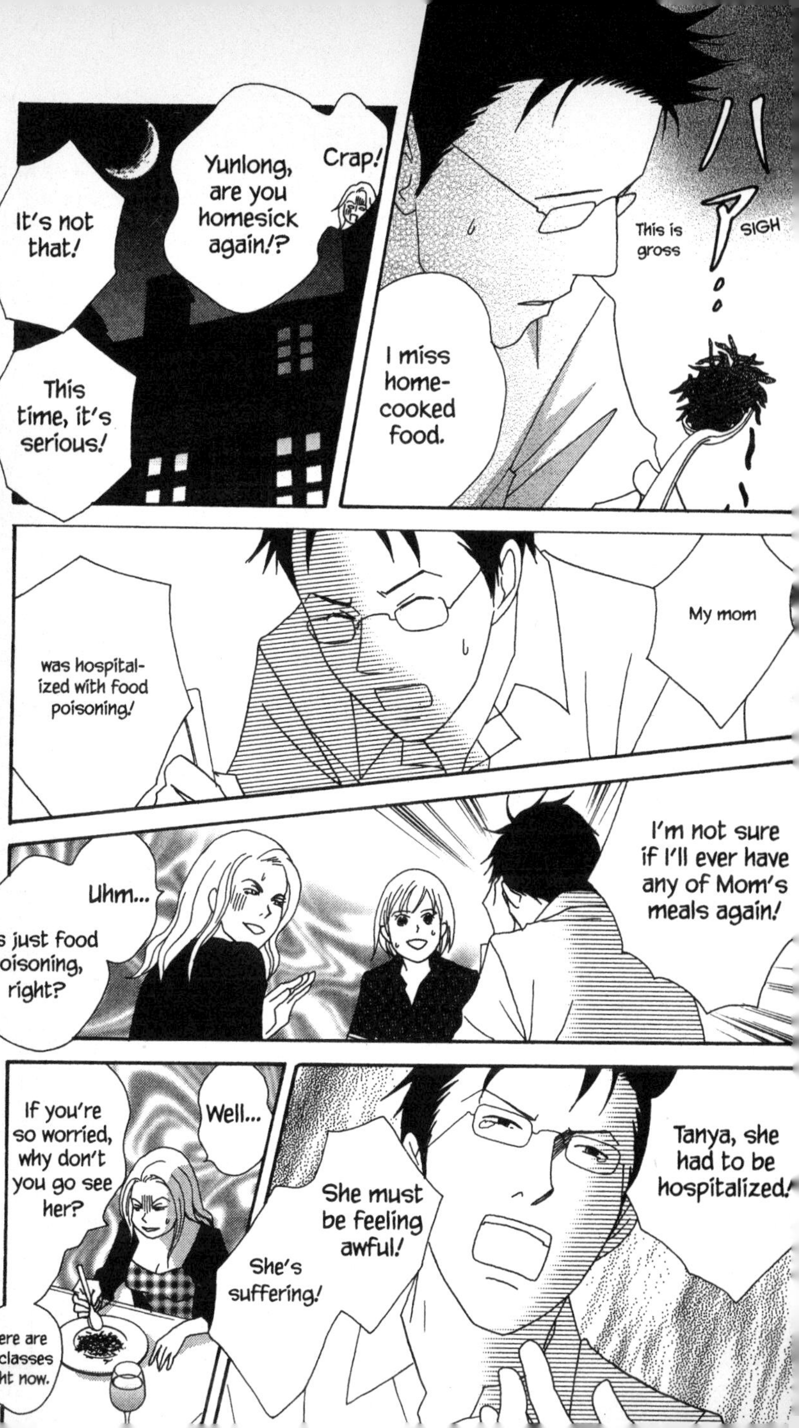
SIGH
This is gross
I miss home-cooked food.
Crap!
Yunlong, are you homesick again!?
It's not that!
This time, it's serious!
My mom
was hospitalized with food poisoning!
I'm not sure if I'll ever have any of Mom's meals again!
Uhm...
It's just food poisoning, right?
Tanya, she had to be hospitalized!
She must be feeling awful!
She's suffering!
Well...
If you're so worried, why don't you go see her?
There are no classes right now.

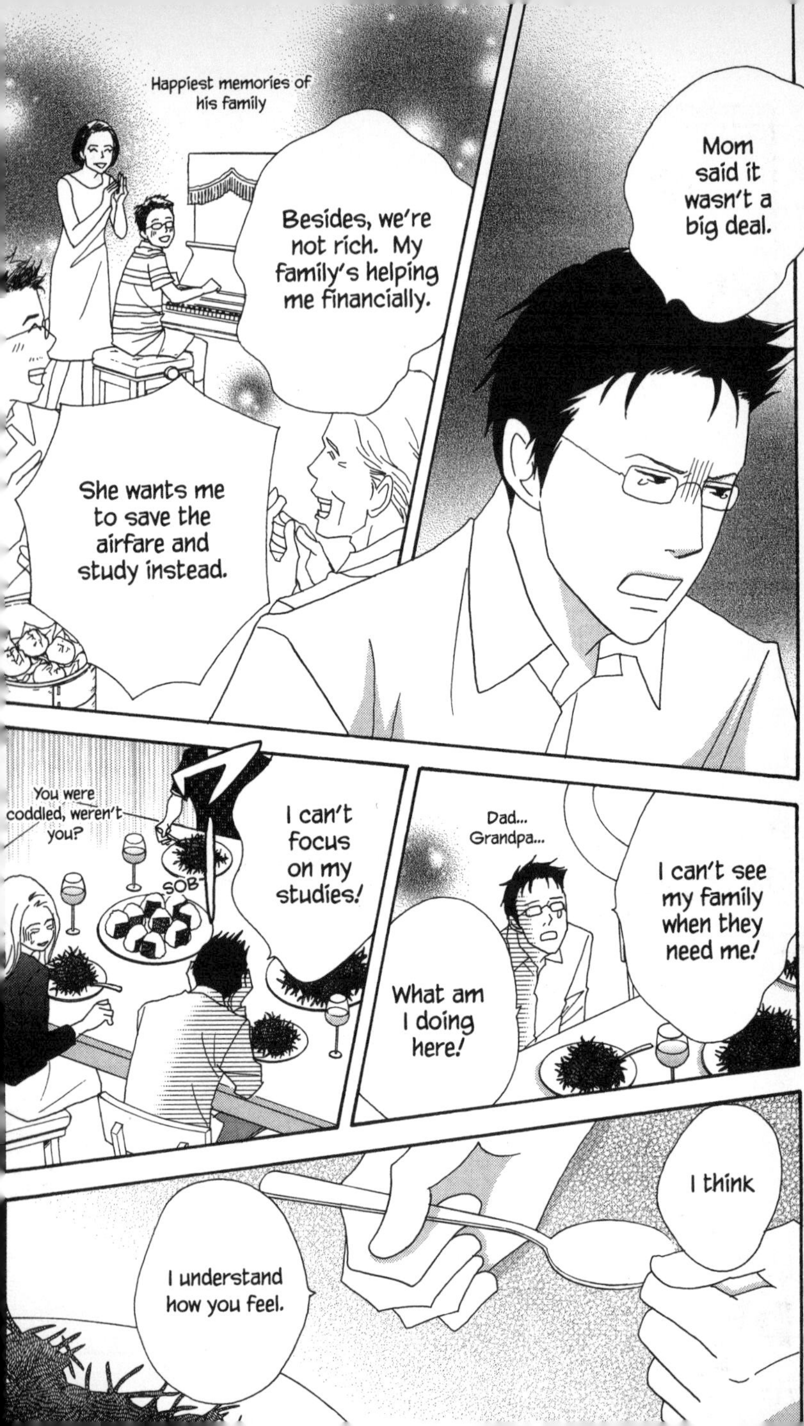
Mom said it wasn't a big deal.
Happiest memories of his family
Besides, we're not rich. My family's helping me financially.
She wants me to save the airfare and study instead.
Dad... Grandpa...
I can't see my family when they need me!
What am I doing here!
I can't focus on my studies!
SOB
You were coddled, weren't you?
I think
I understand how you feel.

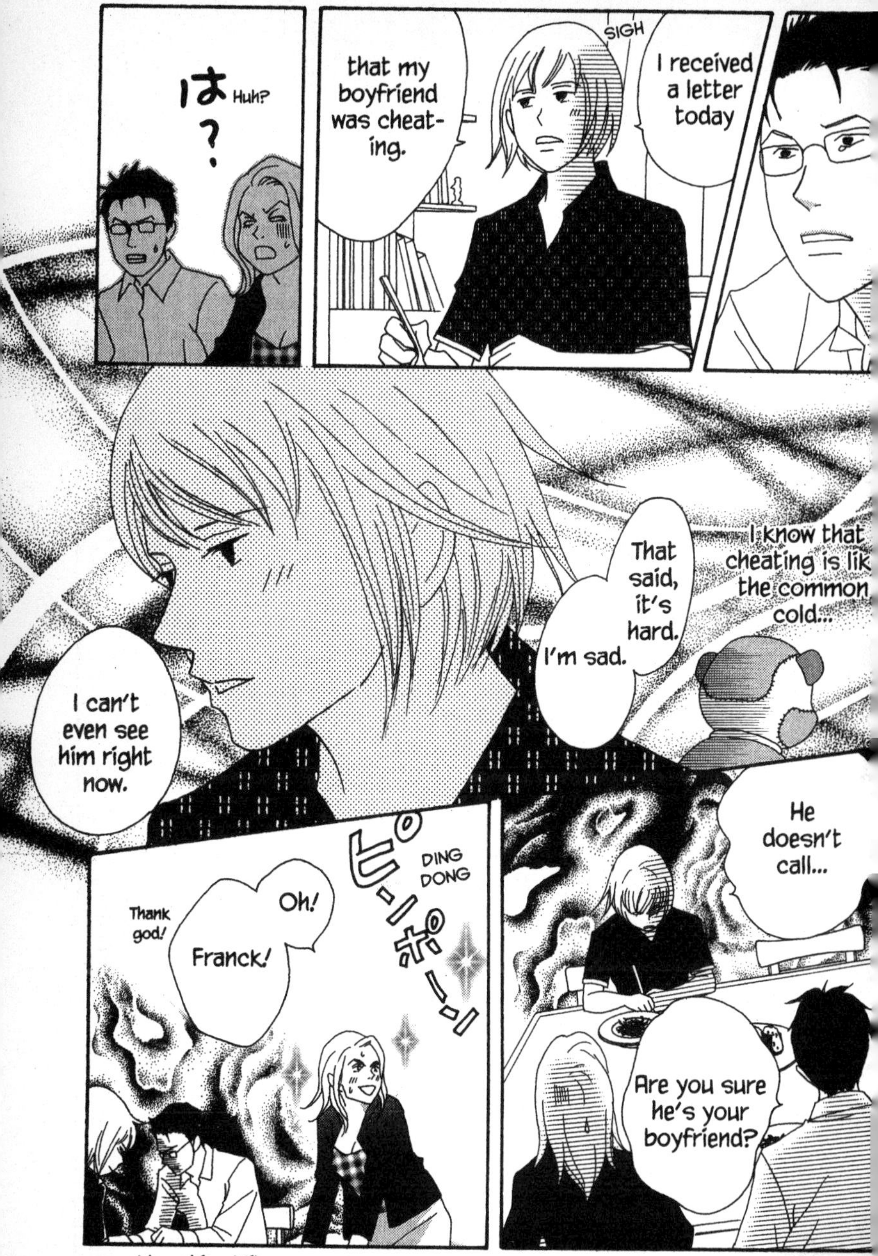
SIGH
I received a letter today
that my boyfriend was cheat-ing.
は？
Huh?
I know that cheating is lik the common cold...
That said, it's hard.
I'm sad.
I can't even see him right now.
He doesn't call...
Are you sure he's your boyfriend?
ピーンポーン!
DING DONG
Oh! Franck!
Thank god!

Negative Vibes

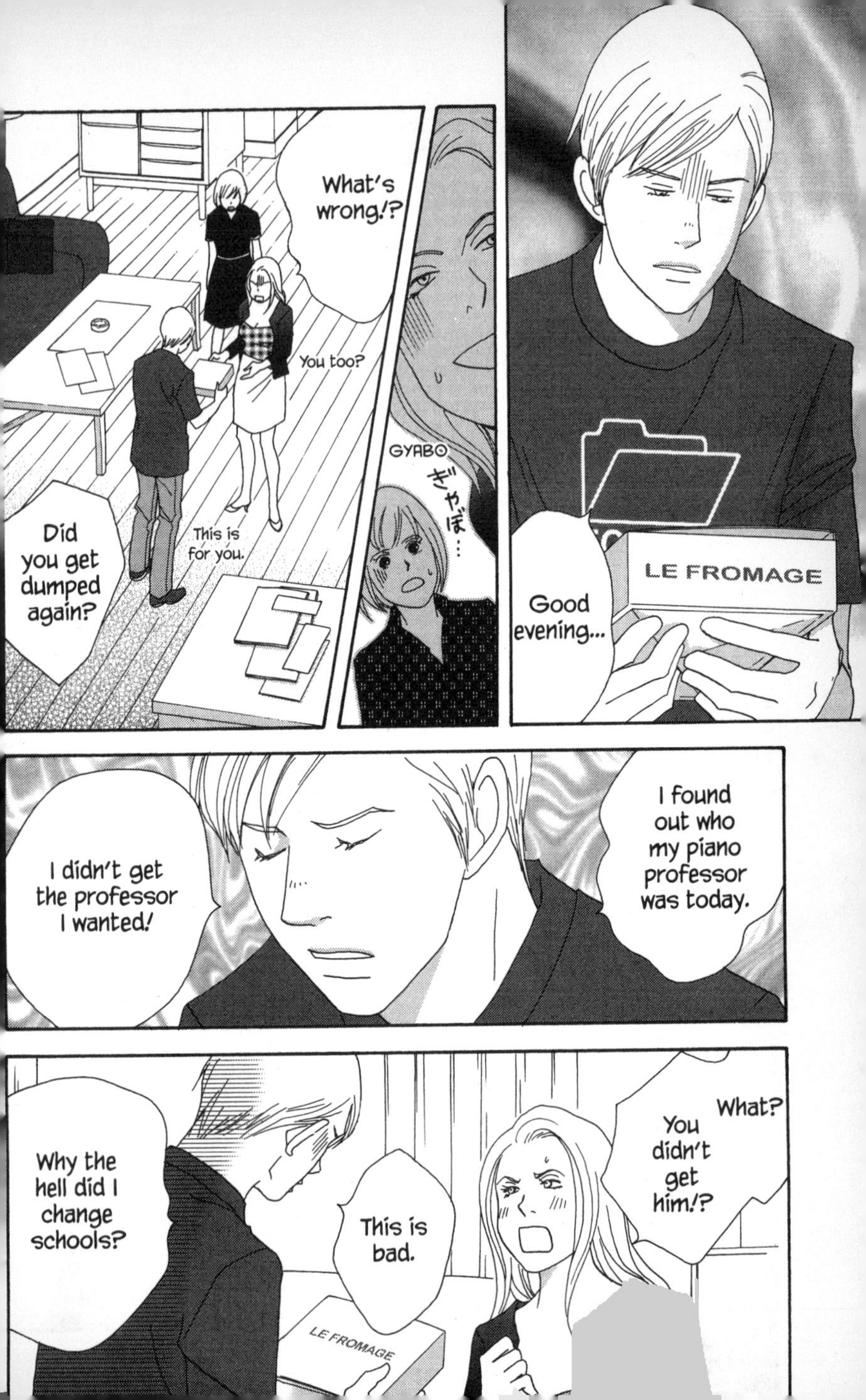
LE FROMAGE
Good evening...
GYABO
ぎゃぼ…
What's wrong!?
You too?
This is for you.
Did you get dumped again?
I found out who my piano professor was today.
I didn't get the professor I wanted!
What?
You didn't get him!?
This is bad.
Why the hell did I change schools?
LE FROMAGE

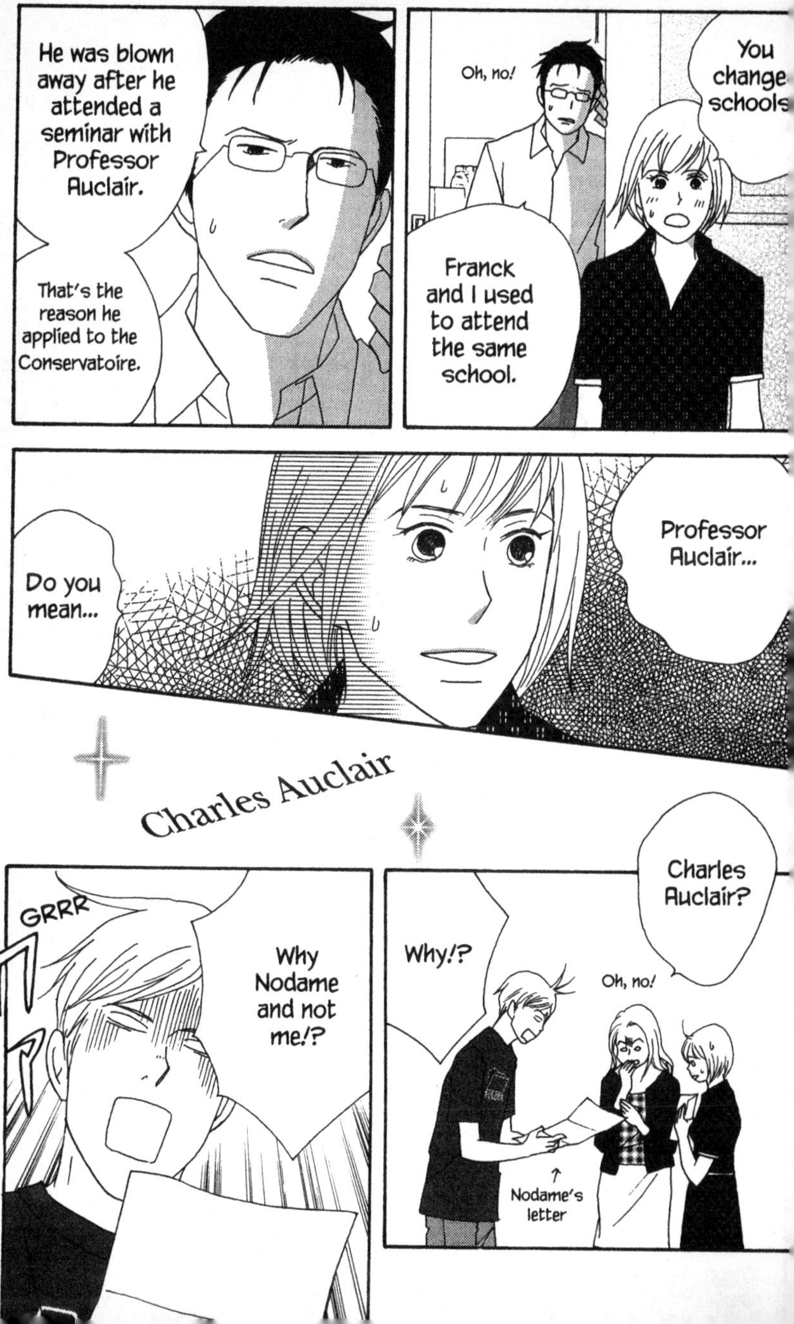
You change schools
Oh, no!
Franck and I used to attend the same school.
He was blown away after he attended a seminar with Professor Auclair.
That's the reason he applied to the Conservatoire.
Professor Auclair...
Do you mean...
Charles Auclair
Charles Auclair?
Why!?
Oh, no!
↑ Nodame's letter
GRRR
Why Nodame and not me!?

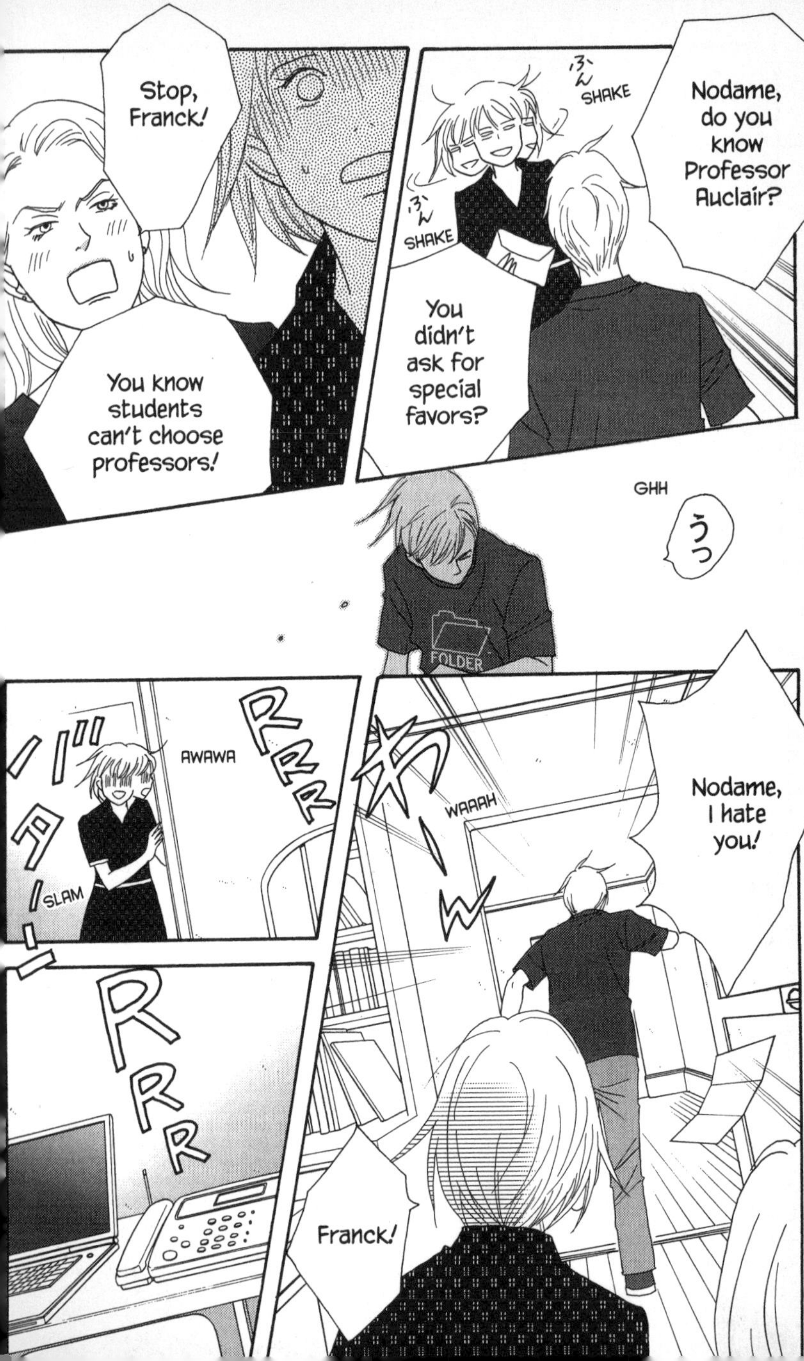
Nodame, do you know Professor Auclair?
ふん
SHAKE
ふん
SHAKE
You didn't ask for special favors?
Stop, Franck!
You know students can't choose professors!
うっ
GHH
Nodame, I hate you!
WAAAH
Franck!
RRRR
AWAWA
SLAM
RRR

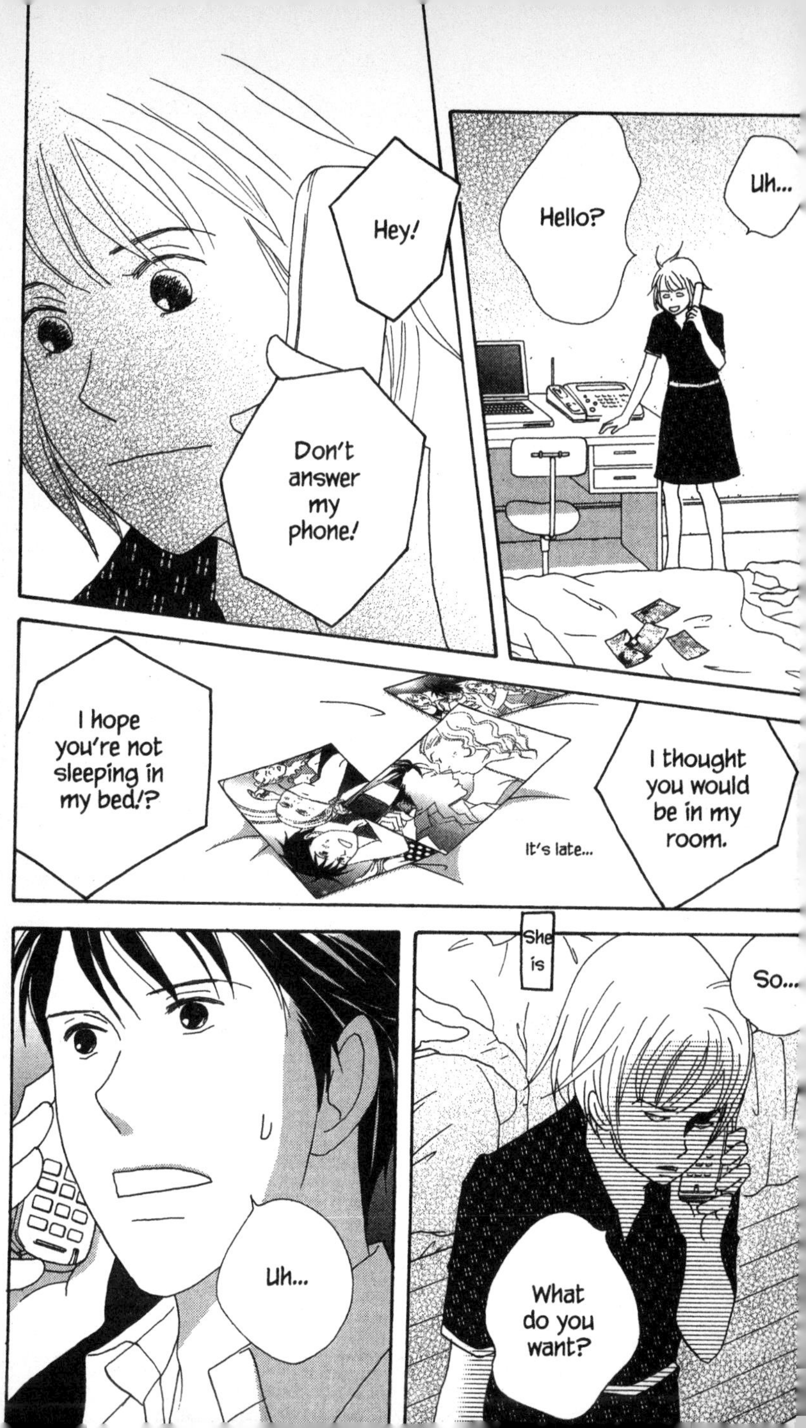
Hello?
Uh...
Hey!
Don't answer my phone!
I thought you would be in my room.
It's late...
I hope you're not sleeping in my bed!?
So...
She is
What do you want?
Uh...

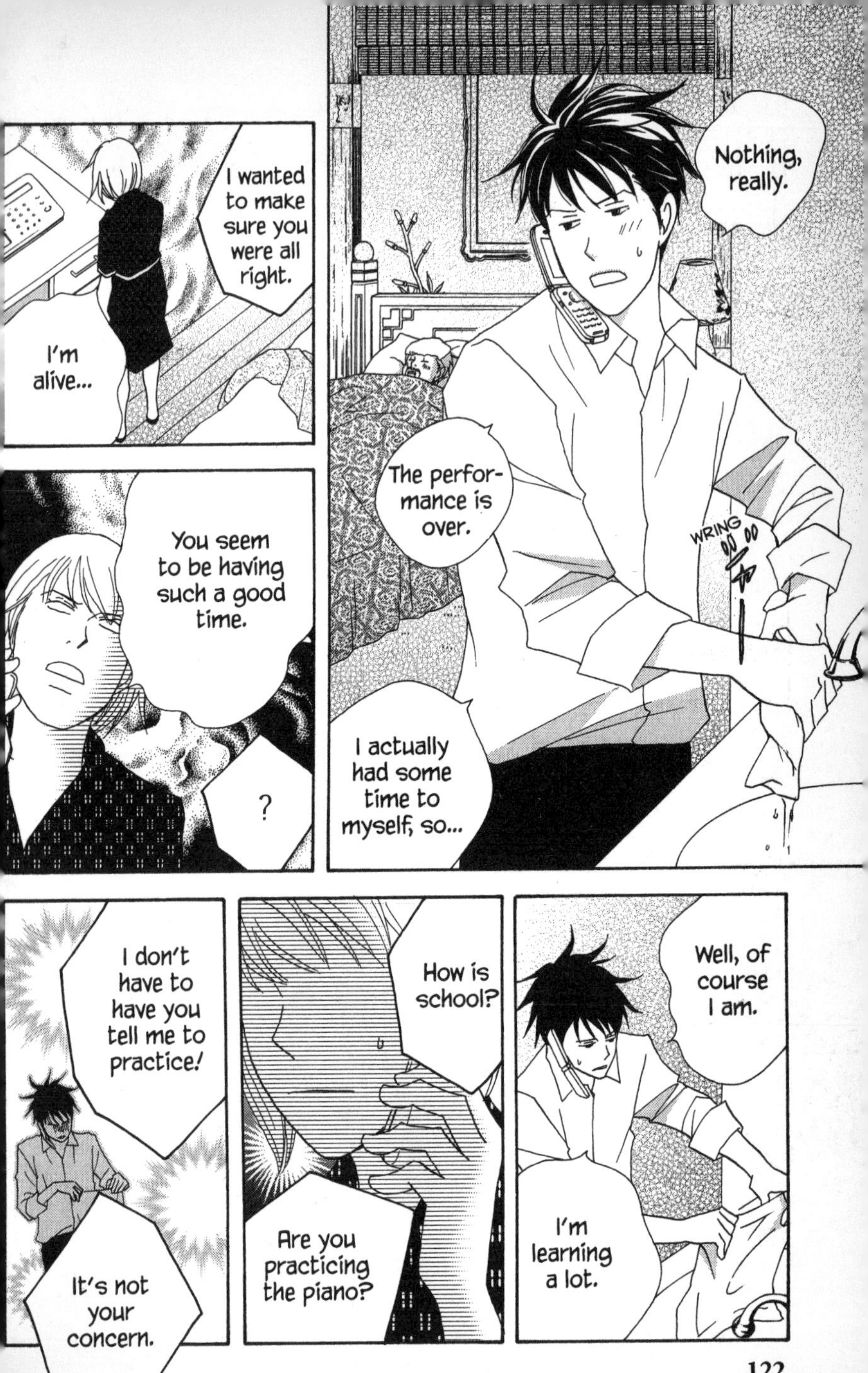

Nothing, really.
The performance is over.
WRING
I actually had some time to myself, so...
I wanted to make sure you were all right.
I'm alive...
You seem to be having such a good time.
?
Well, of course I am.
I'm learning a lot.
How is school?
Are you practicing the piano?
I don't have to have you tell me to practice!
It's not your concern.

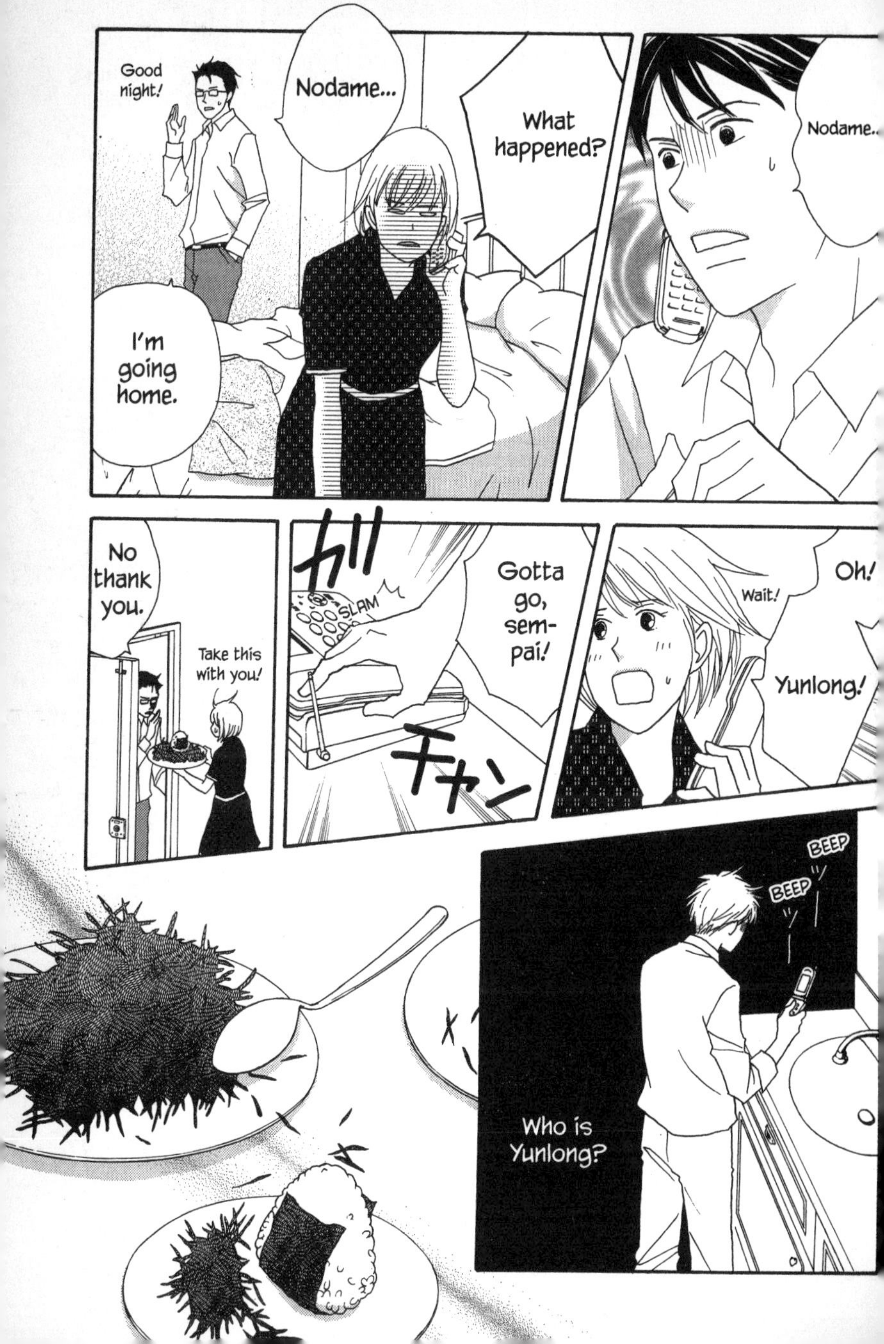
Nodame...
What happened?
Nodame...
Good night!
I'm going home.
Oh!
Yunlong!
Wait!
Gotta go, sempai!
カ
SLAM
チャン
No thank you.
Take this with you!
BEEP
BEEP
ツー
ツー
Who is Yunlong?

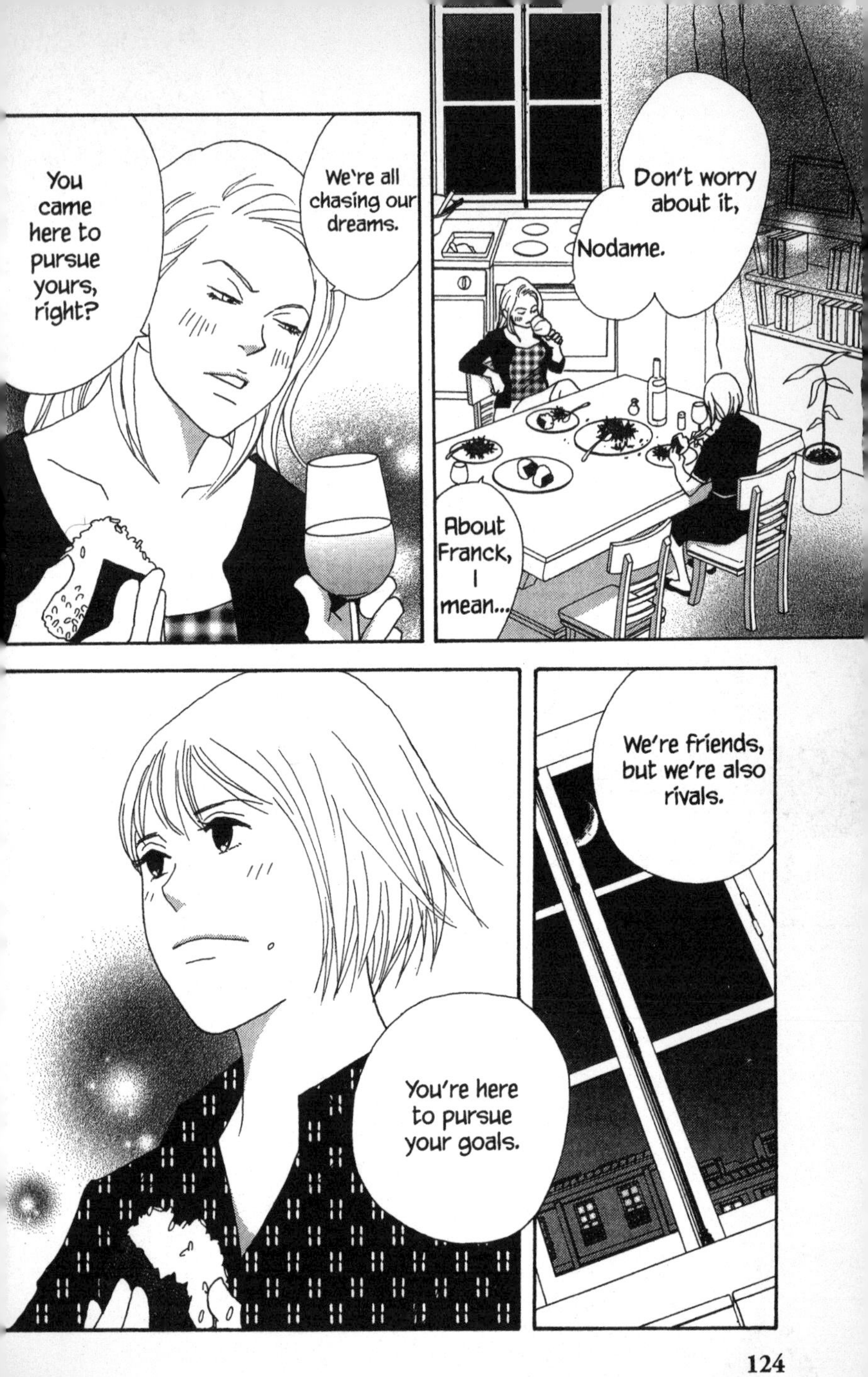
Don't worry about it,
Nodame.
About Franck, I mean...
We're all chasing our dreams.
You came here to pursue yours, right?
We're friends, but we're also rivals.
You're here to pursue your goals.

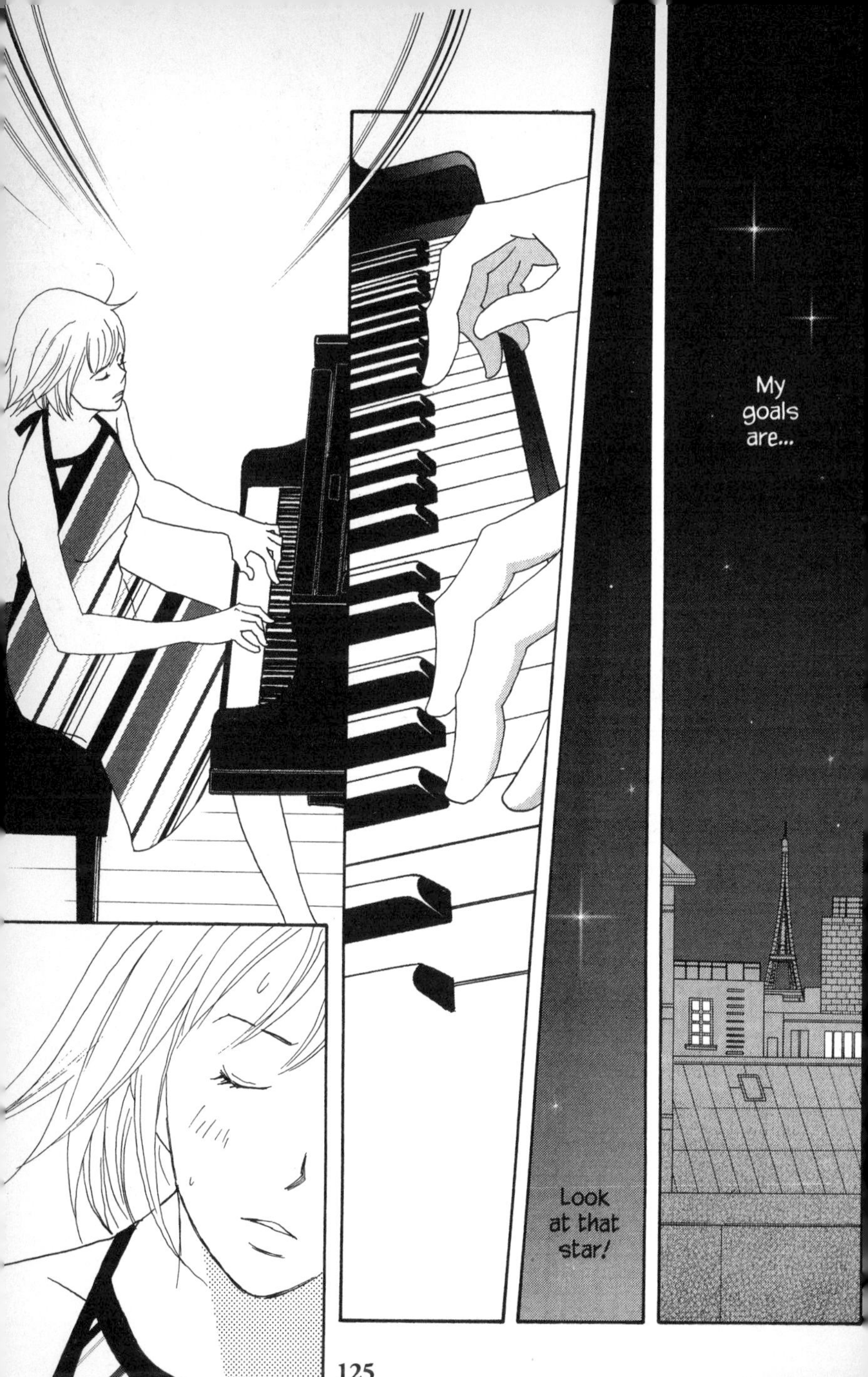
My goals are...
Look at that star!

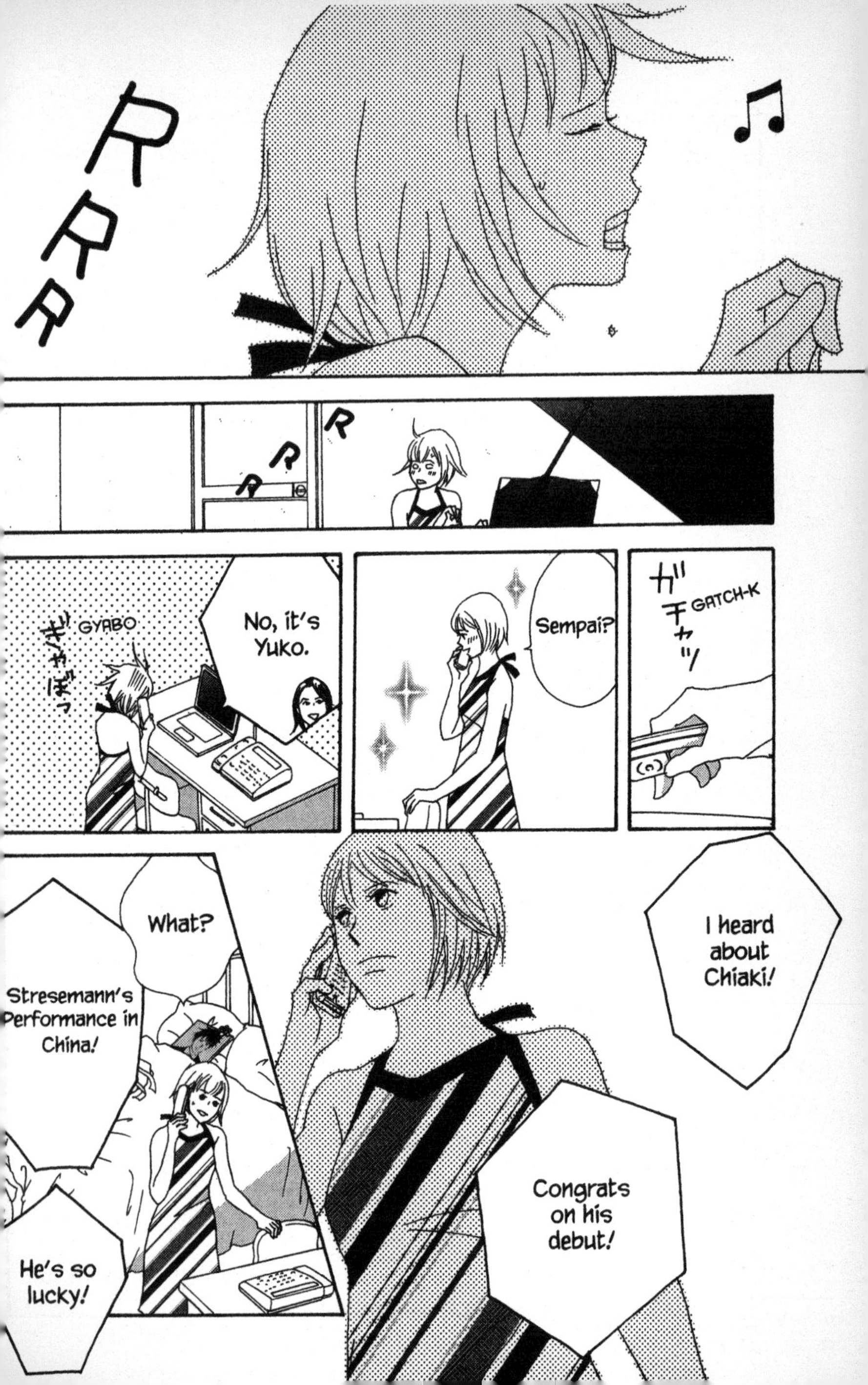
RRR
R R R
ガチャッ
GATCH-K
Sempai?
No, it's Yuko.
ぎゃぼっ
GYABO
I heard about Chiaki!
Congrats on his debut!
What?
Stresemann's Performance in China!
He's so lucky!

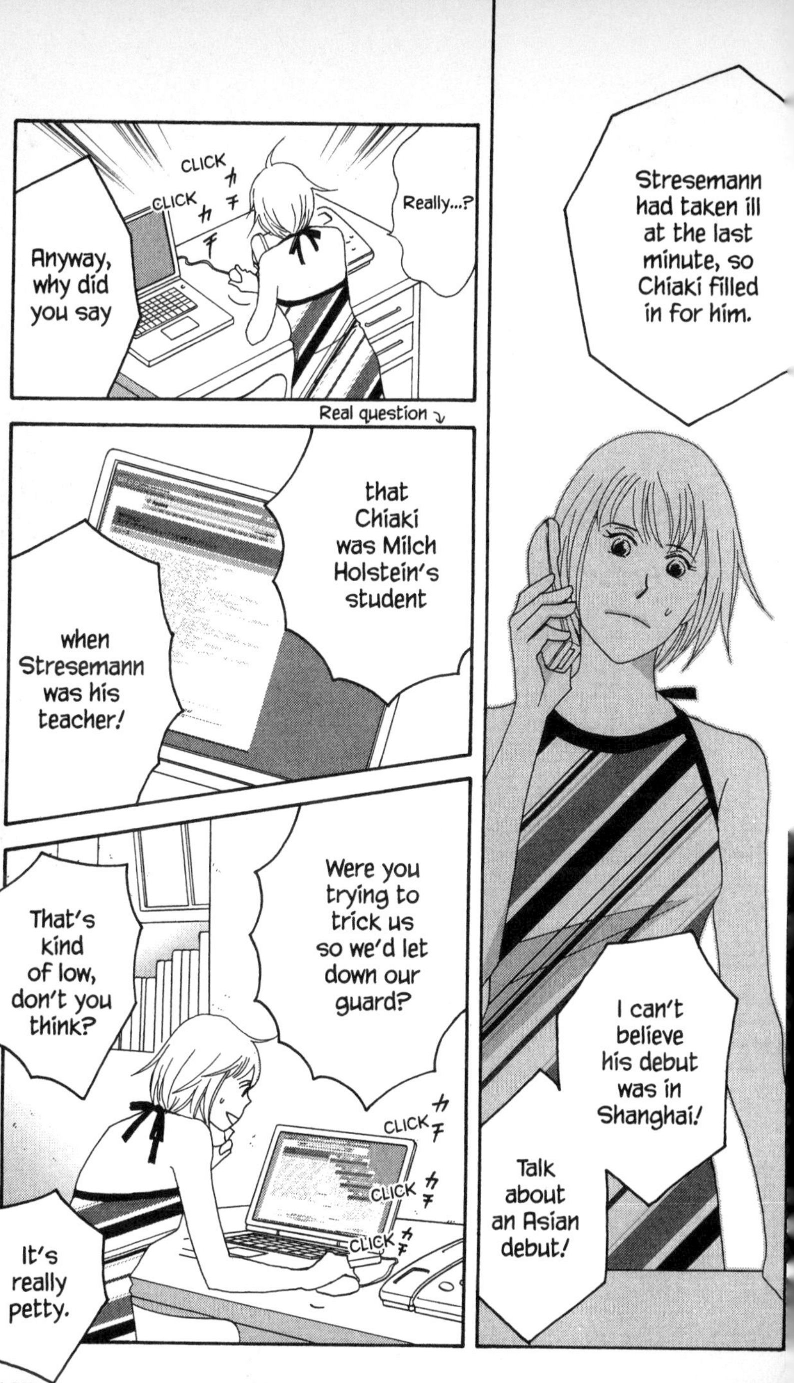
Stresemann had taken ill at the last minute, so Chiaki filled in for him.
I can't believe his debut was in Shanghai!
Talk about an Asian debut!
Really...?
CLICK
CLICK
Anyway, why did you say
Real question
that Chiaki was Milch Holstein's student
when Stresemann was his teacher!
Were you trying to trick us so we'd let down our guard?
That's kind of low, don't you think?
CLICK
CLICK
CLICK
It's really petty.

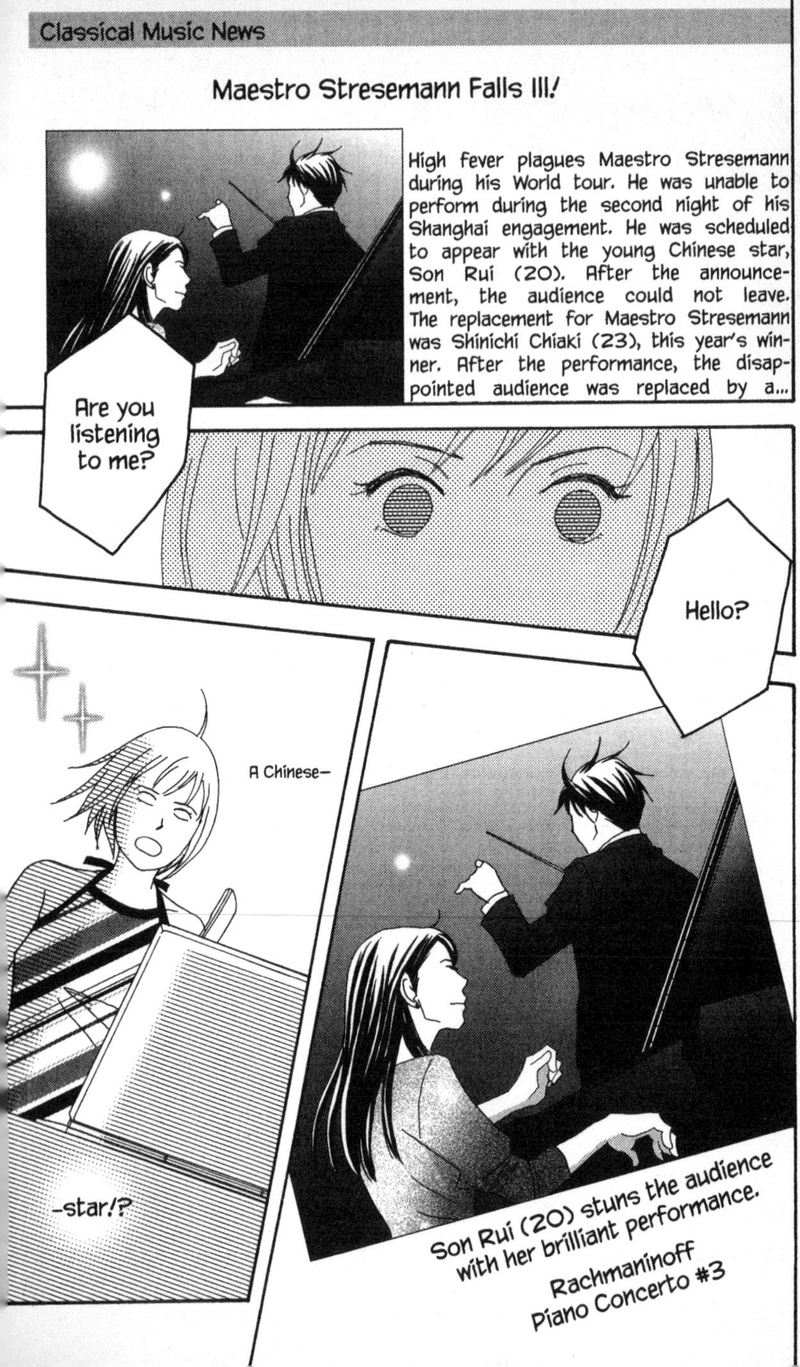
Classical Music News
Maestro Stresemann Falls Ill!
High fever plagues Maestro Stresemann during his World tour. He was unable to perform during the second night of his Shanghai engagement. He was scheduled to appear with the young Chinese star, Son Rui (20). After the announcement, the audience could not leave. The replacement for Maestro Stresemann was Shinichi Chiaki (23), this year's winner. After the performance, the disappointed audience was replaced by a...
Are you listening to me?
Hello?
Son Rui (20) stuns the audience with her brilliant performance.
Rachmaninoff Piano Concerto #3
A Chinese—
-star!?

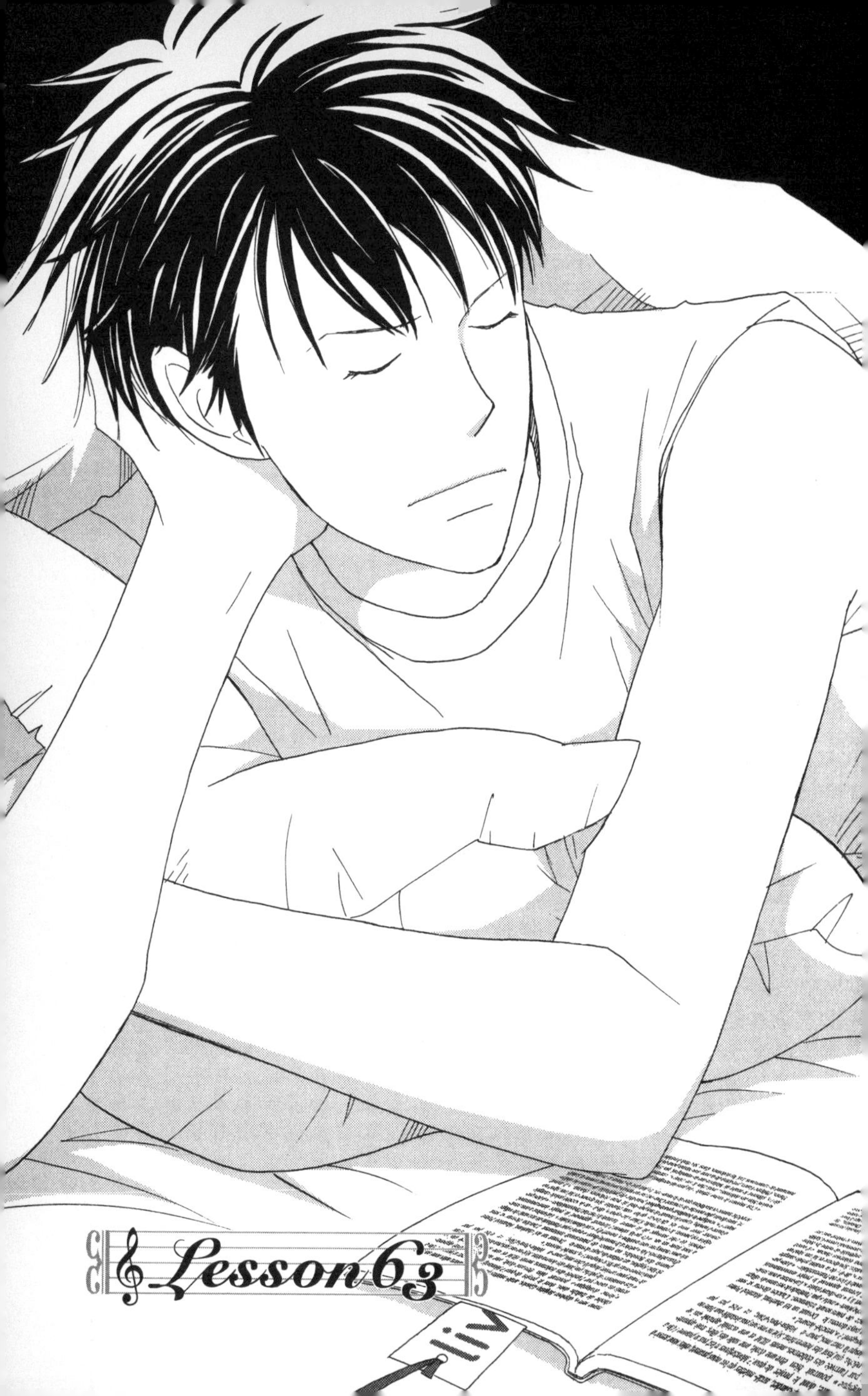
Lesson 63

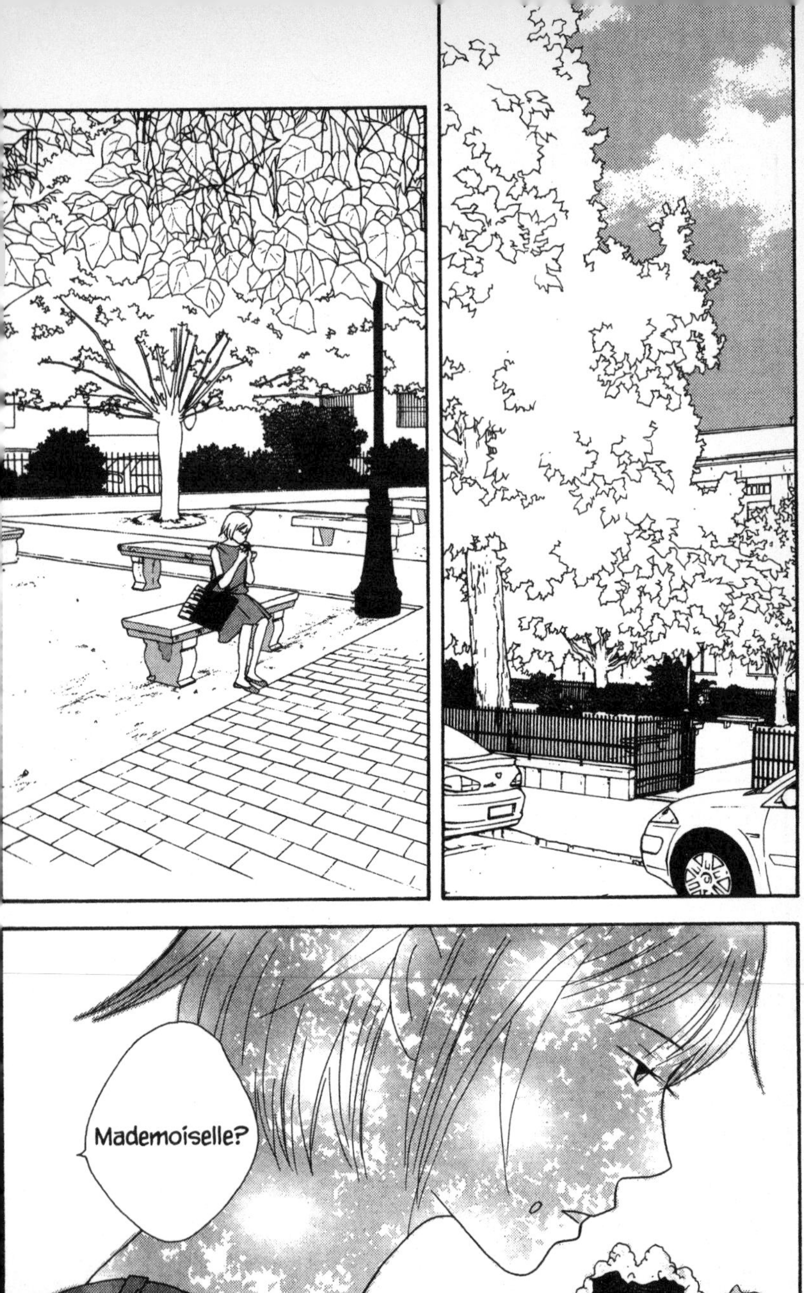
Mademoiselle?

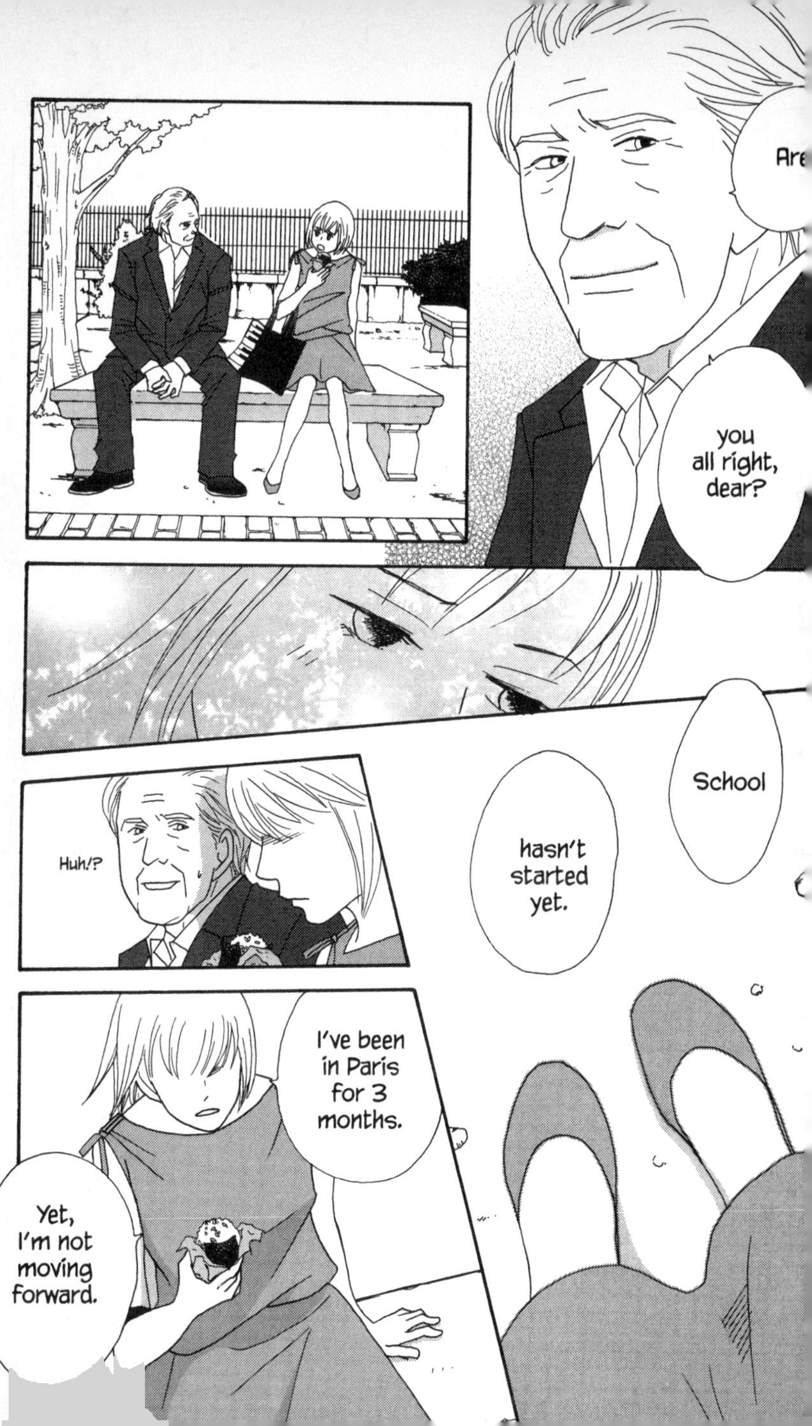

Are
you all right, dear?
School
hasn't started yet.
Huh!?
I've been in Paris for 3 months.
Yet, I'm not moving forward.

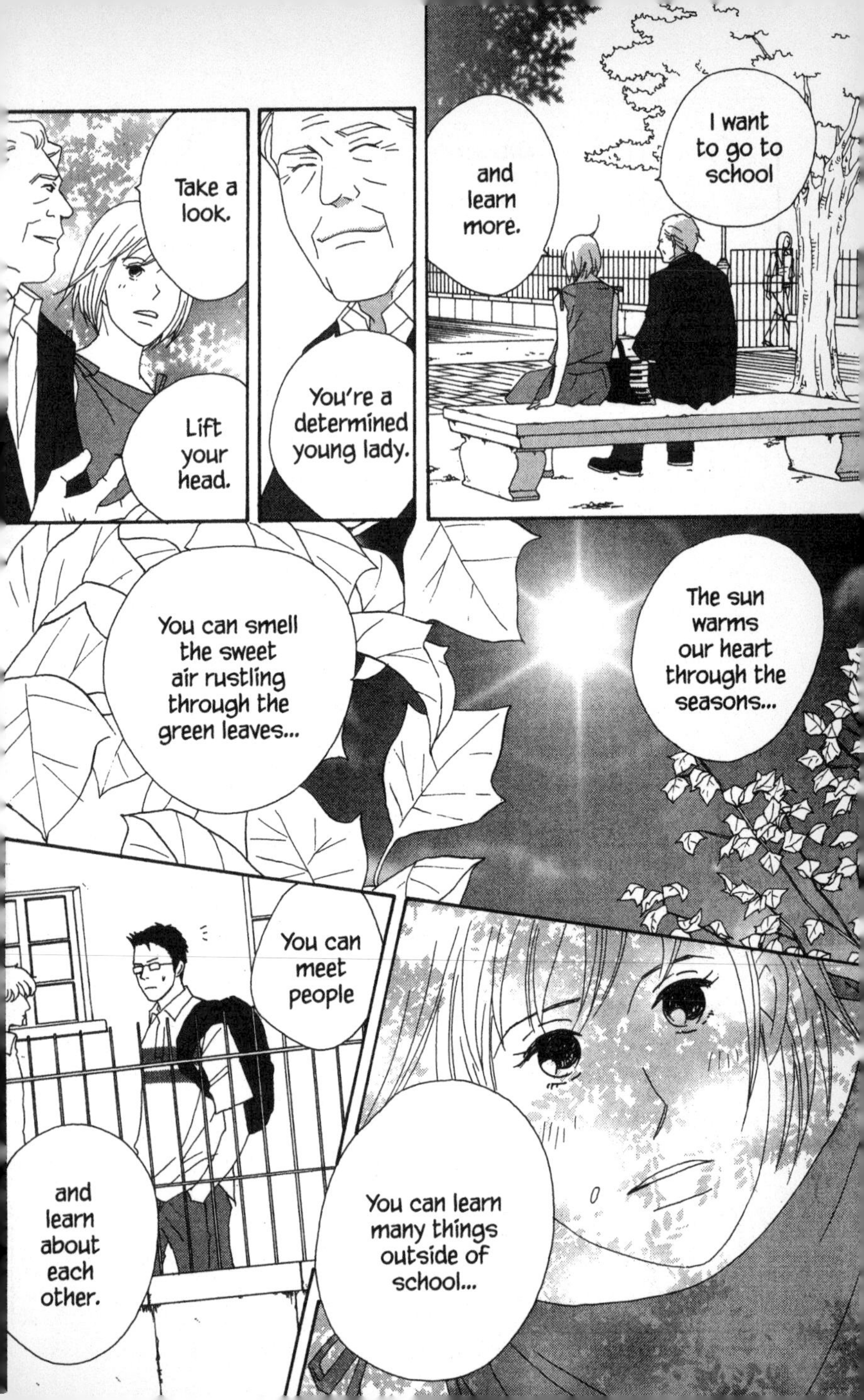
I want to go to school
and learn more.
You're a determined young lady.
Take a look.
Lift your head.
The sun warms our heart through the seasons...
You can smell the sweet air rustling through the green leaves...
You can learn many things outside of school...
You can meet people
and learn about each other.

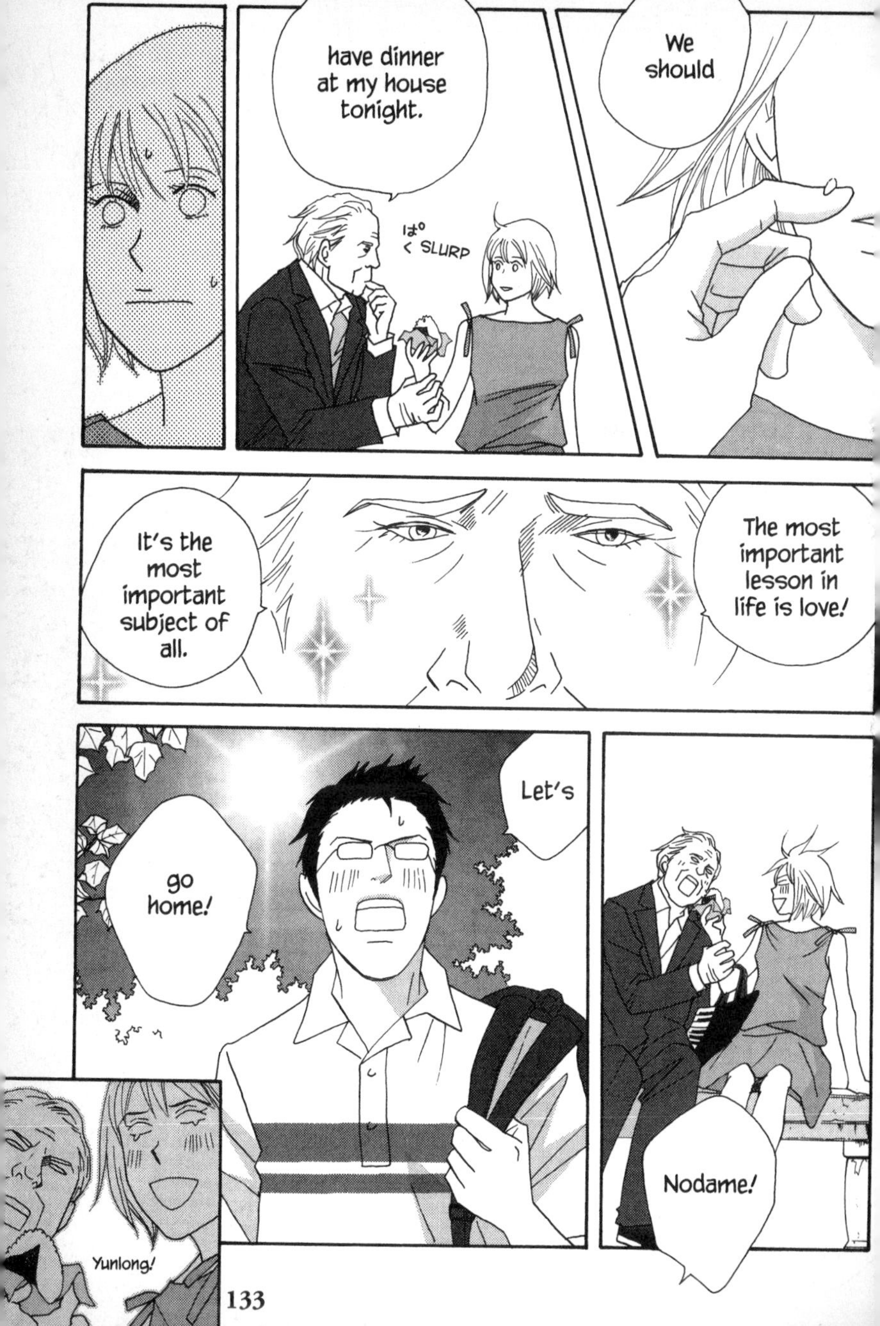

We should
have dinner at my house tonight.
ぱく SLURP
The most important lesson in life is love!
It's the most important subject of all.
Nodame!
Let's
go home!
Yunlong!

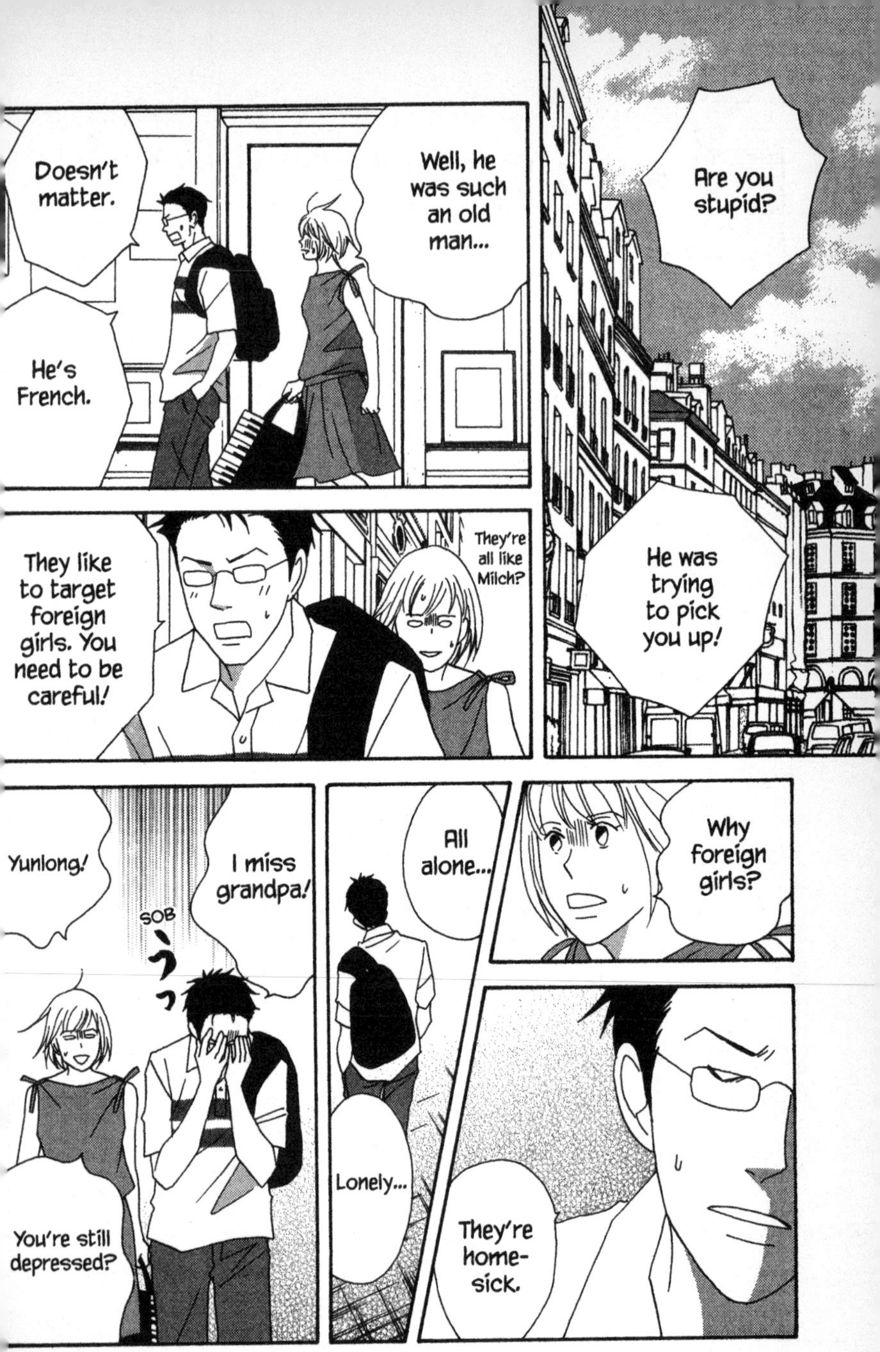
Are you stupid?
He was trying to pick you up!
Well, he was such an old man...
Doesn't matter.
He's French.
They're all like Milch?
They like to target foreign girls. You need to be careful!
Why foreign girls?
They're home-sick.
All alone...
Lonely...
I miss grandpa!
SOB
Yunlong!
You're still depressed?

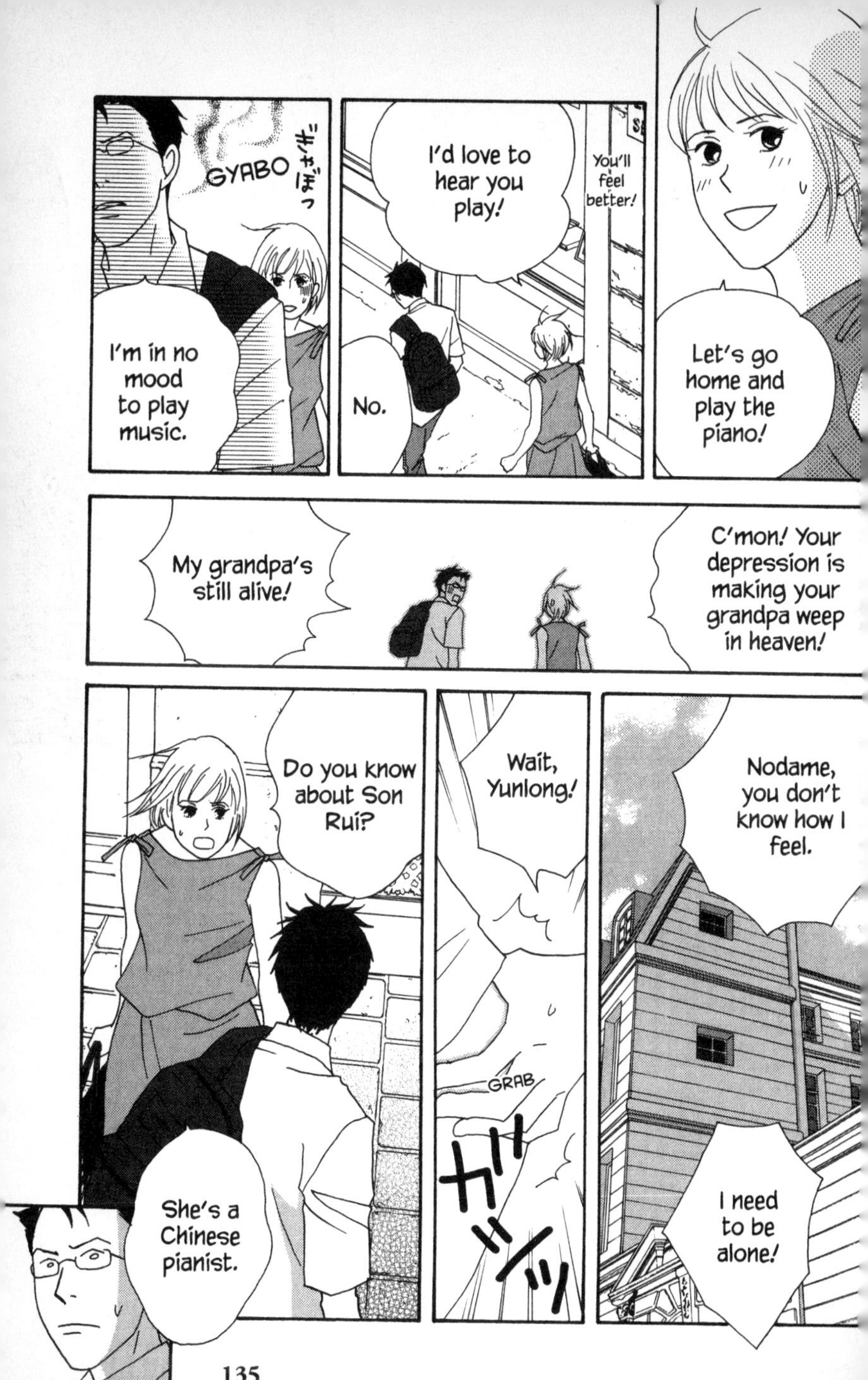
Let's go home and play the piano!
I'd love to hear you play!
You'll feel better!
No.
GYABO
ぎゃぼっ
I'm in no mood to play music.
C'mon! Your depression is making your grandpa weep in heaven!
My grandpa's still alive!
Nodame, you don't know how I feel.
I need to be alone!
Wait, Yunlong!
GRAB
ガッ
Do you know about Son Rui?
She's a Chinese pianist.

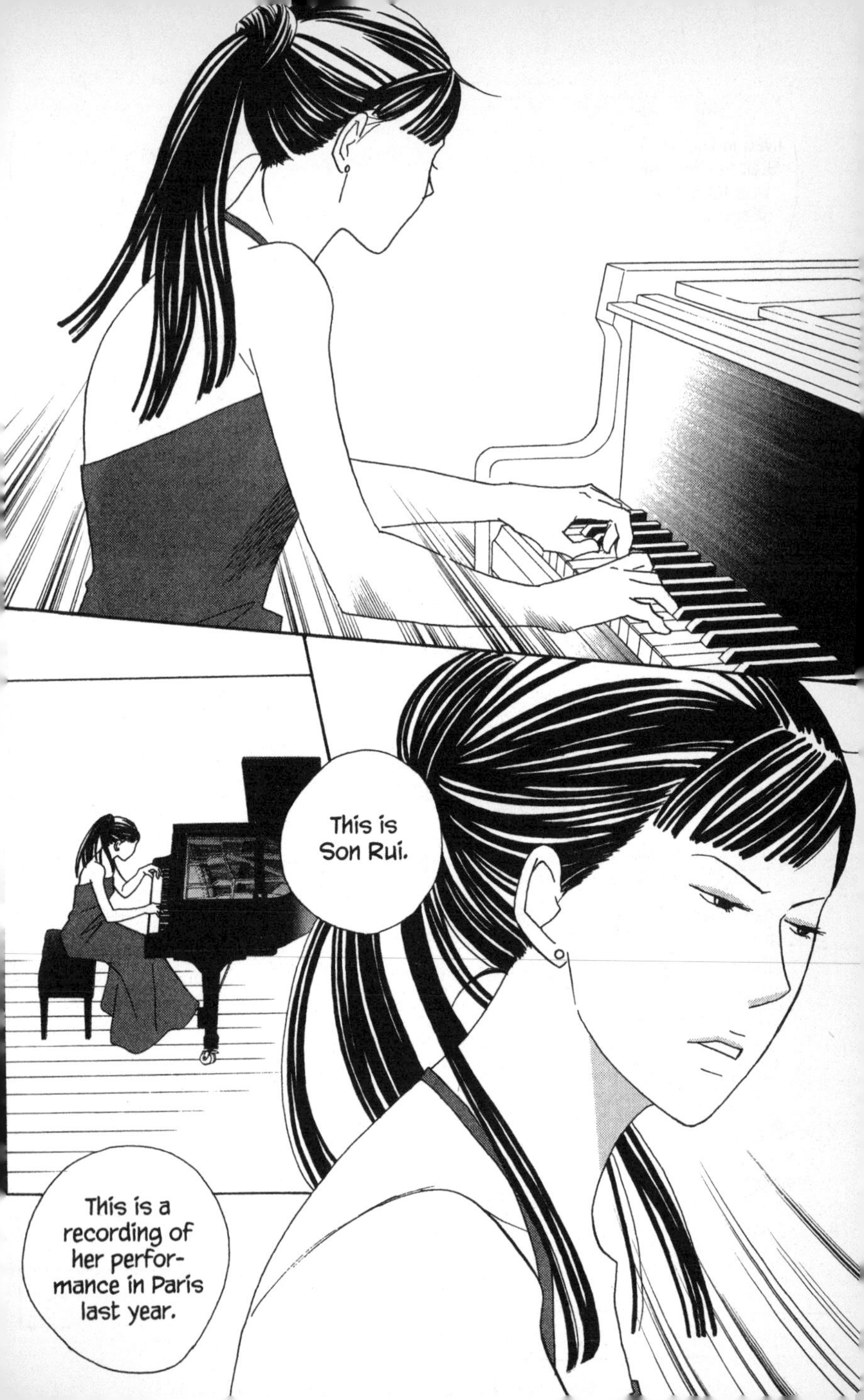
This is Son Rui.
This is a recording of her performance in Paris last year.

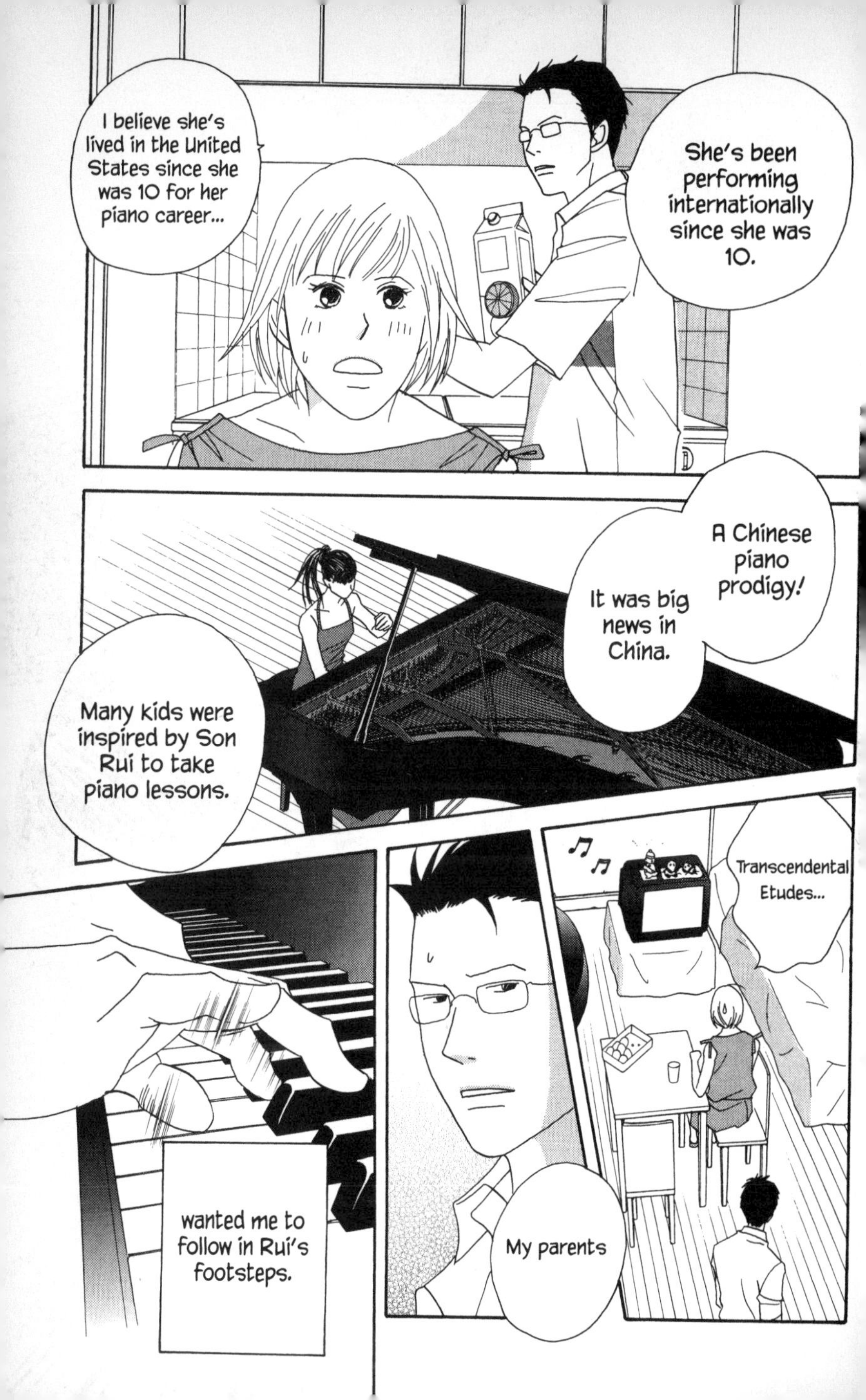
She's been performing internationally since she was 10.
I believe she's lived in the United States since she was 10 for her piano career...
A Chinese piano prodigy!
It was big news in China.
Many kids were inspired by Son Rui to take piano lessons.
Transcendental Etudes...
My parents
wanted me to follow in Rui's footsteps.

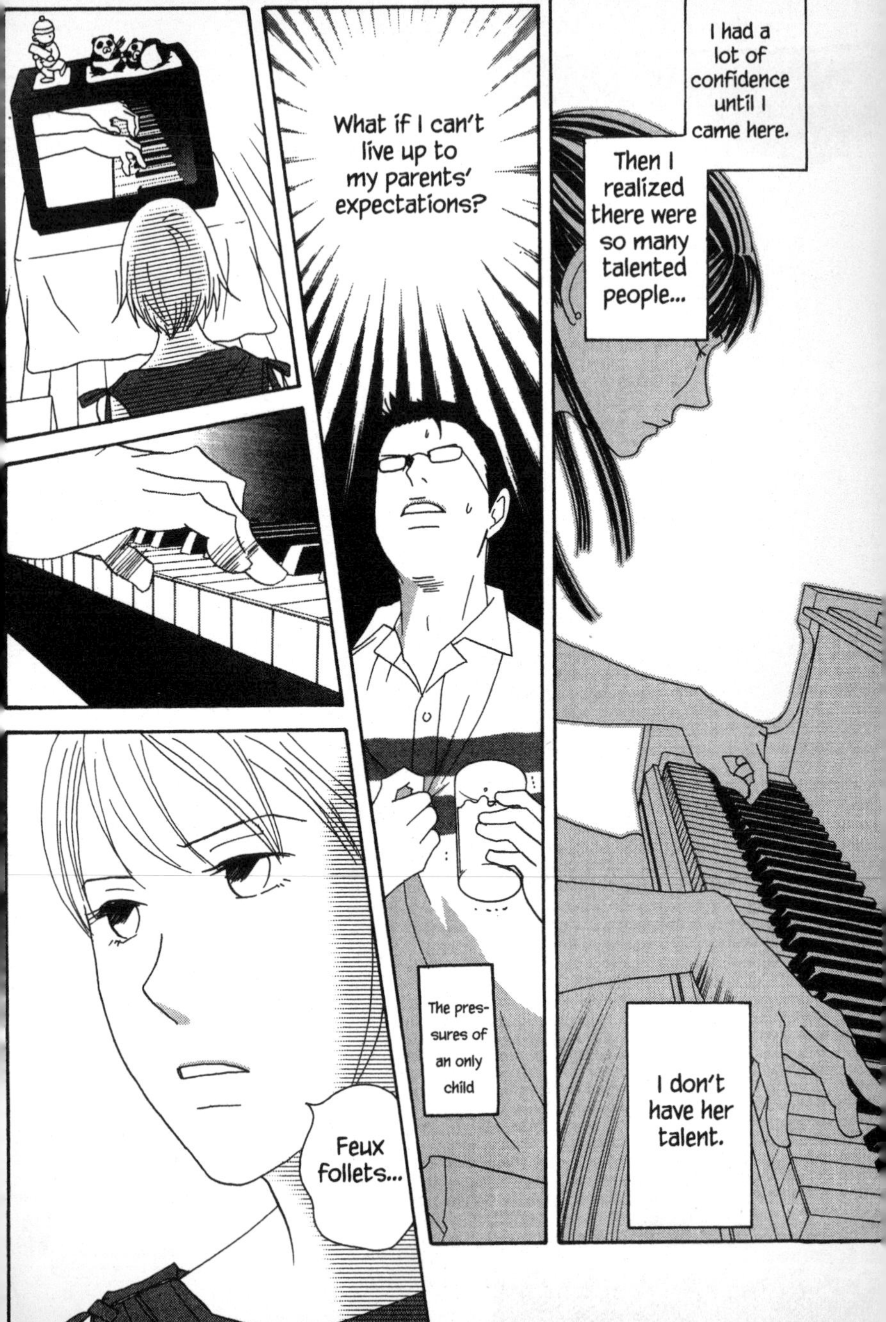
I had a lot of confidence until I came here.
Then I realized there were so many talented people...
I don't have her talent.
What if I can't live up to my parents' expectations?
The pres-sures of an only child
Feux follets...

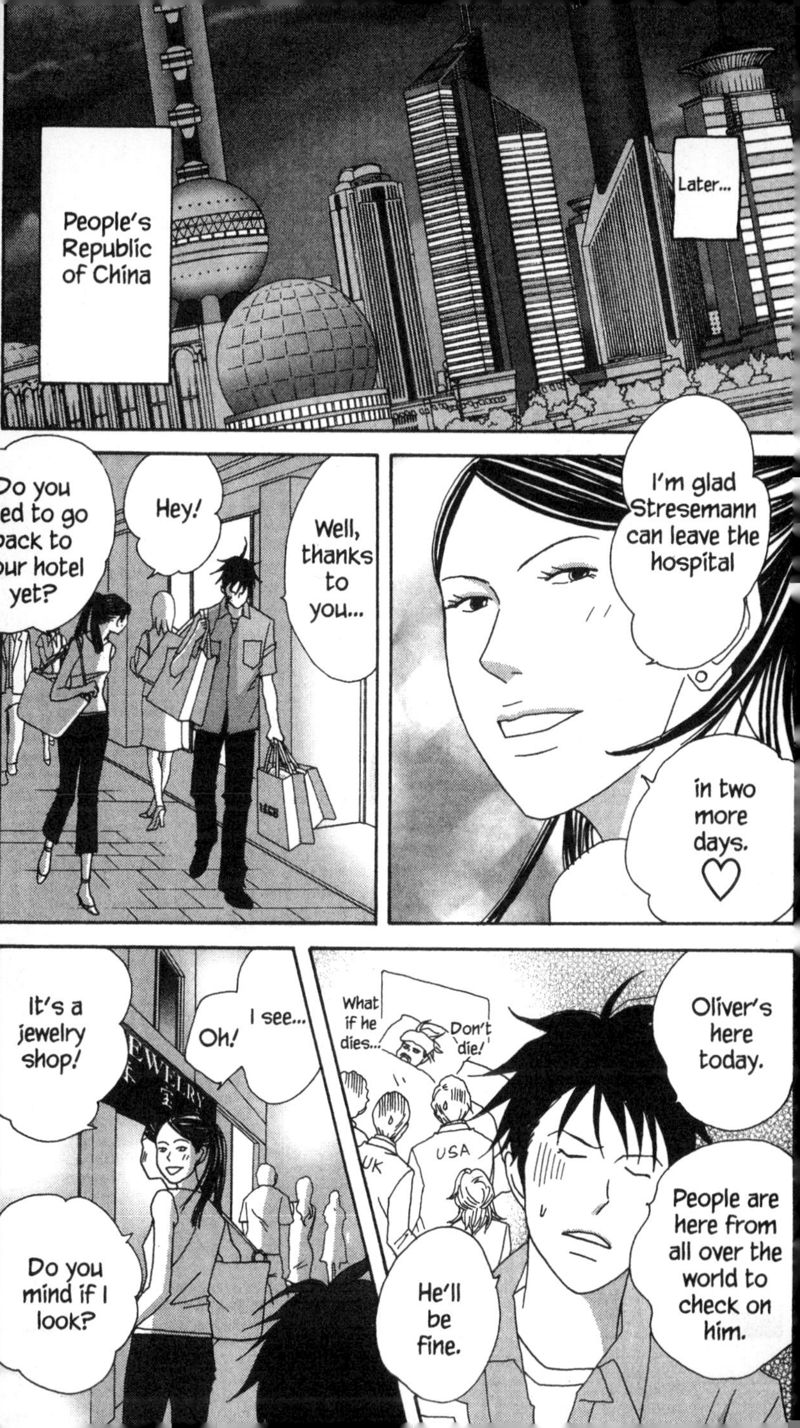
Later...
People's Republic of China
I'm glad Stresemann can leave the hospital
in two more days. ♡
Well, thanks to you...
Hey!
Do you need to go back to your hotel yet?
Oliver's here today.
Don't die!
What if he dies...
USA
UK
People are here from all over the world to check on him.
He'll be fine.
I see...
Oh!
It's a jewelry shop!
Do you mind if I look?

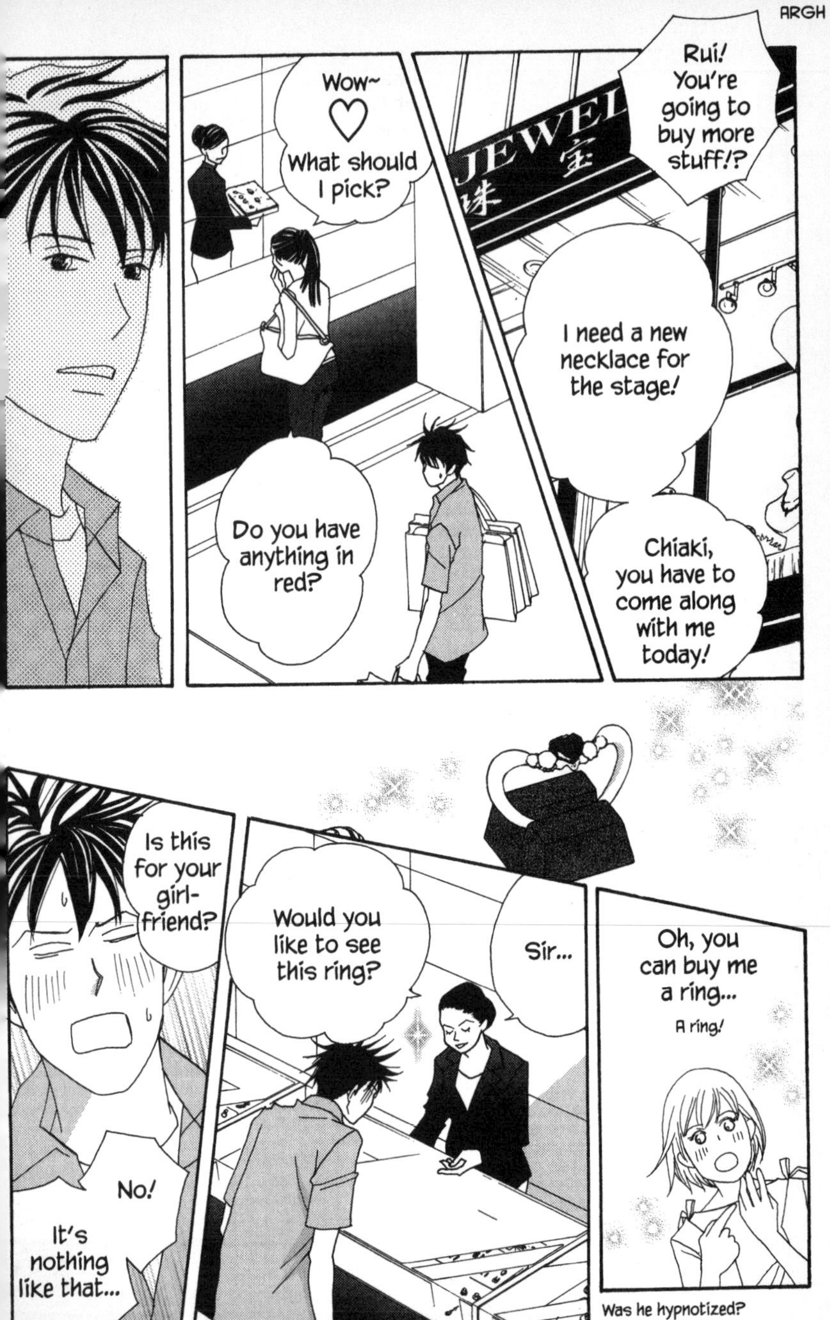
ARGH
Rui! You're going to buy more stuff!?
I need a new necklace for the stage!
Chiaki, you have to come along with me today!
Wow~ ♡ What should I pick?
Do you have anything in red?
Oh, you can buy me a ring...
A ring!
Was he hypnotized?
Sir...
Would you like to see this ring?
Is this for your girl-friend?
No!
It's nothing like that...

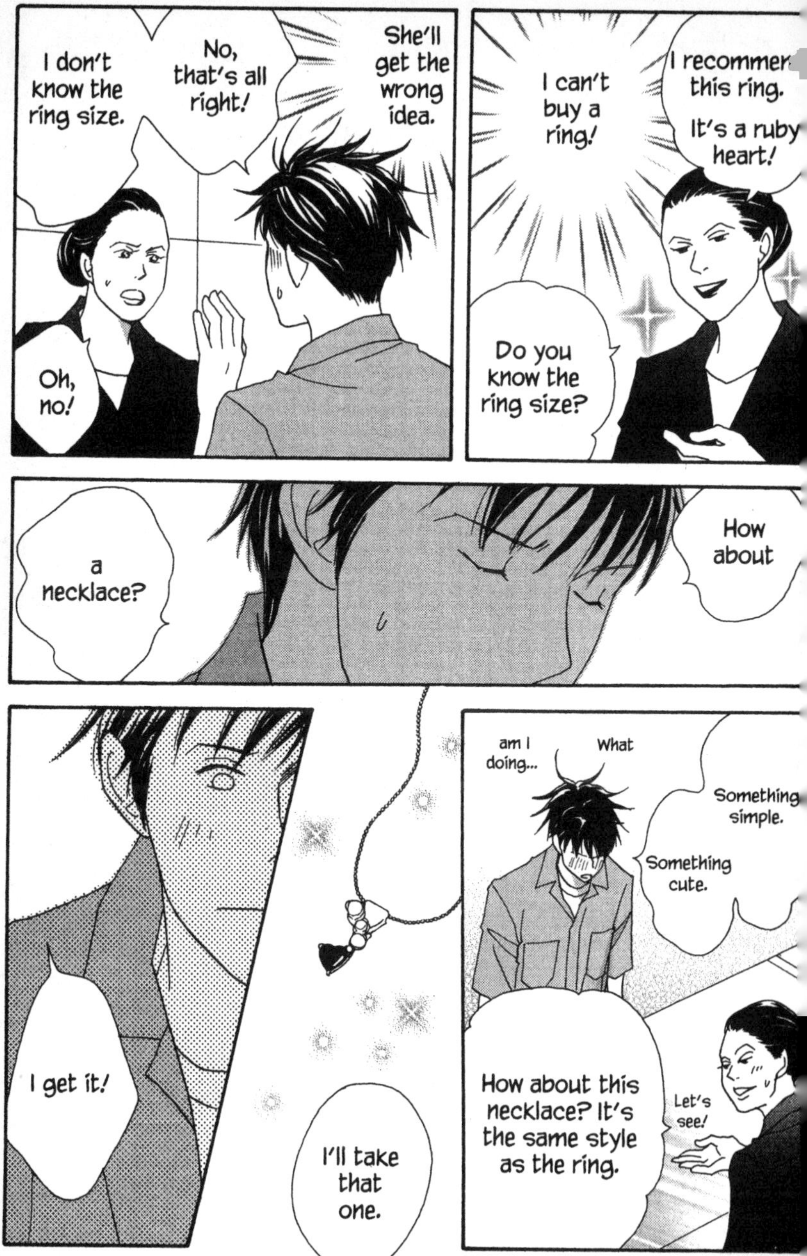
I recommen this ring.
It's a ruby heart!
I can't buy a ring!
Do you know the ring size?
She'll get the wrong idea.
No, that's all right!
I don't know the ring size.
Oh, no!
How about
a necklace?
What am I doing...
Something simple.
Something cute.
Let's see!
How about this necklace? It's the same style as the ring.
I'll take that one.
I get it!

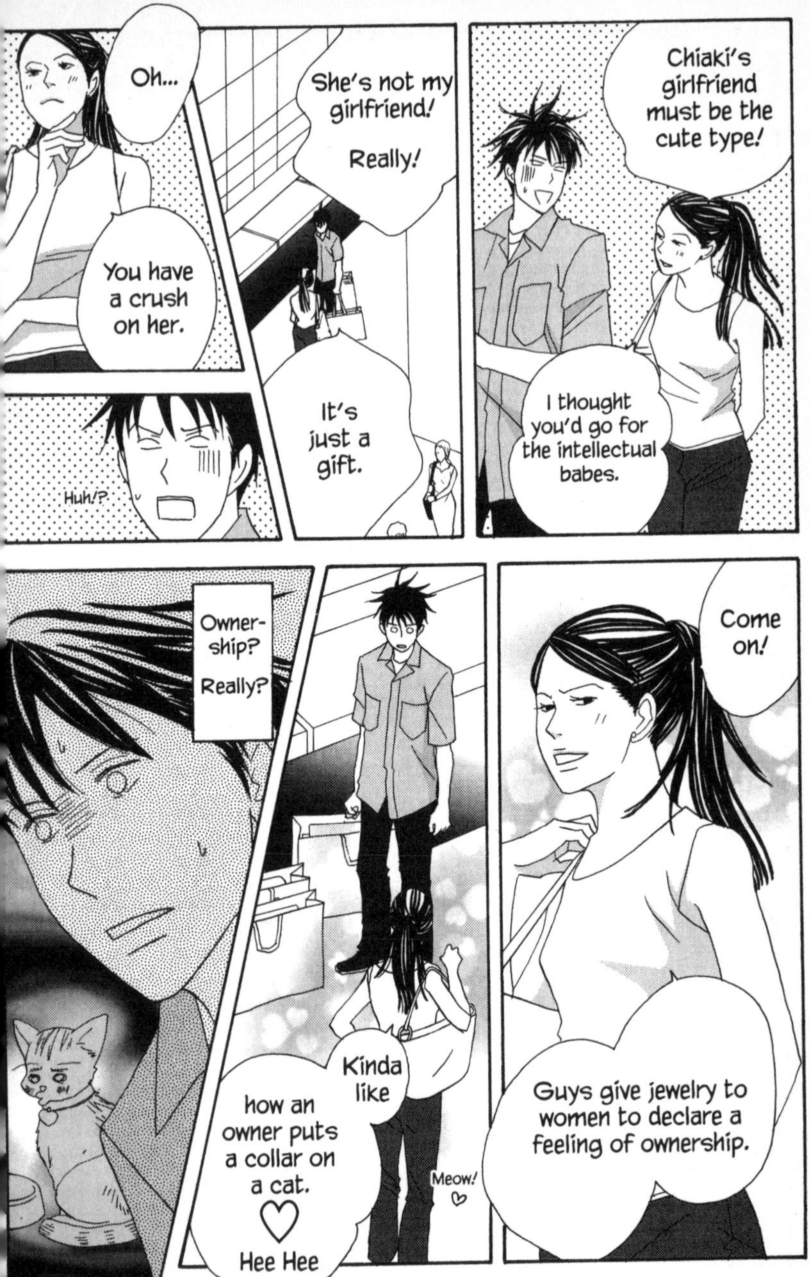

Chiaki's girlfriend must be the cute type!
I thought you'd go for the intellectual babes.
She's not my girlfriend!
Really!
It's just a gift.
Oh...
You have a crush on her.
Huh!?
Come on!
Guys give jewelry to women to declare a feeling of ownership.
Kinda like how an owner puts a collar on a cat. ♡
Hee Hee
Meow! ♡
Owner-ship?
Really?

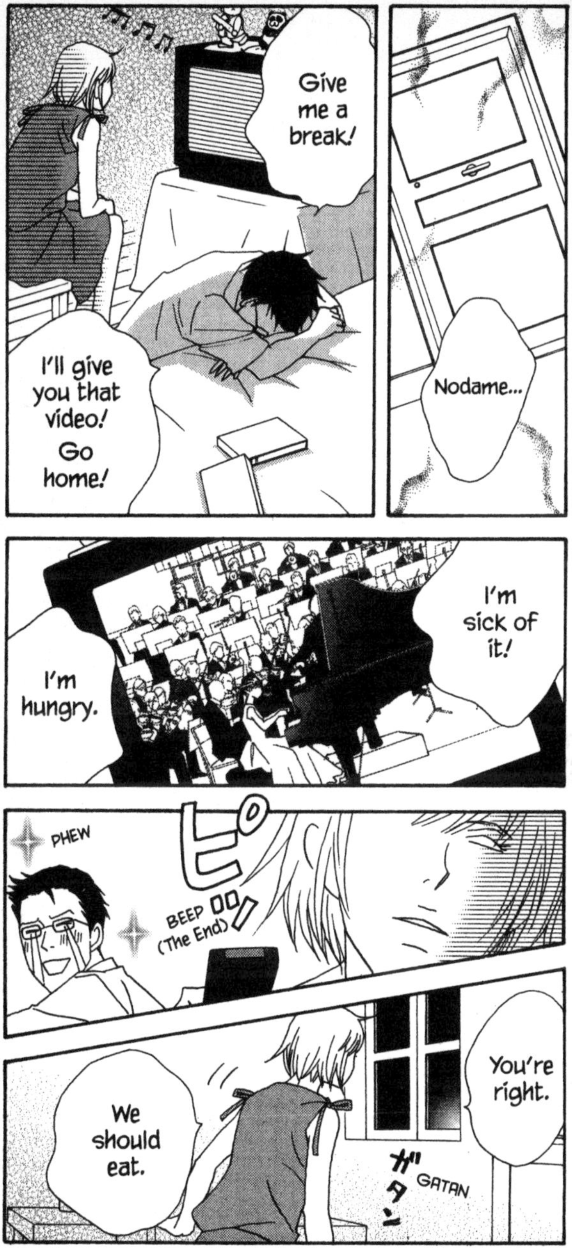
Nodame...
Give me a break!
I'll give you that video! Go home!
I'm sick of it!
I'm hungry.
BEEP
(The End)
PHEW
You're right.
GATAN
We should eat.

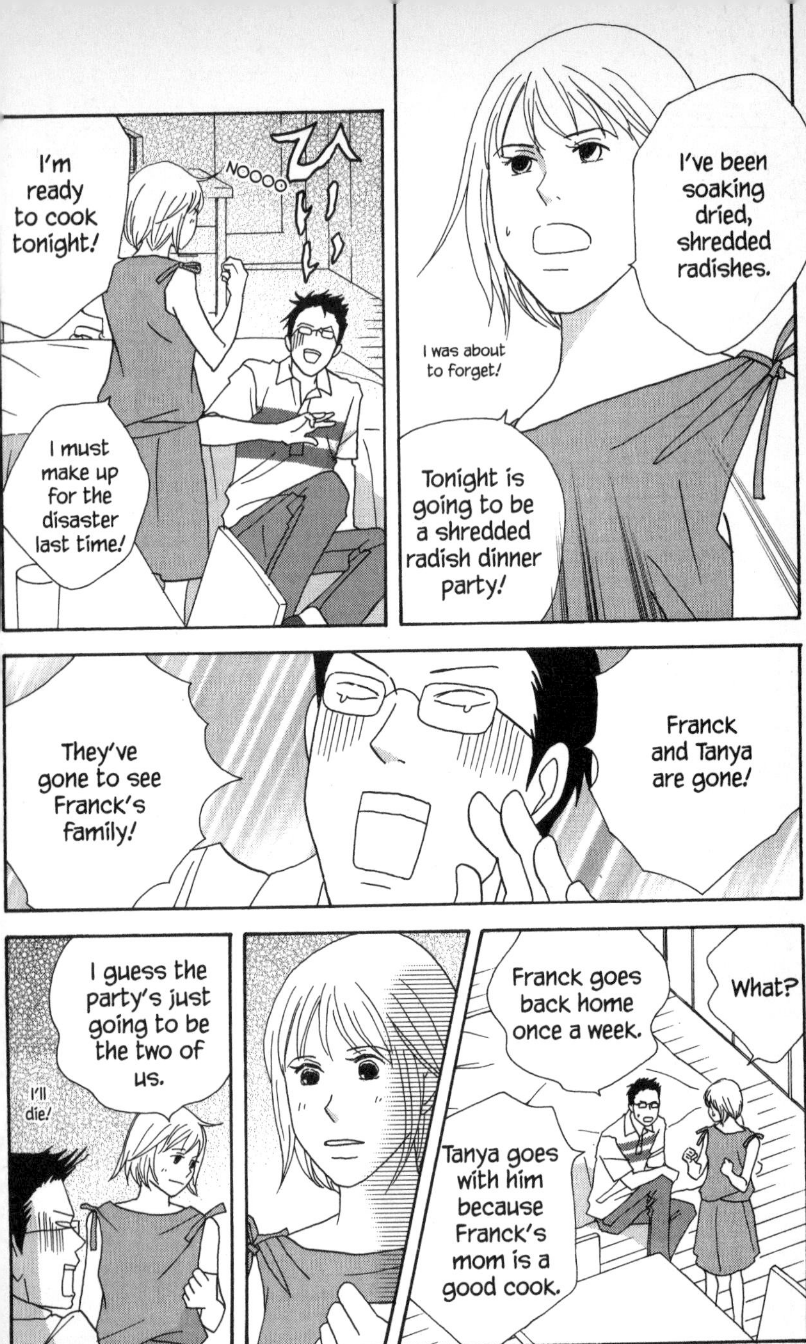
I've been soaking dried, shredded radishes.
I was about to forget!
Tonight is going to be a shredded radish dinner party!
I'm ready to cook tonight!
NOOOO
I must make up for the disaster last time!
Franck and Tanya are gone!
They've gone to see Franck's family!
What?
Franck goes back home once a week.
Tanya goes with him because Franck's mom is a good cook.
I guess the party's just going to be the two of us.
I'll die!

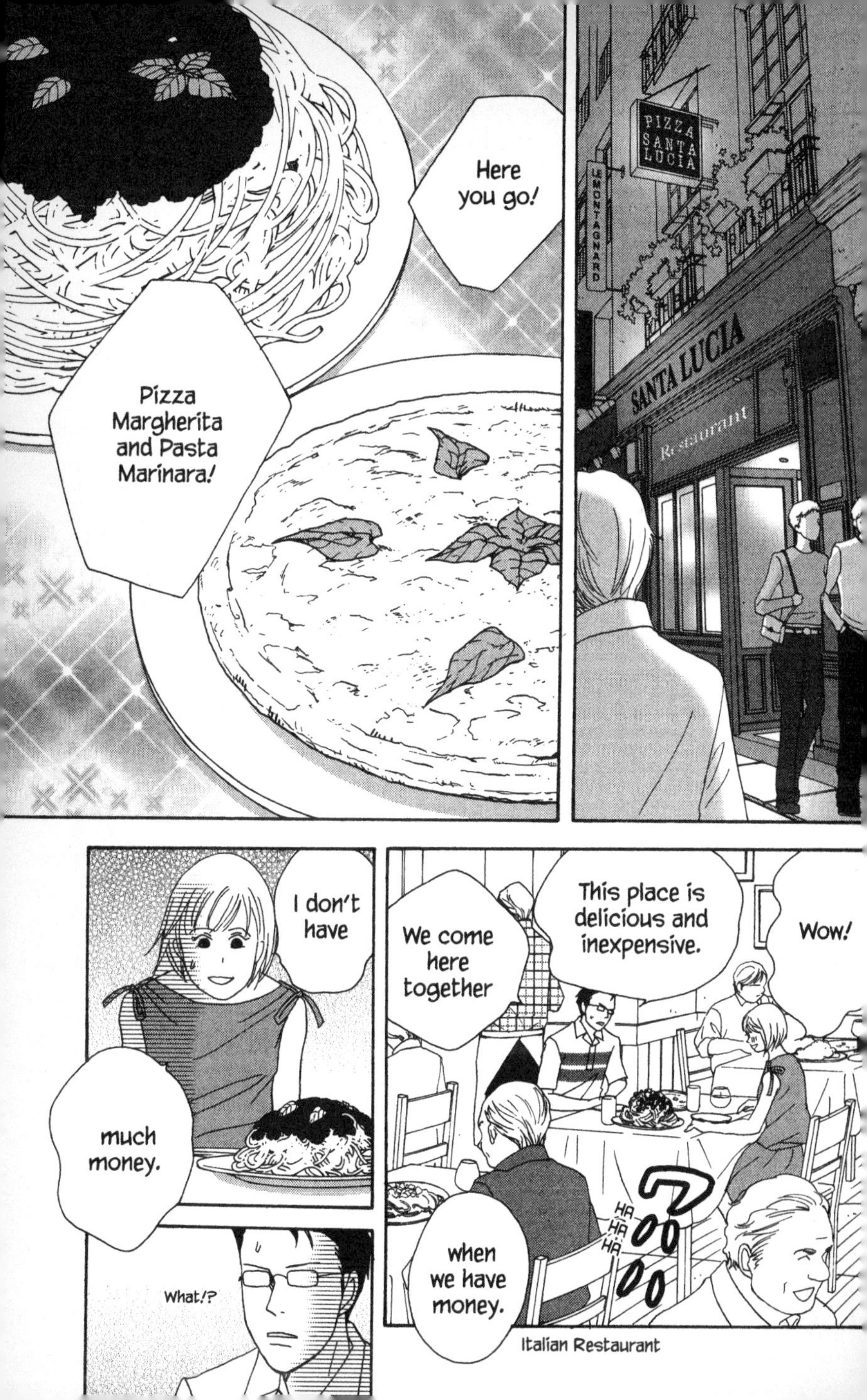
PIZZA SANTA LUCIA
LE MONTAGNARD
SANTA LUCIA
Restaurant
Here you go!
Pizza Margherita and Pasta Marinara!
Wow!
This place is delicious and inexpensive.
We come here together
when we have money.
HA HA HA
Italian Restaurant
I don't have
much money.
What!?

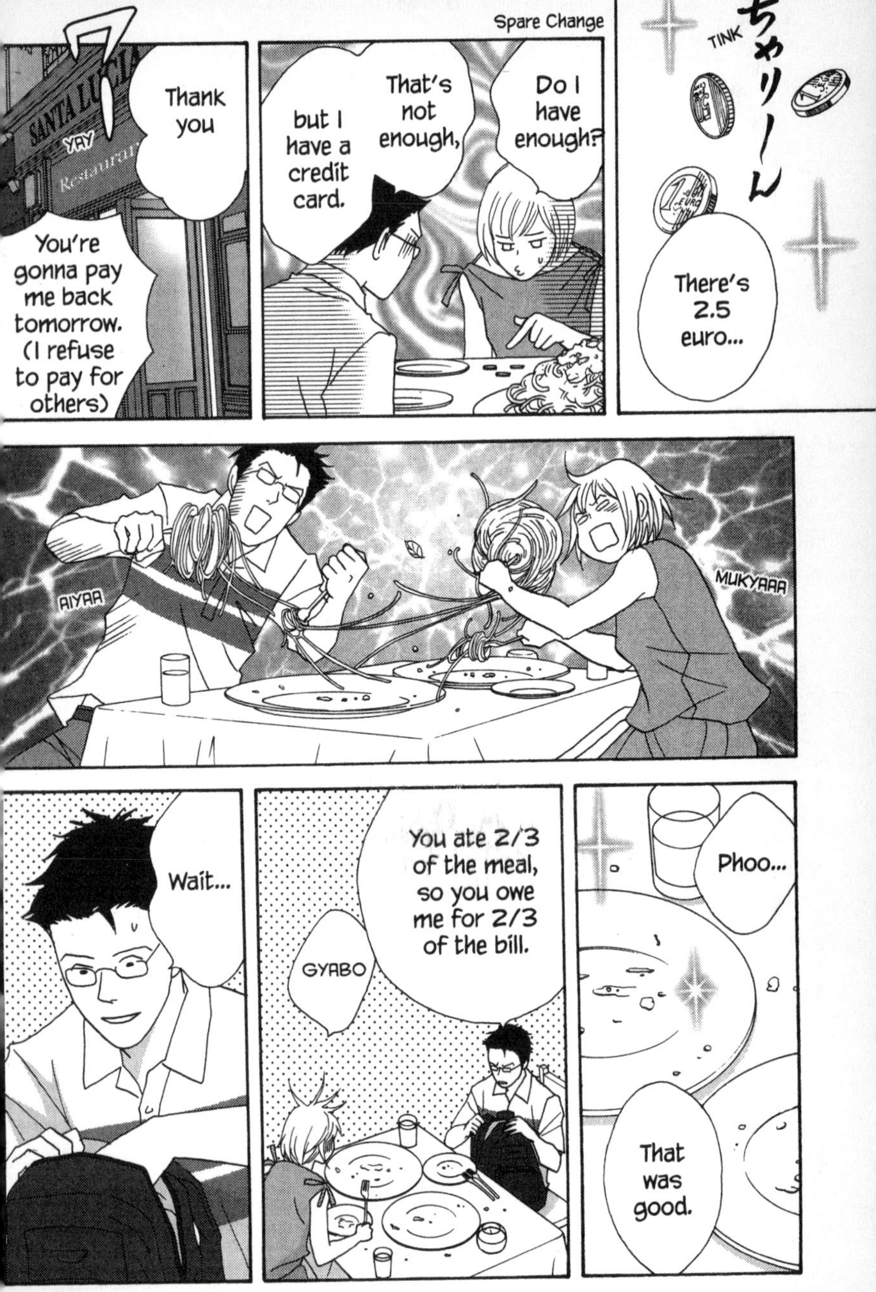
Spare Change
TINK
ちゃりーん
There's 2.5 euro...
Do I have enough?
That's not enough,
but I have a credit card.
Thank you
YAY
You're gonna pay me back tomorrow. (I refuse to pay for others)
MUKYAAA
AIYAA
Phoo...
That was good.
You ate 2/3 of the meal, so you owe me for 2/3 of the bill.
GYABO
Wait...

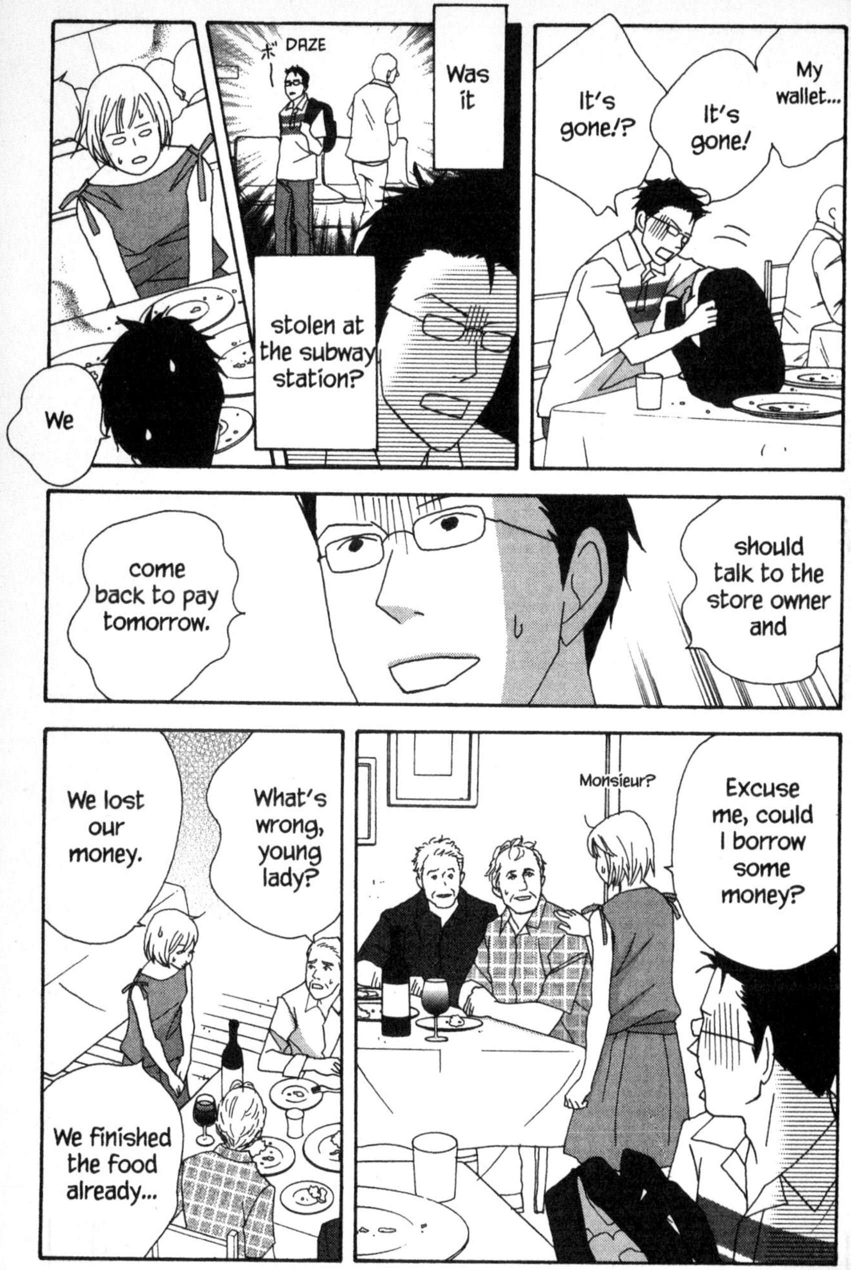
My wallet...
It's gone!
It's gone!?
Was it
ボー
DAZE
stolen at the subway station?
We
should talk to the store owner and
come back to pay tomorrow.
Excuse me, could I borrow some money?
Monsieur?
What's wrong, young lady?
We lost our money.
We finished the food already...

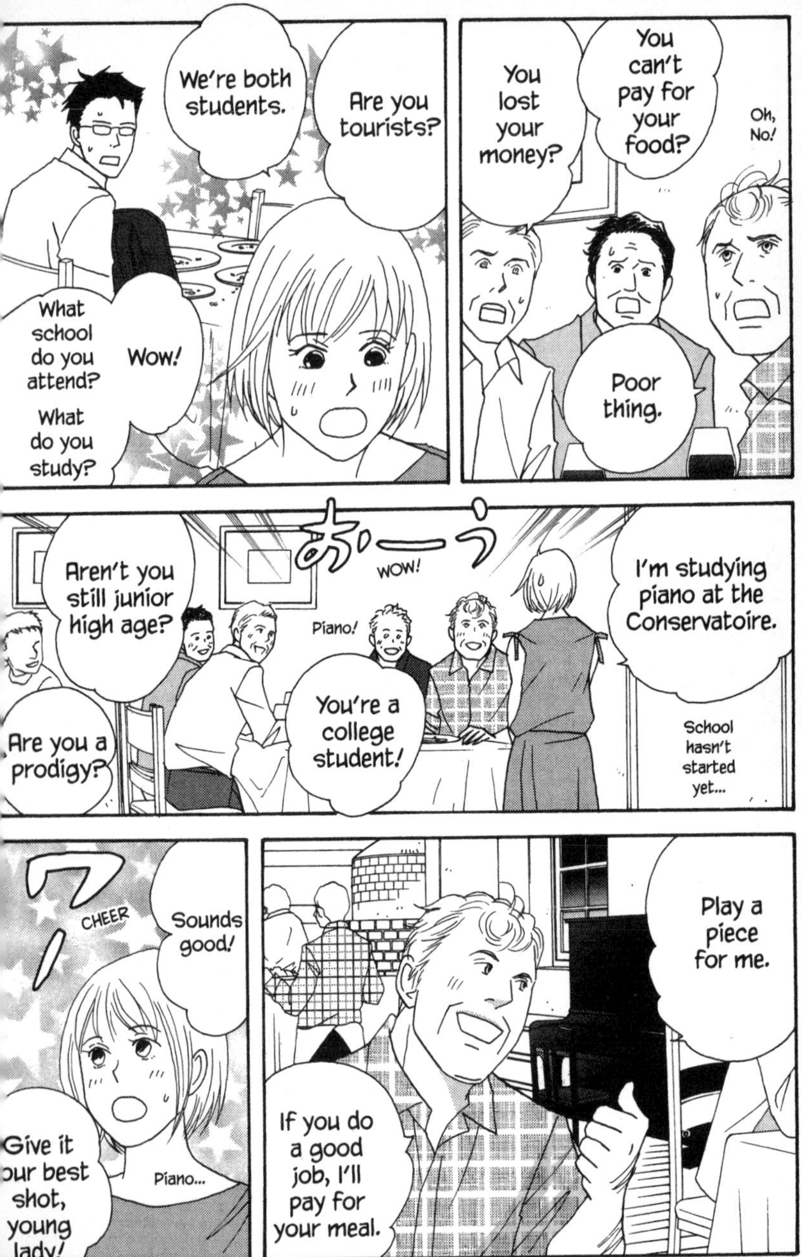
Oh, No!
You can't pay for your food?
You lost your money?
Poor thing.
Are you tourists?
We're both students.
Wow!
What school do you attend?
What do you study?
I'm studying piano at the Conservatoire.
あーう
WOW!
Aren't you still junior high age?
Piano!
School hasn't started yet...
You're a college student!
Are you a prodigy?
Play a piece for me.
If you do a good job, I'll pay for your meal.
Sounds good!
ワー
CHEER
Piano...
Give it our best shot, young lady!

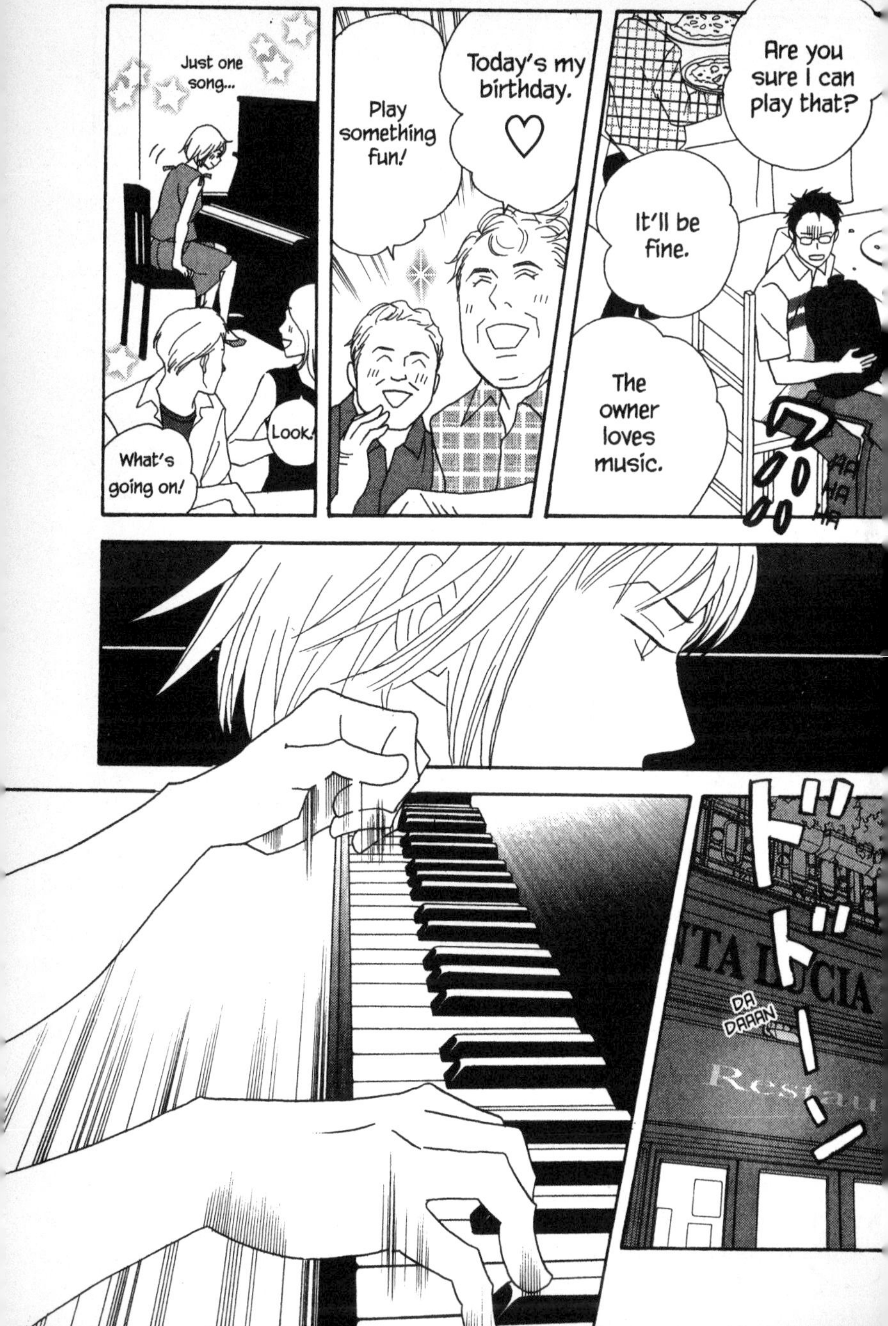
Are you sure I can play that?
It'll be fine.
The owner loves music.
HA HA HA
Today's my birthday. ♡
Play something fun!
Just one song...
Look!
What's going on!
DA DAAAN

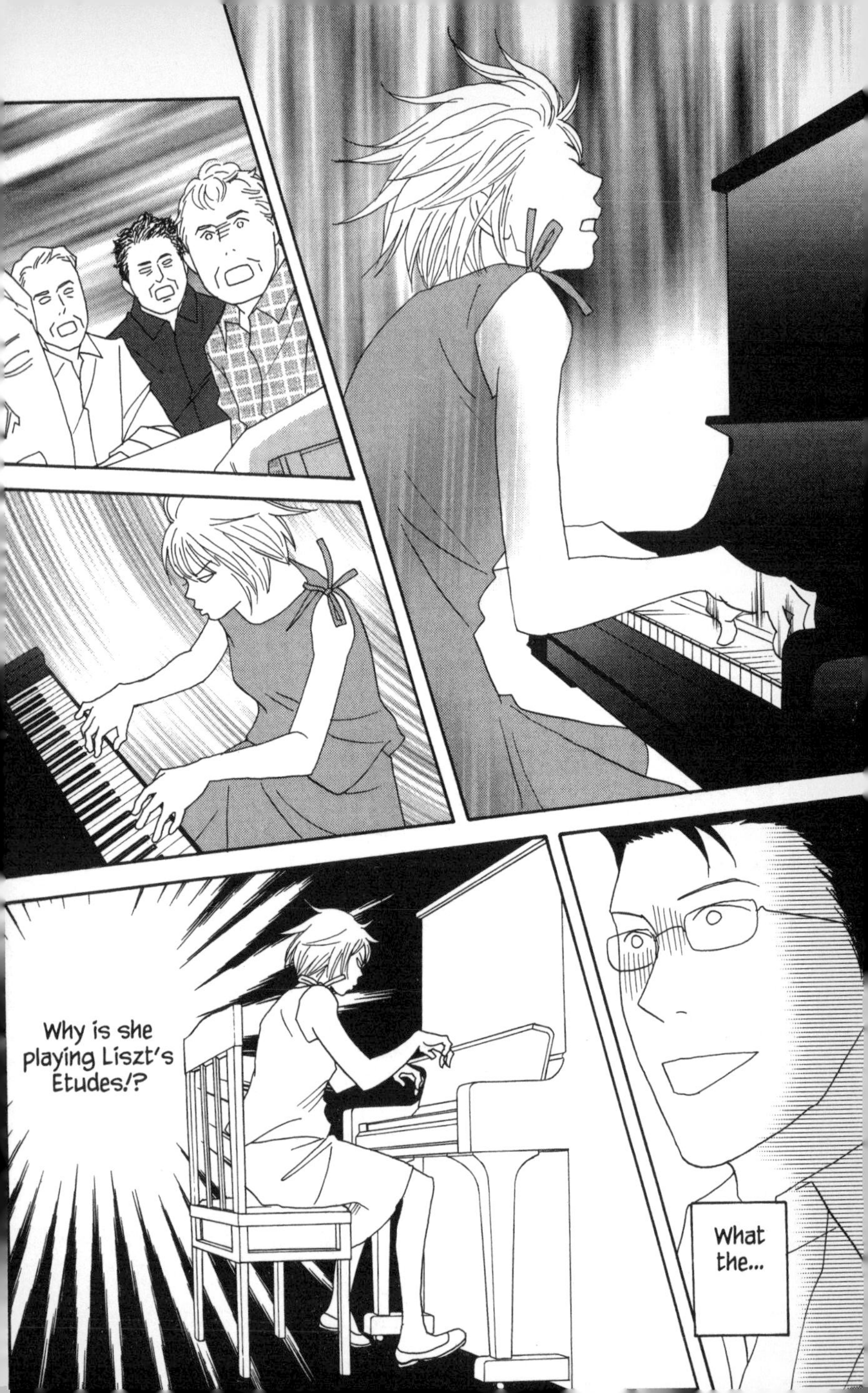
What the...
Why is she playing Liszt's Etudes!?

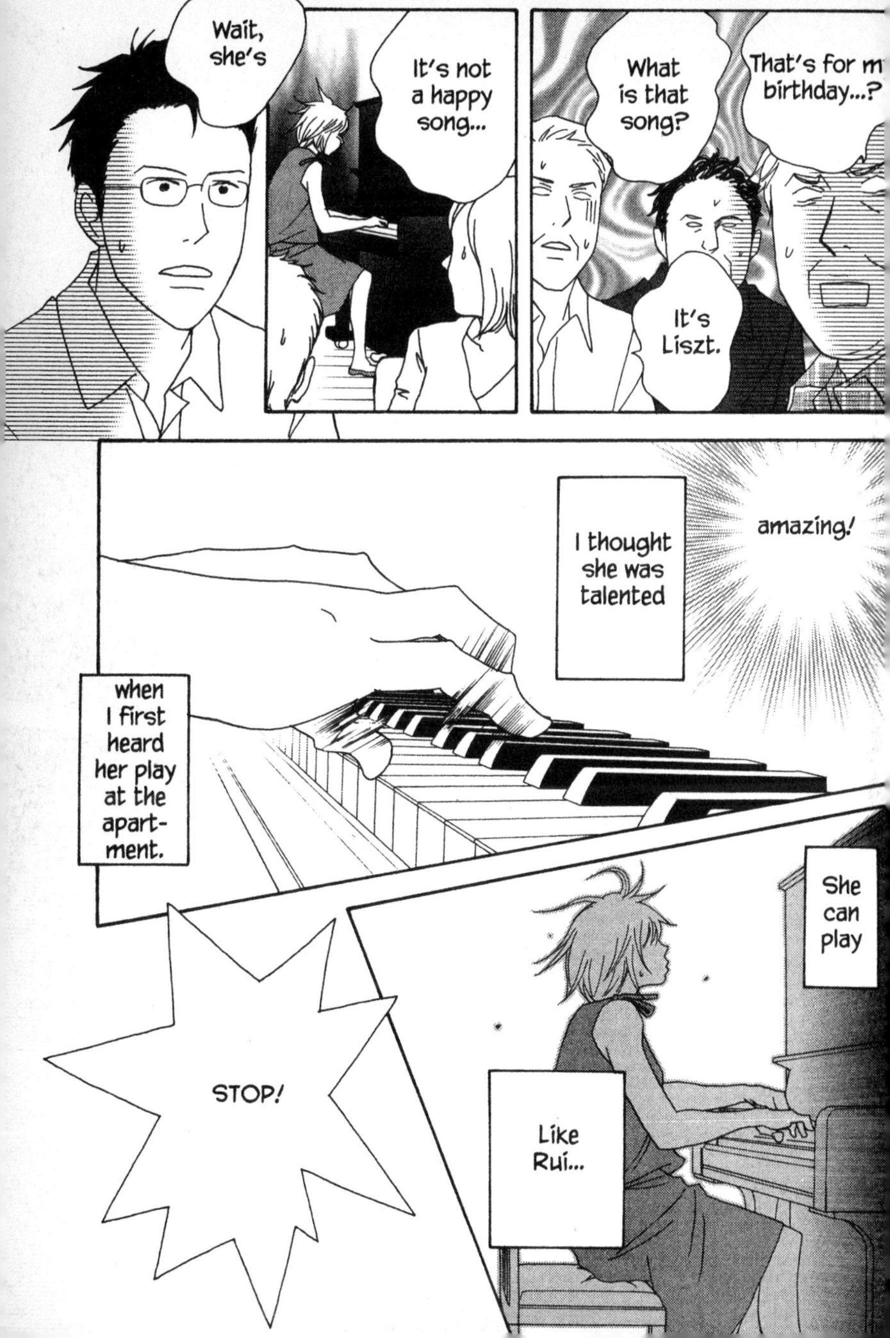

That's for m birthday...?
What is that song?
It's Liszt.
It's not a happy song...
Wait, she's
amazing!
I thought she was talented
when I first heard her play at the apartment.
She can play
Like Rui...
STOP!

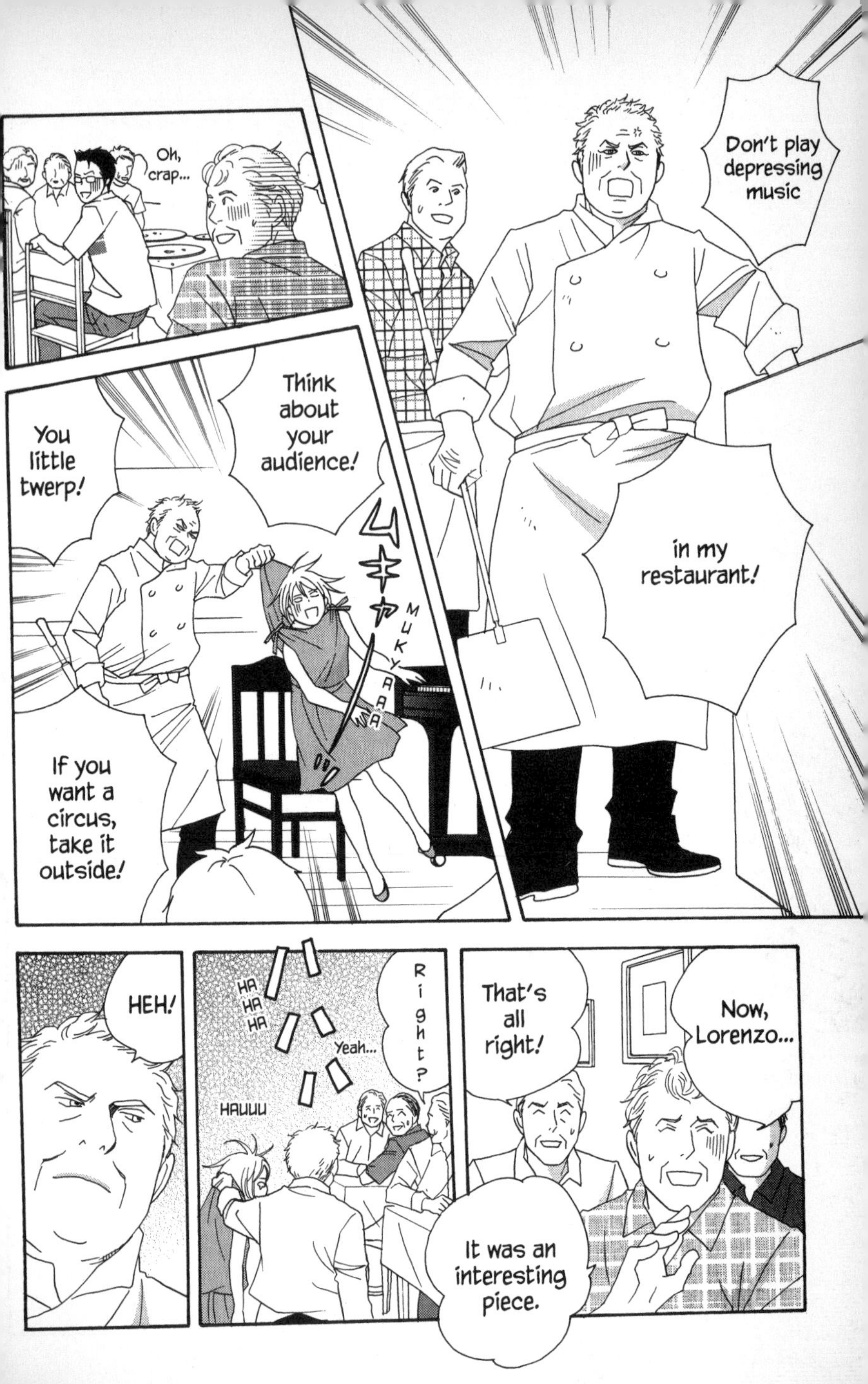
Don't play depressing music
in my restaurant!
Oh, crap...
Think about your audience!
You little twerp!
ムキャ
MUKYAAAA
If you want a circus, take it outside!
Now, Lorenzo...
That's all right!
It was an interesting piece.
Right?
Yeah...
HA HA HA
HAUUU
HEH!

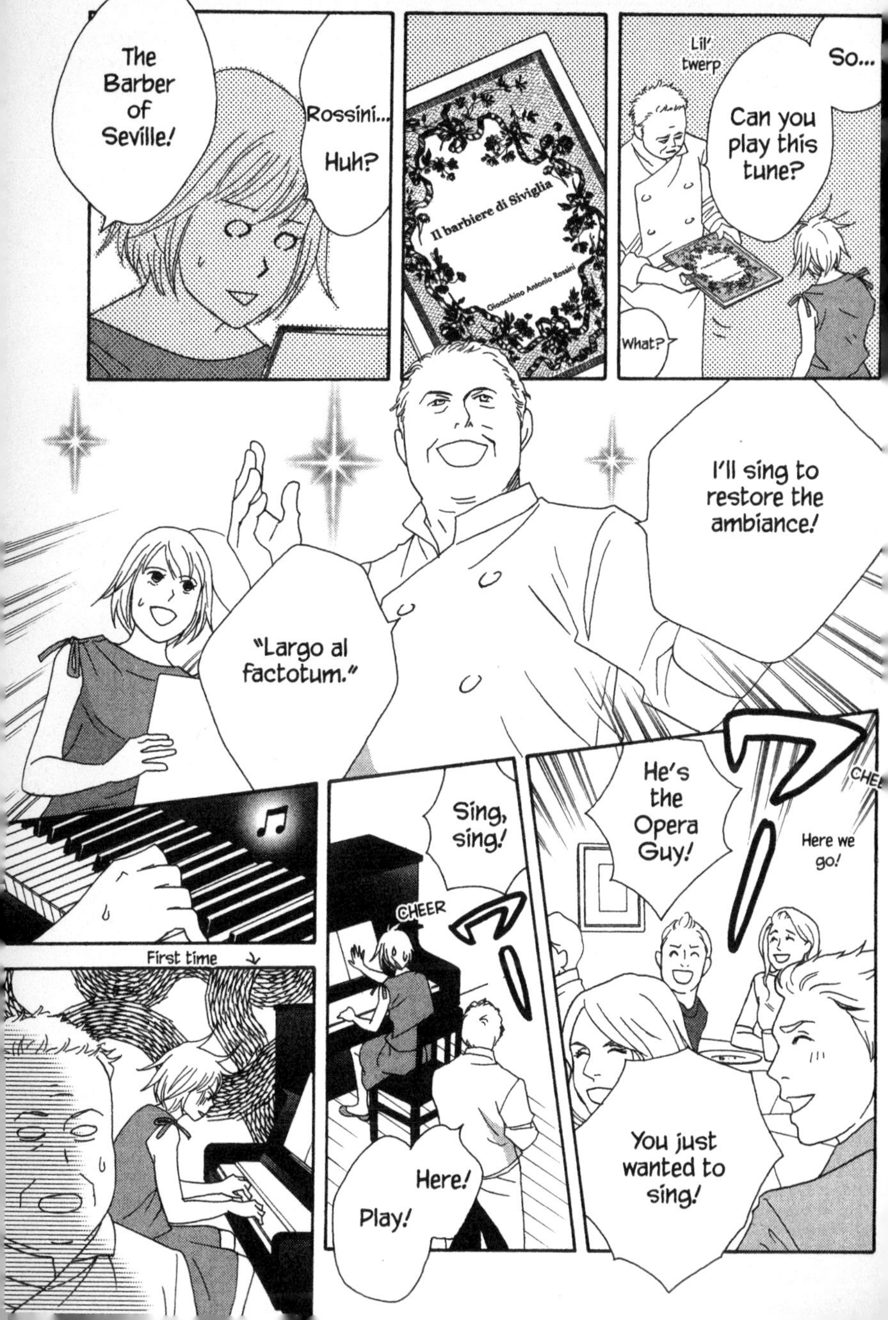
So...
Can you play this tune?
Lil' twerp
What?
Il barbiere di Siviglia
Gioacchino Antonio Rossini
Rossini...
Huh?
The Barber of Seville!
I'll sing to restore the ambiance!
"Largo al factotum."
Here we go!
He's the Opera Guy!
You just wanted to sing!
Sing, sing!
CHEER
Here!
Play!
First time

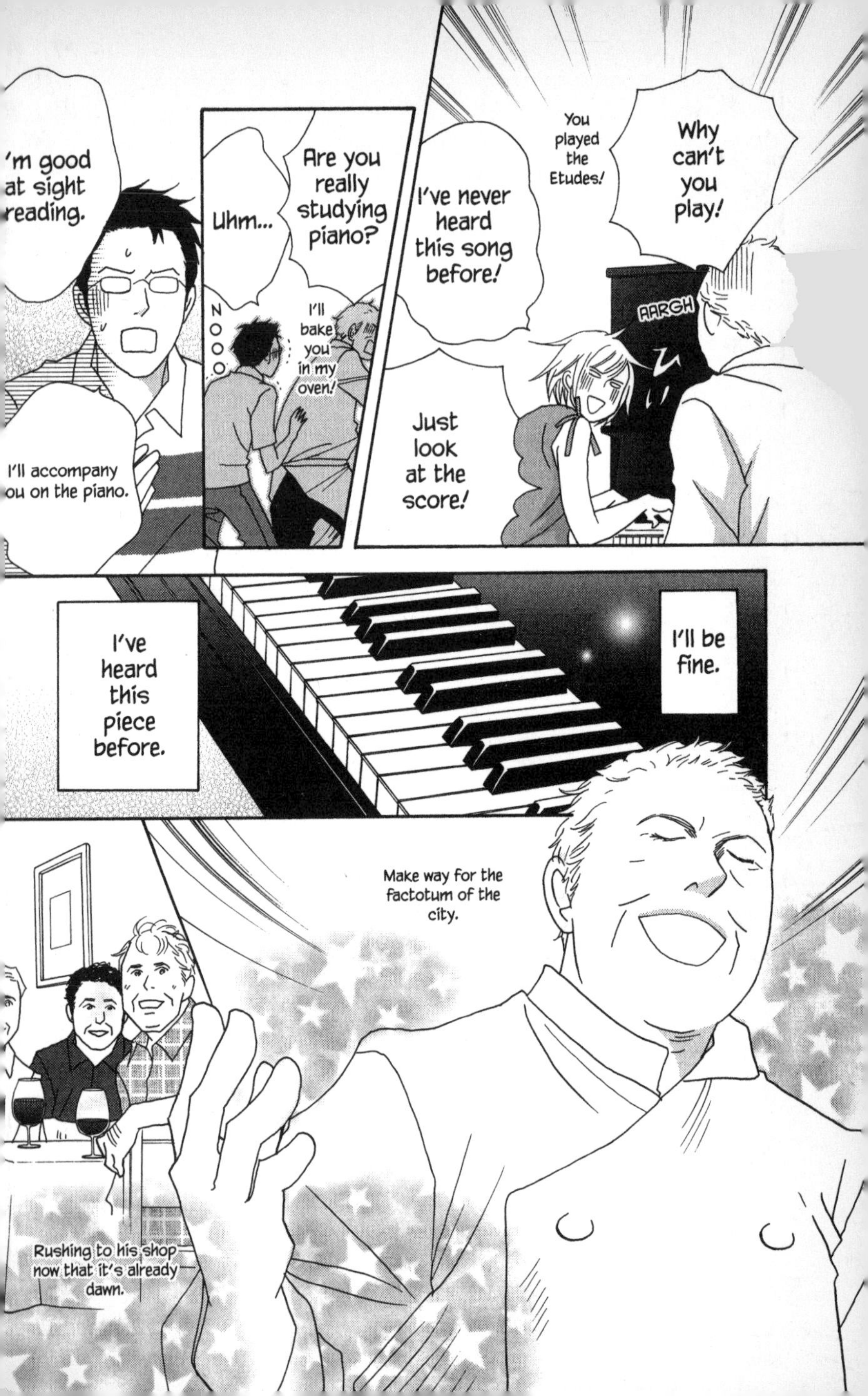
Why can't you play!
You played the Etudes!
AARGH
I've never heard this song before!
Just look at the score!
Are you really studying piano?
Uhm...
I'll bake you in my oven!
NOOOO
'm good at sight reading.
I'll accompany ou on the piano.
I'll be fine.
I've heard this piece before.
Make way for the factotum of the city.
Rushing to his shop now that it's already dawn.

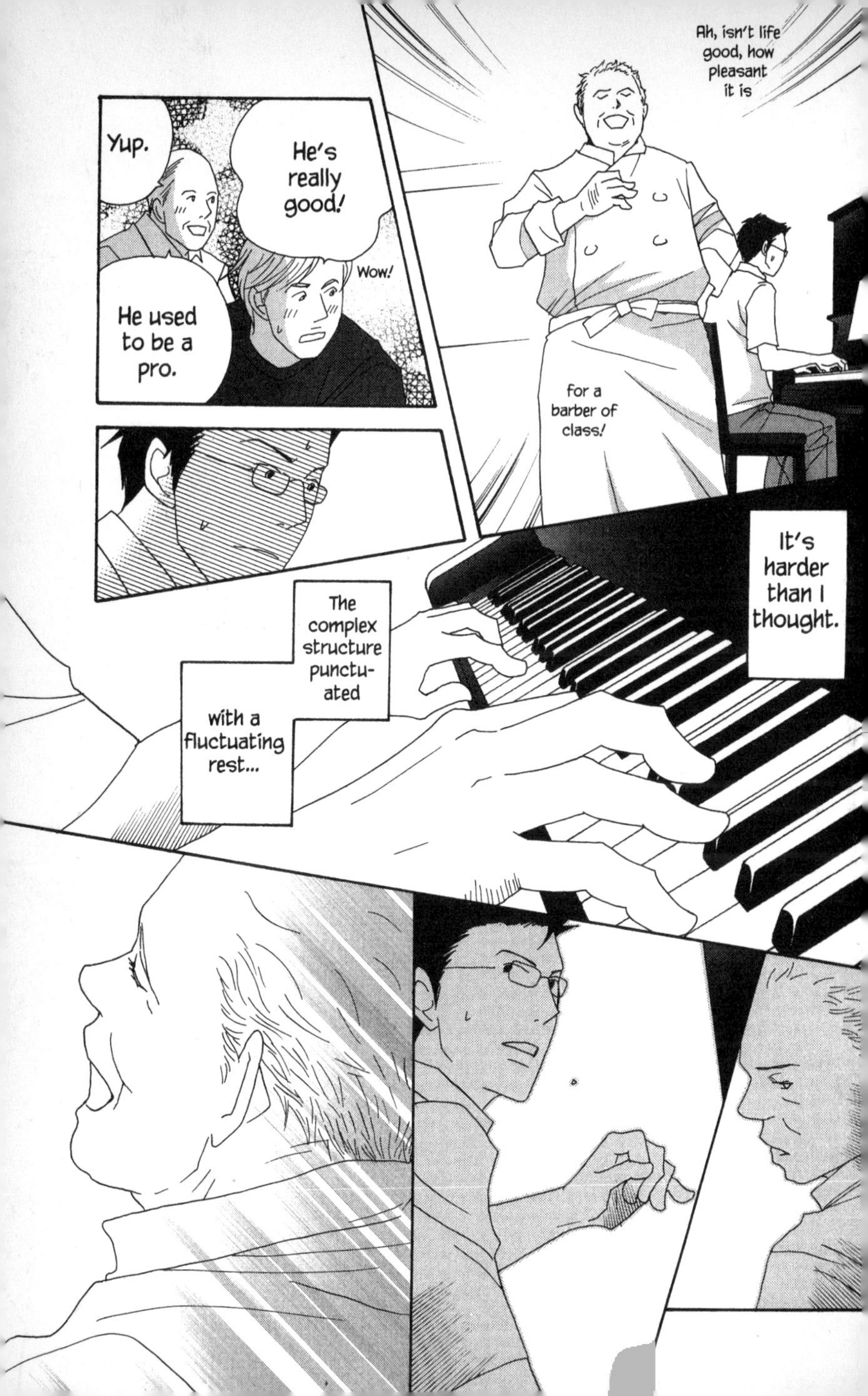
Ah, isn't life good, how pleasant it is
for a barber of class!
He's really good!
Yup.
Wow!
He used to be a pro.
It's harder than I thought.
The complex structure punctuated
with a fluctuating rest...

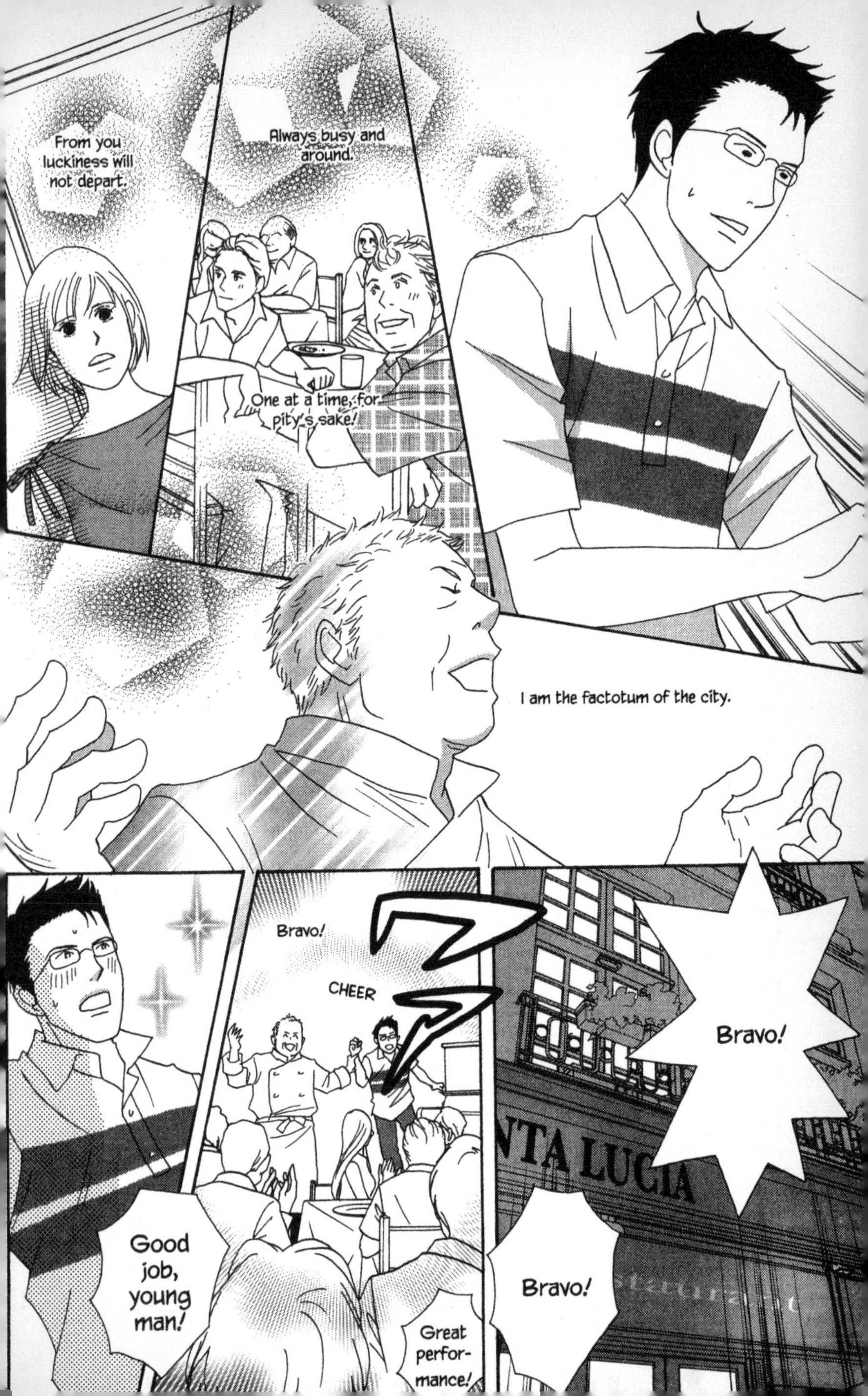
Always busy and around.
One at a time, for pity's sake!
From you luckiness will not depart.
I am the factotum of the city.
Bravo!
NTA LUCIA
Bravo!
Bravo!
CHEER
Great perfor-mance!
Good job, young man!

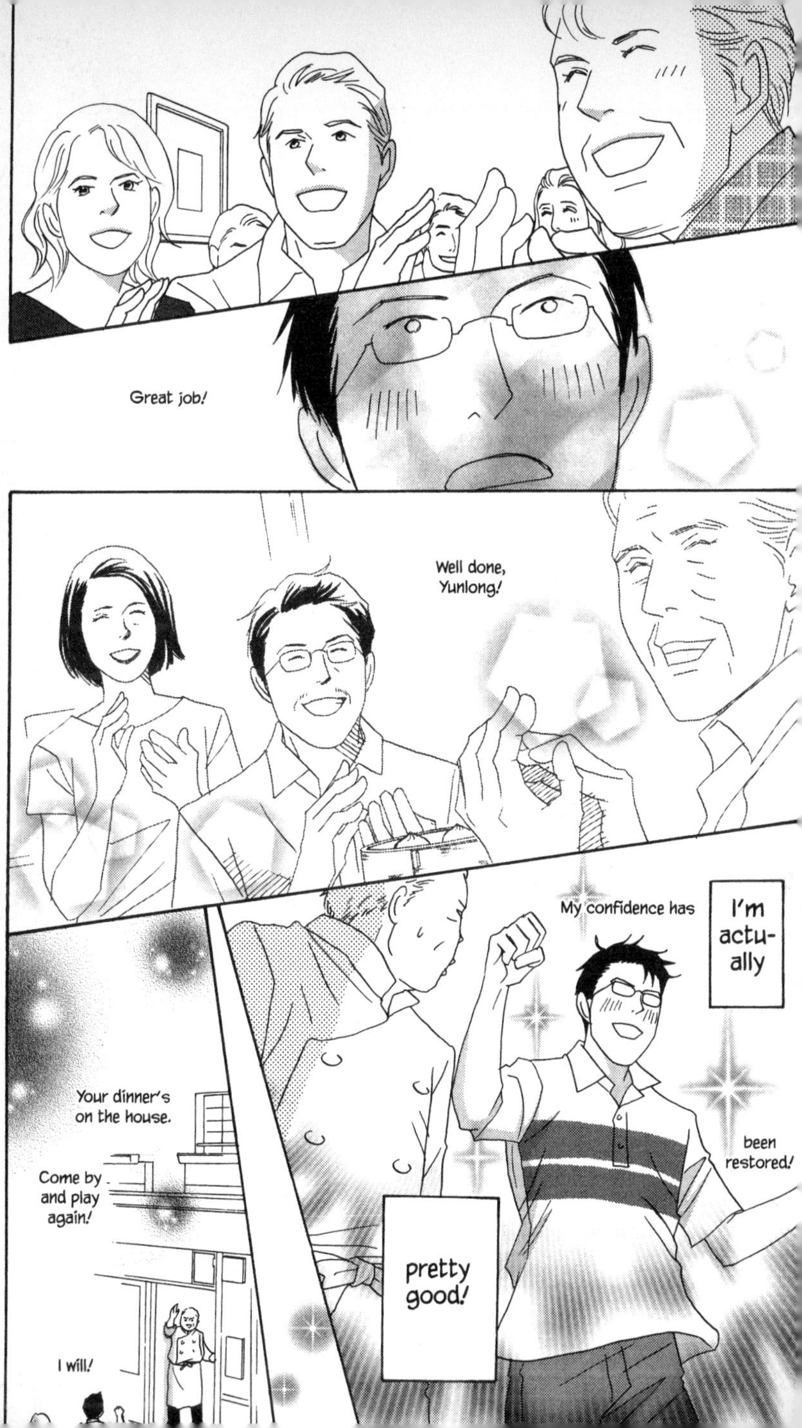
Great job!
Well done, Yunlong!
I'm actually
My confidence has
been restored!
pretty good!
Your dinner's on the house.
Come by and play again!
I will!

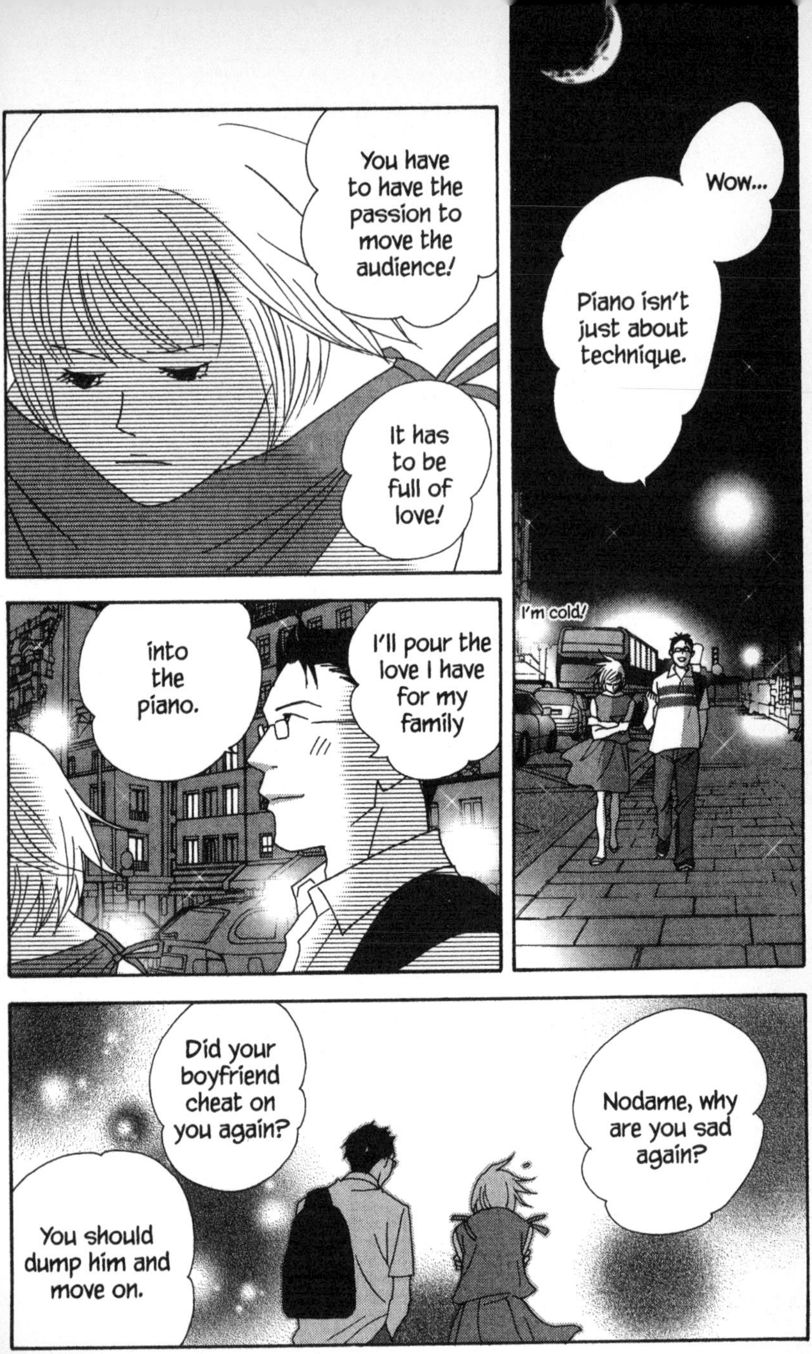
Wow...
Piano isn't just about technique.
I'm cold!
You have to have the passion to move the audience!
It has to be full of love!
I'll pour the love I have for my family
into the piano.
Nodame, why are you sad again?
Did your boyfriend cheat on you again?
You should dump him and move on.

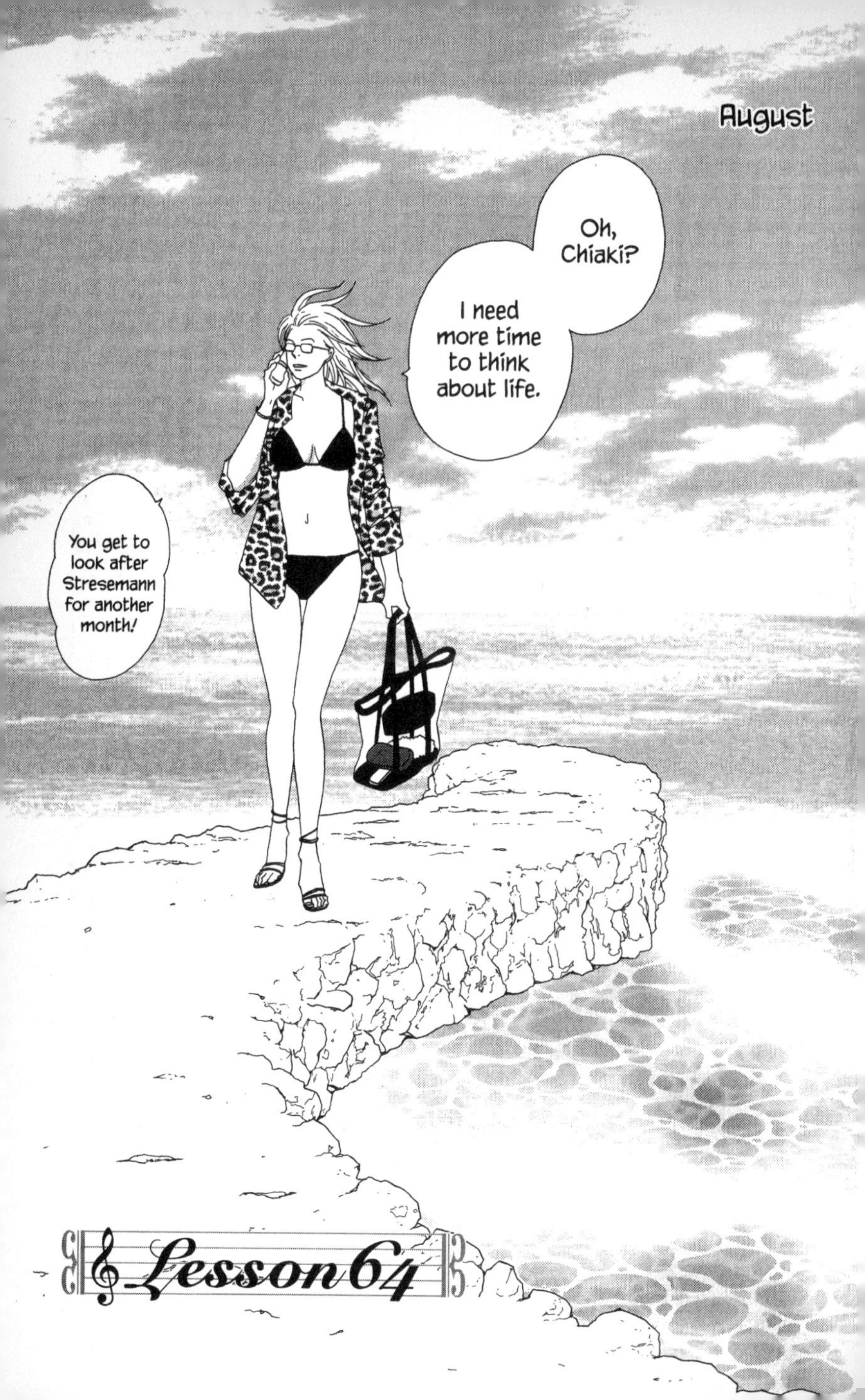
August
Oh, Chiaki?
I need more time to think about life.
You get to look after Stresemann for another month!
Lesson 64

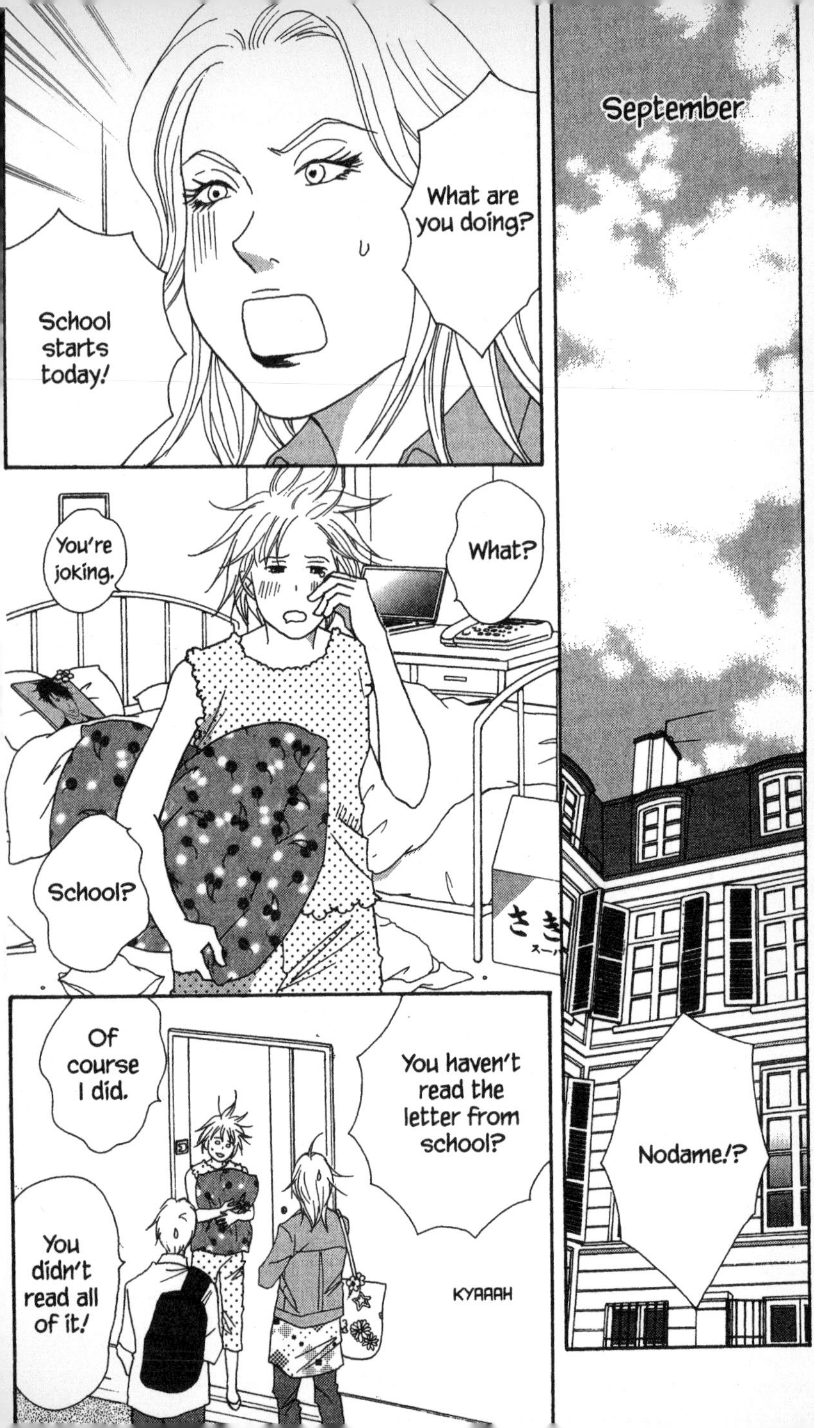
September
Nodame!?
What are you doing?
School starts today!
What?
You're joking.
School?
You haven't read the letter from school?
Of course I did.
KYAAAH
You didn't read all of it!

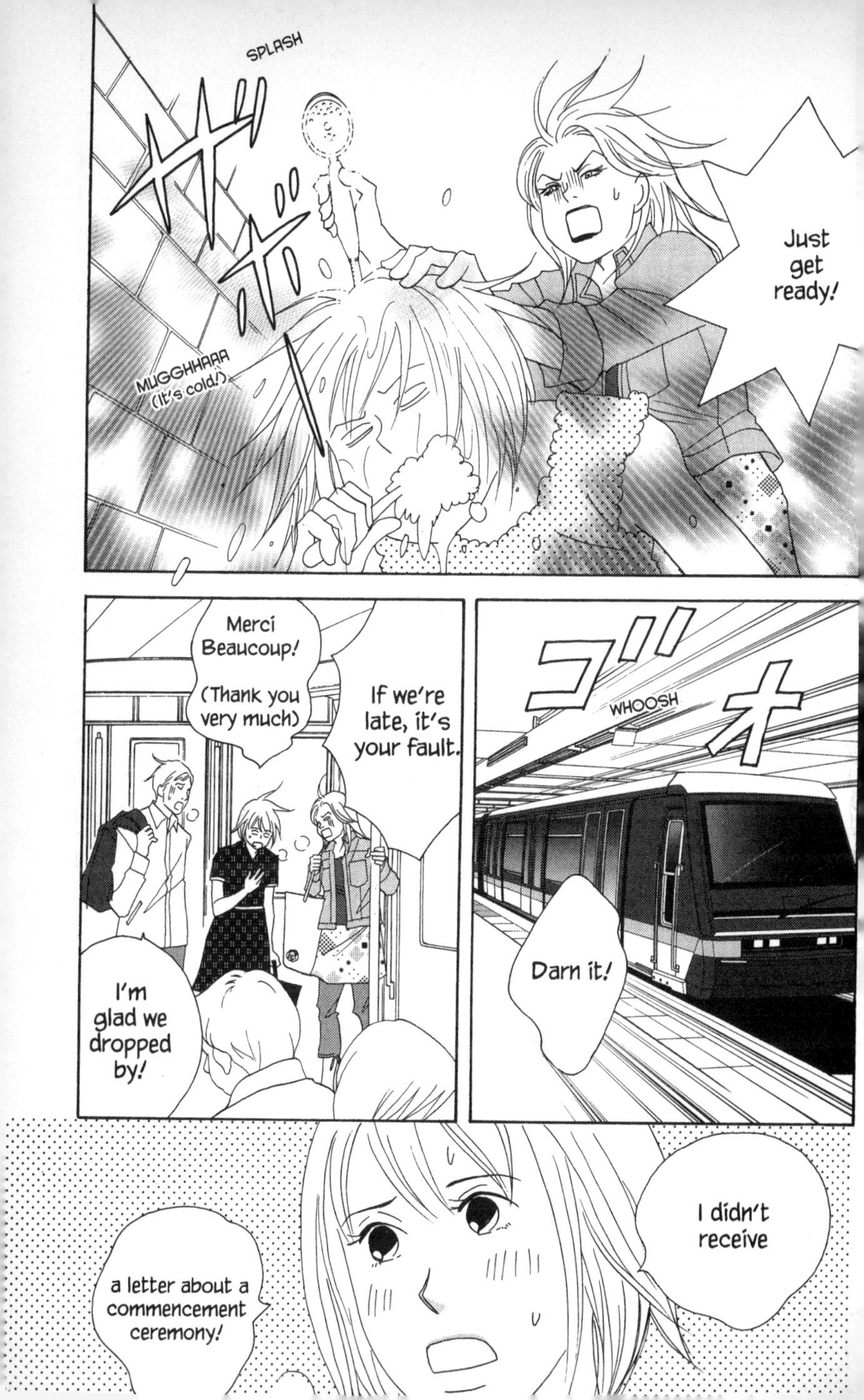
Just get ready!
SPLASH
MUGGHHAAA (It's cold!)
WHOOSH
Darn it!
If we're late, it's your fault.
Merci Beaucoup! (Thank you very much)
I'm glad we dropped by!
I didn't receive
a letter about a commencement ceremony!

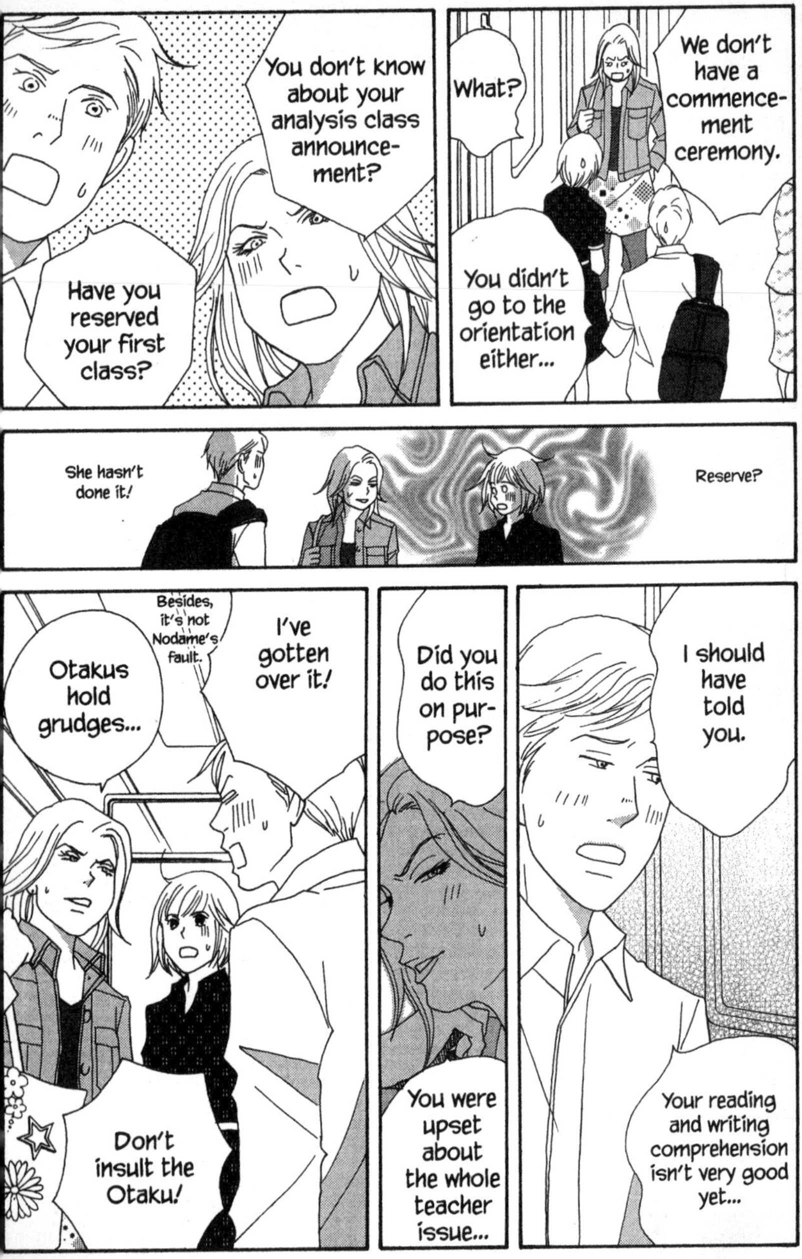
We don't have a commencement ceremony.
What?
You didn't go to the orientation either...
You don't know about your analysis class announcement?
Have you reserved your first class?
Reserve?
She hasn't done it!
I should have told you.
Your reading and writing comprehension isn't very good yet...
Did you do this on purpose?
You were upset about the whole teacher issue...
I've gotten over it!
Besides, it's not Nodame's fault.
Otakus hold grudges...
Don't insult the Otaku!

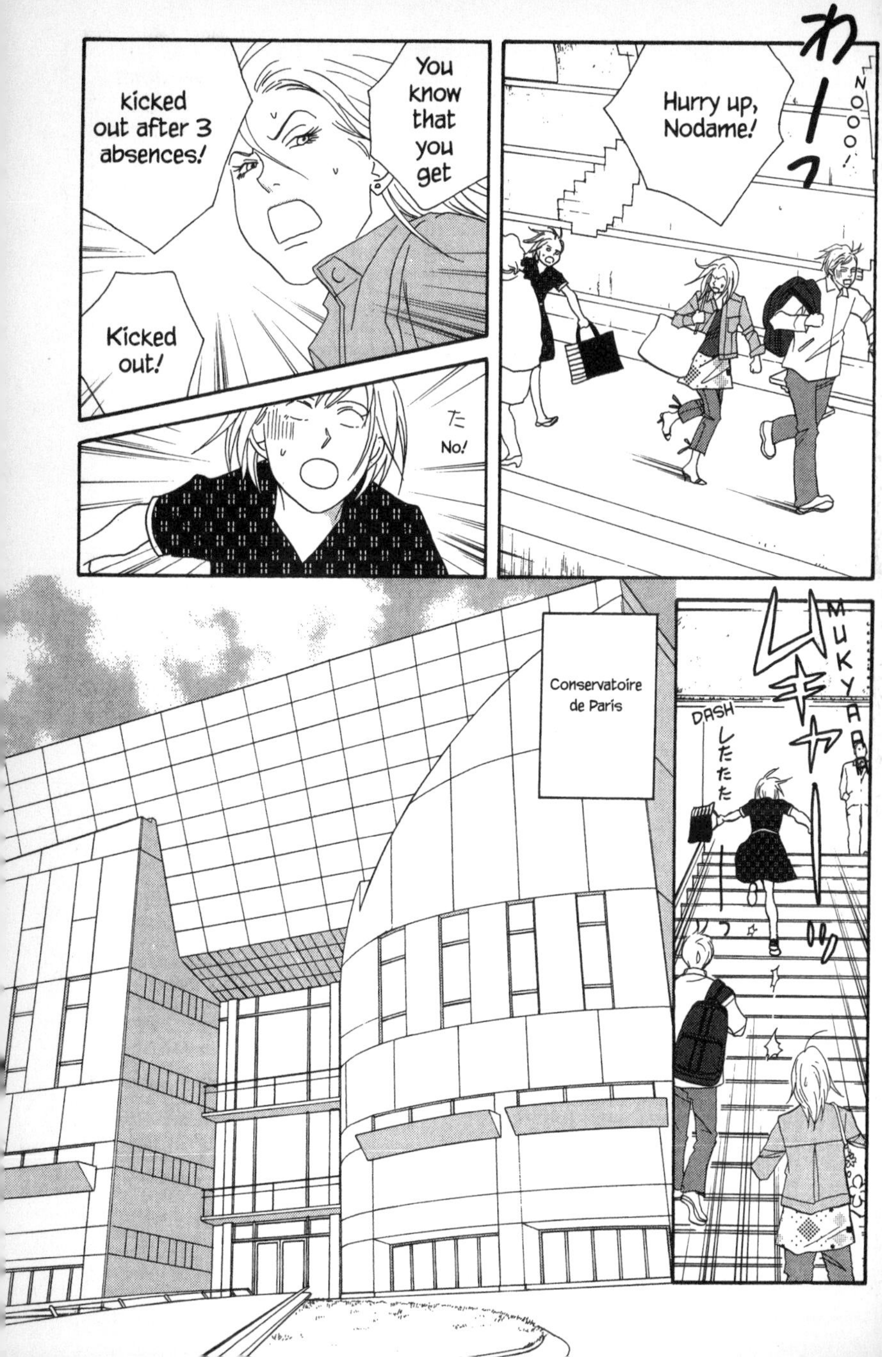
NOOOO!
Hurry up, Nodame!
You know that you get
kicked out after 3 absences!
Kicked out!
た
No!
MUKYAA
DASH
したたた
Conservatoire de Paris

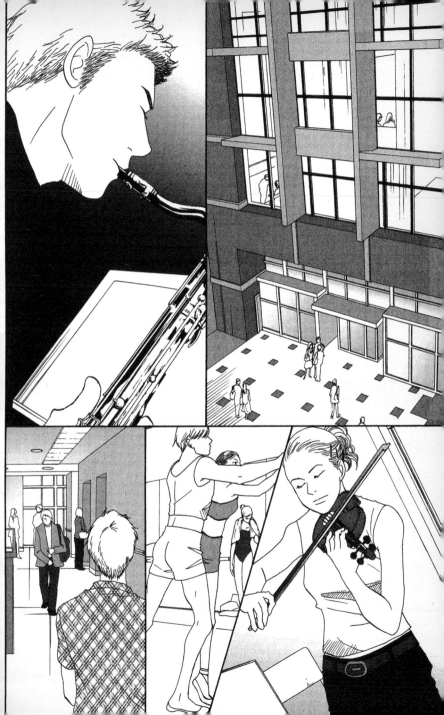

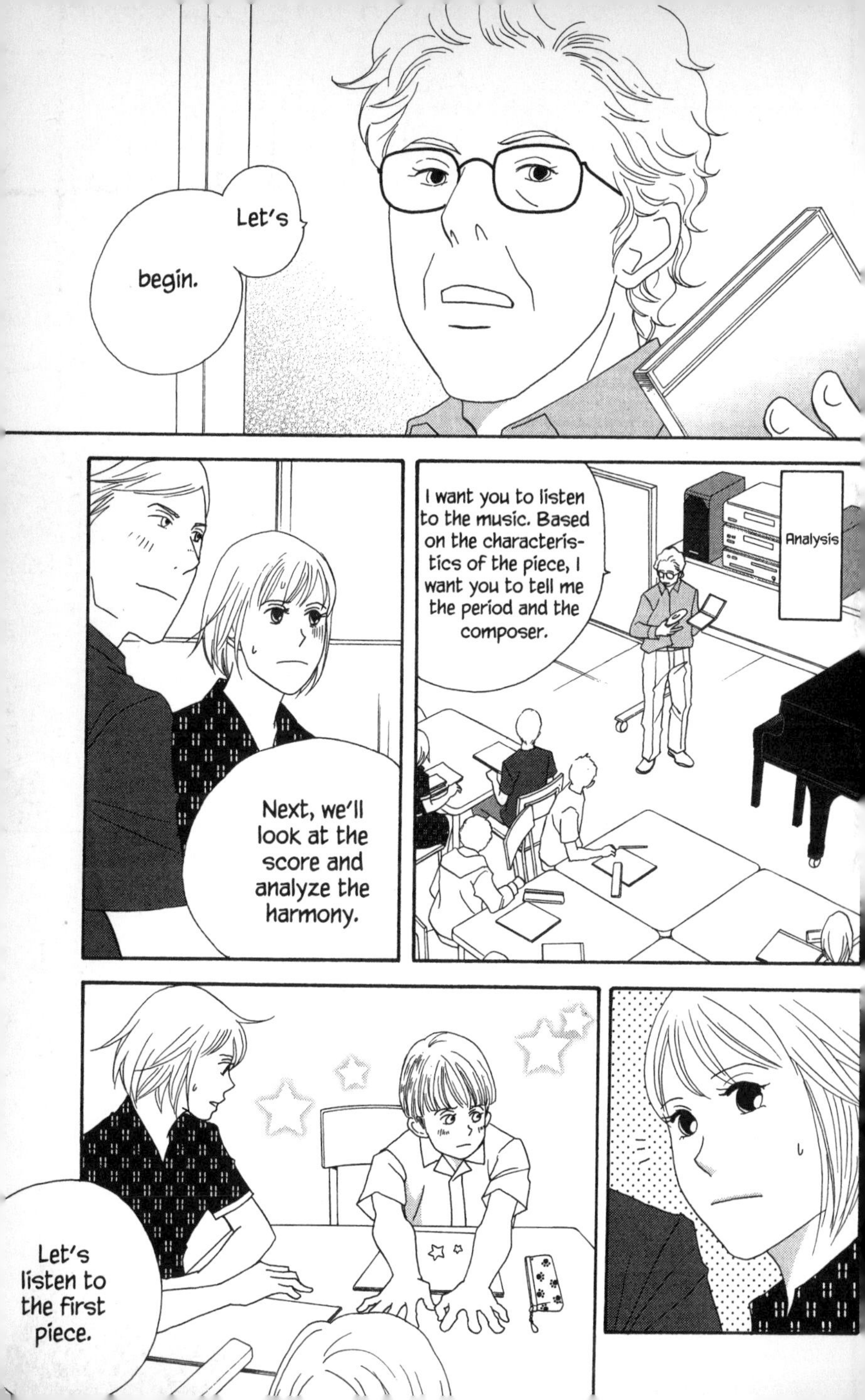
Let's begin.
Analysis
I want you to listen to the music. Based on the characteristics of the piece, I want you to tell me the period and the composer.
Next, we'll look at the score and analyze the harmony.
Let's listen to the first piece.

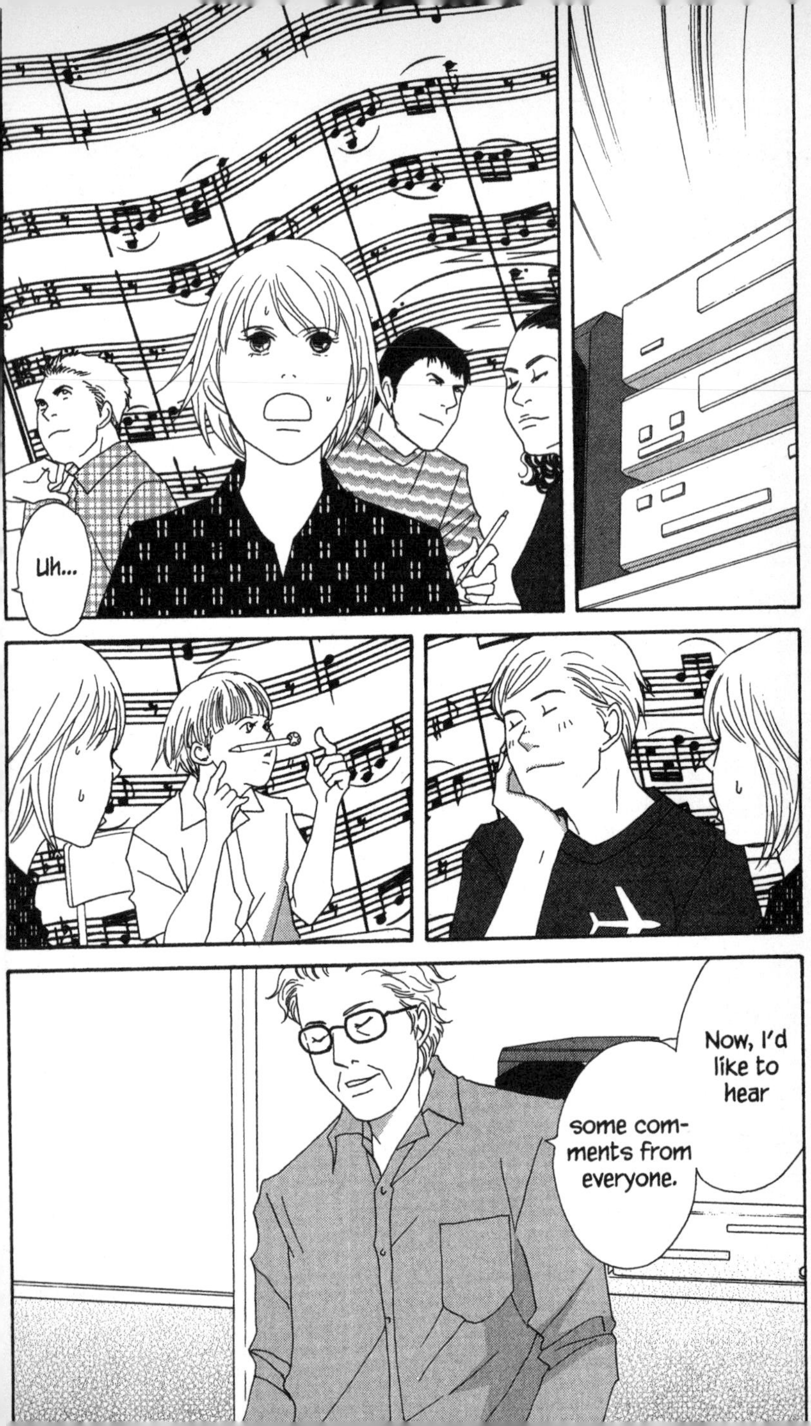
Uh...
Now, I'd like to hear
some com-ments from everyone.

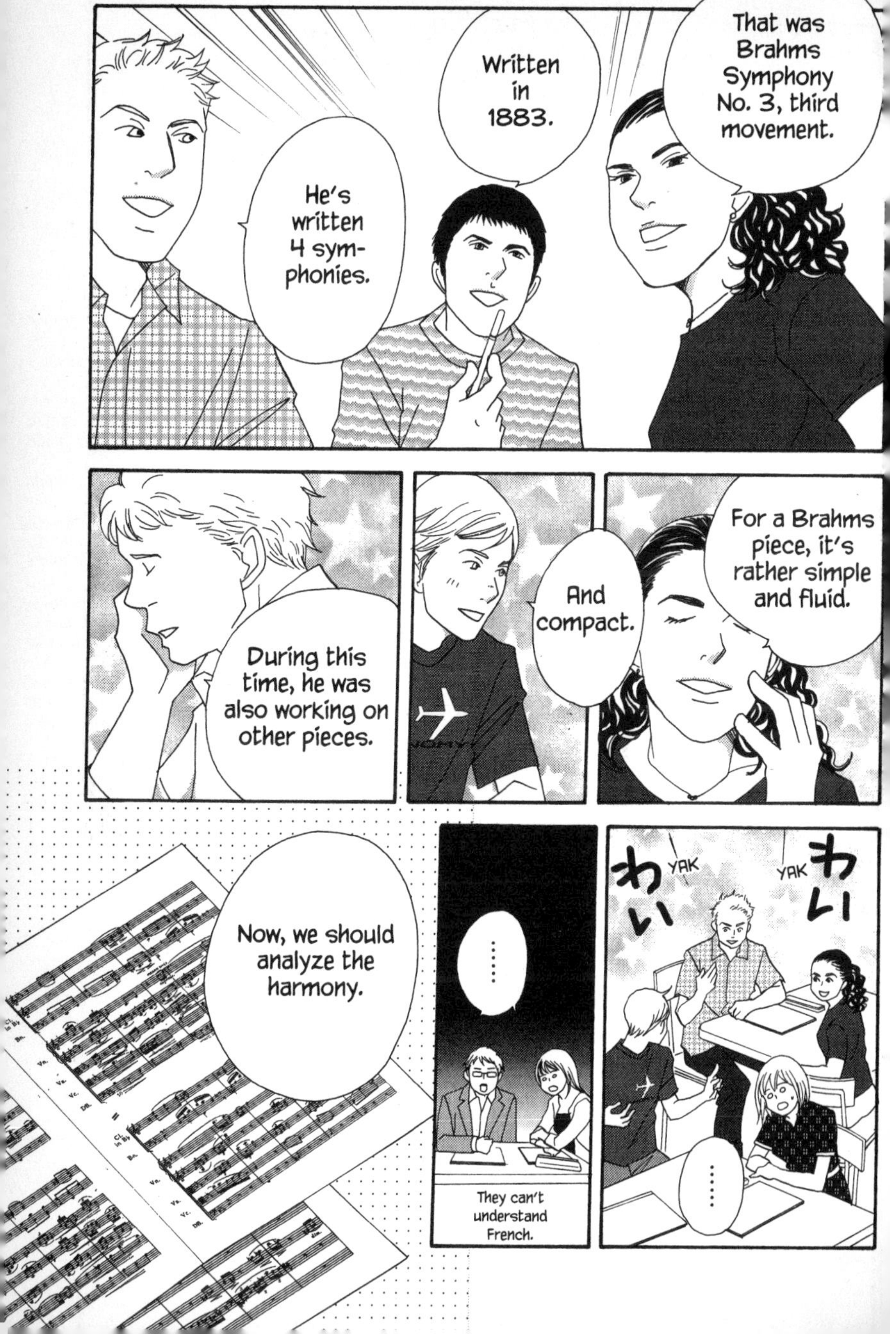
That was Brahms Symphony No. 3, third movement.
Written in 1883.
He's written 4 symphonies.
For a Brahms piece, it's rather simple and fluid.
And compact.
During this time, he was also working on other pieces.
YAK
わい
YAK
わい
......
......
They can't understand French.
Now, we should analyze the harmony.

short tune or musical figure that characterizes and unifies a composition

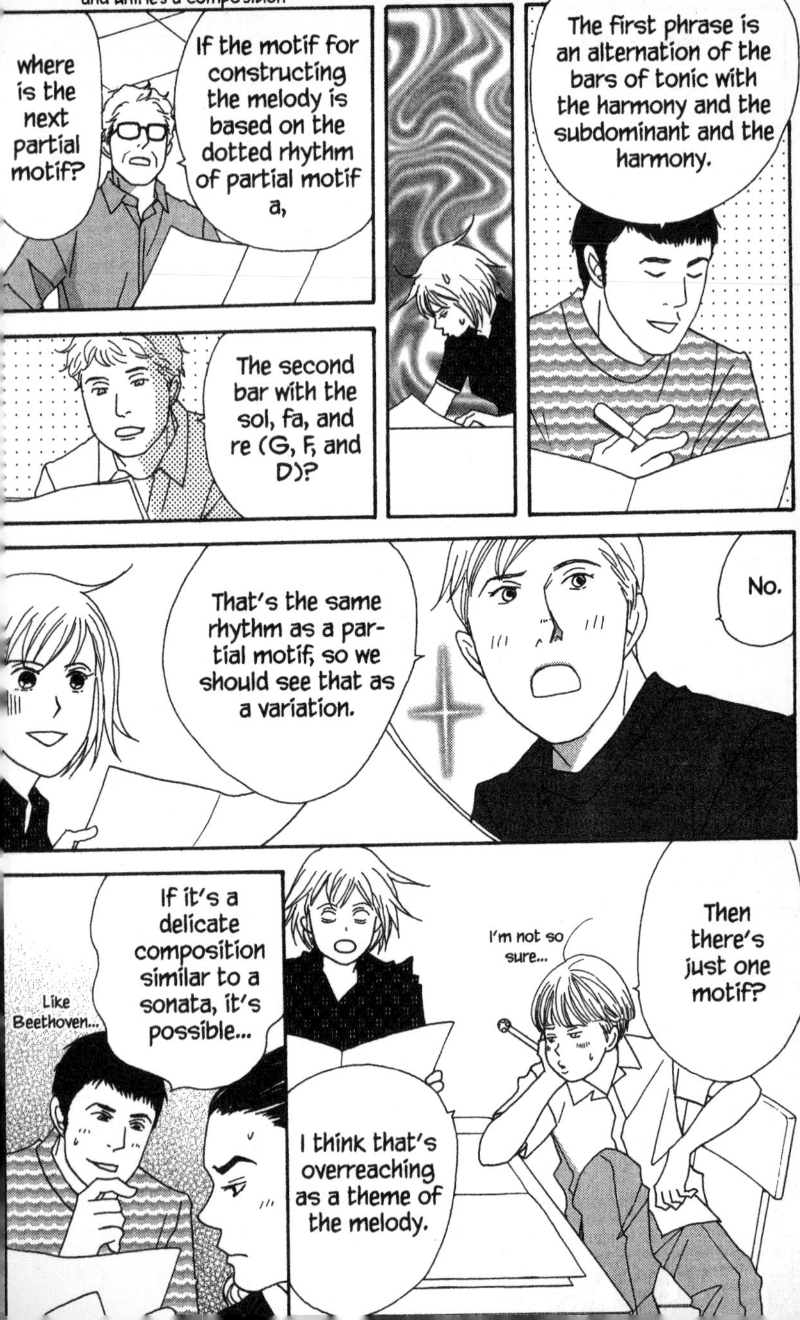

The first phrase is an alternation of the bars of tonic with the harmony and the subdominant and the harmony.
If the motif for constructing the melody is based on the dotted rhythm of partial motif a,
where is the next partial motif?
The second bar with the sol, fa, and re (G, F, and D)?
No.
That's the same rhythm as a partial motif, so we should see that as a variation.
Then there's just one motif?
I'm not so sure...
I think that's overreaching as a theme of the melody.
If it's a delicate composition similar to a sonata, it's possible...
Like Beethoven...

A chord is the sounding of two or more notes (usually at least three) simultaneously. Harmony is the concordant (or consonant) combination of notes sounded simultaneously to produce chords. The tonic is the note upon which a scale or key is based, and the subdominant chord is a chord that uses as its root the subdominant note of a key.

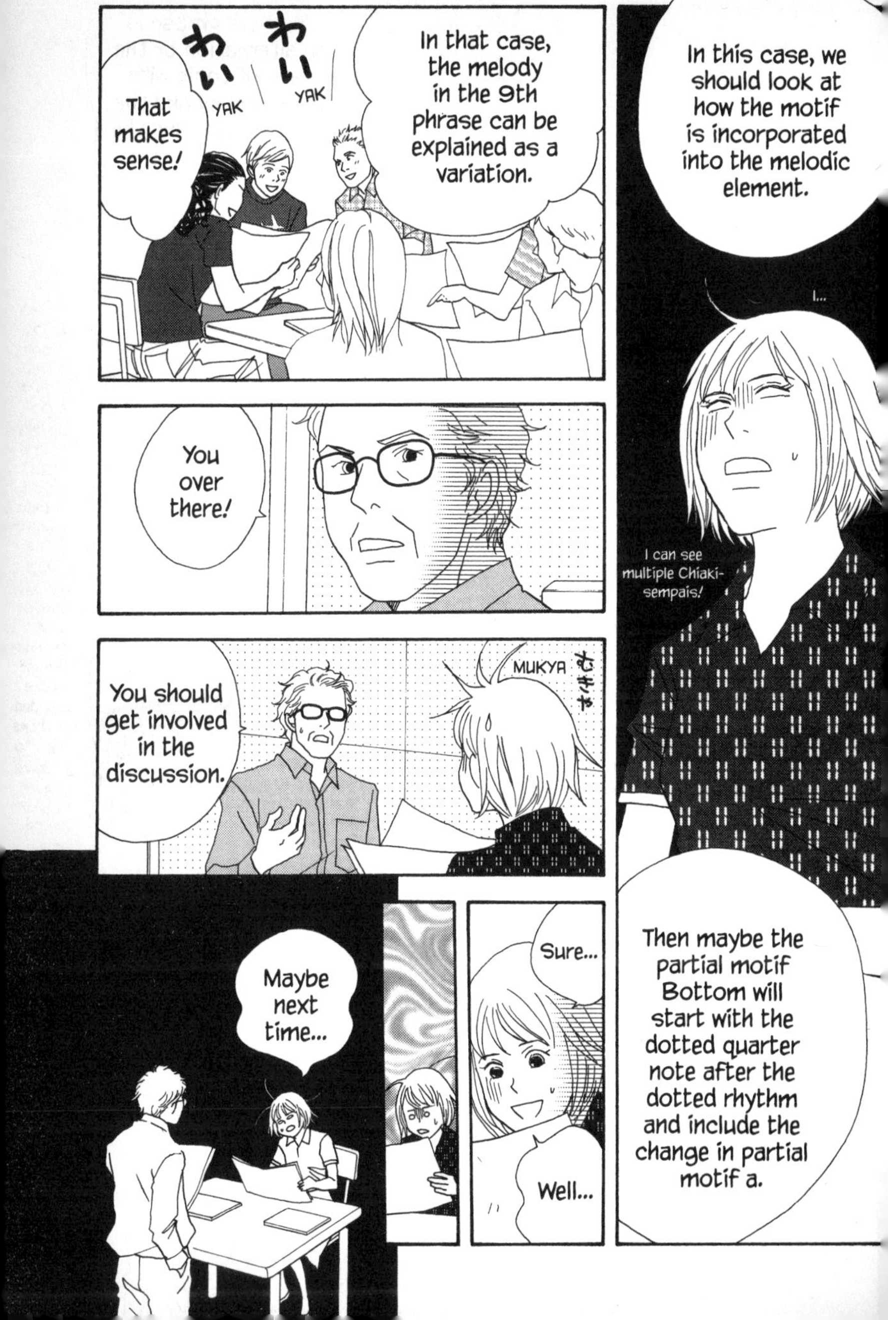
In this case, we should look at how the motif is incorporated into the melodic element.
I...
I can see multiple Chiaki-sempais!
Then maybe the partial motif Bottom will start with the dotted quarter note after the dotted rhythm and include the change in partial motif a.
In that case, the melody in the 9th phrase can be explained as a variation.
わい YAK
わい YAK
That makes sense!
You over there!
MUKYA むきゃ
You should get involved in the discussion.
Sure...
Well...
Maybe next time...

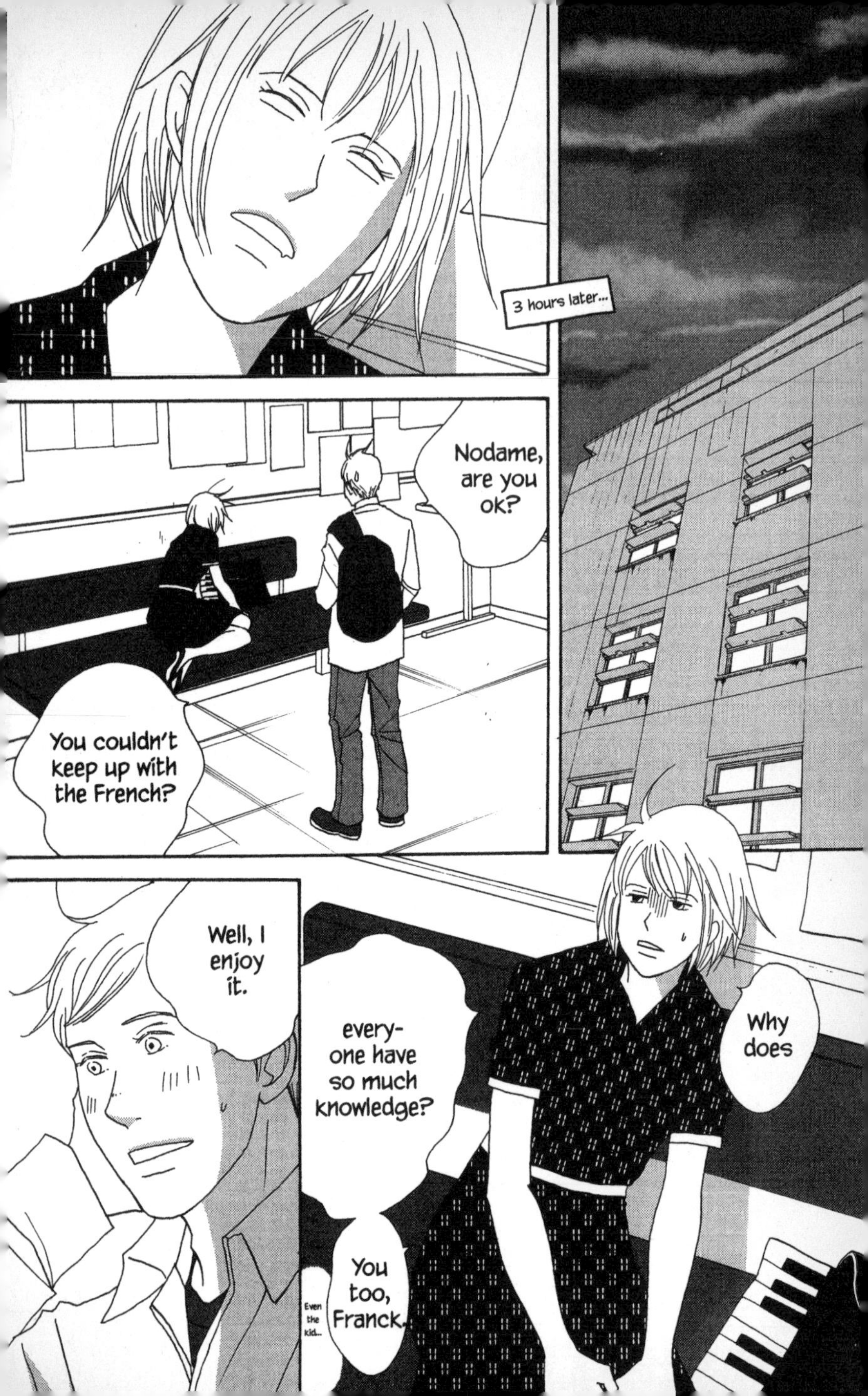
3 hours later...
Nodame, are you ok?
You couldn't keep up with the French?
Why does
every-one have so much knowledge?
You too, Franck.
Even the kid...
Well, I enjoy it.

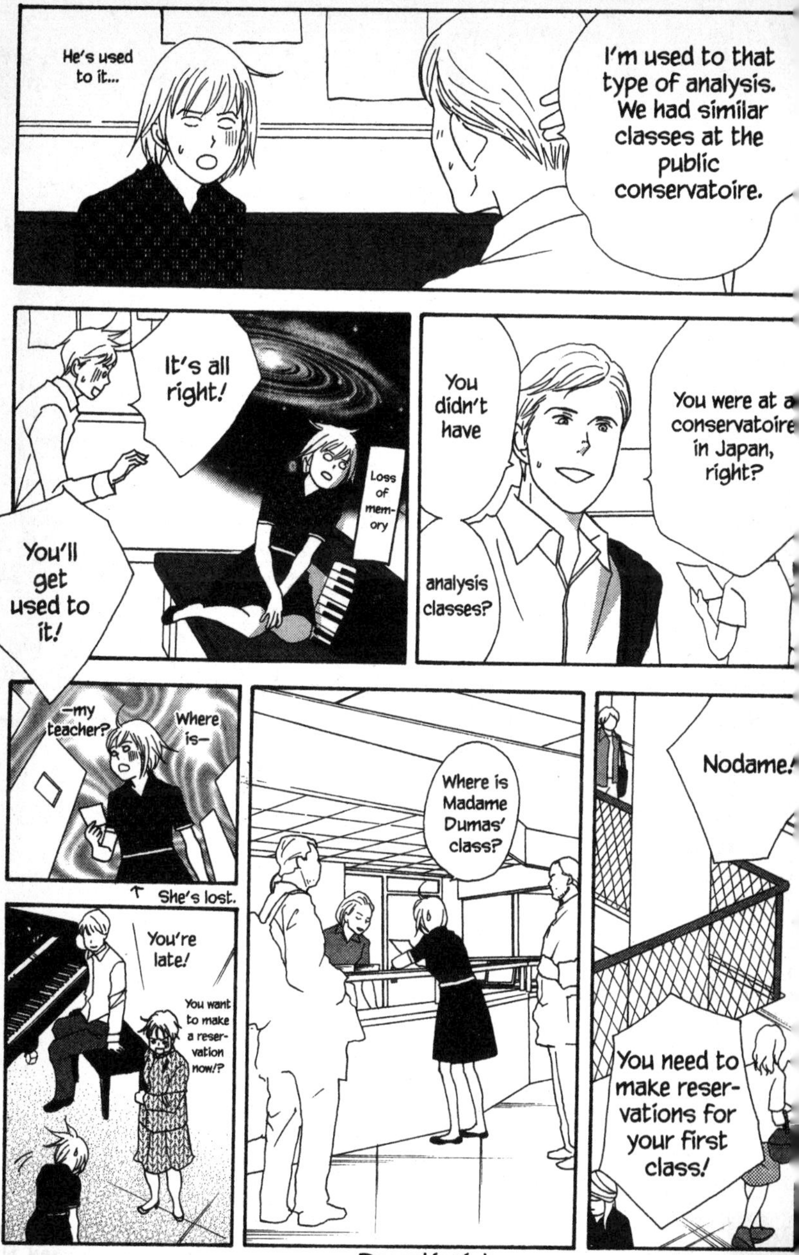
I'm used to that type of analysis. We had similar classes at the public conservatoire.
He's used to it...
You were at a conservatoire in Japan, right?
You didn't have analysis classes?
It's all right!
Loss of memory
You'll get used to it!
Nodame!
You need to make reservations for your first class!
Where is Madame Dumas' class?
Where is—
—my teacher?
She's lost.
You're late!
You want to make a reservation now!?
Receptionist

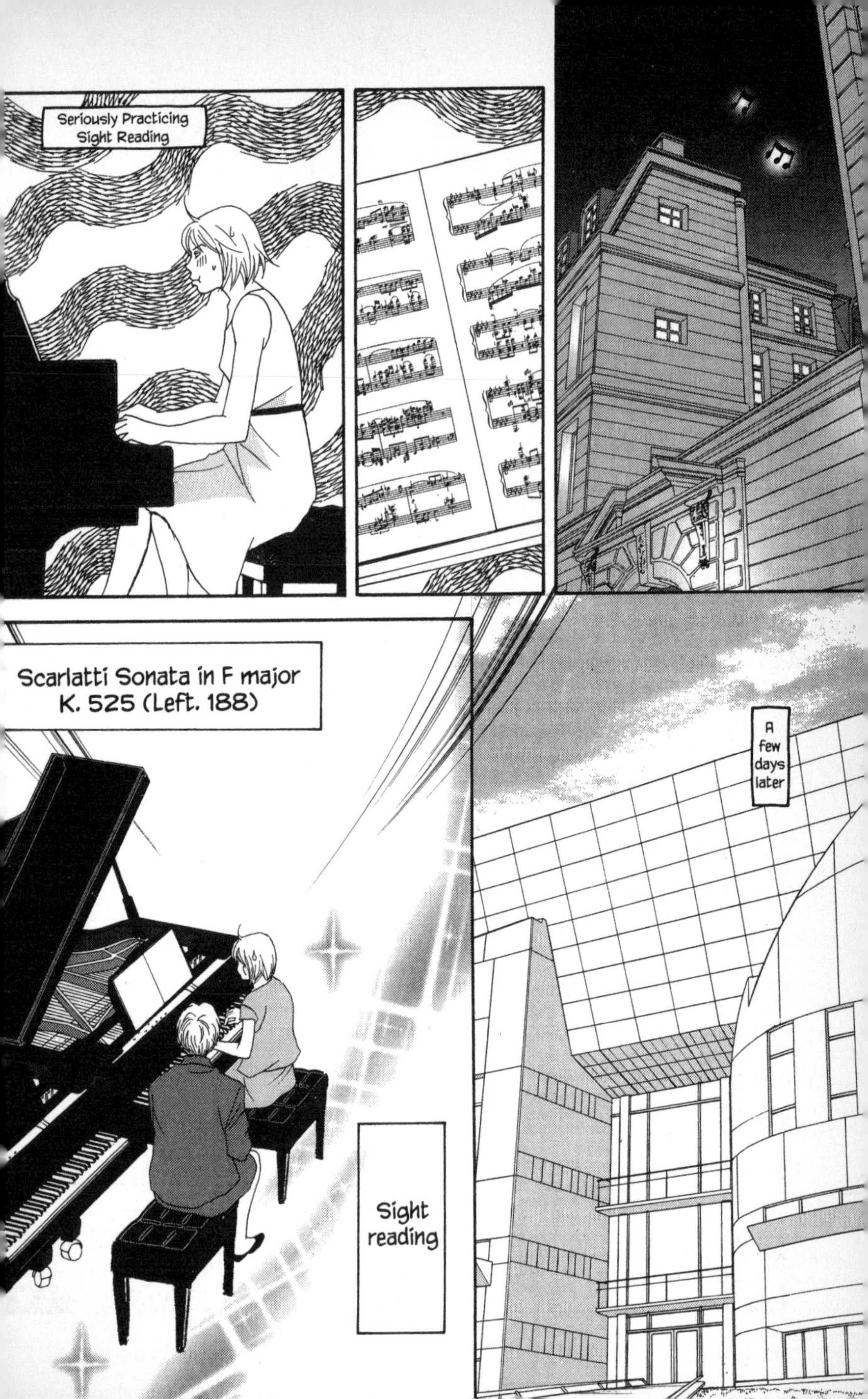
Seriously Practicing Sight Reading
A few days later
Scarlatti Sonata in F major K. 525 (Left. 188)
Sight reading

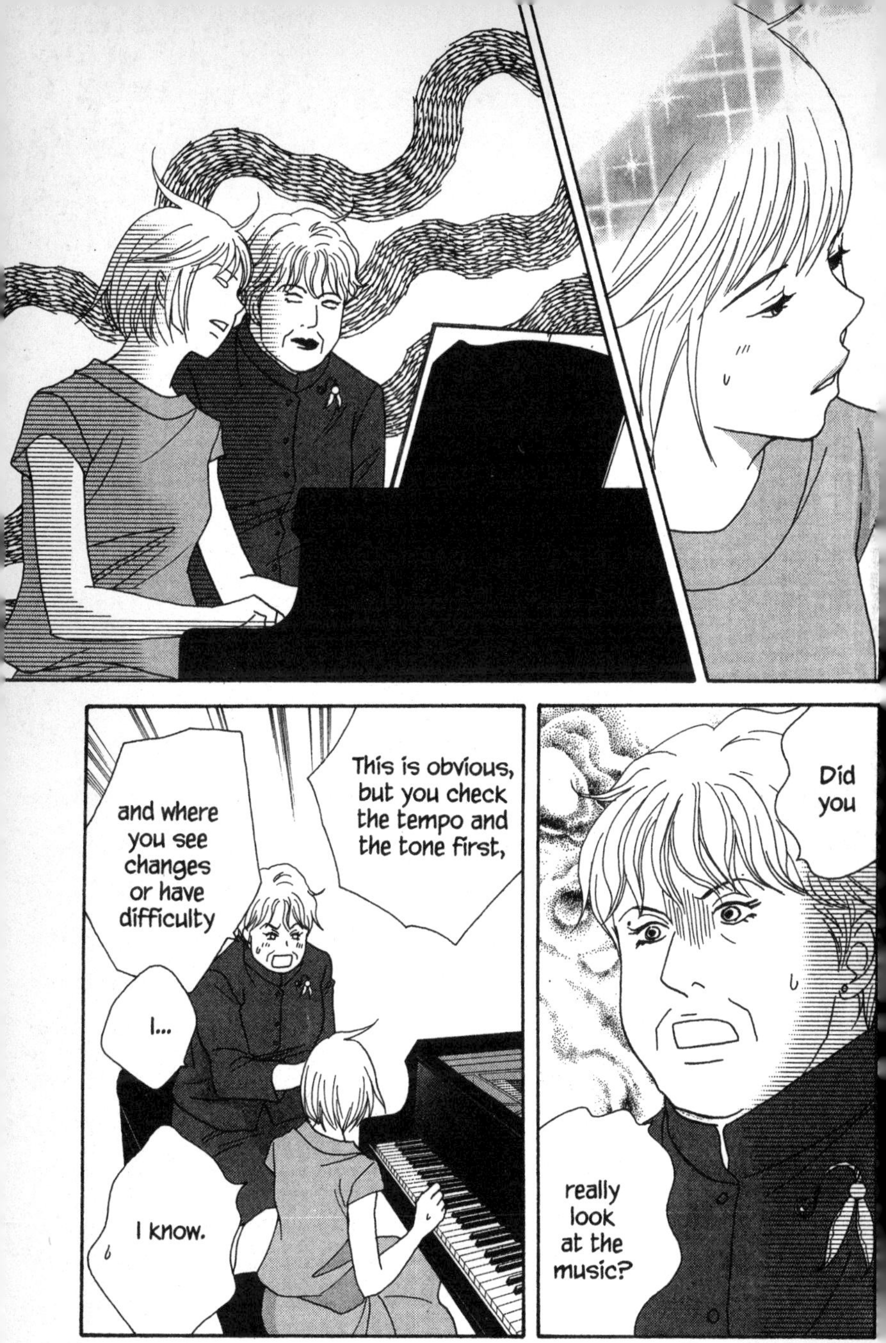
Did you
really look at the music?
This is obvious, but you check the tempo and the tone first,
and where you see changes or have difficulty
I...
I know.

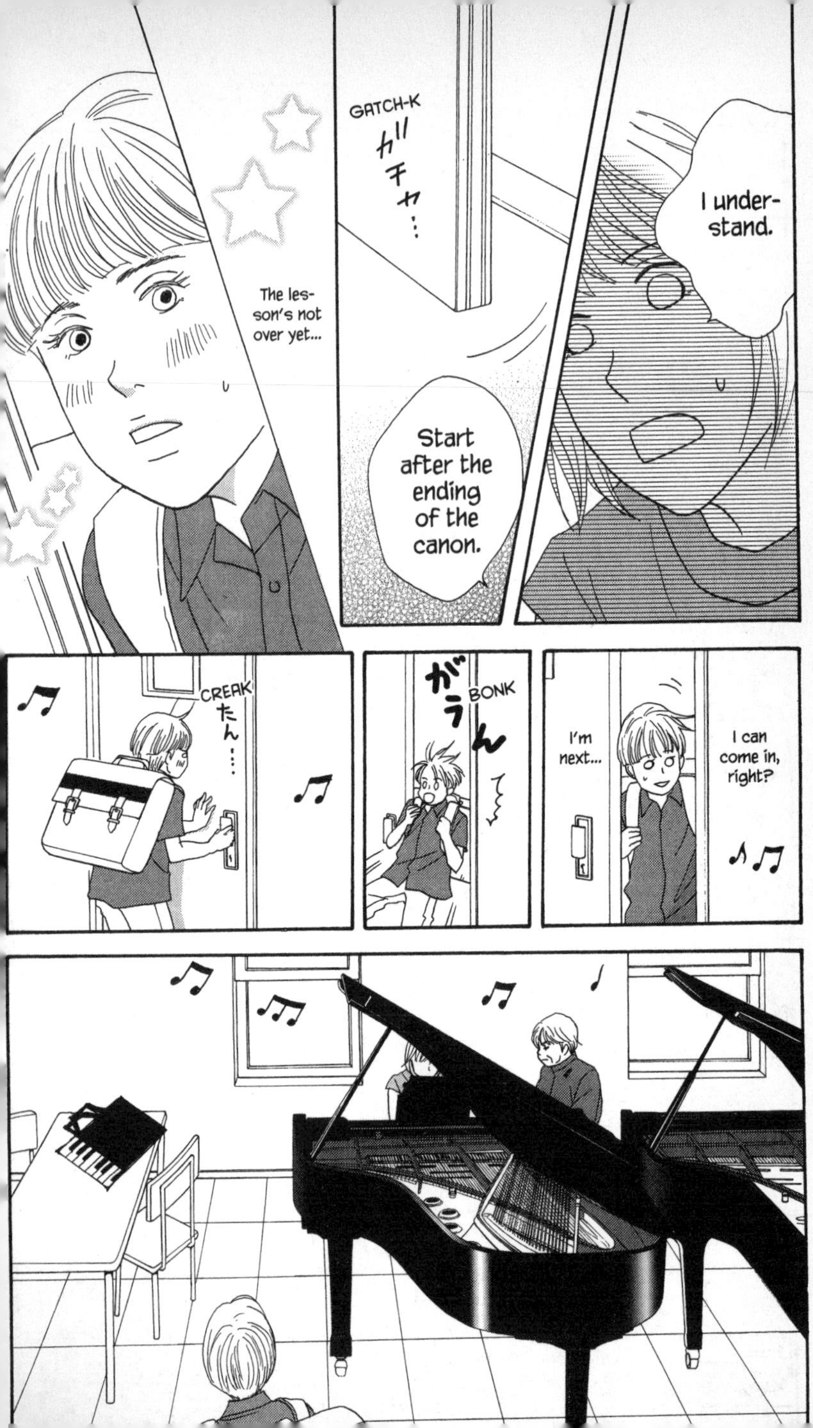

I under-
stand.
GATCH-K
ガチャ…
Start
after the
ending
of the
canon.
The les-
son's not
over yet...
I can
come in,
right?
I'm
next...
BONK
がらん
CREAK
たん…

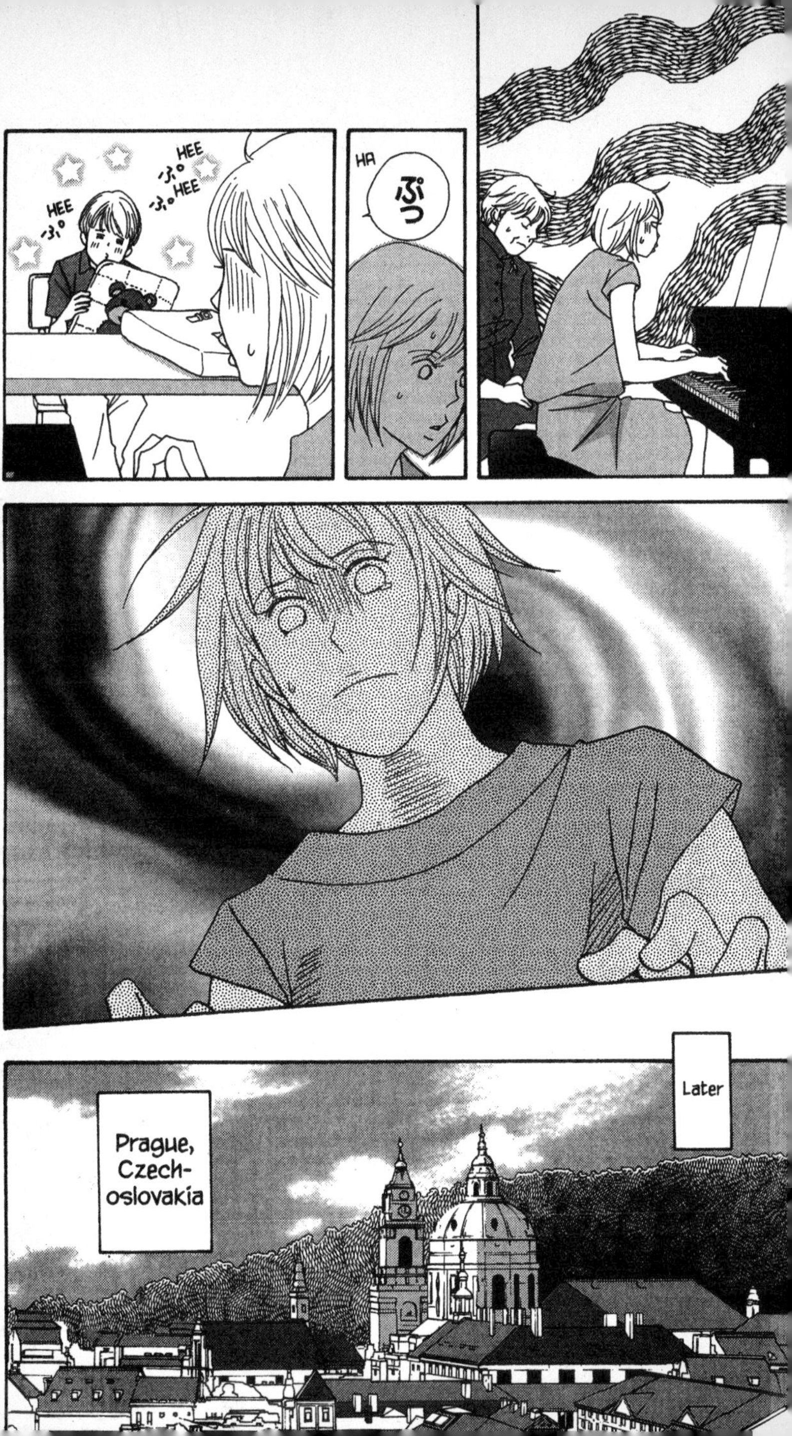
HA
ぷっ
HEE
ぷ。
ふ。HEE
HEE
ぷ
Later
Prague, Czech-oslovakia

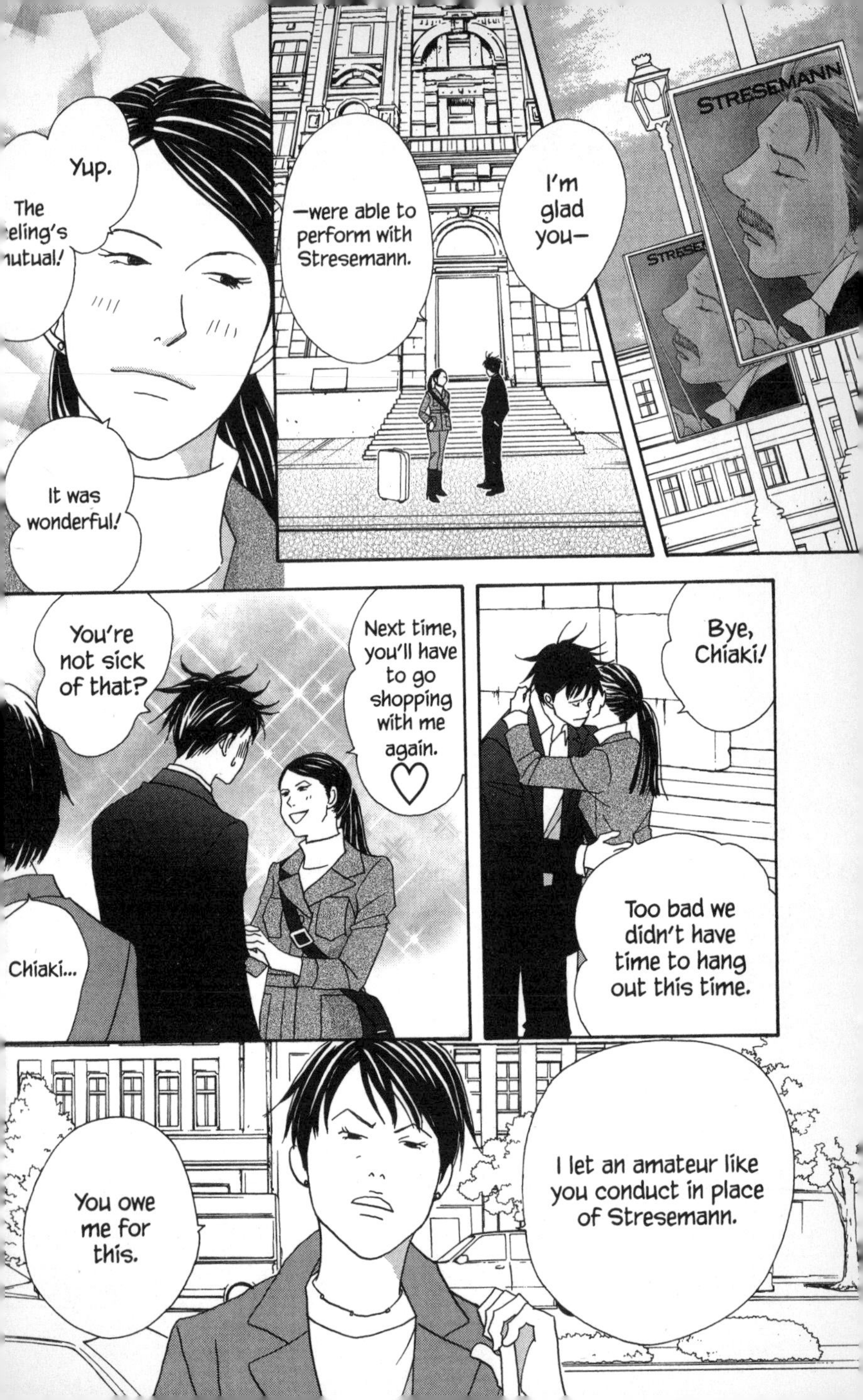
STRESEMANN
I'm glad you—
—were able to perform with Stresemann.
Yup.
The feeling's mutual!
It was wonderful!
Bye, Chiaki!
Too bad we didn't have time to hang out this time.
Next time, you'll have to go shopping with me again. ♡
You're not sick of that?
Chiaki...
I let an amateur like you conduct in place of Stresemann.
You owe me for this.

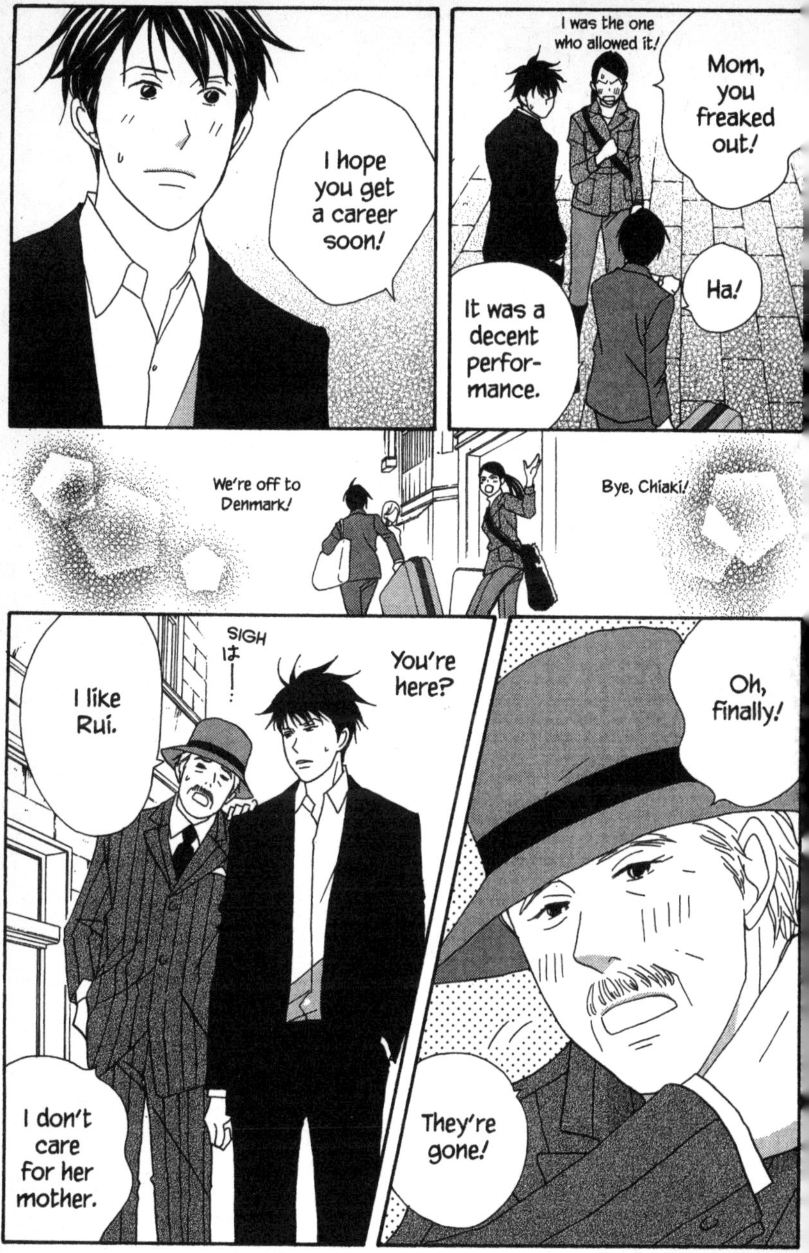
Mom, you freaked out!
I was the one who allowed it!
Ha!
It was a decent performance.
I hope you get a career soon!
Bye, Chiaki!
We're off to Denmark!
Oh, finally!
They're gone!
You're here?
SIGH
は—…
I like Rui.
I don't care for her mother.

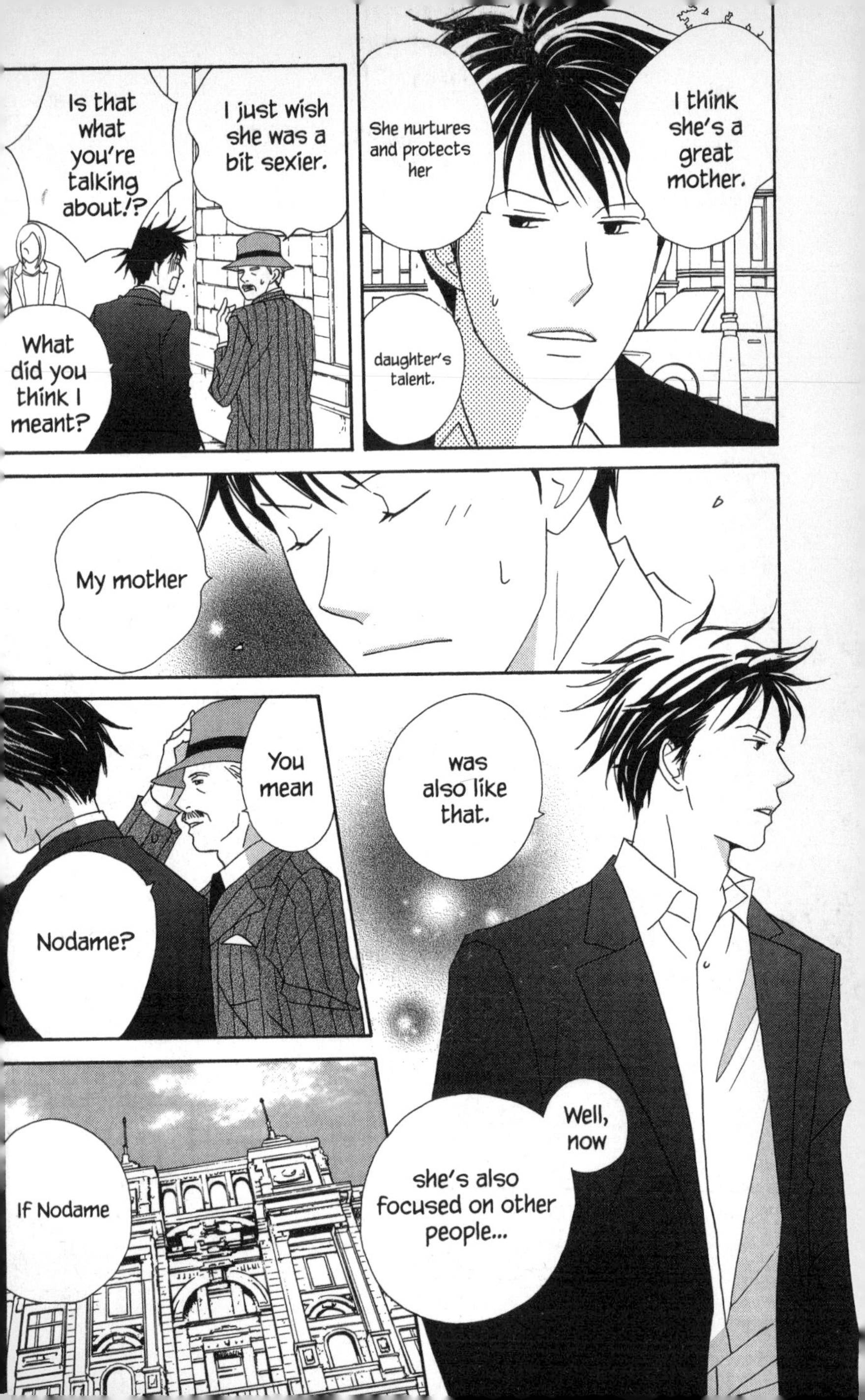

I think she's a great mother.
She nurtures and protects her
daughter's talent.
I just wish she was a bit sexier.
Is that what you're talking about!?
What did you think I meant?
My mother
was also like that.
You mean
Nodame?
Well, now
she's also focused on other people...
If Nodame

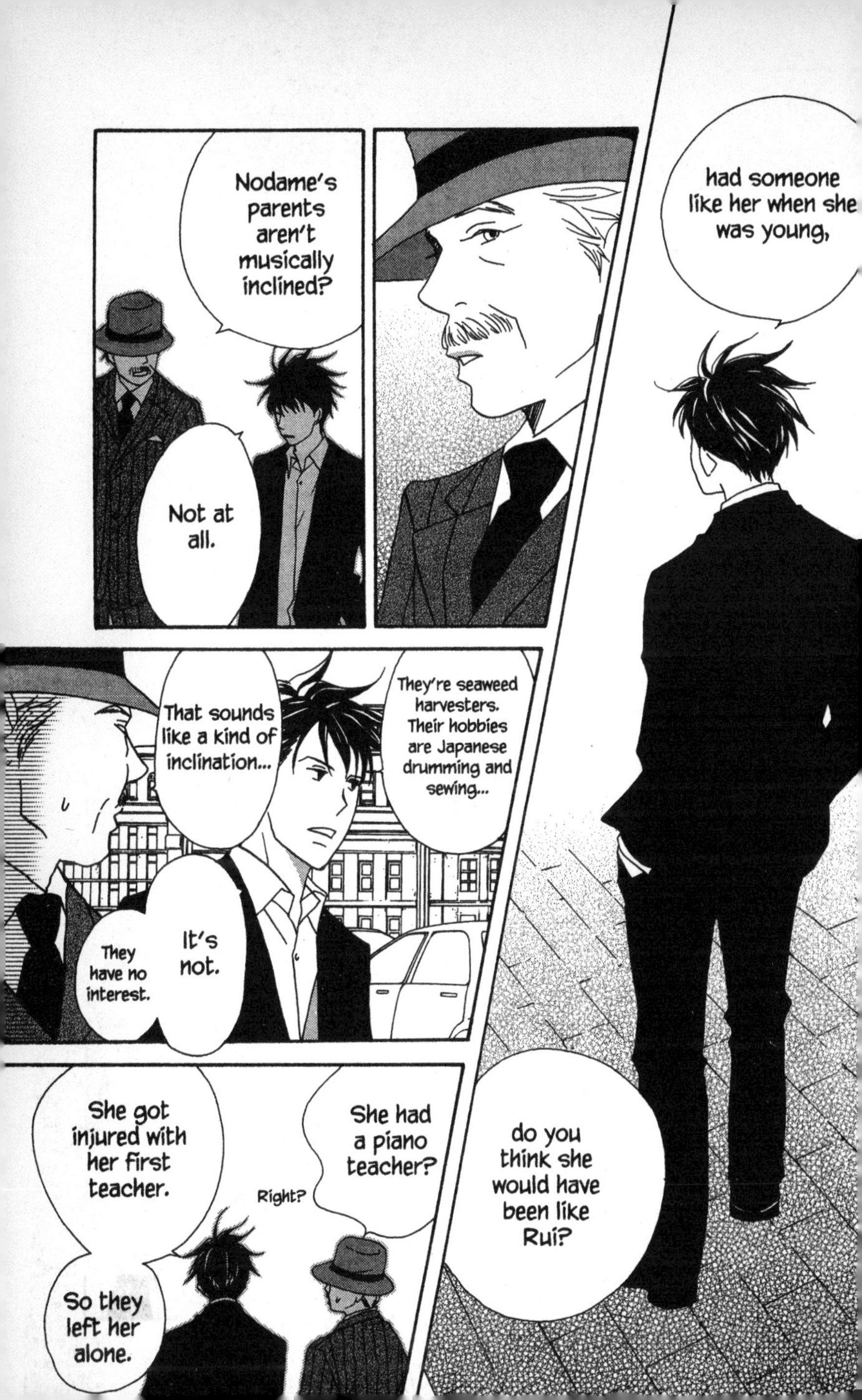
had someone like her when she was young,
do you think she would have been like Rui?
Nodame's parents aren't musically inclined?
Not at all.
They're seaweed harvesters. Their hobbies are Japanese drumming and sewing...
That sounds like a kind of inclination...
It's not.
They have no interest.
She had a piano teacher?
Right?
She got injured with her first teacher.
So they left her alone.

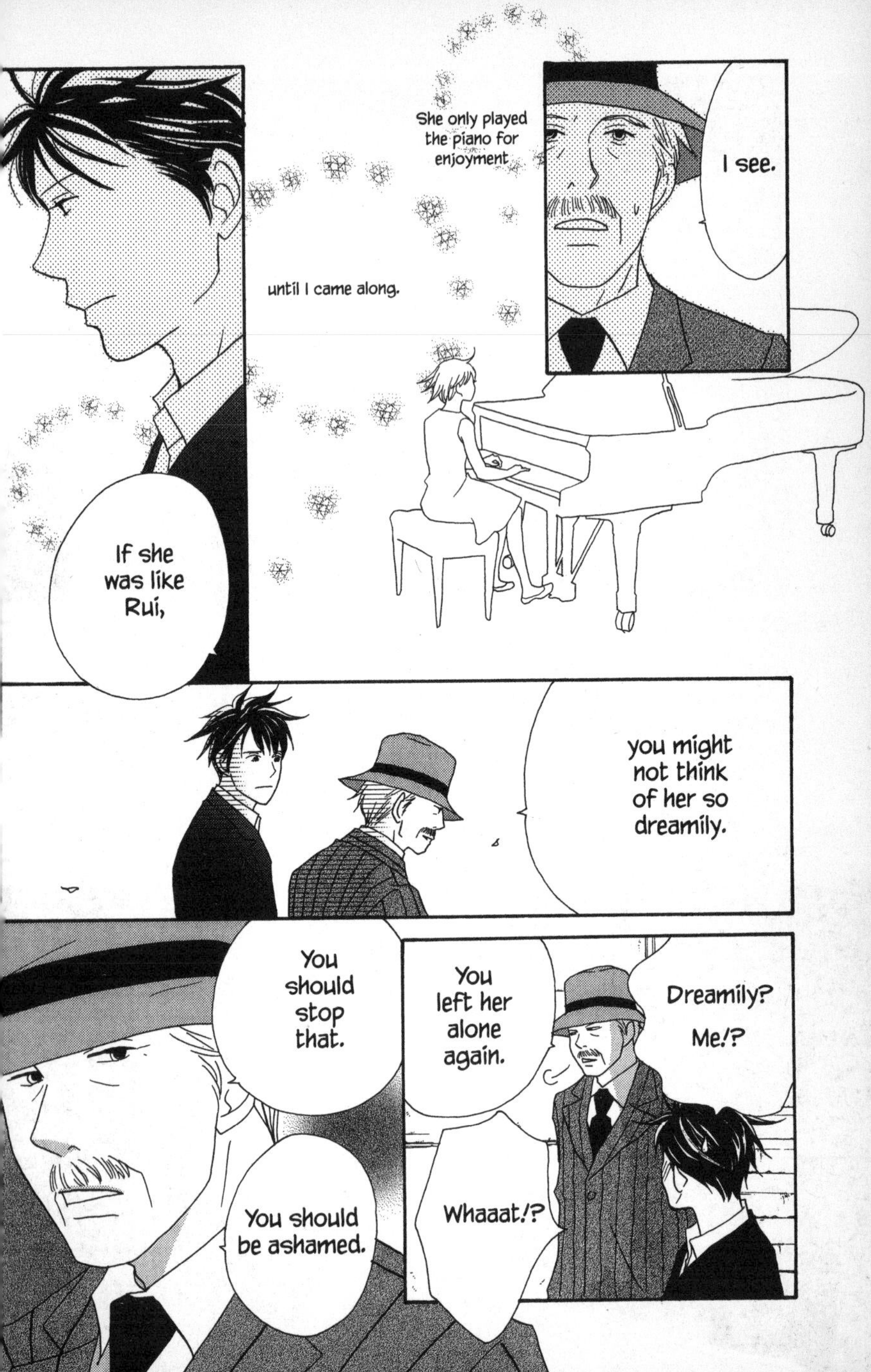
I see.
She only played the piano for enjoyment
until I came along.
If she was like Rui,
you might not think of her so dreamily.
Dreamily? Me!?
You left her alone again.
Whaaat!?
You should stop that.
You should be ashamed.

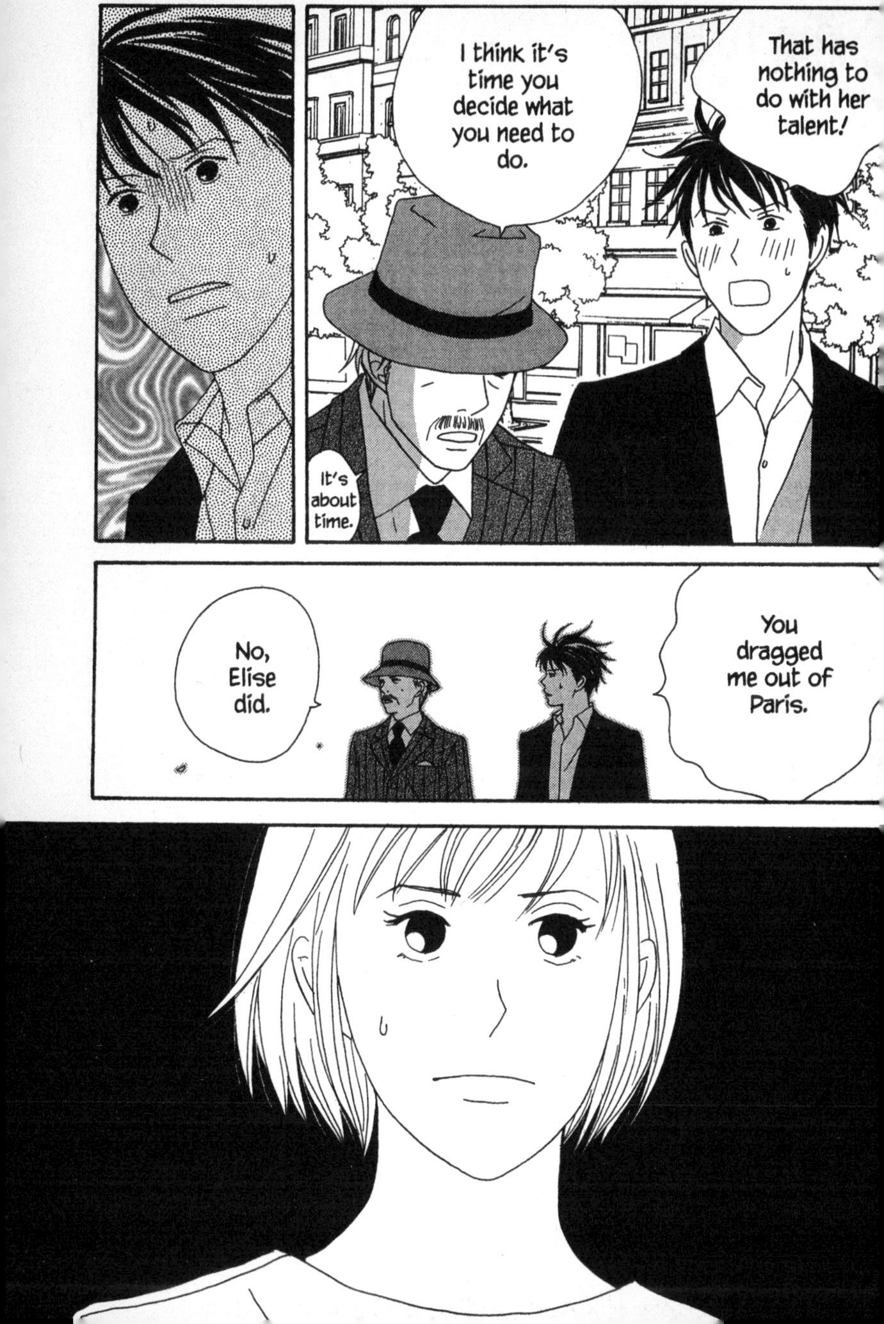
That has nothing to do with her talent!
I think it's time you decide what you need to do.
It's about time.
You dragged me out of Paris.
No, Elise did.

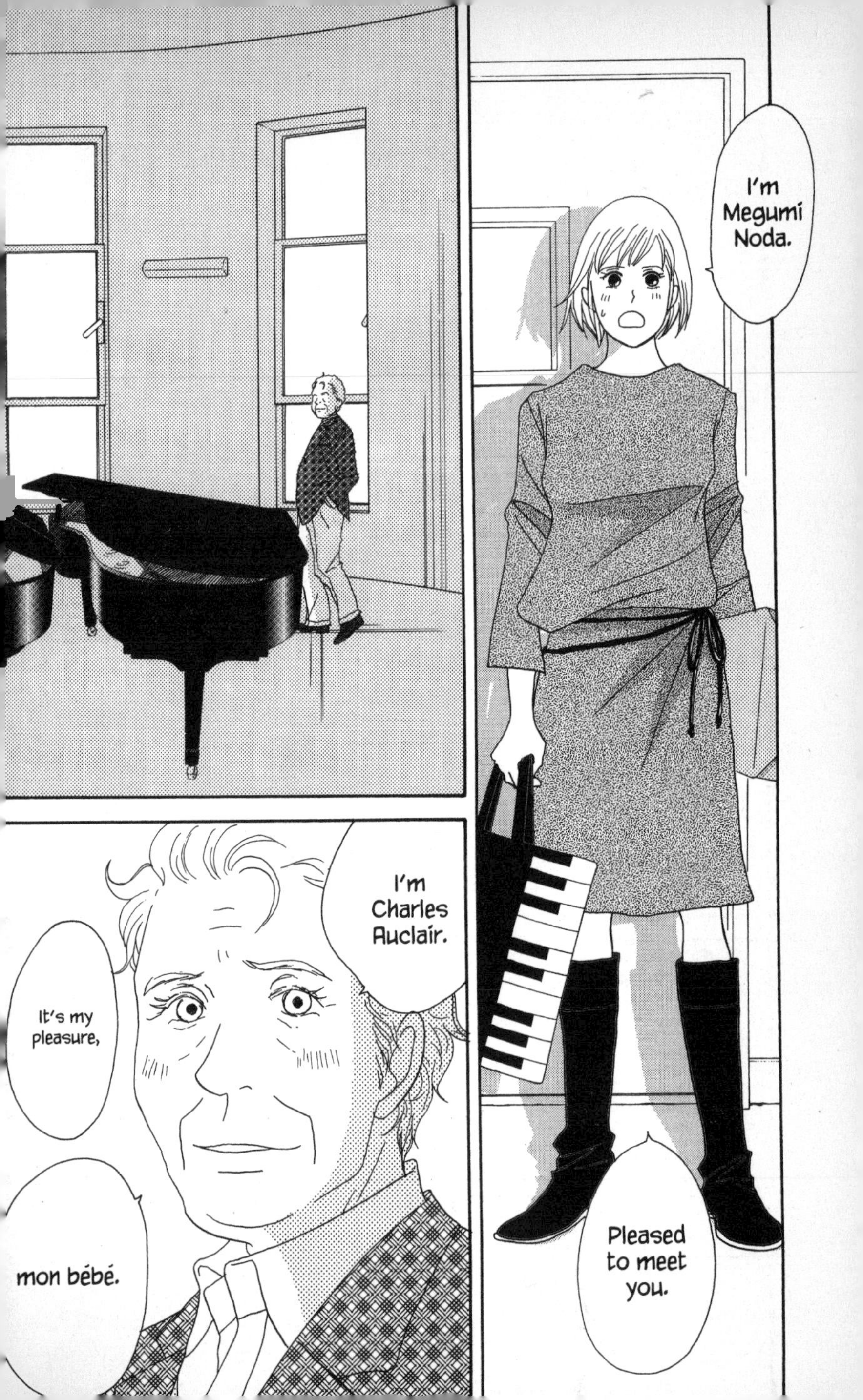
I'm Megumi Noda.
Pleased to meet you.
I'm Charles Auclair.
It's my pleasure,
mon bébé.

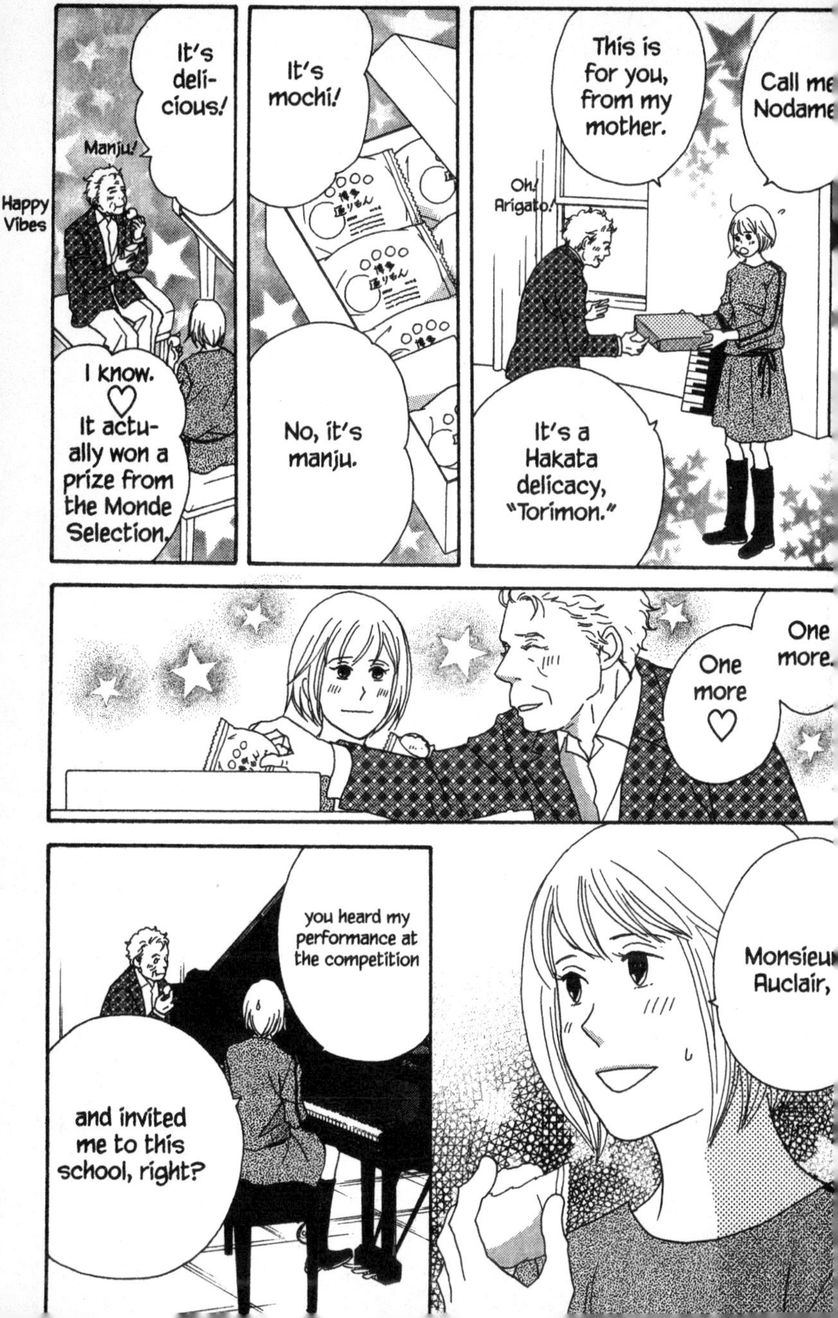

Call me Nodame
This is for you, from my mother.
Oh! Arigato!
It's a Hakata delicacy, "Torimon."
It's mochi!
No, it's manju.
It's deli-cious!
Manju!
Happy Vibes
I know. ♡ It actu-ally won a prize from the Monde Selection.
One more.
One more ♡
Monsieu Auclair,
you heard my performance at the competition
and invited me to this school, right?

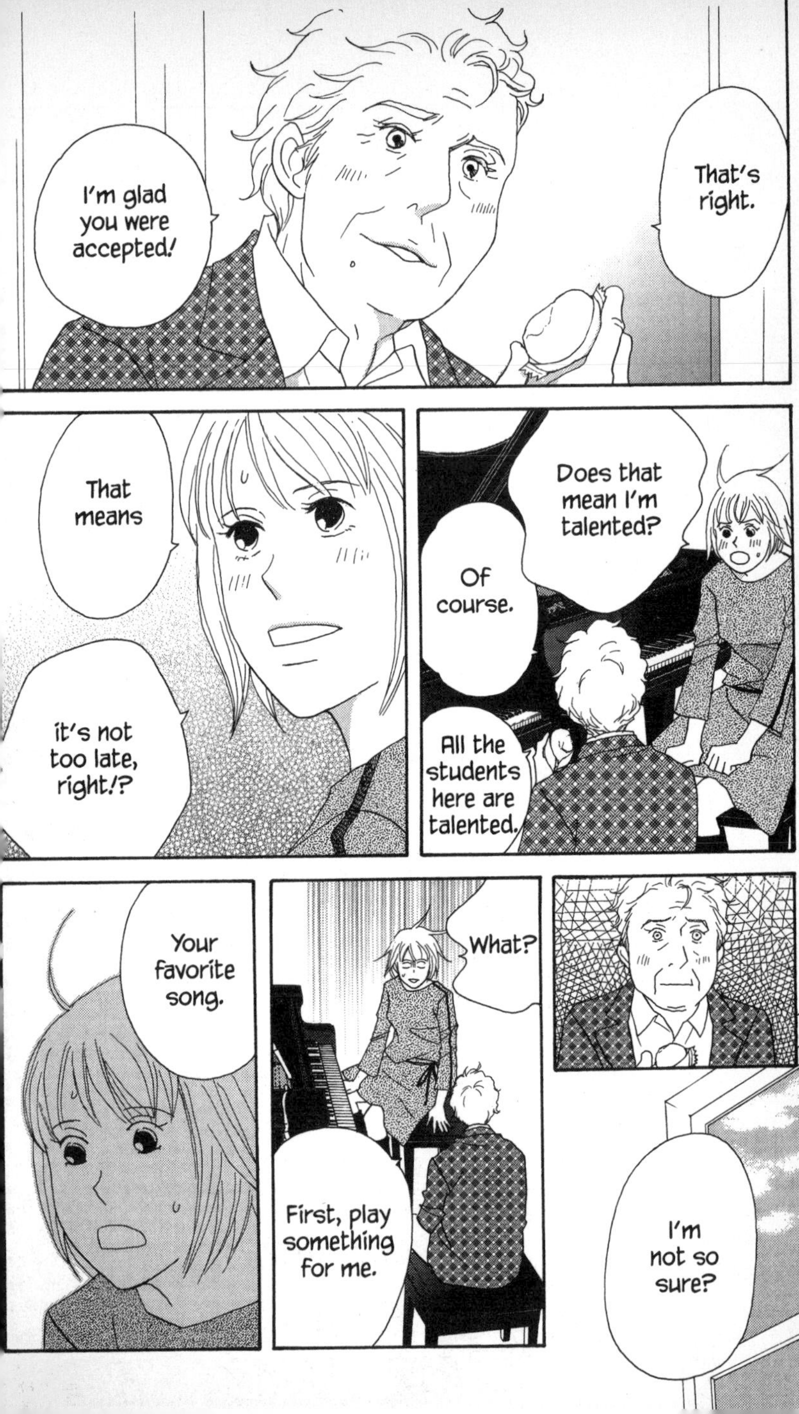

That's right.
I'm glad you were accepted!
Does that mean I'm talented?
Of course.
All the students here are talented.
That means
it's not too late, right!?
I'm not so sure?
What?
First, play something for me.
Your favorite song.

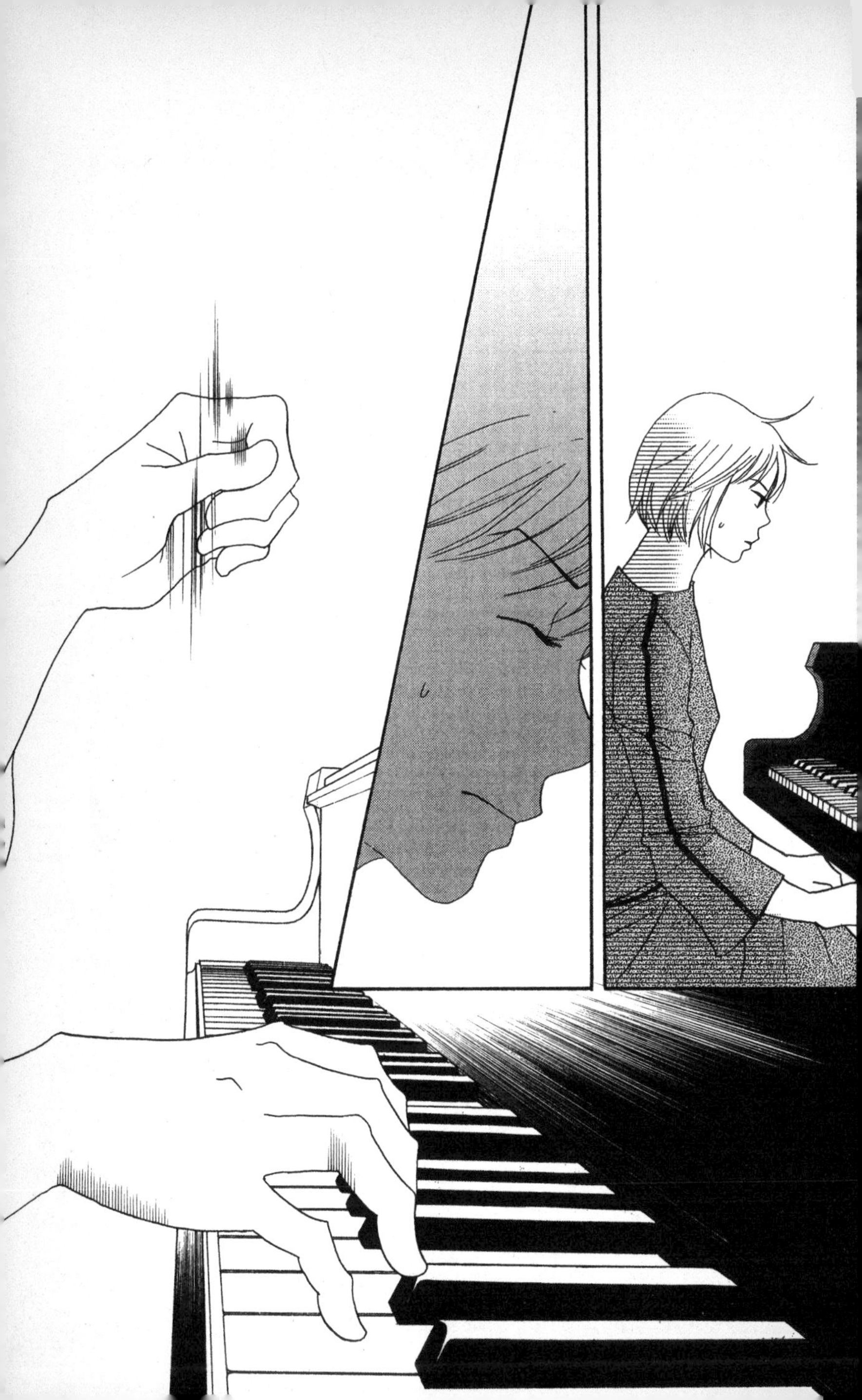

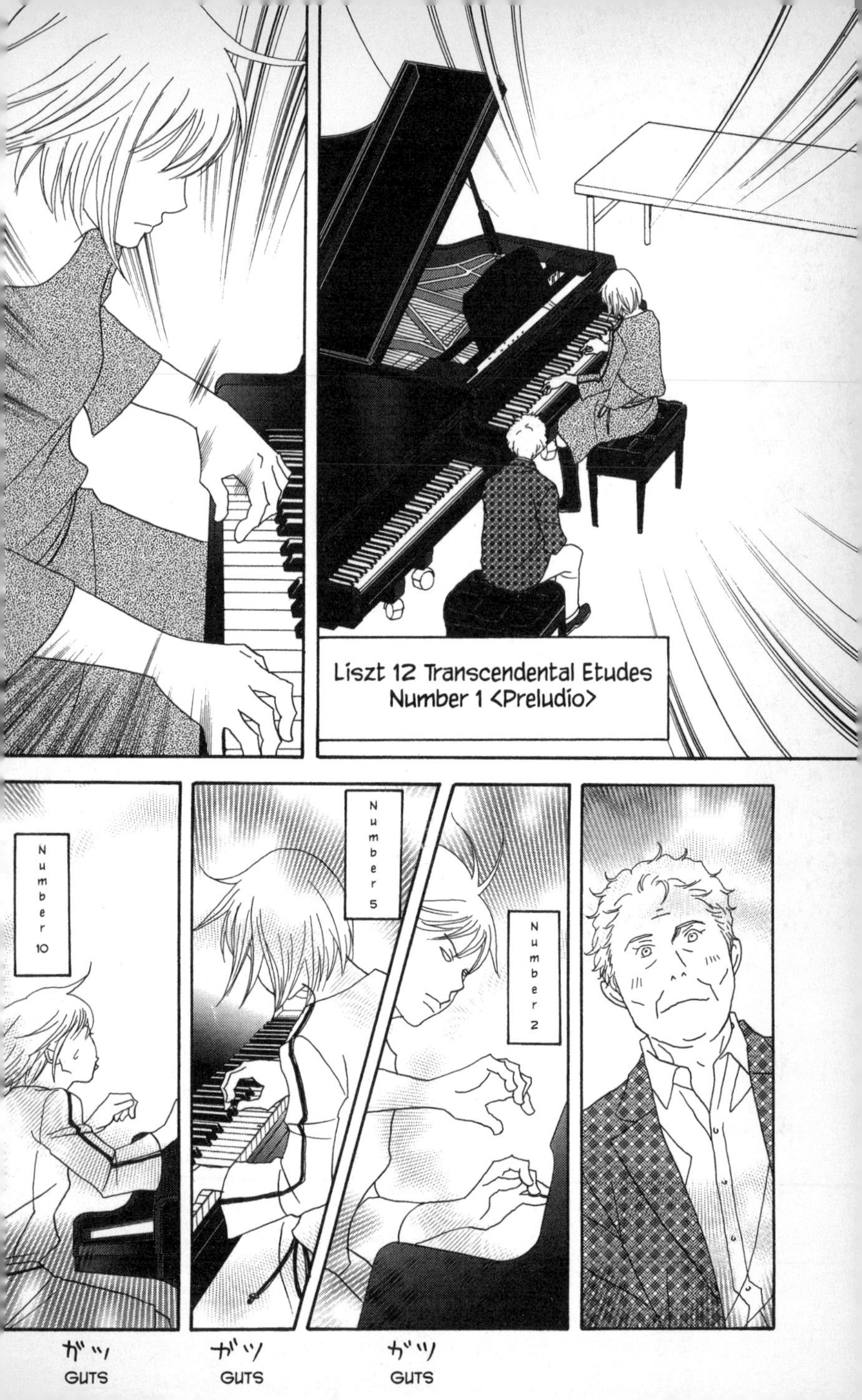
Liszt 12 Transcendental Etudes
Number 1 <Preludio>
Number 2
ガツ
GUTS
Number 5
ガツ
GUTS
Number 10
ガツ
GUTS

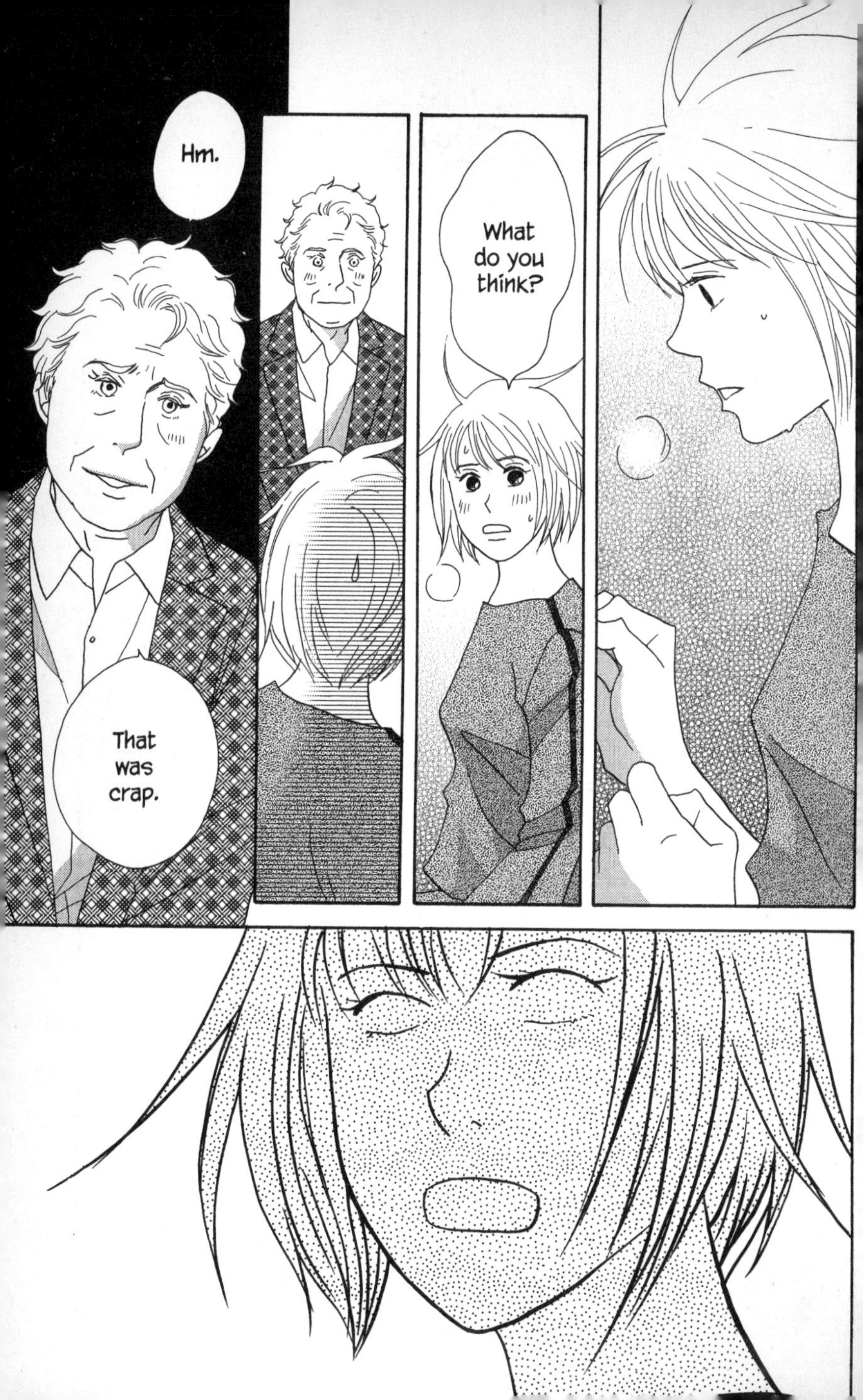
What do you think?
Hm.
That was crap.

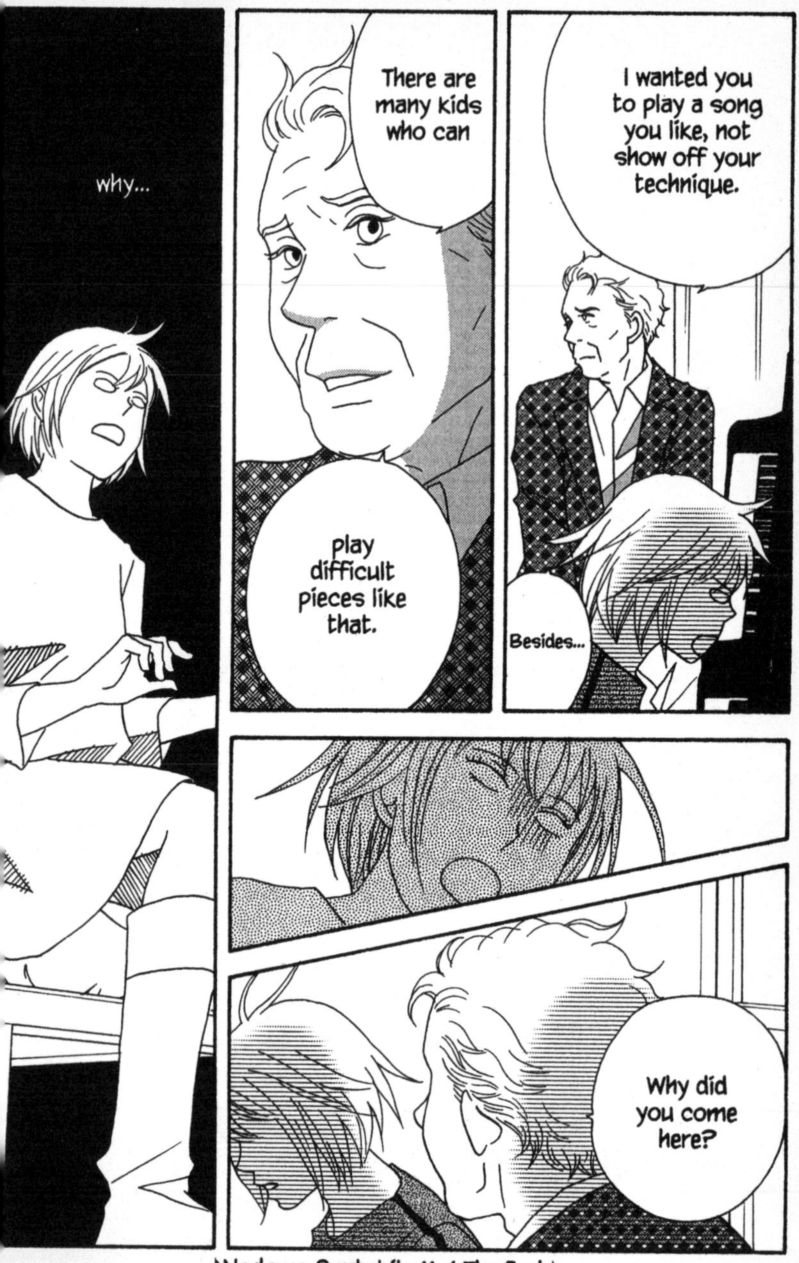
I wanted you to play a song you like, not show off your technique.
Besides...
There are many kids who can
play difficult pieces like that.
Why did you come here?
why...

♪Nodame Cantabile 11 / The End♪

Chiaki Training Diary

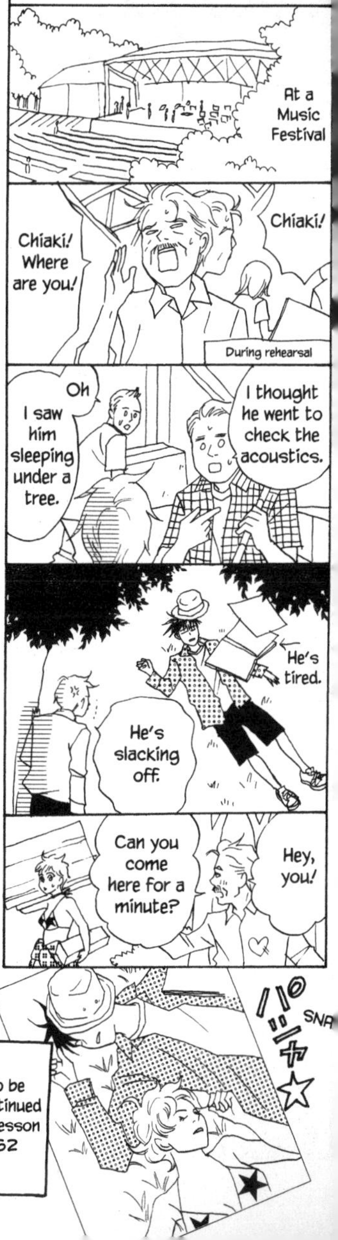
At a Music Festival
Chiaki!
Chiaki! Where are you!
During rehearsal
I thought he went to check the acoustics.
Oh
I saw him sleeping under a tree.
He's tired.
He's slacking off.
Hey, you!
Can you come here for a minute?
SNA
To be continued in Lesson 62

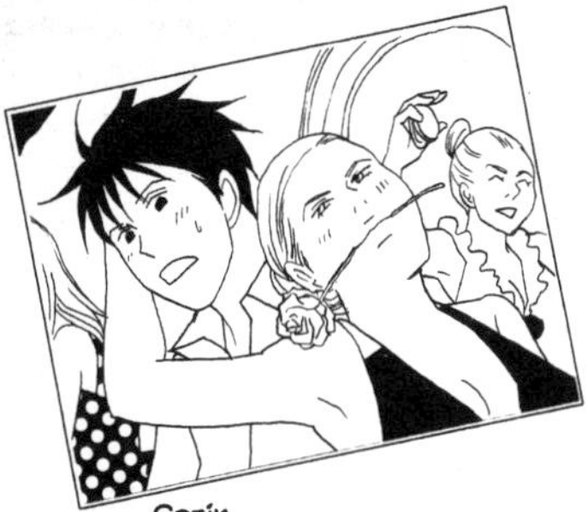

Spain

Chiaki decided to dance the flamenco to further his understanding of Spanish music. People complimented his moves so here's a picture of him feeling bold.

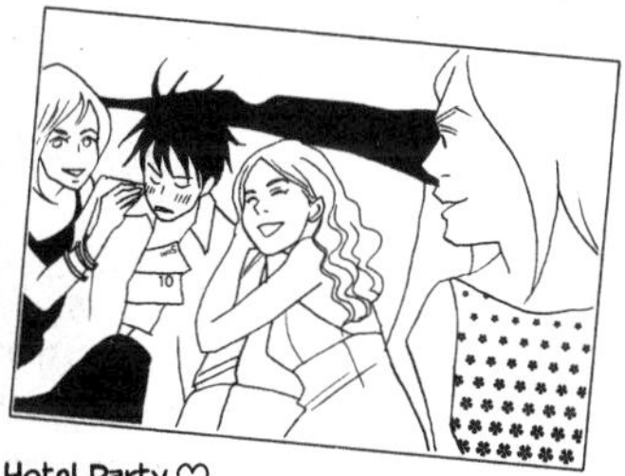

Hotel Party ♡

Chiaki's completely drunk. I made him sing, and people thought he was good. We got tips. It annoyed me.

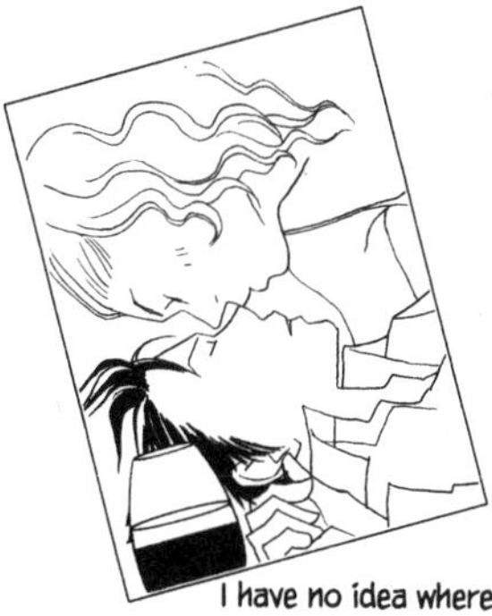

I have no idea where this came from.

That's all

Milch Report

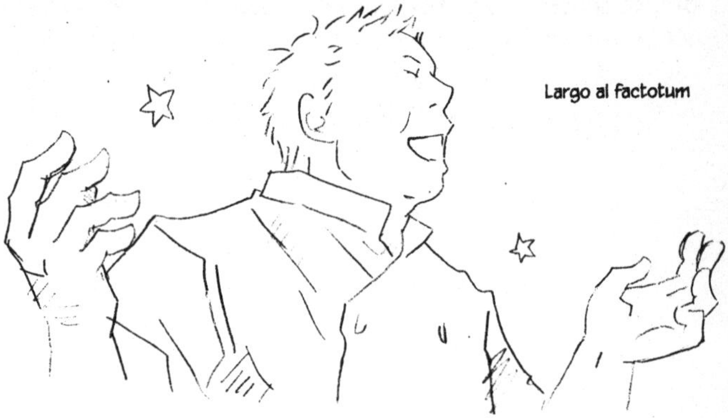
Largo al factotum
Kinda like the Uraken?

Thank you for helping me research this project!

The real Nodame is seeking piano students in Okawa city, Fukuoka prefecture.

Daichi Hoshino (Electric Violinist)

Kogawa-sensei the Horn Player (thank you for your pinpoint advice!)

Tetsugun Oosawa-sensei (Composer "Let's Search for tomorrow." Composer of Ebihara Daisaku)

"Rondo Toccata" helped me edit the "Analysis" section and more.

Miki Oosawa-san (pianist), thank you for your help.

Daisuke Mogi-San (NHK Symphony First Chair Oboist. Author "Orchestra Gakki Betsu Ningen Gaku")

Everyone in Paris, thank you so much for helping me!
M-Chan, Michiko-San, Frank, Yuko, Jean, Nagata Family

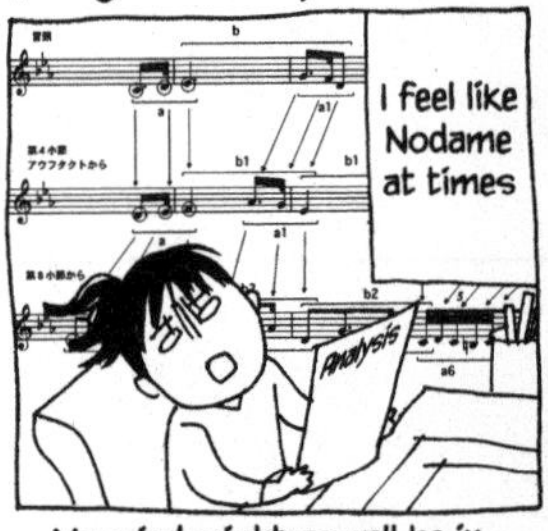
I feel like Nodame at times
Analysis
My mind might as well be in a foreign school

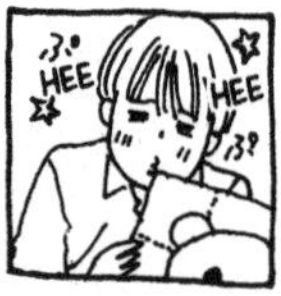
HEE
HEE
Don't laugh!

About the Author

Tomoko Ninomiya was born in Saitama in 1969. She made her debut as manga-ka with "London Doubt Boys" in 1989. Her main works include "Green" and "Miho the Trend Queen." She is currently working on "Nodame Cantabile," which is serialized in *Kiss* (Kodansha).

Here is Tomoko Ninomiya's comment upon winning the 28th Kodansha Manga Award in 2004:

"I hope someone enjoys reading this series. This hope and wish is what always motivates me when working on a manga.

"The original inspiration for 'Nodame Cantabile' came from an idea that I had, that it might be fun to write about a young piano student who practices the piano in a room full of junk. Looking back, I am amazed that my editor and the magazine let me serialize it, and I'm grateful.

"This is also a series which would not have been possible without the generous cooperation of music students and professionals whom I interviewed. The Manga Award goes to everyone who was involved with 'Nodame,' including Mikawa-san, my editor, and all the staff members who work with me.

"I will continue to enjoy working on this series, and I hope my readers will continue to enjoy it, too."

Translation Notes

Japanese is a tricky language for most Westerners, and translation is often more art than science. For your edification and reading pleasure, here are notes on some of the places where we could have gone in a different direction in our translation of the work, or where a Japanese cultural reference is used.

Maurice Ravel's "Pavane pour infante défunte" ("Pavane for a Dead Princess"), page 12

Maurice Ravel (1875–1937) was a French composer and pianist. He composed Pavane in 1899 while studying composition at the Conservatoire de Paris. "Pavane" is a processional dance that was popular in the 16th century. This song has a Spanish flair, which is shared by his other works such as Boléro and Rapsodie Espagnole.

Concerto, page 18

A concerto is a musical work where one solo instrument is accompanied by an orchestra. The modern concerto was developed during the Baroque Period.

First, the contestants will select a concerto.

Édouard Lalo's Symphonie Espagnole (Spanish Symphony), page 19

Éduardo Lalo (1823–1892) was a French composer of Spanish descent. While Symphonie Espagnole is officially a symphony, it is considered a violin concerto by modern musicians. The piece is known for its Spanish theme, and was created during a period when Spanish influence in music was popular (Carmen, the famous opera by Bizet, premiered a month after the Symphony Espagnole).

Pyotr Tchaikovsky's Violin Concerto D Major, page 20

Tchaikovsky (1823-1893) was a Russian composer who wrote some of the most famous classical pieces known today, such as The Nutcracker Suite. His Violin Concerto in D major is also one of the most famous violin concertos. It was composed in 1878, but was not publicly performed until 1881.

Antonín Dvořák's Cello Concerto, page 21

Antonín Dvořák (1841-1904) was a Czech composer. He was known for incorporating elements of folk music from his native Bohemia into his work. He wrote two cello concertos. In 1865, he wrote a cello concerto in A major. He wrote Cello Concerto in B minor during 1894-1895. While Katahira does not specify the cello concerto, the concerto in B minor is one of the most frequently performed cello pieces today.

Richard Strauss, Till Eulenspiegel, page 28

Richard Strauss (1864-1949) was a German composer known for his tone poems and operas. *Till Eulenspiegel* is based on a medieval German joker/jester and folk hero.

Tone Poem, page 29

A tone poem, also called a symphonic poem, is an orchestral piece comprised of a single movement. Tone poems are based on a poem, novel, painting, or some nonmusical source.

Accelerando, page 34

A symbol used in musical notation that indicates the acceleration of the tempo.

Béla Bartók's The Dance Suite, page 42

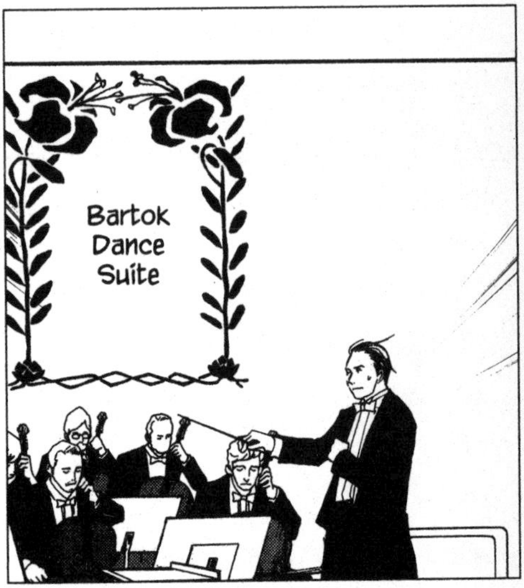
Bartok
Dance
Suite

Béla Bartók was a Hungarian composer as well as one of the founders of ethnomusicology (the study of music in cultural context). The Dance Suite was written in 1923 for a concert marking the 50th anniversary of Budapest.

Tocatta, page 107

Tocatta is a virtuoso composition, usually for the organ or another keyboard instrument, intended to exhibit the player's technique.

Franz Liszt's Etude No. 5 in B-flat, "Feux follets" ("Will o' the wisp"), page 138

Franz Liszt (1811-1886) was a Hungarian composer and virtuoso pianist. "Feux follets" is one of the 12 Transcendental Etudes that was composed between 1826 and 1851. The Etudes are known to be some of the most difficult pieces written for the piano.

Pizza Margherita, page 145

Pizza Margherita is a pizza dedicated to Queen Margherita in 1889 by Raffaele Esposito, a famous pizzaioli (pizza chef). It is a simple pizza topped with tomato, sliced mozzarella, basil, and oil.

Here you go!

Pizza Margherita and Pasta Marinara!

Gioacchino Antonio Rossini's Il barbiere di Siviglia (The Barber of Seville), page 153

The Barber of Seville is one of the most famous operas written by Gioacchino Rossini (1792-1868), an Italian composer. The opera is based on the first play of the French trilogy written by Pierre Augustin Caron de Beaumarchais.

Largo al factotum, pages 154-156

Largo al factotum is one of the most famous arias from the opera *The Barber of Seville*. The word "factotum" means "do everything." The following is the actual Italian lyric of the translated lyric found in this volume.

Largo al factotum della città	Make way for the factotum of the city.
Presto a bottega che l'alba a già.	Rushing to his shop now that it's already dawn.
Ah, che bel vivere, che bel piacere	Ah, isn't life good, how pleasant it is
per un barbiere di qualità!	For a barber of class!
sempre d'intorno in giro sta.	Always busy and around.
Uno alla volta, per carità!	One at a time, for pity's sake!
a te fortuna non mancherà.	From you luckiness will not depart.
sono il factotum della città.	I am factotum of the city.

Mochi, page 183

Mochi is a Japanese rice cake that's been pounded into a paste and molded into shape. It is used in both sweet and savory dishes.

Manju, page 183

Manju is a traditional Japanese confection. There are many varieties, but the most common version is a steamed flour or buckwheat bun filled with sweetened red bean paste.

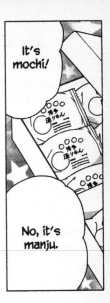

It's mochi!

No, it's manju.

Preview of Volume 12

We're pleased to present you a preview from volume 12. Please check our website (www.delreymanga.com) to see when this volume will be available in English. For now you'll have to make do with Japanese!

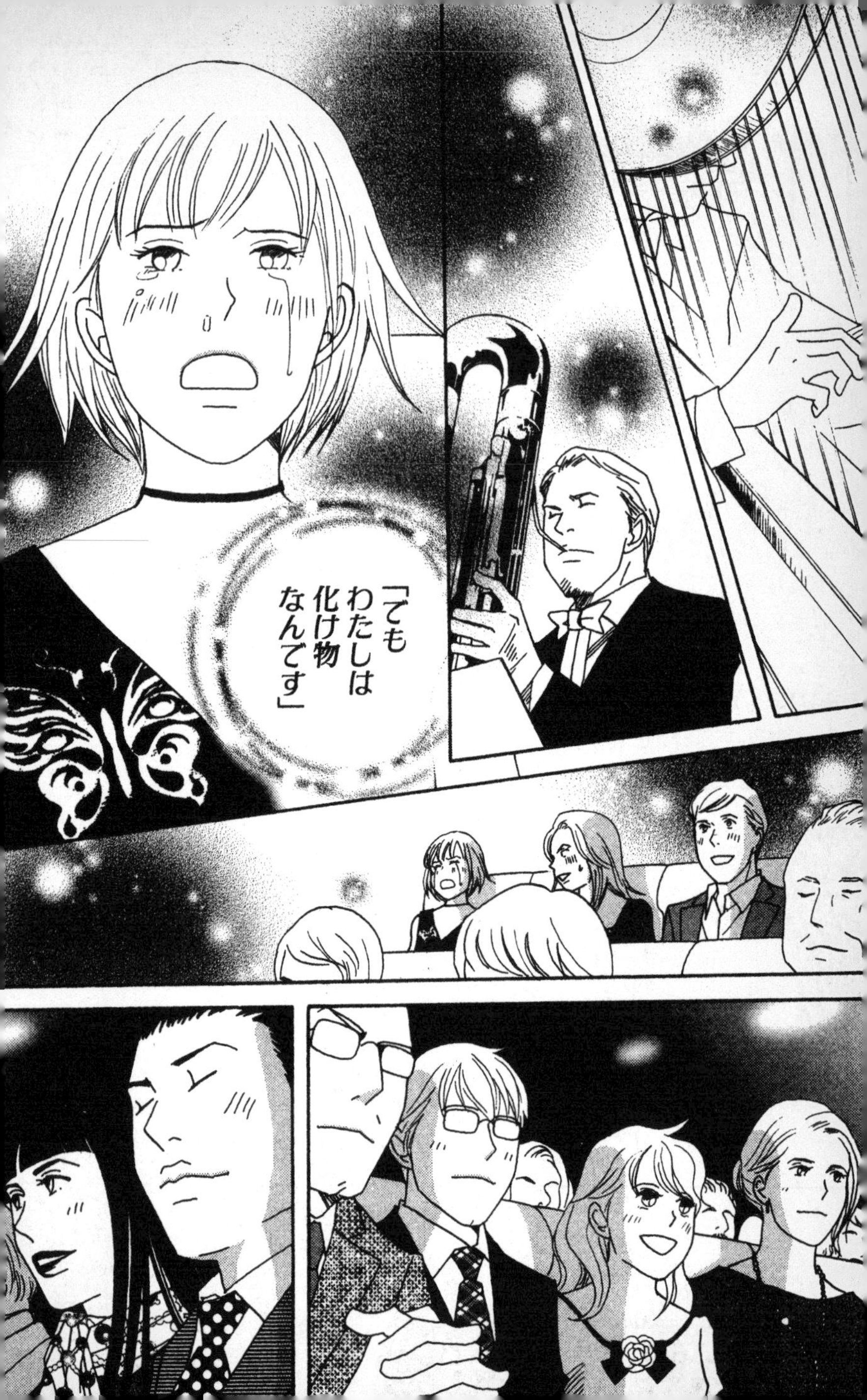
「でも
わたしは
化け物
なんです」

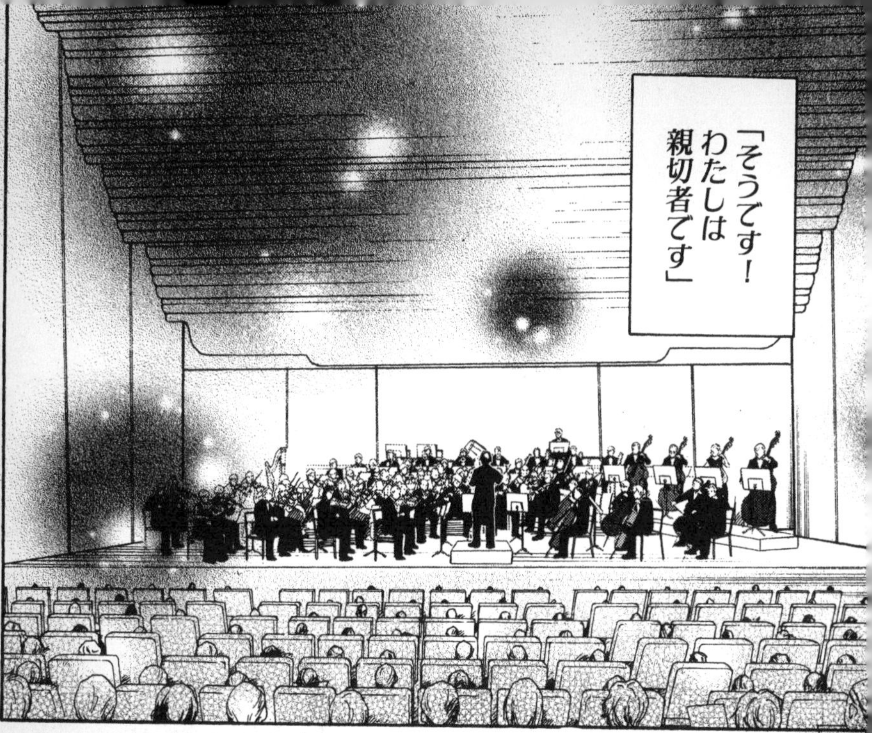
「そうです!
わたしは
親切者です」

RAVEL 〈MA MÈRE L'OYE〉
ラヴェル　マ・メール・ロア

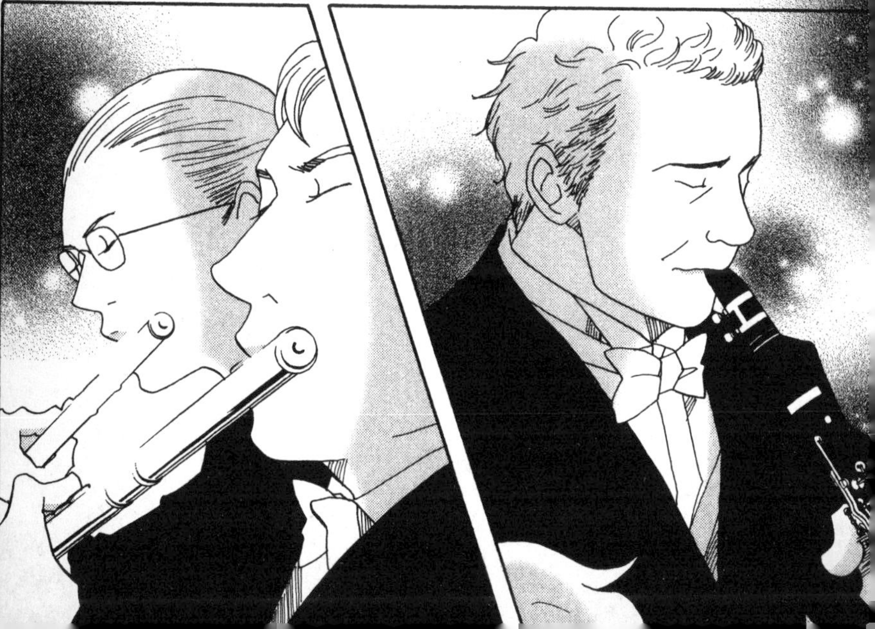

SHUGO CHARA!

PEACH-PIT

Creators of *Dears* and *Rozen Maiden*

Everybody at Seiyo Elementary thinks that stylish and super-cool Amu has it all. But nobody knows the *real* Amu, a shy girl who wishes she had the courage to truly be herself. Changing Amu's life is going to take more than wishes and dreams—it's going to take a little magic! One morning, Amu finds a surprise in her bed: three strange little eggs. Each egg contains a Guardian Character, an angel-like being who can give her the power to be someone new. With the help of her Guardian Characters, Amu is about to discover that her true self is even more amazing than she ever dreamed.

Special extras in each volume! Read them all!

VISIT WWW.DELREYMANGA.COM TO:
• Read sample pages
• View release date calendars for upcoming volumes
• Sign up for Del Rey's free manga e-newsletter
• Find out the latest about new Del Rey Manga series

RATING T AGES 13+

 DEL REY MANGA

The Otaku's Choice

Shugo Chara! © 2006 PEACH-PIT/ KODANSHA LTD. All rights reserved.

MICHIYO KIKUTA

BOY CRAZY

Junior high schooler Nina is ready to fall in love. She's looking for a boy who's cute and sweet—and strong enough to support her when the chips are down. But what happens when Nina's dream comes true . . . twice? One day, two cute boys literally fall from the sky. They're both wizards who've come to the Human World to take the Magic Exam. The boys' success on this test depends on protecting Nina from evil, so now Nina has a pair of cute magical boys chasing her everywhere! One of these wizards just might be the boy of her dreams . . . but which one?

Special extras in each volume! Read them all!

VISIT WWW.DELREYMANGA.COM TO:
• Read sample pages
• View release date calendars for upcoming volumes
• Sign up for Del Rey's free manga e-newsletter
• Find out the latest about new Del Rey Manga series

RATING T AGES 13+

DEL REY MANGA デルレイ

The Otaku's Choice

Mamotte! Lollipop © 2003 Michiyo Kikuta/KODANSHA LTD. All rights reserved.

DETROIT PUBLIC LIBRARY

3 5674 04662726 2

TOMARE!

[STOP!]

You are going the wrong way!

Manga is a completely different
type of reading experience.

To start at the *beginning*, go to the *end!*

That's right! Authentic manga is read the traditional Japanese
way—from right to left. Exactly the *opposite* of how American
books are read. It's easy to follow: Just go to the other end of
the book, and read each page—and each panel—from right side
to left side, starting at the top right. Now you're experiencing
manga as it was meant to be.

JUN 25 2008